What Every Executive Should Know About Chapter 11

THIRD EDITION

Benjamin Weintraub

OF COUNSEL
Kaye, Scholer, Fierman, Hays & Handler

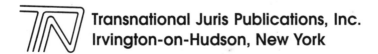
Transnational Juris Publications, Inc.
Irvington-on-Hudson, New York

Library of Congress Cataloging-in-Publication Data

Weintraub, Benjamin, 1905-
What every executive should know about Chapter 11 / Benjamin
Weintraub. -- 3rd ed.
p.   cm.
Includes index.
ISBN 1-56425-032-6
1. Corporate reorganizations--United States. 2. Bankruptcy-
United States. 3. Executives--United States--Handbooks, manuals,
etc. I. Title.
KF1544.W45 1993
346.73'06626--dc20
[347.3066626]   93-47559
                                                            CIP

Manufactured in the United States of America

Table of Contents

Chapter 1
Prepackaged Chapter 11

Chapter 2
Lender's Participation

Chapter 3
Use, Sale, or Lease of Property

Chapter 4
Power of Court

Chapter 5
Involuntary Petition

Chapter 6
Automatic Stay

Chapter 7
Jurisdiction of Bankruptcy Court

Chapter 8
Venue

Chapter 9
Jury Trials

Chapter 10
Committees of Creditors and Equity Security Holders

Chapter 11
Trustees, Examiners, and Officers of the Court

Chapter 12
Reclamation of Goods

Chapter 13
Assumption or Rejection of Executory Contracts and Unexpired Leases of Real Property

Chapter 15
Preferences

Chapter 16
Fraudulent Transfers and Obligations

Chapter 17
Substantive Consolidation of
Multi-Tiered Corporations

Chapter 18
Confirmation of Consensual Plan

Chapter 19
Confirmation of Cram Down Plan

Chapter 20
Postconfirmation Matters

Chapter 21
Before and After Chapter 11

About the Author

In an inscription on the New York University School of Law building at Washington Square appear these words of wisdom from Justice Oliver Wendell Holmes: "Law is the business to which my life is devoted, and I should show less than devotion if I did not do what in me lies to improve it."

No more apt words could be used to describe Ben Weintraub, whose more than sixty years as a practicing lawyer, law professor, author, lecturer, and scholar represent the epitome of dedication to the legal profession. His achievements since founding Levin & Weintraub in 1933 are too numerous to recount fully, but include countless articles on bankruptcy and related problems, monthly columns for New York Credit and Financial Magazine for more than thirty-five years, and two previous editions of this book.

In all his writing, Ben's trademark has been his uncanny ability to explain in understandable prose the most difficult and complex legal issues. Frequently written for lay persons—credit, business, and professional executives—rather than lawyers, his work has enabled them to grasp and understand basic principles underlying the law of Debtors' and Creditors' rights. Indeed, so crystal clear is his writing and so sharp his thought process that practicing lawyers find his material invaluable to them in their own efforts to understand the subject.

That same ability to communicate the law clearly and insightfully has made Ben an extraordinarily effective teacher, as evidenced by his adjunct professorships at New York Law School and Nova University School of Law where his classes were enjoyed by hundreds. It also made him a most effective chairman of Committees on Bankruptcy and Debtor Relief for the National Bankruptcy Conference, the New York County Lawyers Association and the Bronx County Bar Association.

Long recognized as a nationally respected and highly regarded expert, Ben has on more than one occasion testified before Congressional Committees on improvements in the former Bankruptcy Act and the current Code. In recognition of his singular stature and a lifetime of service to the law, Hofstra University established a Distinguished Professorship Chair in his honor in 1985, and the Financial Lawyers Conference of the Los Angeles County Bar Association honored him with this tribute in 1991:

> "Presented to Benjamin Weintraub, In Honor of His Outstanding Scholarship, In Recognition of His Years of Contribution, And in Gratitude for His Dedication In and To the Development and Enhancement of American Bankruptcy Law."

As in the earlier editions, as well as the volumes of the Bankruptcy Law Manual, which he co-authored with Professor Alan Resnick of Hofstra University, Ben has focused on the practical everyday problems and issues confronting business executives in a commercial world where virtually no transaction is without its bankruptcy ramifications and overtones. From the opening chapter on "Prepackaged Chapter 11," the clarity of his thinking is manifest, assuring that this volume will, like its predecessors, be required reading for executives in business communities.

Michael J. Crames
New York City
October 1993

Preface

Our first handbook came into existence in 1980, just two years after the Bankruptcy Code was enacted. Fast-moving events from the Bankruptcy Act to the Bankruptcy Code necessitated a second edition in 1985. Now, only nine years later, a third edition rears its head and requests publication. Bankruptcy moves with the world.

There are a number of current problems that we have highlighted, such as the "leveraged buyout," which has obtained significant importance to business in this period. Finance companies that do the advancing of the funds to keep the business floating will find problems when the trustee seeks to set aside an order giving the financier "cross-collateralization" of a prechapter loan or finds a payment of its loan is held to be a preference because of a guarantor's status. In addition, Congress realized the problems involved with the utilization of intellectual property as benefiting the debtor, and we have extended the subject of executory contracts. Not to be overlooked are the Racketeering Influenced Corrupt

Organizations (RICO) cases, which are included as fraudulent transfers.

These subjects are only a few of the totality of the handbook. What then has been our goal? What is chapter 11 about? We start chronologically with prepackaged chapter 11. The insolvent debtor has no cash flow. Consultation with creditors opens the doors to obtain acceptances for a search leading to chapter 11.

We start with the *Southland* case and move all the way from a successful prepackaged agreement among the debtor, creditor and equity holder followed by a chapter 11 petition filed in the bankruptcy court carrying the prepackaged plan along the path to confirmation of the plan of reorganization. In *Southland* we see the parts played by creditors' committees in participating with other classes working out a prepetition plan when accepted as if in a court proceeding is ready for filing in the Bankruptcy Court and prepared for confirmation. In addition, we cannot overlook the professionals, attorneys, accountants, and investment advisors, each representing specific parties and classes of creditors and equity security holders in their efforts to reach confirmation of the requisite plan. Each party has already participated in and approved a disclosure statement and approval of the plan has been obtained.

Assume that prepackaging cannot be accomplished—what then? The chapters of the book are geared to discuss the activities in chronological order as they would appear to a Debtor working its way through chapter 11 from prepetition to postconfirmation proceedings. A prepetition query confronts a Debtor: What has been pulling the house down diminishing the cash flow? In answer, we start with the Lender's participation and the Debtor obtaining credit. Good footholds exist for a starter. We move to the power of the automatic stay that holds recalcitrant creditors at bay until the Debtor has a reasonable opportunity to rehabilitate, and then on to procedure in court. Early operations under chapter 11 may result in the Debtor meeting problems involving reclamation of property sold by specific creditors within ten days prior to bankruptcy. Consideration is also given to decisions resulting in assumption or rejection of executory contracts and unexpired leases. Such decisions are of importance to debtors and creditors.

Recovery of preferential payments made to creditors or fraudulent transfers made to third parties are the subject of recovery of additional assets for the estate. LBOs are discussed as to their pattern of constituting a fraudulent conveyance or a good faith transfer. In addition, we discuss the *Wieboldt* case, an LBO where the district court upholds a complaint of the bankruptcy court dealing with provisions of state law involving not only the liability, of the Debtor and the Acquirer, but also the participation of Directors and Managers.

Confirmation of a consensual plan is analyzed from the viewpoint of consent of all the impaired classes or failure to obtain such consent. Confirmation of the cram down plan discusses the problems that arise in failing to obtain the acceptances from all classes of creditors or the requirements that cram down plans require. In Chapter 20 of this handbook we consider postconfirmation matters such as "effect of confirmation" as a "bind" of parties to the confirmed plan. We then consider the implementation required to carry out several proceedings after confirmation, e.g., the plan's provisions for the transferring of property under the control of the Debtor, or a non-Debtor, or the commencement or continuance of consummation of a fraudulent conveyance action by the Debtor. Finally, the procedure in "closing the case," brings to a conclusion the chapter 11.

This edition, as well as the earlier editions, is written with the same thought in mind that credit, business, and professional executives should not shy away from understanding basic principles of bankruptcy law any more than they should eschew accounting principles. Armed with this information, the executive will have knowledge as to what procedure to adopt when the Debtor contemplates a "prepackaged" chapter 11, files a voluntary petition for chapter 11, or when creditors file an involuntary petition. Likewise, the Debtor and all participants will be similarly prepared.

What Every Executive Should Know About Chapter 11 is not intended as a substitute for one's lawyer or as a detailed discussion of the Bankruptcy Code. The title of "executive" in the handbook is defined to include directors, officers, and managers not only of the Debtor organization, but the same constituents of the creditors and parties in interest. For those readers who desire to acquaint themselves with a more comprehensive and professional interpretation of the Bankruptcy Code, we refer them to a hardcover bound volume, the *Bankruptcy Law Manual*, now in its third edition, with annual supplements, published from December 1991 to the present, by Warren, Gorham & Lamont, and coauthored by Benjamin Weintraub and Alan N. Resnick. Benjamin Weintraub is Distinguished Professor of Bankruptcy Law of Hofstra University Law School.

We cannot, however, leave without presenting the anti-chapter 11 comments constructed by some writers intent on scuttling chapter 11, and the responses by pro-chapter 11 writers. The history of commercial law from the days of the Statute of Queen Elizabeth (1570) to the present, as we indicate in several chapters, has shown that not only the financial interests of debtors and creditors are considered under federal and state laws but virtually every business problem that a debtor must overcome to survive.

My appreciation and thanks to Katherine Frink-Hamlett, Bruce Rubin, Miriam Gladden, and Joshua E. Fruchter, associates of our firm, who assisted diligently and with much enthusiasm in research involving many of the cases and in discussions of the courts' analyses. Added also to those who are to be commended is Gloria Hartmann, my secretary, who spent many a day working diligently and joyfully preparing text and notes. Finally, cheers to our bankruptcy division and all of Kaye, Scholer who have kept me answering the question: "When will the book be out?"

Benjamin Weintraub
New York City
October 1993

Chapter 1
Prepackaged Chapter 11

A "prepackaged" bankruptcy plan is the nomenclature of an out-of-court proceeding in preparation of a debtor filing a chapter 11 petition. A meeting is generally convened by the debtor inviting its senior financiers, its creditors, and equity interests in an effort to arrive at a chapter 11 plan that complies with the statutory requirements of the Bankruptcy Code. Its goal is to prepare a disclosure statement and plan of reorganization that will be accepted by the necessary approval of a specific number of acceptances of all classes of creditors and equity interests.[1] Prepackaging is designed to accelerate the time and eliminate the expense involved in the consummation of a chapter 11 plan

---

[1] *See* §1125(a) describing adequate information for disclosure statement and §1125(b) for disclosure and solicitation of acceptances to the plan.

1

and most of all, bears the imprimatur of Bankruptcy Code approval.

Although it is somewhat premature at this early stage of the handbook to discuss several of the proceedings that are necessary for confirmation of a plan, a fundamental understanding of prepackaging requires a preliminary discussion of the statutory requirements for plan confirmation. "Prepackaged chapter 11" does not appear in the Bankruptcy Code *in haec verba*; its statutory equivalent is to be found nestled in §1125, which deals with disclosure of adequate information to support a plan before the steps necessary for solicitation of acceptances are taken.

Section 1126[2] deals with the procedure necessary to constitute proper acceptance of a plan. A holder of a claim or interest who has accepted or rejected a plan before the commencement of a chapter 11 case, such as in a prepackaged plan, is deemed to have accepted or rejected such plan if solicitation of the voting was in compliance with any applicable nonbankruptcy law or rule governing disclosure in connection with the solicitation.[3] Absent such law or rule, the Bankruptcy Code provides that adequate information means information in sufficient detail that would enable holders of claims and interests of the relevant class to make an informed judgment about the plan.

Adequate Disclosure

Courts resort to an expansive list of factors to evaluate the adequacy of a disclosure statement, which include: (1) a description of the available assets and their value; and, (2) financial information, data, valuations or projections relevant to the creditors' decision to accept or reject the chapter 11 plan.[4]

---

[2]   *See* §1126 (Acceptance of Plan) and subsections (a), (b)(1) and (2).

[3]   *See* this Chapter subtitle "SEC Compliance." *See also* B.Rule 3016(c): "In a chapter 9 or 11 case, a disclosure statement pursuant to §1125 or evidence showing compliance with §1126(b) of the Code shall be filed with the plan or within a time fixed by the court."

[4]   *See In re* Ferretti, 128 BR 16, 18-19 (B. NH 1991) and cases cited therein for a discussion of the factors related to adequate disclosure.

Prepackaging

We come now to negotiations of the out-of-court settlement before the commencement of the case, part of the procedure resulting in a prepackaged plan under subsection 1126(b). The Debtor convenes a meeting of a group of one or more of the large creditors of its classes, having previously convened the holders of each of its equity interests to obtain approval to its procedure. At this meeting of creditors, committees or representatives of each class are formed and develop a plan and disclosure statement in the same manner as is developed in an in-court meeting in a chapter 11 case except that the formulas set forth in §1125 and §1126 must be carefully followed. Failure to comply with these provisions may jeopardize the confirmation of the prepackaged plan as it affects the particular procedure of providing a proper disclosure statement or correctly tabulating the acceptances.

Acceptances

Assume the proper disclosure statement is approved and with the plan are distributed for solicitation for acceptance or rejection of the plan. The following numerical acceptances are required for confirmation of the plan: acceptance of the plan by each class of allowed claims holding at least two-thirds in amount and more than one-half in number of the allowed claims, and as to a class of interests holding at least two-thirds in amount of allowed interests voting on the plan.[5] Having such acceptances, the plan has the attributes of a prepackaged plan,[6] and the chapter 11 petition can then be prepared for filing.[7] Compliance, of course, must be made with the applica-

---

[5] *See* §1126(c) (class of claims); 1126(d) class of interests; *excluding* §1126(e) interests that are not in good faith.

[6] In addition, the Debtor's plan must also conform to the other provisions of the Code, e.g., §1123 (Contents of plan) and §1129 (Confirmation of plan).

[7] *See* B.Rule 1002 (Commencement of Case): "A petition commencing a case under the Code shall be filed with the clerk." *See* Official Bankruptcy Form No. 1 (Voluntary Petition).

ble sections of the Bankruptcy Code, the Federal Rules of Bankruptcy Procedure, and the Local Rules.[8]

Southland Case: A Leveraged Buyout

Southland,[9] the largest convenience store chain in the world, conducted business under the trade name of "7-Eleven," and owned and franchised stores worldwide. In 1987, Southland was the subject of a leveraged buyout (LBO)[10] transaction. Southland was unable to meet borrowings from secured term loans of $2.5 billion and $1.5 billion from the sale of debt securities and warrants to purchase Southland's common stock. In connection with the LBO, Southland also issued preferred stock to be paid to certain former public shareholders.[11] It was primarily this debt and securities that were being restructured under Southland's prepackaged chapter 11.

In 1989, two years after the LBO, Southland recognized that it could not make the large capital expenditures that would be needed to compete effectively because of its debt load and restrictive covenants in its credit agreements. Accordingly, Southland and its financial advisor began exploring possible alternatives for easing the restrictive covenants and reducing the overall amount of its indebtedness through various exchange offers directed to outstanding public debt securities and preferred stock. Pursuant to these exchange offers, the

---

[8] *See* B.Rule 9029 (Local Bankruptcy Rules) authorizing each district court to make and amend rules governing practice and procedures in all cases and proceedings within the district court's own jurisdiction, which are not inconsistent with Federal Rules of Bankruptcy Procedure (FRBP). *See also* SDNY Local Rule 52 as to contents of "first day order."

[9] Southland Corporation ("Southland" or "Debtor"), 124 BR 211 (B.ND Tex. 1991).

[10] *See infra* Chapter 16, this handbook, Fraudulent Transfers and Obligations subtitle "Leveraged Buyout."

[11] Southland, 124 BR 214. "In each case would-be holders of Southland's LBO-issued securities and debt . . . were informed of the use of the proceeds of the borrowings and were advised of the fraudulent transfer risks connected with the debt and the securities. . . ." *See also infra* Chapter 16, this handbook, Fraudulent Transfers and Obligations subtitle "What Is An LBO?"

holders of securities would exchange them for a lesser amount of new debt securities and/or cash.

Stock Sale

Thereafter, from October 1989 through March 1990, Southland continued to discuss with third parties, an interest in restructuring Southland. On March 21, 1990, after several negotiations, Southland entered into a stock purchase agreement with Ito-Yokado and Seven-Eleven Japan ("Purchaser") whereby Southland agreed to sell 75% of its New Common Stock to the Purchaser for $400 million, conditioned upon the consummation of exchange offers for the "Old Debt Securities."[12]

Steering Committee Due Diligence

In April 1990, a committee of holders of Southland's "Old Debt Securities" was formed to seek to maximize the value such holders would obtain in any restructuring and formed a Steering Committee for that purpose. The Steering Committee, having engaged financial and legal advisors, conducted a due diligence review of Southland, namely "a critical review of [Southland's] forecasts, a valuation analysis of [Southland], an analysis of [Southland's] proposed exchange offers and the preparation of counterproposals . . . an analysis of alternative restructuring proposals . . . a critical analysis of [Southland's] management . . . operations, investments, assets, liabilities and expenses. . . ."[13]

Business Deterioration

Commencing with Southland's March 22 announcement of the stock purchase agreement and continuing up to the time of Southland's chapter 11 filing, business was deteriorating: creditors tightened trade terms, and in some cases put

---

[12] *Id.* at 214. *See also* 124 BR at 213 for definition of "Old Debt Securities": "various exchange offers directed to holders of Southland's outstanding public debt securities. . . ."
[13] *Id.* at 215.

Southland on "cash on delivery" terms. Bondholders sued upon failure to pay interest due on certain bonds in June 1990. Other bank problems resulted in a further deterioration of Southland's cash position during August and September.

Negotiations
Necessity for Quick Action
Prepackaged Plan

The financial advisor had valued the April Proposal at $340 million, and informed the Steering Committee that the amount of consideration was inadequate. The Steering Committee made a counterproposal to those already made. Concerned that nontendering holders ("Stub")[14] would receive a windfall at the expense of those who tendered, the Steering Committee insisted that the tenders by Steering Committee members would be conditioned upon at least 95% of the outstanding amount of "Old Debt Securities" in each class being tendered. This condition took away Southland's and the Purchaser's ability to waive the 95% requirement.

> The Steering Committee also suggested a pre-packaged plan of reorganization as the way to insure participation by an acceptably high percentage of holders. Southland, however, desired to complete its restructuring outside of bankruptcy if at all possible. More importantly, the purchaser was at that time unwilling to discuss a pre-packaged plan.[15]

Problems of valuation, disputes of the restructuring plan by the advisors, and offers made by the Purchasers continued amidst a precipitous financial crisis accentuated by interest

---

[14] *See* court's note 8, observing that investors who do not tender in an exchange offer often do so in anticipation of achieving higher benefits by holding out. A prepackaged plan eliminates the holdout ("Stub") problem by treating all creditors within a class equally, such as the members of the Unofficial Bondholders' Committee who did not tender. Chapter 11 eliminates their windfall.

[15] Southland, 124 BR 216.

payments due July 15, 1990. "Southland feared that its continued failure to pay interest, particularly if coupled with lack of progress in its restructuring negotiations, would create uncertainty among Southland's suppliers and franchisees."[16] Add to this problem an uncertainty of Southland's failure to reduce its revolving credit agreement obligations to $50 million by July 16, 1990, as required by that agreement. Other debt instruments of Southland and its subsidiaries contained cross-default and cross-acceleration problems. Southland, therefore, believed it was imperative to reach and publicly announce an agreement in principle.

Restructuring Plan

Hectic negotiations and meetings continued from July 11, 1990 until the parties reconvened at 3:00 AM on July 16, 1990, when Southland announced an agreement in principle with the Steering Committee on the economic terms of a restructuring plan. The agreement contemplated: (1) acquisition by the Purchaser of 70% of Southland's new common stock for $430 million; (2) an increased aggregate principal amount of "New Debt Securities" to be offered to holders of the "Old Debt Securities;" (3) new cash payments to holders of Old Senior Notes; and (4) an increased percentage of New Common Stock to be offered to holders of the Old Securities.

SEC Compliance

On August 2, 1990, Southland, responding to the SEC comments, filed an amendment to its registration statement. The SEC ultimately declared the registration statement effective, and on August 2, 1990, Southland commenced mailing the prospectus (the "August Prospectus") relating to the July Proposal and other definitive solicitation materials containing the July Prospectus to holders of the "Old Debt Securities."[17]

---

[16]   *Id.* at 218.

[17]   *Id.* at 218. *See also* §1125(e): "A person that solicits acceptance or rejection of a plan, in good faith and in compliance with the applicable provisions of this title, or that participates in good faith . . . in the offer,

Soliciting Acceptances

Even though the Purchaser had not agreed to participate in a chapter 11 reorganization, the Steering Committee's approval of the July Proposal was conditioned upon Southland's agreement to file preliminary materials with the SEC relating to the solicitation of acceptances of a prepackaged plan. "Southland was required to make this 'silent filing' within two weeks of the date upon which it commenced mailing solicitation materials relating to the July Proposal. Southland's failure to file such materials would have permitted the Steering Committee to revoke its approval of the July Proposal."[18]

Although between August 2 and August 16, Southland was soliciting tenders for the July Proposal in the hope of avoiding chapter 11, nevertheless, Southland and the Purchaser were preparing the reorganization plan. On August 16, 1990, Southland filed preliminary confidential proxy materials with the SEC, which included a description of the plan and proposed acceptances of the plan.

Out-of-Court Plan: Insufficient Acceptances

On September 25, 1990, Southland determined that it had not received and most likely would not receive the necessary tenders and its restructuring might have to be consummated with the aid of a bankruptcy reorganization. Further discussions with the Purchaser required a delay in filing. On September 26, 1990, Southland filed a posteffective amendment to the registration statement relating to the July Proposal, thereby proposing to incorporate the plan into its exchange offers and making the terms of the plan public. On October 4, 1990, continuing solicitation of tenders and accep-

---

issuance sale or purchase of a security offered or sold under the plan of the Debtor . . . is not liable, on account of such solicitation or participation, for violation of any law . . . governing solicitation of acceptance or rejection of a plan. . . ."

[18]   *Id.* See court's note 12: "A 'silent filing' is not publicly available."

tances rendered the posteffective amendment relating to the plan effective by the SEC.[19]

Prepackaged Sufficient Acceptances

On October 22 or 23, the final exchange offers and the solicitation of the period for acceptances of the plan expired. Southland had not received the requisite number of tenders to consummate the final exchange offers, but it allegedly had obtained sufficient acceptances of the plan to seek confirmation of the plan by the court.[20]

Filing Chapter 11

On October 23, 1990, Southland and the Purchasers entered into a new stock purchase agreement that allowed Southland to file a chapter 11. The petition was filed on October 24, 1990. In accordance with prepackaging procedure, the plan and the disclosure statement had been filed with the chapter 11 petition. Consequently, an expedited hearing on confirmation was held on December 14, 1990. On that date "[t]he issue before the court [was] the validity of a vote for acceptance of a pre-filing plan of reorganization."[21]

Voting Acceptances
Ad Hoc Committee Objections

Southland submitted proof of an overwhelming acceptance of the Plan based upon a tabulation of the vote of record holders. This vote was challenged by a "self styled 'Unofficial

---

[19] *See* §1125(d): (1) "Whether a disclosure statement required under subsection (b) of this section contains adequate information is not governed by any otherwise applicable nonbankruptcy law, rule or regulation, but an agency or official whose duty it is to administer or enforce such a law, rule, or regulation may be heard on the issue of whether a disclosure statement contains adequate information. . . ."

[20] *See, e.g., In re* NJB Prime Investors, 3 BR 553 (B. SDNY 1979) (Debtor failed to receive sufficient tenders, yet acquired sufficient acceptances to qualify requirements for confirmation).

[21] *Id.* at 219.

Bondholders Committee' (the 'Ad Hoc Committee') which represented five investors who were dissatisfied with the voting process and the representation provided by the Steering Committee which now form[ed] the Official Bondholders Committee (the 'Committee')."[22] The Debtor argued that it was required to recognize only the vote of the record holders. The court found the vote of the record holders "questionable and ill conceived."[23]

In an intensive analysis of "The Vote of Record Holders," which included a subsection of "The Taint of Record Holders' Vote," "Securities Practices: The Record Holder," "The Questionable Tabulation of the Votes," and "The Ballot," the court stated that the "evidence demonstrated a continued *evaluation and judgment of the ballots by the tabulators* in connection with the rejection or acceptance of a ballot as a valid vote."[24]

In its determination as to whether there had been sufficient votes to meet the requirements of §1126 the court reasoned that in accordance with "the plain words of Congress in §1126, only the holder of a claim, or a creditor, or the holder of an interest, may accept or reject a plan."[25] If a record holder of a debt is not the owner or a true creditor or authorized agent of the true creditor, the vote will be disallowed.

Voting Invalidated

After discussing prepetition voting, the court concluded: (1) only the holder of a claim or interest or an authorized agent may accept or reject a plan; (2) references to record holders in Rule 3018 are of no effect; and (3) time for acceptance was unnecessarily short. Accordingly, the votes cast were not those of holders of claims and all votes were invalidated.

---

[22]   *Id.* at 220. *See* court's note 18: "On October 24, 1990, the date of the commencement of the case, the Steering Committee was approved by the U.S. Trustee as the Official Bondholders Committee. The Steering Committee was formed in July, 1990 following an initial offer by the Japanese investor." *See also infra* Chapter 10, this handbook, Committees of Creditors and Equity Security Holders and Chapter 11, this handbook, Trustees, Examiners, and Officers of the Court.

[23]   *Id.*

[24]   *Id.* at 220–23 (emphasis in original).

[25]   *Id. See also* §1126(a).

Voting Renewed

As a result, the court stated that a hearing on disclosure materials and a further vote of all creditors and preferred stockholders on the plan and a certification of authority to vote as a representative of each class was to be held on December 13, 1990. The hearing on confirmation was set for December 15, 1990.

We left Southland at the point where the court had set a date to reapprove the disclosure statement and acceptances of the plan. In the event of the required approval, confirmation was to follow. Indeed, Southland's order of confirmation[26] dated February 21, 1991 followed two months[27] thereafter and contained the following recital:

> The Southland Corporation, debtor in posses-
> sion . . . filed a petition for reorganization relief
> under Chapter 11 . . . on October 24, 1990 . . .
> and simultaneously filed the Debtor's Plan of
> Reorganization which as technically amend-
> ed . . . was transmitted to holders of Claims and
> Interests entitled to vote on the Plan.[28]

The significance of the time schedule is a feature of the expedition with which a prepackaged plan works. Within four months a macroplan was confirmed. Many classes of claims, such as priority, miscellaneous secured claims, bank claims, two trade classes, and classes of old senior and subordinated notes and debentures and common stock were dealt with by the plan.[29]

---

[26] Case No. 390-37119-HCA-11 (B. ND. Tex. Dallas Div. 1991).

[27] *See* §1128 Confirmation hearing. (a) "After notice, the Court shall hold a hearing on confirmation of a plan. —(b) A party in interest may object to confirmation of a plan."

[28] *See* Order of Confirmation Southland Plan of Reorganization.

[29] *See* Southland Plan of Reorganization.

Prepackaged Secured Creditors: G. Heileman Case

A consensuality with secured creditors is reflected in an out-of-court workout of the *G. Heileman Brewing Company* that missed its mark slightly as prepackaging, but still had its rewards in its accomplishment. The New York Times reported:

> In moving into chapter 11, Heileman becomes one of the latest companies to use the bankruptcy courts to help refinance debt. In what has come to be called a prepackaged bankruptcy, Heileman said today that it had already reached agreement with its senior bank lenders on the key terms for slower or reduced debt payments. It said all that remained was for the company to work out terms with its junior lenders—the holders of the $200 million in junk bonds.[30]

De Facto Plans

Creditors may have some concern about a plan bearing the nomenclature of a *de facto* plan. No need to show concern about such plan; it may be the real chapter 11, if the plan follows the routine of the *Crowthers*[31] case. In *Crowthers*, the bankruptcy court approved a merger agreement conditioned on the confirmation of the plan of reorganization holding that the agreement did not constitute a *de facto* plan. The court rejected the creditor's objection that the agreement constituted a *de facto* plan by "locking up" the agreement thus precluding competing plans. The court specifically noted that the agreement did not bar competing plans; that it did not transfer control of the Debtor or possession of the estate property until approval of a disclosure statement and confirmation of a plan incorporating the agreement; and that the proposed transaction met business justification requirements finding that there

---

[30]   NEW YORK TIMES January 25, 1981 at D-1. *See also* G. Heileman Brewing Co., Inc., et al., Case No. 91 B 10326 (FGC) (B. SDNY 1991).

[31]   Crowthers McCall Pattern v. Lewis, Inc., 114 BR 407 (B. SDNY 1990).

was a pressing need to hold a purchaser so that a plan could be considered. Satisfied that the protection afforded to chapter 11 creditors would not be thwarted, the court approved the agreement as a necessary step to achieve a plan.

Observation

The out-of-court settlement has now assumed the nomenclature of "Prepackaged Chapter 11." The question may be asked: Why go through the disturbance of a prepackaged plan when a filing under chapter 11 immediately gives the company the benefit of an automatic stay and many months to negotiate a plan while continuing operations as a debtor in possession? Out-of-court agreements do give Creditors and Debtors an opportunity for mingling and discussing their problems without court restrictions of time and a quicker appreciation of whether a plan is feasible.

In *Southland*, a prospective purchaser reluctantly agreed to the Debtor's filing a chapter 11, but the purchaser's participation in out-of-court negotiations eased the path to chapter 11. In any event, even if the parties do not agree upon a plan, prepackaging may have opened the door to consensuality of a plan among a class of creditors as in the *G. Heileman* case, secured creditors. The procedure is a good start when the chapter 11 petition is subsequently filed.

Furthermore, in *Southland*, another important advance was made in facilitating the reorganization. The Steering Committee that had been the unofficial bondholders' committee prepetition was appointed as the Official Bondholders' Committee by the U.S. Trustee upon the filing of the petition. This continuity of service is of great significance in having a class assisting in propelling the plan to confirmation.[32]

Moreover, the conclusion of the *G. Heileman* case is another example of the workings of a semi-prepackaged plan: "A Federal Bankruptcy Court judge [confirmed] a reorganization plan for the G. Heileman Brewing Company, . . . [which] filed for Chapter 11 protection from creditors in January."[33]

---

[32] *See infra* Chapter 10, this handbook, Committees of Creditors and Equity Security Holders.

[33] NEW YORK TIMES, November 21, 1991 (LD4, Col. 3).

In Chapter 2 of this handbook, we review the important role played by the lender in the prepackaged plan as well as in the ordinary procedure.

Chapter 2
Lender's Participation

Our discussion of the *Southland* case essentially involved the necessity of new capital, which required a change of control of the company. However, there are many businesses that desire to maintain their own control over their operations as in the *G. Heileman Brewing Co.* case.[1] This brings us to a discussion of the lender's participation in a chapter 11. The funds to be borrowed and the lender's experience in insolvency cases contribute substantial support to the Debtor's reorganization plans.

In many chapter 11 cases the Debtor's current lender, one or more, having had profitable returns in dealing with the company, and sometimes occupying the status of an unsecured creditor, is anxious to continue to service the Debtor when the Debtor's needs require rehabilitation. Not only is the continuance of business a primary objective for both, but the lender

---

[1] *See supra* Chapter 1, this handbook, subtitle "Prepackaged Secured Creditors: *G. Heileman* Case."

also measures the benefit of its advancement of additional funds to the Debtor often in anticipation of repayment of its pre-chapter 11 loans and by maintaining a business relationship with the Debtor.

As for the debtor in possession,[2] the advances give the company the support necessary to continue its operations. Nonetheless, absent the support of its own lender, there may be available other lenders, and moreover, specific Bankruptcy Code sections afford a Debtor with other opportunities to continue operations. These opportunities are contained in §363 dealing with the "Use, Sale or Lease of Property" and in §364, "Obtaining Credit."

Obtaining Credit

Since the lender and Debtor first consider the advancing of funds to the debtor in possession, we will consider §364 and leave §363 to Chapter 3.[3] A ladder of opportunity is opened to the debtor in possession from climbing from step one,[4] which authorizes the debtor in possession to obtain unsecured credit and unsecured debt in the ordinary course of business allowable under §503(b)(1) as an "administrative expense."

Higher Priorities For Borrowing

Let us assume that a debtor in possession is unable to obtain unsecured credit as an administrative expense on a parity with other administrative claims. Under these circumstances, the court, after notice and a hearing, may authorize the debtor in possession to obtain credit or by incurring a debt with priority over all administrative expenses

---

[2] *See* 11 USC §1101. Definitions for this chapter: (1) "In this chapter—'debtor in possession' means Debtor except when a person that has qualified under section 322 of this title is serving as trustee in the case." *See also* §1108. "Authorization to operate business."

[3] *See* USC §1107 (Rights, powers, and duties of debtor in possession).

[4] *See* §501 (Filing of proofs of claim or interests); §502 (Allowance of claims or interests); §503 (Allowance of administrative expenses); §506 (Determination of secured status); and §507 (Priorities which provide for sequential priorities for administrative expenses allowed under §503).

of §§503 or 507.[5] A third step provides that in the event such second priority is not obtainable, the court may authorize the obtaining of credit or incurring of debt by securing a lien on unencumbered property or secured by granting a lender a junior lien on property that is encumbered by a lien.

Finally, the last rung of the ladder: if all else fails, the court may authorize the obtaining of credit or incurring of a debt that may be secured by a senior or equal lien on property of the estate that is subject to an existing lien. However, in granting such lien, the court must determine that there is adequate protection of the holder of the lien to the extent of the holder's interest in the property.[6] As we shall see in several cases, the objective is not only to enable the debtor in possession to rehabilitate the estate, but that the subordinated lienor does not lose entirely on any such transaction. Of course, hindsight may be better than foresight, but in such event §507(b) should offer some relief. Moreover, in any hearing under subsection 364(d)(2), the trustee has the burden of proof on the issue of adequate protection.

Adams Apple Case

The *Adams Apple* case[7] dealt squarely with the bankruptcy court's authorization overruling creditor's objection of a financing arrangement that went a step further than our discussion of granting a creditor a senior lien on the debtor's property. The lien was incorporated in a cross-collateralization[8] order that granted a finance company a senior position on its prepetition unsecured loan as well as its postpetition advance. On June 10 and 14, 1983, separate

---

[5] *See* 11 USC §364(c).

[6] *See also* §507(b) providing that to extent adequate protection of the interest of a holder of a claim under §§362, 363, or 364 secured by a lien on debtor's property proves to be inadequate, the claim of such creditor is given a "priority over every other claim under such subsection."

[7] *In re* Adams Apple, Inc. ("Adams Apple" or "Debtor"), 829 F2d 1484 (9th Cir. 1987).

[8] *Id.* at 1486. *See* court's note 1: "Post-petition securing of previously unsecured prepetition loans is referred to as cross-collateralization."

chapter 11 petitions[9] were filed in the *Adams Apple* case consisting of Robert Sterling ("Sterling") and three of his wholly-owned corporations engaged in apple growing and marketing.

Cross-Collateral Financing

The issue before the court was an interim financing agreement providing that Central Washington Bank ("Bank" or "CWB") would advance $450,000 and an optional $325,000 to provide funds to the Debtors to produce crops in 1983, and to preserve the horticultural quality of the Debtors' orchards. In exchange, the Bank would receive a security interest with priority over other creditors in the 1983 crop as collateral for the loan. The first lien as a security interest would secure Bank's loan of $450,000 as well as postpetition advances.

A prepetition loan had been made in 1982 by one of Sterling's wholly-owned corporations. All the Debtors had issued promissory notes to guarantee the debt and subsequently granted a security interest in crops to secure the notes and financing statements, which were filed on April 4, 1983. Soon thereafter when priority disputes[10] arose, "the Debtors began discussing other financing arrangements with the Bank, as well as two other potential lenders, Bank of California ("California") and Dover. Several arrangements for loans were rejected by the Debtors or withdrawn by the potential lenders. The arrangement at issue, which required the Debtors to file Chapter 11 proceedings to clarify the Bank's rights, was then proposed."[11]

Extreme Need for Loan

The bankruptcy court held three hearings to consider the loan. Creditors objected to the cross-collateralization. Sterling

---

[9] *See* FRBP 1015, Consolidation Or Joint Administration Of Cases Pending In Same Court. *See also infra* Chapter 18, this handbook, Confirmation of Consensual Plan.

[10] *See* 829 F2d at 1486, court's note 3, with reference to the classes of Debtor's creditors: "These creditors appear to have a mixture of secured and unsecured claims."

[11] *Id.*

testified that: (1) without the loan his 1983 crops would fail and he could lose his orchards; (2) Bank would provide financing only if the contract included a cross-collateralization clause; and (3) financing was not otherwise available. In addition, Sterling acknowledged he refused California's offers, but these offers were not renewed despite the bankruptcy judge's call for alternative offers.

Appeal

After a tentative oral ruling on June 15, 1983, the bankruptcy court issued its final authorization on July 14, 1983. However, the Bank began its postpetition financing before final authorization and ultimately $450,000 was loaned by July 14, 1983. On the same day, California filed a motion for a stay pending appeal. At first the bankruptcy court denied the motion that day, but reversed itself and ordered a stay on August 19, 1983. However, a notice of appeal to the district court had been filed before August 19, and the district court found that the bankruptcy court properly exercised its authority. The appeal to the circuit court followed.

Jurisdiction: Court of Appeals Finality of Order

The court of appeals found that the court had jurisdiction because of the finality of the order.[12] "[A]n order is final if it is distinct and conclusive of the substantive rights of individuals."[13] The issue to be considered in the case was whether a bankruptcy court might authorize a lender to contract with a Debtor to subordinate the claims of other creditors to property of the Debtor. Accordingly, since the order disposed of the property rights of individuals, the order was deemed final.

Argument: Objection To Sale

The Bank argued that California's claim was moot because the authorization to obtain credit was not stayed as provided

---

[12] *Id.* at 1487 citing 28 USC §158(d), which provides that the district court "shall have jurisdiction to hear appeals from final judgments. . . ." *See also infra* Chapter 7, this handbook, Jurisdiction of Bankruptcy Court.

[13] *Id.* citing *In re* Mason, 709 F2d 1313, 1317 (9th Cir. 1983).

under §364(e). California "maintained that (1) section 364(e) does not apply to a lien to secure a prepetition loan, and even if section 364(e) does apply, then (2) the bankruptcy court did not stay its authorization, and (3) Bank acted in bad faith."[14]

Mootness

In interpreting the language of §364, the court observed that "section 364 authorizes a bankruptcy court to permit the use of a variety of financing devices. Cross-collateralization clauses are not expressly included in the list. . . ." However, examining Congressional intent,[15] the court concluded that "cross-collateralization clauses appear to be covered by section 364 and in turn subject to section 364(e)."

In rejecting California's argument that postpetition liens were not the kind Congress intended to protect, the court stated:

> A lender may be willing to extend credit if the arrangement includes a cross-collateralization clause, and a chance for greater profit (or, put it differently, to reduce earlier losses), but would withhold credit if the clause could be overturned on appeal. . . . We therefore conclude that section 364(e) is meant to protect the lender by preventing reversal of a cross-collateralization clause unless a stay is obtained pending appeal. . . .[16]

In a footnote the court stated that its conclusion that "cross-collateralization clauses are 'authorized' under section 364 is limited to the context of §364(e) mootness, and it is not intended to prevent a future panel from holding, if it so

---

[14] 829 F2d at 1488.

[15] *Id.* (citing United States v. American Trucking Assoc., 60 S.Ct., 1059, 1063 (1940)).

[16] *Id.* (citing *In re* Ellingsen MacLean Oil Co., 65 BR 358 (WD. Mich. 1986), *aff'd.* 834 F2d 599 (6th Cir. 1987), dismissing appeal as moot pursuant to §364(e), but declining to decide whether cross-collateralization was authorized by the Bankruptcy Code; *cert. denied,* 109 S.Ct. 55 (1988). *See infra* this chapter subtitle "Cross-Collateralization Challenged."

determines, that cross-collateralization is illegal per se...."[17] As to the case at bar, since the bankruptcy judge thought that cross-collateralization was legal and entered an order to that effect upon which the creditor relied, the court concluded that the creditor should receive the protection of §364(e) in this case.

The court held that the policies behind §364(e) indicate that a claim is moot as soon as a lender has relied on the authorization. Such authorization takes place as soon as the order becomes final and no party has appealed. In addition, to permit a court to impose a stay after a creditor had loaned money to a Debtor "would intrude on a reorganization process underway and would interfere with the lender's ability to plan for its outlay of funds."[18] The court also observed that the order was issued after California filed an appeal of the cross-collateralization authorization in the district court. A bankruptcy court has wide latitude to reconsider and vacate its own decisions.[19] However, a pending appeal divests a bankruptcy court of jurisdiction. Therefore, if *CWB* acted in "good faith," the issue is moot under §364(e).[20]

Good Faith

Tackling the issue of good faith, the court again indicated that the Code failed to provide any definition. However, a number of circuit court cases indicated that good faith constituted such conduct as looking to "the integrity of an actor's conduct during the proceedings."[21] California argued that the Bank procuring a cross-collateral claim did not act in good faith. The Bank in response maintained that courts have drawn opposite conclusions in determining whether cross-collateralization clauses are authorized under the Code.[22]

---

[17] *Id.* at 1489.

[18] *Id.*

[19] *Id.*

[20] *Id.*

[21] *Id.* citing *In re* Suchy, 786 F2d 900, 902 (9th Cir. 1985).

[22] *Id.* at 1490. *Compare In re* Roblin Indus., Inc., 52 BR 241 (B. WDNY 1985); *In re* Vanguard Diversified, Inc., 31 BR 364 (B. EDNY 1983) *with In re* Monach Circuit Industries, Inc., 41 BR 859 (B. ED Pa. 1984). *See also*

Cross-Collateralization Necessity for Rehabilitation

Appellants advanced two specific arguments in support of their assertion that *CWB* did not act in good faith. First, cross-collateralization was a violation of the fundamental intent of bankruptcy law that like creditors must be treated alike. The court responded to the first argument, stating: "It is flawed because the 'fundamental tenet' conflicts with another 'fundamental tenet'—rehabilitation of debtors, which may supersede the policy of equal treatment."[23] The court then indicated that cases have permitted unequal treatment of prepetition debts when necessary for rehabilitation in contexts of prepetition wages to key employees, hospital malpractice premiums incurred prior to filing, debts to providers of unique and irreplaceable supplies, and peripheral benefits under labor contracts.[24]

> Cross-collateralization clauses may provide the only means for saving a failing debtor. As noted above, a lender may be willing to take the risk of lending funds to a debtor only if the gain derived from cross-collateralization is available. If the lender is the sole lender willing to finance the debtor, a cross-collateralization clause may mean the difference between an ongoing enterprise and a company in liquidation.[25]

The court of appeals concluded its opinion by holding that the Bank did not act in bad faith as a matter of law "simply because some courts have held cross-collateralization clauses to be illegal *per se*."[26] Finally, the argument that the Bank acted in bad faith because other creditors withheld consent to

---

Texlon, 596 F2d 1092 (1979) (suggesting in lengthy dictum that cross-collateralization clauses might be held to be illegal *per se*, but took cognizance of §364(e)).

[23] *Id.*

[24] *Id.* citing Ordin, Case Comment, *In re* Texlon Corporation, 596 F2d 1092 (2d Cir. 1979): *Finality of Order of Bankruptcy Court*, 54 AMER. BANK. L.J. 173, 177 (1980).

[25] *Id.*

[26] *Id.*

the granting of cross-collateralization was also without merit. All that §364 requires is a "notice and hearing," but not consent. "Not only does section 364 permit a judge to authorize secured loans in appropriate circumstances, but section 105(a)[27] provides for a broad exercise of authority by a bankruptcy judge to further the provisions of the Bankruptcy Code."[28]

Forum Case—Current Lending

We turn now to the *Forum* case,[29] which indicates the extent to which cross-collateralization has advanced as a lending "prepackaged agreement prechapter."

Adams Apple emphasized that the fundamental tenet of chapter 11 was rehabilitation, "which may supersede the policy of equal treatment," and presented several examples. Not to be overlooked is the *Forum* case[30] that presents a financial relationship between Forum, as Debtors, and *MHT* its Lenders. The businesses of Forum and its subsidiaries involved substantial enterprises principally engaged in the development, ownership, and operation of retirement communities in several states. MHT had been acting as financier to Forum for a term loan and a revolving credit facility secured by the Debtors' collateral.

---

[27] *Id.* at 1491. *See infra* Chapter 4, this handbook, Power of Court subtitle "Injunction: Section 105(a) Postconfirmation."

[28] *Id.* (citing Bohm, *The Legal Justification for the Proper Use of Cross-Collateralization in Chapter 11 Bankruptcy Cases,* 59 AMER. BANK. L.J. 299, 295–96 (1985)).

[29] *In re* Forum Group, Inc., et al., (or "Debtors") (Case Nos. IP 91-1678-FSO-11 through IP 91-1690-FSO-11) (B. SD Ind 1991) (Order designated as "Final Order Authorizing Debtors To Obtain Post-Petition Financing Pursuant To §364 and To Utilize Cash Collateral Pursuant to §363, and Granting Adequate Protection" dated March 1, 1991 ("Final Order"), commenced as "first day order."

[30] Manufacturers Hanover Trust Co. ("MHT" or "Lender") in its capacity, as agent for the several banks and in its individual capacity ("Lenders" or "DIP Banks").

Preparation of Prefiling Order: First Day Order

Financial difficulties resulted in Forum's consulting with MHT concerning its necessity of filing petitions under chapter 11 and obtaining additional financing for a proposed chapter 11.[31] These activities resulted in an agreement subject to the bankruptcy court's approval as to financing conditioned upon Forum's filing a chapter 11. In pursuance of this consensual agreement Forum and its subsidiaries each filed chapter 11 petitions on February 19, 1991.[32] Authorization for thirty-day financing was approved and thereafter upon notice to all interested parties and a hearing on March 27, 1991 agreements extending such financing between the debtors and MHT were approved in an order by the court.

Let us take a look at some of the significant provisions of *Forum's* order,[33] for comparison with powers supplied by the Code authorizing the lending of funds to a debtor in possession (DIP): (1) immediate[34] authorization to borrow $5 million pursuant to the terms of the interim order and final order providing the moneys were to be used in the operation of Forum's and its affiliates' businesses in accordance with the terms of its postpetition credit agreement; (2) Forum's inability to obtain credit either in the ordinary course of business or under any of subsections 364(a), (b) or (c).[35] Since the DIP was unable to obtain credit under any of these subsections, the highest rung on the ladder of priorities and senior liens was

---

[31] *See* Final Order at page 6 alleging irreparable harm to Debtor's business doesn't appear unless order granted.

[32] By order of March 22, 1991 the cases were consolidated for joint administration. *See* B.Rule 1015. *See also* Chapter 17, this handbook, Substantive Consolidation of Multitiered Corporations.

[33] *See* Chapter 3 of the Bankruptcy Code, "Case Administration."

[34] *See* B.Rule 9006 (Time): (a) Computation; (b) Enlargement; (c) Reduction (1)—". . . the Court for cause shown may in its discretion with or without motion or notice order the period reduced."

[35] *See* §364(b): "The court . . . may authorize the trustee to obtain unsecured credit...other than under subsection (a)...." *See also* §107 (Rights, powers, and duties of debtor in possession) giving the debtor in possession rights of a trustee with certain limitations.

available by virtue of subsection 364(d)(1);[36] and (3) one superpriority senior to the Banks' superiority allowed by the order was a provision for the allowance of administrative expenses by the court, commonly known as the "carve out" provision.[37] This provision stated that "administrative expenses accrued postpetition during the term of the Post-Petition Credit Agreement shall be senior to the administrative priority granted to the DIP banks: (a) accrued and unpaid professional fees . . . of the Debtors or any official committee not to exceed $2,500,000. . . ."[38]

Observation

The *Forum* priming was utilized by the lender even to the extent of priming its own debt. There was due $121 million to MHT at the time of the filing of the petition, which was secured by the Debtors' collateral having a value in excess of the secured obligations. The consent order of the court approved by priming MHT's own prepetition claim secured by the Debtors' collateral of $121 million, including interest and costs, made it possible for MHT to collect interest on its prepetition debt as it was an oversecured creditor.[39]

Reflect for a moment that the prepetition agreement between the Debtors and the lenders was not a true prepackaged chapter 11, but provided, prior to the chapter 11 filing, a framework that arranged postpetition financing: a closer step to confirmation of a plan. As in the *Heileman* case discussed in the previous chapter, "all that remained was to work out

---

[36] *See* §361 (Adequate Protection). *See also* Bankruptcy Rule 4001 (Relief from Automatic Stay; Use of Cash Collateral; Obtaining Credit; Agreements). *See also* §364(e), which was incorporated in the order providing that a reversal or modification of the order on appeal would not affect MHT's lien or priority since MHT extended such credit in good faith.

[37] *See* Gen. Elec. Credit Corp. v. Levin & Weintraub (*In re* Flagstaff Seafood Service Corp.), 739 F2d 73 (2d Cir. 1984), where disallowance may have prompted the current and common use of the "carve out" provision. *See also* §§326 (Employment of Professional Persons), 328, 329, and 330.

[38] *See* Final Order at page 9.

[39] *See* §506(a). Determination of secured status. *See also* United Sav. Assoc. of Texas v. Timbers of Inwood Forest Assocs. Ltd., 108 S.Ct. 626 (1988).

terms" with its creditors. In addition, this cross-collateralization received approval from creditors and the court.

Having considered the lender's participation in elevating the Debtor's financial status, we consider the "use, sale or lease" of the Debtor's property in aiding in its financial growth.

Cross-Collateralization Challenged

Saybrook

With cross-collateralization having been approved by several circuit courts and bankruptcy courts as an emergency financing order under §364, along comes the *Saybrook* case,[40] and challenges the power of the bankruptcy court to issue such financing order to Manufacturer's Hanover Trust Co. At the time of filing chapter 11 on December 22, 1988, *Saybrook* owed MHT $34 million with collateral for the debt of $10 million.

Pursuant to the order, MHT agreed to lend an additional $3 million to facilitate the reorganization in exchange for a security interest in all the Debtor's property, both prepetition and that acquired postpetition. The security interest protected the $3 million and MHT's $34 million and of course, as we indicated, was commonly known as cross-collateralization. Reciting the history of cross-collateralization from the Second Circuit's opinion in *Texlon* case to date, the Eleventh Circuit considered the mootness of the appeal. Referring to the interpretation of "mootness" in *Adams Apple*[41] where the court held that cross-collateralization was authorized under section 364 for the purposes of section 364(e) but declined to decide whether cross-collateralization was illegal per se under the Bankruptcy Code, the court held:[42]

> We reject the reasoning of *In re* Adams Apple
> and *In re* Ellingsen because they put the cart
> before the horse. By its own terms, section

---

[40] Jeffrey Shapiro and Seymour Shapiro v. Saybrook et al., Manufacturing Company, Inc. ("Saybrook"), Manufacturer's Hanover Trust Co. ("MHT"), et al., 963 F2d 1490 (11th Cir. 1992).

[41] *See supra* this chapter, subtitle "Mootness."

[42] *See supra* this chapter, notes 7 and 16.

364(e) is only applicable if the challenged lien or priority was authorized under §364. . . .[43]

The circuit court referred to a law journal article that criticized both *Adams Apple* and *Ellingsen* for the practice of shielding cross-collateralization from appellate review via mootness under §364(e), and the article criticized the *Ellingsen* decision by approving the dissenting opinion that "[l]enders should not be permitted to use their leverage in making emergency loans in order to insulate their prepetition claims from attack."[44]

Determination of Legality

Referring to the controversy existing concerning cross-collateralization in a number of bankruptcy courts, the Eleventh Circuit observed that even the courts that have allowed cross-collateralization were generally reluctant to do so. As an example, the court of appeals referred to the *Vanguard* case,[45] and noted "that cross-collateralization is 'a disfavored means of financing' that should only be used as a last resort. . . . In order to obtain a financing order including cross-collateralization, the [*Vanguard*] court required the Debtor to demonstrate (1) that its business operations will fail absent the proposed financing, (2) that it is unable to obtain alternative financing on acceptable terms, (3) that the proposed lender will not accept less preferential terms, and (4) that the proposed financing is in the general creditor body's best interest. *Id.* This four part test has since been adopted by other bankruptcy courts which permit cross-collateralization."[46]

---

[43] Saybrook at 1493.

[44] *Id. See* Charles J. Tabb, *Lender Preference Clauses and the Destruction of Appealability and Finality: Resolving a Chapter 11 Dilemma,* OHIO ST. L.J. 109, 116, 135 (1989) (criticizing *In re* Adams Apple, *In re* Ellingsen, and the "practice of shielding cross-collateralization from appellate review via mootness under section 364(2)." . . .).

[45] *Id.* at 1493. *In re* Vanguard Diversified, Inc. ("Vanguard"), 31 BR 364 (B. EDNY 1983).

[46] *Id.* citing *In re* Roblin. 52 BR 241, 244–45 (B. WDNY 1985).

The court of appeals also noted the "issue of whether the Bankruptcy Code authorizes cross-collateral is a question of first impression in that Court. Indeed, it is essentially a question of first impression before any court of appeals. Neither the lenders' brief nor our own research has produced a single appellate decision which either authorizes or prohibits the practice."[47]

The court addressed the lender's argument that bankruptcy courts may permit the practice under their general equitable power.[48] The court agreed that the courts had "power to adjust claims to avoid injustice or unfairness. . . ."[49] This equitable power, however, is not unlimited. . . . Furthermore, absent the existence of some form of inequitable conduct on the part of the claimant, the court cannot subordinate a claim to claims within the same class."[50] The court then commented that Code §507 fixed the order of priority of claims and expenses against the bankruptcy estate. "Creditors within a given class are to be treated equally, and bankruptcy courts may not create their own rules of superpriority within a given class. . . ."[51]

The court of appeals disagreed with the bankruptcy court that the fundamental nature of the practice was not changed by the fact that the bankruptcy court sanctioned the practice. The court also disagreed with the district court's conclusion that "[w]hile cross-collateralization may violate some policies of bankruptcy law, it is consistent with the general purpose of Chapter 11 to help businesses reorganize and become profitable. . . ."[52] This end, however, does not justify the use of any means. Cross-collateralization is directly inconsistent with the priority scheme of the Bankruptcy Code. Accordingly, the

---

[47] *Id.*

[48] *Id.* at 1495. citing Young v. Higbee Co., 65 S.Ct. 594 (1945), 11 U.S.C. §105(a). *See also infra* Chapter 14, this handbook, Trustee's Strong Arm Powers.

[49] *Id.* citing Pepper v. Litton, 60 S.Ct. 238 (1939).

[50] *Id.* citing *In re* FCX, Inc., 60 BR 405, 409 (EDNY 1986).

[51] *Id.* at 1496 citing 3 COLLIER ON BANKRUPTCY §507.02[2] (15th ed. 1992).

[52] *Id.*

practice may not be approved by the bankruptcy court under its equitable authority."[53]

The court of appeals concluded that cross-collateralization was not authorized by §364 and accordingly §364(e) was not applicable, and thus the appeal was not moot. "Because Texlon type cross-collateralization is not explicably authorized by the Bankruptcy Code and is contrary to the basic structure of the Code, we hold that it is an impermissible means of obtaining postpetition financing. The judgment of the district court is REVERSED and the case is REMANDED for proceedings not inconsistent with this opinion."[54]

Observation

The *Saybrook* court's disagreement with the *Adams Apple* decision was its holding that the appeal was moot under §364(e) but expressly declined to decide whether cross-collateralization was "illegal per se under the Code." The Ninth Circuit in *Adams Apple* had held that where cross-collateralization is granted under §364, and since no stay pending appeal is sought, §364(e) renders the appeal moot because even reversal could not affect the postpetition lender's rights. The *Saybrook* Court of Appeals explicitly stated: "We also decline to rule whether cross-collateralization is appropriate in this case, or whether as a matter of law it is even permissible."[55]

As the issue of cross-collateralization stands, the Eleventh Circuit in *Saybrook* has held that cross-collateralization has not been authorized by §364 and does not fall under the equitable powers of §105(a).[56] The Ninth Circuit in *Adams Apple* and the Sixth Circuit in *Ellingsen*[57] recognized cross-collateralization as being controversial at times, but moot on appeal if no stay is granted. However, the denial of *certiorari* of appeal may induce *certiorari* in *Saybrook* or the next circuit

---

[53] *Id.*

[54] *Id.* at 1492.

[55] 963 F2d 1494.

[56] *See infra* Chapter 14, this handbook, Trustee's Strong Arm Powers.

[57] *See supra* note 16, indicating that the Supreme Court had denied *certiorari* in the *Ellingsen* case.

court involved may compromise the issue. As for the present, a cross-collateral transaction is still available to financiers in two jurisdictions opposed to one.

We now turn to "§363. Use Sale or Lease of Property," another section designed to assist the debtor in possession by the utilization of the property of the estate in the furtherance of the operation of its business.

Chapter 3
Use, Sale, or Lease of Property

As we discussed in Chapter 2 of this handbook, §364 opens the door for a Debtor to obtain credit for the operation of its business. Now, we arrive at §363,[1] which affords a Debtor another opportunity to support its operations. Recognizing the importance of the continuance of the Debtor's operations, the Code provides that upon the filing of the chapter 11 petition, the debtor in possession may enter into transactions, including the use, sale, or lease of property of the estate in the "ordinary course of business without notice or a hearing."[2] In addition, the debtor in possession, after "notice and a hearing, may use, sell, or lease other than in the ordinary course of business, property of the estate. . . ."[3]

---

[1] See §363. Use, sale or lease of property.

[2] See "§363(c)(1). If the business of the debtor is authorized to be operated under section 721, 1108 . . . of this title and unless the court orders otherwise, the trustee may enter into transactions, . . ."

[3] See §363(b)(1). See also §541. Property of the estate.

Although the Code broadly indicates what property of the estate includes, specific exceptions exist to the use of certain property under §363 without the approval of the court. Most significant is the prohibition against the use, sale, or lease of "cash collateral" that is broadly defined to mean "cash, negotiable instruments, documents of title, securities, deposit accounts, or other cash equivalents whenever acquired in which the estate and an entity other than the estate have an interest and includes the proceeds . . . whether existing before or after the commencement of a case under this title."[4]

Limitation of Sale of Property by Debtor in Possession

After setting forth the Debtor's authorization to operate as set forth in both sections,[5] the Code limits the use of cash collateral in additional subsections.[6] The trustee may not use, sell, or lease the cash collateral unless upon consent of the entity[7] that has an interest in the cash collateral, or unless the court authorizes such use in accordance with the provisions of subsection 363(c)(2). Subsection 363(c)(3) sets forth the procedure for a preliminary hearing and, if necessary, a final hearing to determine the necessity. Subsection 363(c)(4) requires the debtor in possession to segregate and account for any cash collateral in its possession, custody, or control. As to property other than cash collateral, which does not come within "ordinary course of business," the trustee may use, sell, or lease such property after notice and a hearing.[8]

Prime Case: Use of Cash Collateral

With this background of the use of cash collateral, we turn to a practical application in the *Prime*[9] case that involved a

---

[4] *See* §§363(b) and 363(c)(1).

[5] *See* §363(c)(1).

[6] *See* §363(c)(2)(3) and(4).

[7] *See* §101(15): "'entity' includes person, estate, trust government unit and United States Trustee."

[8] *See* §363(b)(1).

[9] *In re* Prime, Inc. ("Prime" or "Debtor"), 15 BR 216 (WD Mo. 1981).

"good sized over-the-road trucking company, headquartered in Springfield, Missouri."[10] Operating funds were obtained from *CIT Corporation* (CIT) financing its accounts receivable. In August or September 1981, Prime purged a number of accounts as duplicates or as having credits against them.

Filing of Chapter 11: Restraining Order

CIT became concerned as to the validity of the accounts being assigned and raised questions as to the future of the arrangement. Several meetings between Prime and CIT did not resolve the problem. On October 15, 1981, Prime filed a chapter 11 petition. Immediately thereafter, on October 16, CIT obtained a Temporary Restraining Order prohibiting Prime from using accounts receivable collections in accordance with the prohibitions set forth in §363(c). A hearing was held, set for October 20, arranged by telephone, and Prime filed its motion to allow such use on October 11, 1981. At the hearing the parties appeared as well as the largest unsecured creditor. "Evidence was heard."[11]

Adequate Protection of Cash Collateral

The court opined: "When a court permits the use of cash collateral, the creditor is entitled to adequate protection of its security interest. Section 363(e) authorizes the court to condition such 'use as is necessary to provide adequate protection of such interest.' Methods by which adequate protection may be provided are set out, although not to be exclusive, in section 361. 'The precise form and sufficiency of such protection must be developed by the trustee . . . and addressed to the sound discretion of the Court.'"[12]

The Debtor argued that CIT was adequately protected because the amount of the accounts receivable was equal to the debt and CIT had a secured position in real and personal property, and other accounts not held by CIT. However, CIT contended that the validity of the accounts was in serious

---

[10] *Id.* at 217.

[11] *Id.*

[12] *Id.* citing *In re* Heatron, 6 BR 493, 494 (B. WD Mo. 1980).

question; it calculated the value at substantially less than the debt; and argued that there was no credible testimony as to the value of the other property.

Procedure of Collecting Receivables

After reviewing the testimony, the court stated the procedure whereby the Debtor books an account when it picks up the merchandise. The amount of those accounts are reported to CIT, which advanced a fixed percentage of that amount to the Debtor. When the account is collected, all of the collection is paid over to CIT. Ineligibles are returned to Debtor for collection but money collected is to be paid to CIT. At the time of the proceedings ineligible accounts amounted to $700,000. On the day of the filing, the accounts receivable totalled $3,390,000 of which $721,000 were ineligible. The amount advanced was $2.6 million and the collateral "a little more." From billing to collection the time lapse was about 30 days. Debtor's witnesses testified that it needed about $600,000 weekly to operate. Unless the financing arrangement continued, the Debtor would be out of business before the outstanding accounts could be verified.

The court opined that as long as the billing system has integrity, the arrangement works and CIT can advance funds and maintain sufficient cushioning to protect against bad debt. "What the evidence shows here is that the billing system prior to bankruptcy lacked adequate safeguards. Substantial accounts had to be purged, wiping out CIT's margin of safety and, if CIT's evidence is to be believed, causing the amount of accounts receivable assigned to be substantially less than the debt."[13]

After reviewing the activity of Prime from billing to collection, and the money needed to operate each week and supplied by CIT, Prime would be out of business before the outstanding accounts could be verified. "It is not the purpose of a Chapter 11 proceeding to close a business at the beginning. While CIT disputes the precise amount of money necessary to operate the Debtor, it does not contest the notion

---

[13] *Id.* at 218.

that Debtor needs money to survive. Nor does CIT refuse to be the source of the funds."[14]

Arrangement: Executory Contract

This last holding led the court to conclude that the debt financing arrangement was "an executory contract from day to day." However, §365(c) provides in part that the Debtor may not assume an executory contract . . . of the Debtor . . . if[15] such contract is a contract to make a loan or extend other debt financing to or for the benefit of the Debtor. . . ."[16] The court observed that, read literally, the section of the statute prohibits assumption whether the creditor consents or not. The court was satisfied, however, that read in the context of the statutory powers[17] given the trustee to operate a business, §365(c)(2) does permit assumption of a debt financing arrangement. "The statutory pattern permits the inference in the language of Section 365(c)(2) that the trustee may assume a contract for debt financing if the creditor consents. Here, the creditor having consented, the arrangement is lawful."[18]

Having resolved the problem that the transaction between the parties was an executory contract, the court had for consideration the time necessary to ascertain the value of the debts owed CIT on the date of filing. "Considering the volume of transactions, however, the answer will be known in about six weeks. In the interim, the effect of allowing Debtor to use cash collateral is to create some risk of loss to CIT. The challenge is to determine the funding arrangement which will

---

[14] *Id.*

[15] *Id.* at 218.

[16] *Id. See* §365(c). *See infra* Chapter 13, this handbook, Assumption or Rejection of Executory Contracts and Unexpired Leases of Real Property.

[17] *Id.* citing the statutory powers: (1) §1108 permitting trustee (debtor in possession under §1107) to operate Debtor's business without affirmative orders of court; (2) §363 permitting trustee to use, sell or lease property in ordinary course of business; (3) §364 permitting trustee to obtain credit as unsecured debt and secured debt accompanied by administrative claim. *See supra* Chapter 2, this handbook, Lender's Participation subtitle "Higher Priorities For Borrowing."

[18] *Id.* at 219.

keep Debtor operating while maintaining adequate protection for the creditor."[19]

Maintaining Adequate Protection

Taking into consideration the other assets upon which CIT had a lien in addition to the accounts receivable, the court held that CIT had adequate protection, but as to maintain that adequate protection, the court found it necessary to maintain such status that future advances could be made based only on new billings. "Adequate protection will be afforded by more careful monitoring of the accounts, audits by CIT and by reduction in the amount of the advance. . . . Use of cash collateral, therefore is authorized upon the following terms and conditions: . . ." The list contained eleven subdivisions, all with the exception of three items, commenced with requirements starting with "Debtor," such as: "1. Debtor is to make a daily report of new billings to *CIT*. . . 3. Debtor is to collect . . . 6. Debtor is to pay over to *CIT* all funds collected. . . 7. Debtor shall account to the Court. . . ."

As for the eleven Debtor requirements, CIT had to perform three: "2. CIT, by agreement will advance such sums of money, from day to day, averaging 70% of the value of the accounts receivable assigned by Debtor. Such advances are to have an administrative priority . . ."[20] 9. CIT shall have the right to audit Debtor's business two days each week . . . 10. CIT shall furnish to the Court a weekly report of accounts assigned, payments received and advances made. . . ."[21]

Rehearing Borrowing of Funds

All is well that ends well, but after operating a few days, at the 70% level of advance and having developed a summary analysis of expenses, Debtor requested a hearing on the level of advances. "Evidence was presented showing that Debtor's operating expenses and fixed costs were about $.85 a mile and that it requested therefore advances of 85% of the amount of

---

[19] *Id.*

[20] *Id. See also* §503. Allowance of Administrative expenses.

[21] *Id.*

the assigned accounts receivable if it were to survive." *CIT* did not oppose the expenses or the projections. It argued that Debtor was now operating at its most efficient level. The issue had now expanded beyond consideration of cash collateral to obtaining credit under §364: "No unsecured credit in the amounts needed by Debtor are available. *CIT* is willing to continue in an arrangement that . . . [i]n each instance the creditor is granted a lien on property of the estate. Since *CIT* is the secured party in such property, the question of adequate protection by Section 364(d)(1)(B) is moot. . . ."[22] As to advances made at the 70% level, there appears to be sufficient cushion, in light of the testimony, to guard against dilution. These advances, the contract concludes, are adequately secured."[23]

There was a doubt, however, as to the advances at 85%. Confronted with the fact that Debtor's survival was at stake, the court ordered such advances at such level for two weeks. The advances were to be eligible against assigned accounts as at the date following the hearing. No advances were to be required against collections, and all other conditions set out in the court's prior order were incorporated in the present order.

Observation

The *Prime* case touches four sections of the six Administrative Powers of the Bankruptcy Code,[24] which extend from sections 361 (Adequate protection), 362 (Automatic stay), 363 (Use, sale or lease of property), 364 (Obtaining credit), 365 (Executory contracts and unexpired leases), to 366 (Utility Service).[25] Prime's case did not have to discuss sections 362 and 366, which is the Automatic as its name indicates its restraint against creditors, and utilities services, which have a distinct method of payment.

While the court's comment that the powers given to Debtors in the foregoing and other sections constitute an indication that "Congress intended business under reorganiza-

---

[22] *See supra,* Chapter 2, this handbook, subtitle "Mootness."

[23] 15 B.R. at 220.

[24] *See* Bankruptcy Code Subchapter IV "Administrative Powers." *See also infra* Chapter 6, this handbook, Automatic Stay.

[25] *See* §366(a)(4), "Utility Service".

tion to proceed in as normal a fashion as possible," we can conclude that in the *Prime* case it did. Although the strength of the court's opinion to a great extent relied upon the consensual agreement of CIT, the result is not to be a criticism of its position, but may have turned out to be beneficial to *CIT* as compared to a possible liquidation of the Debtor's assets. Upon liquidation the collection of accounts receivable, presents unattractive returns, but the administrative sections present balanced alternatives to debtor and creditor.

Sale of Property Not In Ordinary Course

Having considered the Debtor's "use" of property, we turn now to several cases where the DIP endeavored to sell property out of the regular course of its business. Subsection 363(b)(1)[26] allows such property to be sold other than in the ordinary course of business, subject to notice and a hearing. Also to be noted is §363(f) that allows a DIP "to sell property under section 363 (b) or (c) free and clear of any interest in such property of an entity other than the estate, only if . . ." the following conditions are satisfied: (1) applicable nonbankruptcy law permits; (2) such entity consents; (3) such interest is a lien and the selling price is greater than all the liens; (4) such interest is in bona fide dispute; or entity could be compelled in legal or equitable proceeding to accept a money satisfaction. Not to be overlooked is subsection 363(f) that allows a Debtor with court approval "to use, sell, or lease, under §§363(b) or (c)." Several cases emphasize the court's close scrutiny of such sales. In the *White Motor* case,[27] the bankruptcy court approved a sale of all assets recognizing the existence of an emergency. In the *Lionel* case,[28] the Second Circuit Court of Appeals delineated grounds that constituted such emergency but held the application insufficient. In

---

[26] *See* §363(b)(1): "The [Debtor], after notice and a hearing may use, sell or lease, other than in the ordinary course of business, property of the estate." *See also* §365(c)(1)(A), which prohibits trustee from assuming executory contract if applicable nonbankruptcy law excuses the other party from performance.

[27] *In re* White Motor Credit Corp., 14 BR 584 (N.D. Ohio 1981).

[28] *In re* Lionel Corp., 722 F2d 1063 (2d Cir. 1983).

addition, in the *Braniff* case,[29] the Fifth Circuit Court of Appeals refused to approve a sale of certain assets since several features of the sale constituted in essence part of a *de facto* plan of reorganization.[30]

Bad Faith: Vacating Sale

Now we turn to *Abbotts Dairies*[31] where the court determined that the sale of the Debtor's business was conducted in bad faith and the transaction was reversed. On the same day that Abbotts Dairies filed the chapter 11 petition, it also filed motions seeking court approval of two agreements that would result in the sale of its business. The same afternoon, the court held an emergency hearing, notice of which was given only to the Debtor's two secured creditors. During testimony, the Debtor's chief executive officer (CEO) testified as to the exigent circumstances warranting the immediate sale of the business. On cross-examination it was disclosed that the CEO would act as a consultant to the purchaser at a salary of $150,000 annually.

At the conclusion of the hearing, the bankruptcy court entered an order provisionally approving the sale. Notice of the motion for approval was then sent to all interested parties. The notice summarized the Purchase Agreement and set a deadline for objections to it, as well as for more lucrative bids. The notice, however did not disclose the CEO's contemplated relationship with the prospective purchaser, that an emergency hearing had been held, nor did it summarize the terms of the agreement approved by the court.

Upon one objector's motion for a stay, the bankruptcy court initially enjoined the sale, which ordered it later vacated. After the sale to the prospective purchaser was completed, the

---

[29] *In re* Braniff Airways, Inc., 700 F2d 935 (5th Cir. 1983).

[30] *See infra* Chapter 18, this handbook, subtitle "De Facto Plan." *See also* Crowthers McCall Pattern, Inc. v. Lewis, 114 BR 407 (SDNY 1990) for constituents of a *de facto* plan. *See also* Braniff Airways at 940: "The Debtor and the bankruptcy court should not be able to short circuit the requirements of chapter 11 for confirmation of a reorganization plan by establishing the terms of the plan *sub rosa* in connection with a sale of assets."

[31] *In re* Abbotts Dairies of Pa., Inc. ("Debtor"), 788 F2d 143 (3d Cir. 1986).

district court dismissed the objector's motion as moot.[32] The circuit court reversed, finding that the bankruptcy court did not make an explicit finding of good faith with respect to the prospective purchaser's conduct during the course of the sale proceedings:

> For example, prior to the . . . hearing . . . [the objector] filed a number of written objections to the proposed sale that were relevant to the issue of [the prospective purchaser's] "good faith." These included . . . claims that certain terms of the Interim Agreement had "chilled" the bidding . . . and that insufficient value was being paid. . . .[33]

> Under these circumstances, then, the district court erred when it dismissed the present appeals as moot. . . .

The court of appeals also considered that the prospective purchaser's lucrative offer of employment to the Debtor's CEO and the timing of the filing of the petitions in bankruptcy, and the motion for approval of the interim agreement, created a situation that was "ripe for collusion and interested dealing" between the Debtor and the prospective purchaser.[34] Accordingly, the district court's judgment will be reversed and the matter remanded to the district court with instruction to remand it to the bankruptcy court for proceedings consistent with this opinion.[35]

Undersecured Creditor: Adequate Protection

Although we have discussed Adequate Protection in Chapter 2, we again refer to the subject as it affects the "use"

---

[32] *See infra* Chapter 2, this handbook, subtitle "Mootness."

[33] 788 F2d at 148.

[34] *Id.* at 149, citing: *cf.* Wolverton v. Shell Oil Co., 442 F2d 666, 669–70 (9th Cir. 1971).

[35] *Id.* at 151.

of property by the Debtor in the *Timbers* case.[36] *United Savings*, an undersecured creditor, moved for adequate protection. The bankruptcy court required the Debtor to make monthly payments for adequate protection approving United Savings' contention that it was entitled to interest on its collateral as compensation for delay caused by the restraint of the automatic stay on its collateral.

On June 29, 1982, *Timbers* had executed a note of $4,100,000 in favor of *United Savings*, which was secured by an apartment project and an assignment of rents. On March 4, 1985, almost three years after the transaction, *Timbers* filed a petition under chapter 11. Two weeks thereafter *United Savings* moved for relief from the automatic stay on the ground that there was "a lack of 'adequate protection' of its interest within the meaning of 11 U.S.C. §362(d)(1). . . ."[37] Since the Debtor's collateral was valued at $4,250,000 or less and the amount due was $4,366,388.77, it was undisputed that petitioner was an undersecured creditor. The bankruptcy court agreed with the Debtor that it would allow a continuation of the stay or monthly payments on the market rate of 12% per annum on the estimated amount realizable on foreclosure to effect the normal foreclosure delays and allowed the application of postpetition rents. *Certiorari* was for time "to determine whether undersecured creditors are entitled to compensation under 11 U.S.C. 362(d)(1) for the delay caused by the automatic stay in foreclosing on their collateral."[38]

Referring to subsections 362(d)(1) and 361, the Supreme Court held that the meaning of "interest in property" must be determined by several sections of the Code. Section 506(a) holds that an undersecured creditor's "interest in property obviously means his security interest without taking account of his right to immediate possession of the collateral on default. . . . The phrase 'value of such creditor's interest' in §506(a) means 'the value of the collateral.' We think the

---

[36] *See* United Savings Assoc. of Texas ("United Savings") v. Timbers of Inwood Forest Assoc., Ltd. ("Timbers"),108 S.Ct. 626 (1988).

[37] *See* §362(d)(1) dealing with relief from the automatic stay: ". . . for cause, including the lack of adequate protection of an interest in property of such party in interest; or. . . ."

[38] *Id.*

phrase 'value of such entity's interest' in §361 and (2), when applied to secured creditors, means the same."[39]

More important than the terminology of §506 was its "substantive effect of denying undersecured creditors postpetition interest on their claims—just as it denies *over* secured creditors postpetition interest to the extent that such interest, when added to the principal amount of the claim will exceed the value of the collateral. . . ."[40]

As to the agreement by Timbers to pay Union Savings the postpetition rents from the apartment project, which was covered by the after-acquired property clause in the security agreement, the Supreme Court held: "Section 552(a) states the general rule that a prepetition security interest does not reach property acquired by the estate or Debtor postpetition. Section 552(b) sets forth an exception allowing postpetition 'proceeds, product, offspring, rents, or profits' of the collateral to be covered only if the security agreement expressly provides for an interest in such property and the interest has been perfected under 'applicable nonbankruptcy law.'"[41]

Supreme Court: Defines Indubitable Equivalent

Union Savings contended among other issues that denying it compensation under §362(d)(1)[42] is inconsistent with the phrase, "indubitable equivalent" in §361 and in the provisions of §1129(b).[43] The Court, however, did not disagree that Union

---

[39] *Id.* at 630. *See* "§361. Adequate Protection. When adequate protection is required under section 362, 363, 364 of an interest of an entity or property, such adequate protection may be provided by—(1) requiring the trustee to make a cash payment . . . [or] (2) providing to such entity an additional or replacement lien. . . ."

[40] *Id.*

[41] 108 S.Ct. at 631 citing *In re* Casbeer, 793 F2d 1436, 1442-44 (5th Cir. 1986).

[42] *Id.* at 633. *See also* §362(d)(1): ". . . the court shall grant relief from the stay...by terminating...or conditioning such stay—(1) for cause, including the lack of adequate protection of an interest in property of such party in interest; . . ."

[43] *Id. See also* §361(3) and §1129(b)(2)(A)(iii): "For the purpose of this subsection the condition that a plan be fair and equitable with respect to a class includes the following requirements: (A) with respect to a class of secured claims, the plan provides (iii) for the realization by such holders of

Savings was entitled under §1129(b) to receive the present value of its collateral.

The Supreme Court found no merit in Union Savings' argument that indubitable equivalent connoted "reimbursement for the use value of collateral because the phrase was derived from *In re* Murel Holding Corp. . . .[44] where it bore that meaning. . . ." *Murel* was a proposed reorganization that provided interest to a secured creditor of over ten years with payment of the principal at the end of the term. No provision was included for amortization of the principal or maintenance of the collateral's value during the term. "In rejecting the plan, Murel used the words 'indubitable equivalence' with specific reference not to interest (which was assured) but to the jeopardized principal of the loan. . . ."[45]

Adequate Protection

The Supreme Court concluded that the Fifth Circuit correctly held that Union Savings, an undersecured creditor, was not entitled to interest on its collateral during the stay to assure adequate protection under 11 U.S.C. §362(d)(1). The Court also noted that Union Savings never sought relief from the stay under §362(d)(2)[46] or on any ground other than lack of adequate protection. While adequate protection is a flexible doctrine, limited only by the improved prospects of the Debtor, the approval of the secured creditor, and other creditors, the Supreme Court placed restrictions on its application. Specifically, the Court ruled that adequate protection did not contemplate postpetition interest payments to an undersecured creditor as compensation for lost opportunity costs.

---

the indubitable equivalent of such claims. . . ."

[44] *Id.* citing *In re* Murel Holding Corp. ("Murel"), 75 F2d 941 (2d Cir. 1935).

[45] *Id.* at 633.

[46] *Id.* at 635. *See also* §365(d): "[T]he court shall grant relief from the stay . . . (2) . . . against property under subsection (a) of this section, if—(A) the Debtor does not have an equity in such property; and (B) such property is not necessary to an effective reorganization," and *infra* Chapter 13, this handbook, "Assumption or Rejection of Executory Contracts and Unexpired Leases of Real Property."

Adequate Protection: Super Priority Claim

The reader will recall that "Adequate Protection" also was provided in §364(d)(1)(B) in Chapter 2 to enable a Debtor to obtain credit. Now we call attention to another similarity between sections. Section 363(m) dealing with the reversal or modification on appeal of an authorization under subsection (b) (sale or lease of property other than in the ordinary course of business), and subsection (c) (sale or lease in the ordinary course of business) "does not affect the validity of a sale or lease under such authorization to an entity that purchased or leased such property in good faith. . . ." The interplay of both subsections 363(m) and 364(d)(1)(B) is readily seen whether a DIP user sells or leases its own property or obtains credit through or subordinates liens on its own property. Adequate protection is meant to protect the lienor whose property is being subordinated to a senior lienor.

An inquisitive lienor may very well ask: Assuming the adequate protection doesn't protect the existing lienor by this superpriority, where does that leave the existing lienor? We look to §507(a) which provides for a sequential listing of priorities of claims. Subsection (b) which deals with the debtor in possession providing adequate protection under §§362, 363, and 364 to the holder of a claim secured by a lien on property of the Debtor, presents an answer: "and if notwithstanding such protection such creditor has a claim allowable under subsection (a)(1) of this section [administrative expenses] arising from the stay of action against such property under section 362 of this title, from the use, sale, or lease of such property under section 363 of this title, or from the granting of a lien under section 364(d) of this title, then such creditor's claim under such subsection shall have priority over every other claim under such subsection."

State Law: Defining Property

In the *Mini Storage*[47] case, we hear another call to a mortgagee for funds from a mortgagor who owned a mini-

---

[47] *In re* 163rd Street Mini Storage, Inc. (or "Mortgagor," "Debtor" or "Mini Storage."), 113 BR 87 (B. SD. Fla. 1990).

storage warehouse facility. Although there were three mortgages on the property, the court limited its discussion by the
issue raised by the first mortgagee, Professional Savings
Bank.[48] On February 10, 1988 the Debtor executed and
delivered a Promissory Note ("Note") and a Mortgage and
Security Agreement ("Mortgage") securing payment of the
Note to Professional.

The Mortgage contained a provision for the absolute
assignment of the rents, leases, and security deposits payable
to the Debtor under leases of storage space to third parties.
The Mortgage and Note were extended to August 9, 1989.
Defaults were thereafter made by the Debtor in making
monthly payments and an outstanding balance when the
extended loan matured. Professional thereafter instituted
foreclosure procedures, which were followed by the Debtors
filing a chapter 11.

Promptly thereafter, the Debtor filed a motion under
§363(c)(2)[49] and B. Rule 4001(b)[50] requesting the court to
authorize the use of cash collateral derived from the property.
Professional filed an objection. The court conducted an
evidentiary hearing and the central issues addressed in the
court's opinion were: "[W]hether the mortgagee's issuance of
the notice provided in §697.07, Fla. Stat., creates an absolute
ownership interest of the rents derived from the mortgaged
property, such that those rents are not property of the Debtor's
estate under Section 541(a) of the Bankruptcy Code, and
accordingly not cash collateral as defined in 11 U.S.C. §363(a).

"This threshold issue must be resolved prior to addressing
the cash collateral issue raised by Debtor's motion. If, as
Professional contends, the effect of its §697.07 notice is to
transform the collateral assignment of rents into an absolute
assignment, then the rents are neither property of the estate
nor cash collateral, and the motion must be denied."[51]

The court rejected the Debtor's argument that notwithstanding the state's reason for enacting the statute, the

---

[48] Professional Savings Bank ("Professional").

[49] 113 BR 88. *See* §363(c)(2) (requiring consent for use of cash collateral
by entity having an interest in property or court).

[50] *See* B.Rule 4001(b). "Use of Cash Collateral".

[51] 113 BR 88.

interpretation of §697.07, the equities of the case authorized the court to allow the use of rents as cash collateral under 11 U.S.C. §363(c)(2). . . .[52] Rejecting the Debtor's arguments and indicating that the Mortgage contained an assignment of rents clauses governed by §697.07, the court held: "It would be utterly improper for the Court to rewrite the Note and Mortgage in order to revive rights which have passed to the Mortgagee by operation of the §697.07 demand."[53]

Observation: Chapters 2 and 3 Cross

Analogies between sections of the Bankruptcy Code and their interrelationship are a necessity in carrying out the objective of rehabilitating the Debtor and at the same time granting adequate protection to prospective financiers as well as to the secured creditors. Indeed, the Supreme Court in the *Timbers* case stated: "Statutory Construction, however, is a holistic endeavor. A provision that seems ambiguous in isolation is often clarified by the remainder of the statutory scheme. . . ."[54]

For example, in the *Adams Apple* case in Chapter 2,[55] an objection was raised to the lender who received a cross-collateralization of its unsecured claim so as to rank it above all other unsecured claims, on the grounds that the fundamental intent of bankruptcy was that like creditors should be treated alike. The court responded: "It is flawed because the 'fundamental tenet'—rehabilitation of Debtors, which may supersede the policy of equal treatment." Yet, in the *Saybrook* case, the Eleventh Circuit, criticizing *Adams Apple*, held that like creditors, such as unsecured, should not be diminished by cross-collateralization by secured creditors and equitable relief should not supersede such relief.

---

[52] *Id.* at 90. *See* §363(c)(2) authorizing use of cash collateral subject to a security interest only with consent of entity which has an interest or the court.

[53] *Id.* at 90, citing Principal Mutual Life Insurance Co. v. Lamb, 552 So. 2d 1156, 1157 (3d D. Ca. 1989).

[54] *See supra* note 36 and text of *In re* Timbers of Inwood Forest, 108 S.Ct. 626 (1988).

[55] *See supra* Chapter 2, this handbook, subtitle "Cross-Collateralization Challenged."

Nor can a Debtor forget the power of state law that endeavors to apply helpful provisions to mortgagees. "The issue appears to be one of first impression within the District. In *Butner v. United States*,[56] . . . the Supreme Court concluded that the right to rents and profits derived from mortgaged property is to be determined by laws of the state in which the property is located rather than by federal law. Accordingly, the Court must apply Florida law, specifically §697.07, Fla. Stat., to the case at bar."

The Code having bolstered the Debtor with opportunities to strengthen its reorganization, we turn now to §105(a), "Power of Court," which grants the court the power to assist the Debtor by utilizing its equitable powers in carrying out the provisions of chapter 11.

---

[56] *Id.* at 88; 99 S.Ct. 914 (1979).

Chapter 4
Power of Court

C ontinuing the operation of the DIP's business is a prime consideration towards its ultimate rehabilitation. This fundamental objective of keeping the Debtor functioning requires immediate payments from the Debtor's funds or borrowings upon the filing of the petition and bears the sobriquet of "first-day" orders. As the cash flow is failing to accommodate the Debtor's needs, in an effort to accommodate these immediate needs, a court will invoke its equitable powers under subsection 105(a): "The court may issue any order, process or judgment that is necessary or appropriate to carry out the provisions of [chapter 11]. . . ."[1]

---

[1] *See* §105. Power of Court. *See also, supra* note 29, Chapter 2, this handbook, subtitle "First Day Order."

Business Necessity First-Day Orders

Accordingly, in the chapter 11 case of *Laventhal & Horwath*,[2] the court authorized payment to employees whose prepetition wages and necessary expenses earned within 30 days prior to the filing of the chapter 11 petition had previously remained unpaid. In addition, authorization was issued for payment of checks issued to employees, but had not been presented to the banks for payment. Other approved expenses included health and medical services paid under a health plan, authorized vacation pay, and workers' compensation benefits.

The necessity requiring the immediate approval of these otherwise limited or general claims was indicated in the application presented to the court. The application explained that it was impossible to maintain the Debtor's operation without the critical daily services performed by these employees. Unless payments were authorized by the court, the business would cease to operate, consequently thwarting the rehabilitative purposes of chapter 11.

Hills Department Stores

Similar reasoning was presented by Hills Department Stores,[3] upon the filing of their chapter 11 petitions. In their application seeking payment of prepetition employee-related claims, the Debtor primarily emphasized that "[c]ontinued service by . . . [e]mployees is vital to the Debtors' ongoing operations and ability to successfully reorganize."[4]

Accepting the Debtor's position, the court authorized payment of prepetition wages and salaries; out-of-pocket business-related expenses; certain health benefits; vacation pay; workers' compensation claims; and, other essential services connected to the operation of the Debtors' business.

---

[2] Case No. 90 B 13839(CB)(B.SDNY) and *infra* Chapter 19, this handbook, subtitle "Confirmation: Consensual and Cram Down Combined" for a discussion of the case.

[3] *In re* Hills Department Stores Company ("Debtors" or "Hills"), Case No. 91 B 10488 (TLB) (B. SDNY 1991).

[4] *Id.*

Nonapproved Necessity

Not every business necessity application is approved by the court. The application presented in the *Mabey*[5] case failed to receive circuit court approval. In that case, the district court ordered the establishment of an emergency treatment fund for the purpose of providing tubal reconstructive surgery or in vitro fertilization to eligible Dalkon Shield claimants. Fund disbursement was scheduled to occur prior to plan confirmation and prior to the allowance of claims of the Debtor's other creditors. The court referred to its broad equitable powers pursuant to subsection 105(a) as its grant of authority to establish the fund.[6]

The court of appeals reversed the district court stating that the fund would only benefit certain unsecured claimants and that the disbursement of such funds prior to the plan of confirmation violated the dictates of the Code, which prevents distribution to unsecured creditors except under a plan that has been properly presented and approved.

Observation

The critical inquiry is what distinguishes the *Mabey* case from circumstances like those in *Laventhal and Hills*. The primary distinction can be found in the fundamental objective of chapter 11, which is to rehabilitate and sustain the financial health of the Debtor. This goal often cannot be accomplished without the court's power to allow payment of certain unsecured claims outside of specific statutory authorization. Consequently, where it could be proved that the

---

[5] Official Committee of Equity Security Holders v. Mabey ("Mabey"), 832 F2d 299 (4th Cir. 1987) (an A.H. Robins Co. case action arising in AH Robins Co., Inc. v. Aetna Casualty & Surety Co., 828 F.2d 1023 (4th Cir. 1987)). *See also infra* this chapter subtitle "Injuries Prepetition."

[6] The court's powers under §105(a) are equitable in nature and such powers extend, *inter alia,* to a preliminary injunction restraining the prosecution of product liability actions against codefendants. *See, e.g., In re* A.H. Robins Co., Inc., v. Aetna Casualty & Surety Co., 828 F2d 1023, 1025 (4th Cir. 1987).

preconfirmation, postpetition payments made in *Laventhal*[7] and *Hills Department Stores* were necessary to preserve the life of the DIP, a similar argument was unavailing with respect to disbursements made pursuant to the emergency fund. In the latter situation, although the group of unsecured claimants presented a sympathetic case, payments could not be justified on the necessity of sustaining the operation of the Debtor.

As a secondary consideration, the claims in *Laventhal* may, for the most part, constitute administrative claims that rank high on the ladder of distribution as opposed to the unsecured status of the claims in *Mabey*, which are located at the bottom rung of claims.[8]

Having commented on first-day orders, we turn now to the power of the court to extend its authority without a time limitation so that the court may "carry out the provisions of" chapter 11, and even enjoin suits against third parties that not only would have an impact against Debtor's operations but also would interfere with its reorganization.

Johns-Manville Suit Against Employees Restrained

In the *Johns-Manville*[9] case, the court was confronted with the basic problem of "whether the automatic stay extended to [a suit or examination of] the Debtors' employees, agents and other related entities." Could the court employ the "use of its equitable powers to grant such extension of the stay pursuant to §§362 and 105 of the Code?" The Debtor argued that allowing the continuation of asbestos-related lawsuits against

---

[7] *See* Chapter 18, this handbook, discussing the Laventhal & Horwath case, where plan was confirmed on August 24, 1992. A.H. Robins Co. was also confirmed.

[8] *See* §507. Priorities: "(a) the following expenses and claims have priority in the following order: (1) First, administrative expenses allowed under section 503(b) of this title . . . ;(2) Second, unsecured claims allowed under section 502(f) [gap claims in an involuntary case]; (3) Third, allowed unsecured claims for wages, salaries, or commissions, including vacation, severance, and sick leave pay— . . . ."

[9] *In re* Johns-Manville Corp. ("Debtor"), 26 BR 420 (B. SDNY 1983) *aff'd,* 40 BR 219 (B. SDNY 1984).

its employees, agents and others would impact the Debtors' estate inasmuch as the Debtors are contractually obligated to defend and indemnify such persons.

Accepting the Debtors' argument, the court invoked its equitable powers pursuant to §105. In doing so, the court recognized that "in great measure the suits being pursued against Manville's officers and employees are in reality derivative of identical claims brought against Manville."[10] Accordingly, the injunction was necessary to protect the Debtor's reorganization.[11]

Supreme Court's Application:
§105(a) Restrains IRS

Concern for the reorganizational efforts of the Debtor was also echoed by the Supreme Court when it approved the application of §105(a) as a method to alter creditor-debtor relationships in order to revive financially distressed companies. In the Energy Resources case,[12] the Court held that §105(a) supplied the bankruptcy court with the requisite authority to order the Internal Revenue Service (IRS) to treat tax payments made by chapter 11 debtor corporations as trust fund payments.[13] The debtor was delinquent on the payment of trust fund tax debts as well as nontrust fund tax debts. The confirmed plan of reorganization contained a provision authorizing the Debtor to satisfy trust fund tax debt prior to paying nontrust fund tax debt.

The IRS refused to allocate payments in accordance with the provision, reasoning that trust fund tax debt was guaranteed whereas nontrust fund debt was not, thereby leaving the IRS at risk for potentially unpaid nontrust fund tax obligations. Further, the IRS argued that the plan's provision

---

[10] 26 BR 420, 426 (B. SDNY 1983).

[11] See In re Skinner, 917 F2d 444, 447 (10th Cir. 1990): ". . . [T]he weight of authority supports our holding that section 105(a) empowers bankruptcy courts to enter civil contempt orders. . . ."

[12] U.S. v. Energy Resources Co., Inc. ("Debtor"), 110 S.Ct. 2139 (1990).

[13] Employers are required to withhold certain funds from employees' paychecks. These funds are commonly referred to as "trust fund" taxes.

conflicted with the Bankruptcy Code, which protects the Government's ability to collect delinquent taxes.[14]

Relying predominantly on the bankruptcy court's equitable powers in §105, the Court rejected the IRS's position:

> It is evident that these restrictions on the bankruptcy court's authority do not preclude the court from issuing orders of the type at issue here, . . . [W]hereas the Code gives it the right to be assured that its taxes will be paid in six years,[15] the Government wants an assurance that its taxes will be paid even if the reorganization fails–*i.e.*, even if the bankruptcy court is incorrect in its judgment that the reorganization plan will succeed.[16]

Injunction

Section 105(a)

Postconfirmation

We now go many steps beyond the first-day orders. An order has been signed confirming the Debtor's plan of reorganization. The automatic stay has ceased. The Debtor turns to §105. The *Carolina Parachute* case[17] is on point.

In 1986 the Government entered into several contracts with Carolina Parachute. On October 21, 1987, Carolina filed for Chapter 11. On September 2, 1988 Carolina Parachute (now DIP) filed its plan of reorganization and disclosure

---

[14] *See* §507(a)(7) (granting priority status to certain taxes); §523(a)(1)(A) (excepting from discharge taxes with priority status in §507(a)(7)).

[15] *See* §1129(a)(9)(C) . . . the plan provides that—with respect to a claim of a kind specified in section 507(a)(7) [a tax on or measured by income or gross receipts—] of this title, the holder of such claim will receive on account of such claim deferred cash payments, over a period not exceeding six years. . . ." *See also* Chapter 18, this handbook, Confirmation of Consensual Plan.

[16] 110 S.Ct. at 2142.

[17] U.S. Dept. of Air Force ("Government") v. Carolina Parachute Corp., 907 F2d 1469 (4th Cir. 1990) ("Carolina" or "DIP"). *See also infra* Chapter 20, this handbook, "Postconfirmation Matters."

statement, which was approved by the bankruptcy court, and November 9, 1988 was set as the last day to file objections.

A confirmation hearing was scheduled for November 10, 1988. The plan expressly included the assumption by the DIP of all Government contracts. Despite notification of the confirmation hearing, the Government did not attend and did not file an objection to the plan.[18] The bankruptcy judge confirmed the plan. The Government did not appeal.

Motion to Apply Automatic Stay Postconfirmation Denied

On December 10, 1988, the bankruptcy court held a hearing on the Government's motion to modify the automatic stay. This motion was adjourned to December 23, 1988, and was denied by the bankruptcy court on the grounds that the order of confirmation was a final order and the doctrine of *res judicata* precluded the government from relitigating the issue of whether the DIP might assume the contracts. "The bankruptcy court grounded the injunctive portion of its order on its equitable powers under 11 U.S.C.A. §105."[19]

The Government appealed to the district court asserting that the Anti-Assignment Act prevented assumption of the contracts. The district court, without addressing the preclusive effect of the confirmation order, held that the "interplay between the Anti-Assignment Act and 11 U.S.C.A. §365(c)(1) which precludes the assumption of executory contracts when a party other than the Debtor is excused from performance by applicable law required reversal of the December 23, 1988 order of the Bankruptcy Court."[20]

The court of appeals, brushing aside Rule 3020,[21] nevertheless held that "its failure to appeal the confirmation order is fatal to this argument. Bankruptcy Rules 8001 and 8002 set

---

[18] 907 F.2d 1469, 1471 (4th Cir. 1990), where the Court cited [B.Rule] 3020(b) (discussing procedures for filing an objection).

[19] *Id.* at 1472.

[20] *Id. See infra* Chapter 13, this handbook, Assumption or Rejection of Executory Contracts and Unexpired Leases of Real Property.

[21] *See* B.Rule 3020(b) dealing with "Objections to and Hearing on Confirmation," and 3020(c) "Order of Confirmation."

out the procedures and time limits for appealing orders of the bankruptcy court, none of which were met by the Government. . . ."[22] The court of appeals also supported the holding of the bankruptcy court that the terms of the confirmed plan were *res judicata,* but even though *res judicata* bars the Government from asserting the Anti-Assignment Act or preconfirmation defaults as grounds for terminating these contracts, "we hold that the automatic stay no longer prevents it from taking other steps, should it choose to do so, to terminate them. Under section 362(c)(2)(C) the automatic stay continues until 'the time discharge is granted or denied.' Section 1141(d)(1)(A) states that the order confirming the plan 'discharges the Debtor from any debt that arose before the date of such confirmation.' Additionally, 'the confirmation of a plan vests all property of the estate in the Debtor.' 11 U.S.C.A. §1141(b). 'Consequently, since Confirmation of the Plan has [the] dual effect . . . there can be no further application of the automatic stay after confirmation."[23]

Basis for Injunction of Postconfirmation

In addition to denying the Government's motion to lift the automatic stay, the bankruptcy judge enjoined the government from "interfering in any way with the Debtors . . . confirmed plan of reorganization." The government contends that this injunction is so broad that it: "[i]mpermissibly 'rewrites' the contracts. . . . It has eliminated the government's right to terminate the contracts assumed by the [reorganized Debtor] for post-assumption defaults, ..."[24]

The court of appeals rejected the Government's contention that the bankruptcy court did not have jurisdiction to issue an injunction. Citing 28 U.S.C. §157(a), the court had subject matter jurisdiction over "all civil proceedings arising under

---

[22] 907 F2d at 1473.

[23] *Id.* at 907 F.2d 1473, 1474. *See also* Chapter 18, this handbook, Confirmation of Consensual Plan.

[24] *Id.* at 1474.

title 11, or arising in or related to cases under title 11."[25] However, the record did not indicate what the bankruptcy court intended by the issuance of the injunction. Puzzled as to the bankruptcy court's intention by issuing the injunction and there being no indication that it was issued under §105, giving the bankruptcy court the benefit of the doubt, the court of appeals held that such injunction must conform to Rule 65(d) of the Federal Rules of Civil Procedure and that the injunction did not comply with the rule.

> Every order granting an injunction and every restraining order shall set forth the reasons for its issuance; shall be specific in terms; shall describe in reasonable detail, . . . the act or acts sought to restrain; and is binding only upon the parties to the action, their officers, agents, . . . and upon those persons in active concert or participation with them. . . .[26]

Observation

DIP and creditors alike should be aware that the automatic stay departs upon confirmation of the plan of reorganization. However, the court's power of §105 not only exists during the operations of the DIP to deal with proceedings that hinder the reorganization process, but extend beyond the confirmation date in order to preserve the provisions of the plan which have already been approved.[27]

Injuries Prepetition

In another[28] of the *Robins'* cases, the Fourth Circuit Court of Appeals was called upon to consider whether a claimant's

---

[25] *Id.* citing 28 USC §1334(b): "An action is 'related to' Title 11 if its outcome could impact the handling and administration of the bankrupt estate. *See* A.H. Robins Co. v. Piccinin, 788 F2d 994, 1002 n. 11 (4th Cir.) . . . *cert. denied,* 479 US 876, 107 S.Ct. 251 . . . (1986)."

[26] *See* Federal Rules of Civil Procedure Rule 65 Injunctions; Rule 65(d), Form and Scope of Injunction or Restraining Order.

[27] *See infra* Chapter 20, this handbook, Post Confirmation Matters.

[28] *See supra* note 6, Grady v. A.H. Robins Co., Inc. ("Robins"), 839 F2d 198 (4th Cir. 1988). *See also infra* Chapter 6, this handbook, Automatic Stay.

injury arose prior to the filing of the petition under chapter 11 and therefore, was subject to §362(a)(1) of the automatic stay. The claimant had been injured by the use of one of the Debtors' products, known as the Dalkon Shield, prior to the Debtor's filing of its petition. Claimant's injury caused her to have pain, and surgical treatment resulted in the removal of the Dalkon Shield. Thereafter, complaining of persistent pain, fever and chills, she was again admitted to the hospital at which time she was diagnosed as having pelvic inflammatory disease, and underwent a hysterectomy. She blamed the Dalkon Shield for these injuries.

On October 15, 1985, which was almost two months after Robbins filed its chapter 11 in the Eastern District Court of Virginia, claimant filed a civil action against Robbins in the U.S. District Court for the Northern District of California, which was subsequently transferred to the Eastern District of Virginia. The claimant then filed a motion in the bankruptcy court seeking a decision that her claim did not arise before the filing of the petition so that it could not be stayed by the automatic stay. The court of appeals held that the injury of inserting the Dalkon Shield constituted a claim under §362(a).

A Court of Equity: Section 105(a)

Having discussed the objective of §362, we turn now to examine whether §362 with all its aid for a DIP must still require the DIP to go beyond its parameters and seek additional support in areas in which the automatic stay does not afford relief. When all is said and done, §362 is an enunciation of the law. When the broad provisions of the law do not supply the answer, one turns to equity. Section 105(a) provides this equitable relief. "The [bankruptcy court] may issue any order, process, or judgment that is necessary or appropriate to carry out the provisions of this title."[29]

Probably the most comprehensive stay granted was in the *Johns-Manville* case[30] where the court had under consideration

---

[29] *See* 11 USC §105(a).

[30] *In re* Johns-Manville Corporation ("Debtors" or "Manville"), 26 BR 420 (B. SDNY 1983); *aff'd,* 40 BR 219 (SDNY, 1984), *rev'd in part,* 41 BR 926 (SDNY 1984).

"whether the automatic stay extends to the Debtors, employees, agents and other related entities" and the "use of its equitable powers to grant such extension of the stay pursuant to sections 362 and 105 of the Code."[31]

The Debtors' amended complaint, which contained four counts; sought to stay and enjoin creditors that had instituted various actions. In Counts One and Two the Debtors alleged that the continuation of approximately 250 lawsuits brought by the defendants against employees, agents and others related in some capacity or status to the Debtors would severely and adversely impact property of the Debtors' chapter 11 estates. In addition, such actions would obligate the Debtors to defend and indemnify certain of these people according to the Debtors' by-laws. The bankruptcy court stated that in effect these actions were nothing more than a ruse to avoid the automatic stay by examining employees as to the same issues that were involved in actions against the Debtors. Moreover, such actions and discovery proceedings had a negative impact on the reorganization of the Debtors' business.

In Count Three *Manville* sought extension of the automatic stay to enjoin actions to collect and recover prepetition claims against insurers and sureties of the Debtors. The Debtors contended that these "coverages represented property of the estate which must be preserved for all creditors."[32] Finally, in Count Four, *Manville* sought to enjoin a security holders' class action suit commenced after the *Manville* filing against various of the employees, agents, and others pending in the United States District Court.

Upon the hearing of the application and the rehearing, the court held that it had the power under subsection 105(a) to extend the automatic stay and "enjoin proceedings or actions against non-Debtors where such actions would interfere with, deplete, or adversely affect property of the Manville estates, or which would frustrate the statutory scheme embodied in chapter 11 or diminish Manville's ability to formulate a plan of reorganization."[33] The court thereupon restrained the actions in Counts One and Two against present, former, or

---

[31] *Id.*

[32] *See* §541. Property of the estate.

[33] 26 B.R. 420.

future officers, directors and employees of the Debtors. As to Count Three, the court held: ". . . Manville's rights under its insurance policies and the policies themselves are property of the Manville estates within the meaning of Section 541(a) of the Bankruptcy Code. . . ."[34] Accordingly, the stay was granted as to actions against insurers and sureties.

As to Count Four, the court granted the stay against the continuance of the class action by the security holders. In this connection the court stated that "the suit is nothing more than an effort to circumvent §362 by suing Manville's officers and directors when the real party in interest is Manville."[35]

In conclusion, the court emphasized that the extension of the automatic stay is "beyond this Court's prior orders on grounds that relief is necessary and appropriate and on a showing of irreparable harm should be the subject of a further hearing."[36] Sure enough, a further hearing was held. Manville and its insurer moved to stay various actions[37] against Debtor's key officers and direct actions under Louisiana law against Debtor's insurers because maintenance of these actions would have caused a drain on assets of Debtor's estate due to possible conflicts between Debtor and those other defendants, including those arising from efforts by insurers to limit their liability.[38] In concurrence with an order of the district court, the bankruptcy court held that the automatic stay was binding upon appellate courts to enjoin them from allowing actions in derogation of the stay.

On June 16, 1983, Travelers Insurance Co. ("Travelers") presented an order to show cause seeking an extension of the stay granted by the bankruptcy court pursuant to §§362 and 105(a) of Bankruptcy Code. Manville sought coextensive relief.

---

[34] *In re* Johns-Manville Corp., 33 BR 254 (B. SDNY 1983); United States v. Whiting Pools, Inc., 462 U.S. 198, 103 S.Ct. 2309 (1983).

[35] *Id.* at 263.

[36] *Id.*

[37] *In re* Johns-Manville Corp., 33 BR 254 (B. SDNY 1983).

[38] *See In re* Otero Mills, Inc., 25 BR 1018 (B. NM 1982) where Debtor obtained injunction restraining bank from collecting upon its judgment against the president of the Debtor, a guarantor of loans made to Debtor, asserting "that its reorganization plan would require contribution of assets [by the president] to the Debtor."

The Fifth Circuit Court of Appeals had held[39] that the Louisiana direct litigation against the insurers could go forward. In an endeavor to overcome the holding of the Fifth Circuit, Manville and Travelers submitted an order to show cause to the district judge of the Southern District of New York. On June 21, 1983, the District Court "stayed all direct action suits against Manville insurers."[40]

Termination of Stay

Subsection 362(c) provides for the continuation of the stay of an act against property of the estate under subsection 362(a) until such property is no longer property of the estate. As to any other act under subsection 362(a), the stay continues until the earliest of either the time the case is closed or dismissed or in a chapter 11 case, the time a discharge is granted.

Observation

The Manville opinion is a sound indication of the extent to which equitable relief under subsection 105(a) will protect both property of the estate and those persons whose assistance is necessary for the Debtor's reorganization. One court has even gone so far as to deny a mortgagee's motion seeking to vacate the automatic stay, claiming lack of adequate protection under subsections 362(d)(1) and (2), even though the Debtor had no equity in the property and the property was not necessary for an effective reorganization. The court conditioned the stay upon the Debtor's monthly payments of its debt.[41]

---

[39] *See* Wedgeworth v. Fibreboard Corporation, 706 F2d 541 (1983).

[40] *See* §362(c): "Except as provided in subsections (d), (e), and (f) of this section— .... Subsection (f) provides relief from the stay with or without a hearing if necessary to prevent irreparable damage. Subsection (g) places the burden of proof upon the party requesting relief under subsections (d) or (e) on the Debtor's equity in property and the opposing party has the burden on all other issues."

[41] *See In re* Missimer, 44 BR 219 (B. ED Pa. 1984). *See also*, United Savs. Ass'n. of Texas v. Timbers of Inwood Forest Assocs., Ltd., 108 S.Ct. 626 (1988); and *In re* Sutton, 904 F2d 327 (5th Cir. 1990) following the Timbers case.

Furthermore, consider the far reaches and a powerful application of the bankruptcy court's jurisdiction emphasized in the *Baldwin-United* chapter 11 case[42] pending in Ohio. The court of appeals reversed the district court's injunction in a related case pending in the Southern District of New York, prohibiting the Debtor from applying to the bankruptcy court in Ohio for any relief under the automatic stay as improperly interfering with the reorganization proceedings. The Court of Appeals held that ". . . the injunction's prohibition of the debtor's opportunity to apply to the Bankruptcy Court for any relief under Section 105 against any defendant . . . unduly interferes with the proper administration of the reorganization."[43]

We turn now to the involuntary petition which unlike a chapter 7 liquidation, often is resolved by the Debtor's converting the case to a chapter 11 liquidation.

---

[42] *In re* Baldwin-United Corp. Litigation, 765 F2d 343, 348 (2d Cir. 1985).

[43] *Id.* 765 F2d at 348.

Chapter 5
Involuntary Petition

As we shall see in the *Bioline* case,[1] filing of an involuntary petition case against a debtor occasionally occurs when a debtor is endeavoring to negotiate an out-of-court or prepackaged plan. At such time at least three or more creditors may be dissatisfied with the proposed plan and refuse to await further delay in its completion. Section 303 provides that an involuntary case may be commenced only under chapter 7 or 11 and against a person or a corporation that may be a debtor under the chapter under which the case is commenced.[2]

---

[1] *See infra* text at note 26, this chapter, *In re* Boline Lab, Inc., 9 BR 1013 (B. EDNY 1981).

[2] *See* §303(a) ". . . and only against a person, except a farmer, family farmer, or a corporation that is not a moneyed, business or commercial corporation that may be a Debtor under the chapter under which such case is commenced."

Debtor's Alternatives

A Debtor has several alternatives when an involuntary petition is filed: (1) moving to dismiss the petition; (2) denying the allegations of the petition; (3) consenting to the petition; or (4) applying for an abstention.[3]

Involuntary Conversion: Chapter 7 or 11

The *Farley* case[4] also presents a situation where the Debtor was attempting a workout with its creditors. On July 24, 1991, while Farley was pursuing this objective, three creditors joined in an involuntary petition under chapter 7 against Farley. The petition, among other necessary allegations,[5] listed the names and amounts of the three petitioners'[6] claims and alleged that:[7] the claims were not contingent as to liability and not subject to a bona fide dispute, and in excess of any lien held by them on the Debtor's property securing such liens, to at least $5,000; Debtor's place of business was in the Northern District of Illinois; and "[the] Debtor is generally not paying its debts which are not subject to a bona fide dispute as they become due. . . ."

Answer to Petition

Having been served with the petition, Farley, with the consent of petitioners, obtained an extension of time to

---

[3] *See* §305 and *infra* this chapter, subtitle "Abstention of Chapter 11."

[4] *In re* Farley, Inc. ("Farley"), 156 BR 203 (B. ND Ill. 1993).

[5] *See* §303. Involuntary cases containing subsections: (a) An involuntary case may be commenced only under chapter 7 or 11; (b) by three or more entities. . . (2) if there are fewer than 12 such holders. . . (3) if a person is a partnership by (A) fewer than all the general partners; or (B) by all the general partners . . . and (4) by a foreign representative. . . . *See also* §303(h). "If the petition is not timely controverted. . . ."

[6] *See* §303(b)(1). "(b) . . . or an indenture trustee representing such a holder, if such claims aggregate at least $5,000. . . ."

[7] *See* §303. Involuntary cases.

answer.[8] In the meantime, Farley's attorneys, Kaye, Scholer,[9] the petitioners, and other creditors continued negotiations in anticipation of working out a proper method of dealing with Farley's financial obligations and attempting to develop a consensual plan of reorganization.[10]

"... Until an order for relief in the case, any business of the debtor may continue to operate . . . as if an involuntary case concerning the debtor had not been commenced."[11] During this gap period between filing of the involuntary and the Debtor's answer by motion to dismiss, or to have the court abstain, the Debtor's operations continue. General business with creditors during this period of time constitutes expenses of administration for the creditors.[12]

Status Hearing

Since the petitioners had filed a chapter 7 petition for liquidation and the parties were at a point of settling their differences, a status hearing was set for September 17, 1991. In its application, Farley stated that it intended to file at the status hearing: "a plan of reorganization, a disclosure statement, a scheduling order and Debtor-in-possession financing documents. . . . [T]he status conference . . . will enable all constituencies to review and comment upon all documents to be filed herein and will thus ensure the most orderly transition to chapter 11."

---

[8] *See* B.Rule 1011. (Responsive Pleading or Motion In Involuntary and Ancillary Cases). *See also* §1011(b) (Defenses and Objections; When Presented).

[9] Kaye, Scholer, Fierman, Hays & Handler ("Kaye, Scholer").

[10] *See* proposed Senate Bill No. S.540 introduced March 10, 1993: "Sec. 105. Powers of Bankruptcy Courts. (a) Status Conferences—Section 105 . . . is amended by adding . . . (d) The court on its own motion or on the motion of any party in interest, may—(1) hold a status conference regarding any case or proceeding. . . ."

[11] *See* §303(f). *See also* §363.

[12] *See* §507. Priorities and §503. Allowance of administrative expenses.

Conversion to Chapter 11

Following the status conference, Farley filed its answer to the involuntary petition on September 24, 1991 consenting to the entry of an order for relief under chapter 11 of the Bankruptcy Code and converting the involuntary case under chapter 7 to a case under chapter 11 of the Bankruptcy Code in accordance with §706(a), and reserved its rights under §1112(a) and B. Rule 1019.[13] On the same day, the bankruptcy judge granted the relief.

Hearing on Fees
Pension Benefit Guaranty Corporation's Objection

Kaye, Scholer's final application had sought fees of $2,603,618 and disbursements of $405,687. Only the Pension Benefit Guaranty Corp. (PBGC) objected to the hourly rates charged by Kaye, Scholer's attorneys and its paralegals. However, after confirmation the reorganized Debtor recommended a reduced fee of $2,403,618 negotiated by it with counsel. The application and the PBGC objection thereto were set for a hearing at which this Court took evidence. "Arguments of the applicant and objector have been considered. For reasons given herein, the PBGC's objection to hourly rates is overruled, and Kaye, Scholer's fee application has by prior order been entirely allowed. This Opinion will stand as Findings of Fact and Conclusions of Law following the hearing."[14]

PBGC Party in Interest
Contingent Claim

Kaye, Scholer first argued that PBGC lacked the standing necessary to object to its application for fees. In response, the

---

[13] *See* §706 (Conversion) and §706(a): "The debtor may convert a case under this chapter to a case under chapter 11, 12 or 13 of this title at any time, ..." *See also* §1112 (Conversion or dismissal). *See also* B.Rule 1019. ("Conversion Of Chapter 11 Reorganization Case, . . . To Chapter 7 Liquidation Case").

[14] *See In re* Farley, Inc. ("Farley"), 156 BR 203 (B. Ill. 1993), "Opinion of Court" #1. Hereinafter, footnotes will be referred to by number.

court cited § 1109(b):[15] "A party in interest . . . may raise and may appear and may be heard on any issue in a case under this chapter." Referring to the *Wilson*[16] case as authority "it opined PBGC's role in Farley's reorganization demonstrates that it has an interest that could be affected indirectly by the allowance or disallowance of Kaye, Scholer's fee application. . . ."

The court held that PBGC had filed claims in *Farley's* case to protect itself in the event Farley chose to terminate one or more of its pension plans without providing for sufficient assets to cover PBGC benefits, which had been guaranteed and alleged over $55 million in such benefits. "Farley [dealt] with this contingent liability in its Plan by agreeing to make certain payments earmarked for the reduction or elimination of the underfunding problem . . ."[17] [PBGC] continues to face a $55 million possible exposure should Farley be left with insufficient assets to fund its pension plans. The money to pay the professional fees of Kaye, Scholer and other firms is coming out of the debtor's coffers—money which might otherwise be used to fund its pension liabilities. Based on these facts and because the fees sought are quite large, PBGC has rights and interests that are potentially affected by Kaye, Scholer's fee application."[18]

Cost of Comparable Services With Bankruptcy Fees

The court found that PBGC had the right to examine the value of the fees paid to Kaye, Scholer relative to the services rendered. "The only issue here is whether the hourly rates of debtor's New York counsel are too high for a reorganization in a Chicago-filed proceeding. . . ." Turning to §330, the court observed that the section governed the awarding of attorneys' fees. However, "[p]rior to enactment of this provision, economy of administration was the paramount consideration in determining attorney fee awards. . . . Thus, a judge considering a

---

[15] Use of word "including" in §1109(b) is not inclusive.

[16] Farley, 156 BR 203, 207. *In re* James Wilson Associates ("Wilson"), 965 F2d 160, 169 (7th Cir. 1992).

[17] *Id.*

[18] *Id.* at 208.

fee application under the Bankruptcy Act was to award fees 'at
the low end of the spectrum of reasonableness.'"[19]

The court indicated that "[i]n shifting the focus to the 'cost
of comparable services' compared to non-bankruptcy cases,
Congress rejected the 'spirit of economy' notion in favor of a
market approach to determining fees."[20] The purpose of §330
was to encourage bankruptcy practitioners not to leave the
field in favor of more lucrative areas of the law." The court
cited the relevant part of §330, which governs the awarding of
attorney's and professional fees:

(a) *Section 330 Requires Market Analysis*

After notice to any parties in interests . . . the
court may award. . . to the debtor's attorney . . .
(1) reasonable compensation for actual, necessary services rendered by such . . . attorney . . .
based on the nature, the extent, and the value
of such services, the time spent on such
services, *and the cost of comparable services
other than in a case under this title. . . .*[21]

Kaye, Scholer's Legal Status

The court first analyzed the firm's personnel: "Mr. Herbert
Edelman was the senior and supervising attorney for the
Farley case; . . . [h]e and other Kaye, Scholer counsel in Kaye,
Scholer have served as lead bankruptcy counsel for debtors in
nationally prominent bankruptcy cases. . . . The evidence
shows that Mr. Edelman currently charges and collects the full
rate of $475/hour for service rendered to his other clients. . . .

---

[19] *Id.* at 210.

[20] *Id.* at 210 (citing 1243 Cong. Rec. H 11091 (daily ed. Sept. 28, 1978)
(remarks of Rep. Edwards, and 124 Cong. Rec. S 17408 daily ed., Oct. 6,
1978) (remarks of Sen. De Concini). *See also In re* Industries, Inc., 986 F2d
207, 208 & 209).

[21] *Id.* at 209 (emphasis added). *See also* §§ 327; Employment of
professional persons: "(a) . . . the trustee . . . may employ one or more
attorneys, accountants, appraisers, auctioneers, or other professional
persons. . . ; 328(a); Limitation on compensation of professional persons. . . ;
and 329; Debtor's transactions with attorneys."

His usual rate is commensurate with rates of other attorneys at competing New York firms with similar experience. . . ."

Comparison of Fees: New York and Chicago

The court indicated that Kaye, Scholer fees were higher than those charged by partners in Chicago, which were $315/hour and associates billed $95 to $180/hour, and several firms in Chicago had the expertise and capabilities necessary to successfully represent Farley through its reorganization. "In this regard, PBGC is correct. However, at the outset of this proceeding, Farley's experienced general counsel conducted an inquiry as to which lead bankruptcy counsel to employ. Farley, Inc. accepted his recommendation of Kaye, Scholer because of the substantial experience of that firm . . . and—most importantly—a comfortable relationship of mutual confidence that developed between client and counsel . . . and not unreasonable for it to select the firm chosen by its general counsel."[22]

Added to this commendation, the court also cited a section of the Debtor's testimony:

> ["Kaye, Scholer] was lead counsel to Farley throughout the chapter 11 case and was involved, either directly or indirectly, in the resolution of virtually every major issue to confront Farley during these proceedings. . . ."[23]

Magnitude of Liability

The court described the magnitude of the case as extremely large and complex, but nonetheless it was confirmed only sixteen months after the proceedings had been commenced. Discussions had been held with major constituencies from the start "includ[ing] the Bank of New York, the United Automobile Aerospace and Agricultural Implement Workers of America (the 'UAW'), and holders of certain junior and senior subordinated debt instruments. Creditors within those creditor constituencies were spread throughout the nation, and held

---

[22] *Id.* at 205.
[23] *Id.* at 206.

several hundred million dollars of claims against Farley. Additionally, there were creditors with disputed and unliquidated claims who alleged Farley owed them over $100 million including PBGC's claim.[24] No plan could be confirmed unless and until these claims could be managed or liquidated below a level the debtor could manage."[25]

Necessity for Experienced Counsel

"Given the complexity of issues confronting Farley's reorganization, and because reorganization of its debt would have wide-spread effects, it was clearly appropriate for Farley to choose bankruptcy counsel experienced in major work to handle its reorganization."[26] Indeed, the reorganized Debtor had no objection to paying the fee. In testimony before the court the Debtor testified: "Kaye, Scholer's services were of exceptionally high quality throughout the case and it was due in large part to their efforts that the case was concluded."

Abstention of Chapter 11

Section 305 provides: "The court after notice and a hearing, may dismiss a case under this title, or may suspend all proceedings in a case under this title at any time if—(1) The interests of creditors and the debtor would be better served by such dismissal or suspension; . . ." Such application was presented in the *Bioline* case[27] where the court considered the alternative to continuing its jurisdiction of the involuntary petition or abstaining by dismissal of the case and found the case warranted abstention.

Prior to the filing of an involuntary petition, Bioline had been engaged in the wholesale distribution of pharmaceutical drugs. It encountered financial difficulties that made it impossible to continue business. A sale was urgent. As a

---

[24] *See supra* note 13, Opinion at p. 6.

[25] *Id.*

[26] *Id.* at 205.

[27] *See In re* Bioline Lab, Inc., 9 B.R. 1013 (B. EDNY 1981). *See also* to same effect *In re* Artists Outlet, Inc., 25 BR 231 (D. Mass. 1985).

result, Bioline agreed with the *Hollywood*[28] company to sell its business to them as provided in an "Asset Purchase Agreement." The proceeds of the sale to Hollywood were to be distributed to Bioline's creditors and Hollywood was also to assume other obligations. The parties agreed to comply with applicable provisions of the Bulk Sales Law.

A notice of the sale dated January 3, 1980 was timely sent to Bioline's creditors scheduling a closing for January 22. Prior to January 22, three of Bioline's creditors, however, filed an involuntary petition in bankruptcy, and on the same day submitted an order to show cause to restrain Bioline from proceeding with the bulk sale until the court determined whether relief should be granted pursuant to the involuntary petition or the involuntary petition be abstained or dismissed.

Citing §305(a)(1), the court decided to dismiss the petition. "I examined the bona fides of all sides . . . and devised a solution . . . I enjoined the bulk sale on condition that the petitioning creditors or Darby [other competitive bidder] post a $500,000 bond to indemnify Bioline from any damage suffered by reason of my delaying the bulk sale. . . ."[29] The bond, however, was not posted and the sale went through.

The court cited a part of the Congressional history, which indicated a reason for the enactment of §305:[30]

> Among the purposes of a chapter proceeding under the bankruptcy laws is to preserve the going-concern value of debtors, thereby preventing disruptions in the marketplace. . . ."[31] "Accordingly, the involuntary chap-

---

[28] Hollywood OBL, Inc. ("Hollywood"). *See* Uniform Commercial Code §6-102(1): "A bulk transfer is any transfer in bulk and not in the ordinary course of the transferor's business of a major part of the materials, supplies, merchandise or other inventory of an enterprise subject to this article. . . ." *See also* MCKINNEY'S CONSOLIDATED LAWS OF NEW YORK ANNOTATIONS, at 689: "For discussion of the Code Provisions see . . . Weintraub & Levin, 'Bulk Sales Law and Adequate Protection of Creditors,' 65 HARV. L. REV. 418 (1952)."

[29] *Id.* at 1019.

[30] *Id.* at 1022 citing H.R. Rep. No. 95-595, 95th Cong., 1st Sess. 325 (1977); S. Rep. No. 95-989, 95th Cong. 2d Sess. 35, 1978.

[31] 9 B.R. at 1022.

ter 11 petition is dismissed. This renders moot the motions for summary judgment and to set aside the bulk sale as a fraudulent conveyance made by the petitioning creditors. I shall retain jurisdiction for the sole purpose of granting Bioline's motion authorizing [the escrow agent] to distribute to unsecured creditors the funds collected and earmarked for them pursuant to the Asset Purchase Agreement.[32]

Observation

The *Farley* case emphasizes that a creditor having a contingent claim has the right to participate in a chapter 11 proceeding. Furthermore, until the court determines the validity of the contingent claim, the contingent creditor may well argue and attempt to challenge other claims whose allowance may reduce the ultimate distribution of dividends available to the contestant.

In the *Farley* case, the PBGC, as a contestant, was on the wrong track in challenging Kaye, Scholer's claim. History indicated that Congress had already rejected the payment of professional services allowed in a bankruptcy case on the basis of an "economical theory." The purpose of such allowance as now provided under §330 is based on a principle of "fairness," payments commensurate with what professionals charge their clients in nonbankruptcy cases. This principle is consistent with the same theory that the "butcher, the baker and the candlestickmaker" do not diminish their sales prices to a customer when business continues as Debtor in chapter 11.

Bioline is an indication that not every involuntary petition bearing adequate grounds for relief under chapter 11 will be granted such relief. If there is a proceeding pending out of court aimed at granting unsecured creditors better benefits than a bankruptcy proceeding, the involuntary petition may be stayed. The *Bioline* court restrained the bulk sale and abstained from proceeding with bankruptcy and alleged fraudulent conveyance issues until the court had determined that the out-of-court settlement was preferable.

---

[32] *Id.* at 1023.

Of course, since no discharge was granted the Debtor, the petitioning creditors still had the option of pursuing Bioline and Hollywood for what they considered a fraudulent transfer under New York State law. We doubt, however, that on the basis of the facts they could recover.[33]

---

[33] *See infra* Chapter 16, this handbook, Fraudulent Transfers and Obligations subtitle "Fraudulent Conveyance Under State Law."

Chapter 6
Automatic Stay

Debtor In Possession

P reliminary paperwork[1] including the chapter 11 petition has now been completed and the chapter 11 petition has been filed with the clerk of the bankruptcy court.[2] The company, which has been the former Debtor, now becomes the debtor in possession.[3] In such status, the DIP acts as a fiduciary in charge of the business and is accountable for the

---

[1] *See* Bankruptcy Official Forms (1–35). Some selected forms for chapter 11 are: (1) Voluntary Petition; (6) Schedules of Assets and Liabilities; (9) List of Creditors Holding 20 Largest Unsecured Claims. Official Forms to be used with such alterations as may be necessary.

[2] *See* B.Rule 1002 (Commencement of case).

[3] *See* §1101(1): "In this chapter[11]—'debtor in possession' means *Debtor* except when a person that has qualified under section 322 of this title is serving as trustee in the case; . . ." (emphasis added to indicate "debtor in possession" ["DIP"] is designated as "Debtor" in chapter 11 sections).

property of the estate[4] and its operations.[5] In this capacity as a fiduciary, the DIP has all the powers and responsibilities of a trustee in bankruptcy with certain limitations. Thus, a reference in the Bankruptcy Code to powers of a trustee also refers to a DIP that is designated as "Debtor."[6]

Automatic Stay's Coverage

The breadth of the automatic stay has been set forth in §362, which contains eight subsections indicating restraints against property of the estate. Subsection (a)(1) reads as follows:

> (a) Except as provided in subsection (b) of this section, a petition filed under section 301 [voluntary cases], 302 [joint], or 303 [involuntary], . . . operates as a stay, applicable to all entities, of
> (1) commencement of continuation, including the issuance or employment or process, of a judicial administrative or other action or proceeding against the debtor that was or could have been commenced before the commencement of the case,. . . or to recover a claim against the debtor that arose before the commencement of the case; . . .
> Subsection (b) contains a list of sixteen paragraphs which contain actions or proceedings under subsection (a) each of which paragraph "does not operate as a stay —". . . Subsections (c) to (h), as in subsection (g), are designed to protect creditors' interests by granting relief under the circumstances or proceedings as set forth in each section.

Section 362, the automatic stay, is the cornerstone of chapter 11. The reorganization would be stymied without the

---

[4] *See* 11 USC §541 Property of the estate.

[5] *See* B.Rule 2015: "Duty [of Trustee or debtor in possession] to Keep Records, Make Reports, and Give Notice of Case."

[6] *See* §1107. Rights, powers, and duties of debtor in possession.

support §362 supplies to a debtor in possession by restraining payment of debts, foreclosure of property, and the continuance of the Debtor's operations. The moment a petition under chapter 11 is filed, the automatic stay springs into operation enjoining all entities[7] from the commencement or continuation of all prepetition actions against the Debtor.

The automatic stay is extremely broad in scope and is designed to protect the Debtor's estate against pending or contemplated actions while at the same time protecting the unsecured creditors as well as creditors who have an interest in specific property of the estate. We turn now to several cases to examine not only judicial interpretations, but view with open eyes different types of harassment and see how broadly or narrowly the courts have adhered to the Congressional intention.

Violation of Copyright

In *Sonnax*[8] the court of appeals had for consideration a denial for relief from the automatic stay. Sonnax was a manufacturer of automobile parts, but in 1986 began to manufacture torque converter parts. At that time Tri Component, a manufacturer and distributor of torque converter parts, had already developed a copyrighted numbering system of the parts it sold.

In November 1982 Tri Component hired Lawrence May ("May") as sales manager of its torque converter department. May signed a restrictive covenant in which he agreed not to use information or knowledge gained within three years of leaving his job at Tri Component. In September 1986, May left Tri Component and shortly thereafter was hired by Sonnax as an independent sales representative.

State Court Injunction

In May 1987 Tri Component filed an action in a New York state court against Sonnax and defendants, May, and its president, alleging that May had breached the restrictive

---

[7] *See* §101(15): "'entity' includes, person, estate, trust, governmental unit and United States trustee. . . ."

[8] *In re* Sonnax Indus., Inc. ("Sonnax"), 907 F2d 1280 (2d Cir. 1990).

covenant by using knowledge gained at Tri Component, including its customer list, while employed at Sonnax. Tri Component sought money damages and injunctive relief. A preliminary injunction was granted in early 1987 prohibiting Sonnax from doing business with entities that had been customers of Tri Component prior to September 1986 and granting other relief. The three defendants moved to stay the injunction pending an appeal to the appellate court. The motion was denied on March 8, 1988.

Chapter 11 Filed

The next day Sonnax filed its petition for chapter 11. After Tri Component filed its proof of claim, Tri Component moved to modify the automatic stay under §362 to allow it to continue prosecution of its litigation in New York and to enforce the injunction. The motion was withdrawn from the bankruptcy court to the district court.[9] The district court denied the motion.

> Tri Component has not credibly shown that it will suffer any real hardship if the stay is left in place. By contrast, the Debtor may fail in its attempt to reorganize and may be driven out of business altogether if the stay is lifted. . . .[10]

Tri Component appealed to the circuit court of appeals. After determining that it had jurisdiction over the appeal, the court turned to the motion to modify the automatic stay. Addressing the applicable statutory provisions of the case, the court stated that only §362(d)(1) was applicable because the case concerns a stay of a judicial proceeding for cause.[11] "[N]either the statute nor the legislative history defines the

---

[9] *See, infra* Chapter 7, this handbook, Jurisdiction of Bankruptcy Court.

[10] *In re* Sonnax Indus., Inc., 99 BR 591, 595 (D.Vt. 1989).

[11] *See* 11 USC §362(d)(1): "On request of a party in interest and after notice and a hearing, the court shall grant relief from the stay . . . for cause, including the lack of adequate protection of an interest in property of such party in interest, . . ." *See also, supra* Chapter 3, this handbook, subtitle "Adequate Protection."

term 'for cause'. . . .[12] In defining "cause," the court referred to the case of *In re Curtis*[13] in which the court catalogued a dozen factors to be weighed in defining whether litigation should be permitted to continue in another forum. The court also observed that:

> [F]rom the unstructured nature of the issue, existing case law indicates that the "decision of whether to lift the stay [is committed] to the discretion of the bankruptcy judge," . . . We believe four of the *Curtis* factors are relevant to the instant case: (1) whether the New York proceeding is connected to or might interfere with the bankruptcy case; (2) whether the bankruptcy petition was filed in bad faith; (3) the balance of harms; and (4) the interests of judicial economy and the expeditious and economical resolution of litigation.[14]

Referring to the four factors the court found: (1) The state court proceeding was connected to and would interfere with the bankruptcy case; (2) Tri Component failed to show bad faith; (3) The balance of harms supported the district court's decision; and (4) "the interests of judicial economy and the speedy and economical determination of litigation support a denial of relief from the stay."[15]

In affirming the district court, the court of appeals stated that "the lifting of the stay is committed to the sound discretion of the court and because Chief Judge Billings properly considered the factors determining cause, we must affirm his denial of relief from the stay."[16]

---

[12] 907 F2d at 1285.

[13] 40 BR 795 (B.D. Utah 1984).

[14] 907 F2d at 1286, citing: "*See* Holtkamp v. Littlefield (In re Holtkamp), 669 F2d 505, 507 (7th Cir. 1982). . .; and that we may overturn a denial of a motion to lift the automatic stay only upon a showing of an abuse of discretion. Holtkamp 669 F2d at 507."

[15] *Id.* at 1287.

[16] *Id.* at 1288.

Observation

The *Sonnax* case is not meant to be an indication that all breaches of restrictive covenants copyrighted by a Debtor are subject to the automatic stay, but rather an indication of how far the automatic stay reaches to protect property of the estate.[17] In other words, the balance of harms suffered was upon the Debtor. Tri Component was, of course, free to continue its action against May and the president of Sonnax since the automatic stay applied only to the Debtors. Injunctive relief under §105(a) was available to May and the president, as obviously their services were indispensable to the Debtor and without injunctive relief, the same harm would prevent Sonnax from operating.[18]

Violation of Stay

Free Speech

The *Stonegate* case[19] presents the problem of whether free speech by a prepetition creditor impinges upon the automatic stay. Prior to September 30, 1983, Ramm Industries Co. ("Ramm") sold goods to Stonegate, but Stonegate failed to make payment when due. As a result, the president of Ramm caused a truck to be placed outside Stonegate's business premises. On the front, side, and rear of the truck were painted signs: "Stonegate Auto Alarms does not pay supplier; . . ." "Stonegate Auto Alarms does *not* pay suppliers; . . ." "Crime does not pay, Stonegate Auto Alarms the same way."[20] Ramm then fought Stonegate in state court for the money owed to it. The case ended in an agreement whereby Ramm agreed to remove the truck and Stonegate agreed to pay the

---

[17] See, *e.g.*, *In re* 48th Street Steakhouse, Inc., 835 F2d 427 (2d Cir. 1987) (landlord's sending of notice to a third party lessee due to nonpayment of rent violated the automatic stay of a sublessee in chapter 11 operating in the premises).

[18] *See supra* Chapter 4, this handbook, subtitle "Business Necessity First-Day Orders."

[19] *In re* Stonegate Security Servs., Ltd. ("Stonegate"), 56 BR 1014 (ND Ill. 1986).

[20] *Id.* at 1016.

money due. Stonegate made its initial installment payment and Ramm removed the truck.

Involuntary Petition

Stonegate missed its subsequent payment and Ramm replaced the truck. On September 30, 1983, Ramm, along with other of Stonegate's creditors, filed an involuntary chapter 11[21] against Stonegate. Stonegate consented to the entry of an order for relief under chapter 11, and thereafter continued to operate its business as a DIP. Ramm's truck remained in front of Stonegate's business premises both before and after the filing of the bankruptcy petition.

Contempt Proceeding

On October 28, 1983, Stonegate obtained an order to show cause why Ramm and its president should not be held in contempt of court for violation of §362(a) of the automatic stay.[22] At the hearing, Stonegate argued that Ramm's action constituted harassment to coerce payment violation and that the truck was adversely affecting Stonegate's business. Ramm attempted to argue that it was not harassing Stonegate but merely stating a fact and exercising its First Amendment rights. The bankruptcy judge refused to take evidence as to whether Ramm's purpose was in fact to harass and did not address Ramm's First Amendment argument. The judge found that the admitted conduct constituted a violation of §362(a)(6).

After much activity between the parties to settle the case, the bankruptcy court signed an order granting Stonegate's fee, stating that "the presence of the truck violated section 362(a)(6) and that Ramm and its president knew that they were in violation of the statute." The bankruptcy judge stated that "there was no doubt that Ramm and [its president] were guilty of contemptuous conduct in violating the automatic stay,

---

[21] *See supra* Chapter 5, this handbook, Involuntary Petition.

[22] *See* 11 USC §362(a): ". . . [A] petition filed under section 301, 302, or 303 of this title . . . operates as a stay, applicable to all entities, of–(6) any act to collect, assess or recover a claim against the Debtor that arose before the commencement of a case under this title."

and that fees had to be assessed in order to preserve the 'sanctity' of the stay."[23]

Upon appeal the district court stated that it had to determine whether Ramm and its president had a reasonable basis for resisting the contempt order or whether their conduct in placing the truck in front of Stonegate's premises was defensible. In pursuance of such objective, the court stated: "Section 362(a)(6) is designed to prohibit a creditor from attempting to collect a prepetition debt in any manner, including harassment. . . ."[24]

In determining whether there was a willful disobedience of the court order, the district court looked to an evaluation of the merits of the defense. After examining several infirmities in the order holding Ramm and its president in contempt, the district court turned to an examination of Ramm's and its president's First Amendment rights, observing the bankruptcy court's rejection of such defense. Turning to §362, the court observed that §362 also involved the protection of the judicial process itself:

> All bankruptcy statutes are designed to protect our economic system. Congress enacted Title 11 because it believed that it is in our nation's interest to protect Debtors and enable them to reorganize and to continue their businesses.[25]

In the final analysis the court stated that in the absence of some language presenting a clear and present danger of some significant interference with the Debtor's reorganization or with the functions of the bankruptcy court, §362 could not prohibit public criticism. "It is not enough that the behavior be

---

[23] 56 BR at 1017.

[24] *Id.* at 1018 citing: "*See* Wilson v. Harris Trust and Savings Bank, No. 82 C 2960, Memo Op. at 5 n.3 (ND Ill. Nov. 23, 1983) (Grady, J.) citing H. Rep. No. 95-595, 95th Cong. 1st Sess. (1977) 340-3. . . . For example, legislative history indicates that Congress intended §362(a)(6) to prohibit creditors from evading the bankruptcy laws by encouraging Debtors to pay their debts in spite of bankruptcy. *Id.* Therefore, it is clear that §362 is designed to prohibit conduct which may include free speech components."

[25] *Id.* at 1019.

'annoying' . . . or even that it has actual adverse effect on someone's business. . . ."[26]

The district court decided to remand the proceeding to the bankruptcy judge instead of reversing the bankruptcy court because in its opening argument Stonegate had alluded to physical obstruction having been caused by the truck, but there had been no evidence to show damage to its business caused by the truck's obstruction.

Observation

The application of the First Amendment rights by a creditor presented a close call to constitute a violation of the automatic stay. Stonegate was called upon to prove damages to its business. How many customers and/or suppliers reading the signs would continue doing business with words like "crime" and "nonpayment of bills?" Accordingly, the case was remanded to determine whether the truck did obstruct access to Stonegate's premises and if so, whether a fee assessment was warranted. Ramm's behavior was a clear intent to collect his prepetition debt, indicated by his prepetition activities. His placing of the truck near the Debtor's premises, receiving a payment on account, removing the truck, were harassments designed to compel additional payment of the prepetition debt. It is hard to conceive that more facts were needed to prove a violation of §362(a)(6): "any act to collect . . . a claim against the debtor. . . ."

Creditor Collection

Let us consider for the moment the *Olson* case,[27] in which the Debtors filed a petition under chapter 7 and listed McFarland Clinic, P.C. ("Defendant") as a general unsecured

---

[26] *Id. See also In re* National Service Corp. 742 F2d 859, 862 (5th Cir. 1984) (message on a billboard owned by a creditor, "Beware, this company is in bankruptcy," was not harassment in violation of §362, and did not "warrant use of a prior restraint on the advertiser's speech").

[27] *In re* Ronald D. Olson, 38 BR 515, (B. ND Iowa 1984).

creditor in its Schedule A-3 of its schedules in bankruptcy.[28] Thereafter the Bankruptcy Clerk's Office[29] sent the usual "Notice to All Creditors".to the defendant informing it of the meeting of creditors pursuant to §341(a) and of the applicability of §362.[30]

The Defendant thereafter sent the Debtors a letter containing the following statement:

> Since you have filed bankruptcy, I realize that we cannot legally pursue the collection of this account. However, we are willing to reinstate service if you wish to pay your account voluntarily.[31]

The Debtors subsequently sought medical services that were refused by the defendant, even though they offered to pay cash in advance. They were informed that no medical services would be performed unless the entire amount of the debt owing was paid.

Contempt Proceeding

Thereafter, the Debtors moved to hold the defendant in contempt of court and filed a complaint for damages. The court, after taking testimony, found that the purpose behind the defendant's letter was the collection of the prepetition debt. Even though a "literal reading of the letter reveals no direct effort at collection, the defendant is not excused."[32] The court observed that defendant was not committed to refusing

---

[28] *See* B.Rule Part I, Commencement of Case; Proceedings Relating To Petition And Order For Relief. *See also* B.Rule 1007. Lists, Schedules and Statements; Time Limits; Official Form No. 6, Schedules Of Assets and Liabilities.

[29] *See* B.Rule 2002. Notices to Creditors, Equity Security Holders, United States and United States Trustee: "[The] clerk, or some other person that the court may direct, . . ."

[30] *See* 11 USC §341. Meetings of creditors and equity security holders. *See also, infra* Chapter 10, this handbook, subtitle "Powers And Duties of Committees."

[31] 38 BR at 516.

[32] *Id.* at 517.

services "on the basis of nontainted reason" and if the "defendant were to simply refuse service without any mention of the Debtors' bankruptcy filing, §362 would not come into play."[33]

Discharge Acts As Injunction

The court then turned to a consideration of whether the defendant had violated §524(a)(2)[34] since the Debtors in the meantime had received their discharge in bankruptcy. This latter section provides that a discharge operates as an injunction of any act to recover a prepetition debt. Since the defendant had received constructive notice by the publication[35] of the discharge of the Debtors, it violated §524(a)(2). By refusing treatment to the Debtors, the defendant was engaging in efforts to collect a prepetition debt.

Observation

Are *Stonegate* and *Olson* in conflict? Assume that in the *Olson* case the creditor had approached the Debtor and had expressed by spoken words the same data that appeared in its letter. *Stonegate* would hold no contempt because it was free speech. *Olson* would still hold it a contempt as a violation of the Bankruptcy Code.

The *Olson* case presents a caveat to all creditors, namely, that any subterfuge to collect a prepetition debt will constitute a contempt of court. However, some question arises as to the court's finding that a failure to sell for cash, is "nontainted" or justified if not coupled with an implied effort to collect a

---

[33] *Compare, In re* Blackwelder Furniture, Co., Inc., 7 BR 328 (B.WDNC 1980) where the court indicated that it had jurisdiction to prevent unlawful discrimination by private companies that are refusing to deal with the Debtor if such discrimination is an unlawful violation of antitrust laws.

[34] *See* 11 USC §524(a)(2): "A discharge in a case under this title . . . operates as an injunction against the commencement or continuation of an action . . . or an act to collect, recover or offset any such debt as a personal liability of the Debtor. . . ."

[35] *See* B.Rule 2002(a). Notices To Creditors, Equity Security Holders, United States and United States Trustee.

prepetition debt.[36] Such action may be justified if not coupled with a subliminal request for payment.[37] Moreover, it is significant that Congress in its 1984 Amendments added to § 362(a)(1) in its classification of restraints, "the commencement or continuation . . . of a judicial, administrative, *or other action*, or proceeding against the Debtor. . . to recover a claim against the Debtor that arose before the commencement of a case under this title. . . ."[38] (Emphasis added.)

Exception to Automatic Stay: §1110

The *Pan Am* case[39] involved a multinational organization that provided air transportation and related services to the public and operated a fleet of 154 jet-powered aircraft. After filing its chapter 11 petition, Pan Am moved under §1110 seeking a determination that §1110 did not permit sale-leaseback transactions, which did not involve the acquisition of new equipment. Distinguishing the section from §§362 and 365, the court stated:

> Section 1110 stands in stark contrast to sections 362, the automatic stay provision, and 365, the assumption or rejection of executory contracts or leases provision, of the Code. Congress obviously saw a need for this type of special legislation in order to protect certain persons who deal with air carriers. . . . Specifically, the

---

[36] *See, supra* note 27 at 517.

[37] *See, e.g., In re* National Service Corp., 742 F2d 589 (advertising on a billboard: "Beware this company does not pay its bills"); and *In re* Ohio Waste Servs., Inc., 23 BR 59 (B.SD Ohio 1982) (using the criminal courts for collection of bad checks).

[38] 11 U.S.C. §362(a)(1).

[39] *In re* Pan Am Corp. ("Pan Am"), 124 BR 960 (B. SDNY 1991), *aff'd* in part 125 BR 372 (SDNY 1991) *aff'd* 929 F2d 109 (2d Cir. 1991), *cert. den.* Pan Am Corp. v. Section 1110 Parties, 111 S.Ct. 2248 (1991). *See* 11 USC §1110 (Aircraft equipment and vessels).

Debtors are of the view that the Sale-Leasebacks are not protected by section 1110.[40]

Pan Am, like other airlines, was a party to "Sale-Leasebacks in which the Debtors 'sold' Aircraft and Equipment which had been part of their fleet for many years to financiers, who then leased that same Aircraft and Equipment back to the Debtors. The Debtors did not acquire any new Aircraft and Equipment as a result of these transactions."[41]

Pan Am asserted that §1110 was not clear on its face and mandated a review of legislative history. Such review would demonstrate that Congress intended the section to apply only to transactions involving a Debtor's new acquisition of equipment. In response the court held that §1110 "clearly and unambiguously applies to 'a lessor. . .of aircraft'."[42]

As to the holders of purchase money equipment security interest transactions ("PMESI") in aircraft and or equipment, these holders were not proper PMESIs, and therefore the holders were not entitled to the benefits of the Code. These benefits indicate that application of the provisions of §1110 are "unaffected 'by sections 362 or 363 of this title or by any *power of the court to enjoin such taking of possession,*—unless. . ." certain conditions are met (emphasis added).[43] Obligations as to payment are performed by the Debtor within specified periods of time. The court concluded among other findings that the Sale-Leasebacks, lease extensions and renewals, and PMESIs were protected by §1110.

---

[40] *Id.* at 965. *See also* §1110(a), which exempts secured parties with purchase money security interests in certain aircraft equipment from the automatic stay except where the Debtor agrees to perform pursuant to the purchase money security agreement and cures any defaults pursuant to such agreement. Such agreement and cure must be executed "before 60 days after the date of the order for relief under this chapter [expires]. . . ."

[41] *Id.*

[42] *Id.* at 966. *See also In re* Ionosphere 123 BR 166 (B. SDNY 1991), where court terminated automatic stay after operations had ceased allowing holders of secured equipment certificates to enforce their interest in a pool of 67 aircraft and allowing money in restricted accounts to be transferred to the collateral trustee.

[43] *Id.* at 974.

It is interesting to note that on March 17, 1993, Congress enacted the "Aircraft Equipment Settlement Lease" (Business Law 103-7 [S. 400]) which offers special protections under Bankruptcy Code §1110 to aircraft lessors in a chapter 11 case.[44]

Observation

Pan Am emphasizes §1110 as a statutory modification of §362, but also indicates a restraint on §105(a), which deals with the broad injunctive powers that supplement the automatic stay. The importance of such exception is to protect vendors of aircraft and vessels extending credit to such purchasers as well as by this process, making credit available to the Debtor.[45]

We turn now to consider the jurisdiction of the Bankruptcy Code, which has been limited by the Bankruptcy Amendments Federal Judiciary Act (BAFJA).

---

[44] *See* Public Law 103-7 (S. 400), Sec. 2: Treatment of Aircraft Equipment Settlement Leases with the Pension Benefit Guaranty Corporation, subsections (1)–(3).

[45] *See, supra* Chapter 2, this handbook, subtitle "Obtaining Credit."

Chapter 7
Jurisdiction of Bankruptcy Court

S ale of goods in a merchant's ordinary course of business is essential for continued operations. One of the pressing problems confronting a debtor in possession is the reclamation[1] of goods by creditors, which lowers its inventory, and another is the collection of its accounts receivable. Necessity compels haste and the bankruptcy court, where the Debtor has sought refuge, appears to be the proper forum in which to commence such action. The problem leads to the *Commercial Heat* case,[2] which analyzes the jurisdiction of the bankruptcy court in "Bankruptcy cases and proceedings" and in "Procedures."[3]

---

[1] *See infra* Chapter 12, this handbook, Reclamation of Goods.

[2] *In re* Commercial Heat Treating of Dayton, Inc. ("Commercial Heat" or "Plaintiff"), 80 BR 880 (B. SD. Ohio 1987).

[3] 11 USC §1334 and 11 USC §157, respectively.

Collection of Accounts Receivable

These problems are considered in an adversary proceeding where the Plaintiff[4] instituted an action to collect a prepetition account receivable from Atlas Industries, Inc. ("Defendant"). Plaintiff's complaint[5] alleged that heat treating services and materials in the amount of $7,250.20 were provided to Defendant. The Defendant's answer denied a breach, yet admitted a contract existed between the parties and denied the remainder of plaintiff's claims; and asserted that Plaintiff failed to state a claim upon which relief could be granted. Defendant also filed a motion to dismiss the complaint.

Northern Pipeline Decision

This appeared to be a simple case: "[A]n attempt by the debtor in possession to collect a prepetition account receivable [required] a limited review of the United States Supreme Court's decision in *Northern Pipeline*[6] [Bankruptcy Amendments and Federal Judgeship Act of 1984]. . . .and Congress' legislative response, BAFJA, is necessary."[7] In Northern Pipeline, the Supreme Court in a plurality opinion held unconstitutional the Congressional grant of jurisdiction that provided: "[T]he bankruptcy court for the district in which a case under Title 11 is commenced shall exercise *all* of the

---

[4] *See* Part VII Rules of Procedure "Adversary Proceedings." *See also* B.Rule 7002 (References to Federal Rules of Civil Procedure ("F.R.Civ.P.")). *See also* B.Rule 7004(a) (Process, Service of Summons, Complaint) with reference to adversary proceedings.

[5] *See* B.Rule 7001: "An adversary proceeding is governed by the rules of this Part VII. It is a proceeding (1) to recover money or property, . . ." *See also* §1107 granting the debtor in possession the rights, powers and duties of a trustee with several exceptions.

[6] 80 BR at 882, Northern Pipeline Const. v. Marathon Pipeline Co. ("Northern Pipeline"), 102 S.Ct. 2858 (1982), citing in note 2: "For extended reviews, see Countryman, Scrambling To Define Bankruptcy Jurisdiction: The Chief Justice, the Judicial Conference and the Legislative Process, 22 Harv. J. Legis. 1, (1985); King, Jurisdiction and Procedure Under The Bankruptcy Amendments Of 1984, 38 Vand.L.Rev. 4, at 675 (1985)."

[7] *Id. See* BAFJA Public Law 98-353. (Such necessity is also to be found in *infra* Chapter 9, this handbook, Jury Trials.)

jurisdiction conferred by this section on the district courts. . . .[8] The [Court] reasoned that the separation of power's doctrine was violated because the legislation attempted to confer the complete judicial power of the United States contained in Article III of the Constitution upon judges who did not possess the complete protections of life tenure and irreducible salary contained in that same article."

The Court referring to the *Thomas*[9] case observed that the *Northern Pipeline* Court in a number of cases following the decision was "'[u]nable to agree on the precise scope and nature of Article III's limitations.'"[10] The Thomas Court continued that the "case establishes only that Congress may not vest in a non-article III court the power to adjudicate, render final judgment and issue binding orders in a traditional contract action arising under state law, without consent of the litigants and subject only to ordinary appellate review. . . . The most recent Supreme Court decision on this subject, *Commodity Futures Trading Com'n. v. Schor*, 106 S.Ct. 3245 (1986) reaffirms the above statement as the holding in Northern Pipeline."[11]

Congress' response was "a proposed emergency rule (the Interim Rule), which, with minor modifications, has been adopted in all the circuits. This Interim Rule became, to a very great extent, the model for Congress' revised bankruptcy legislation, Bankruptcy Amendments And Federal Judgeship Act ("BAFJA").[12] As finally enacted by Congress, BAFJA provides that the district courts shall have original and exclusive jurisdiction of all cases under §1334(a) of title 28, and original, but not exclusive jurisdiction of all civil proceedings arising under or related to cases under title 11. Section 1334(c)(1) of title 28 provides that nothing in its section prevents a district court in the interest of justice, or in

---

[8] *Id.* citing "§1471(c)(1976 ed. Supp. IV) (emphasis added). *Id.* at 54 n. 1-3 102 S.Ct. at 2862 n. 1-3.

[9] Thomas v. Union Carbide Agr. Products Co. ("Thomas"), 105 S.Ct. 3325 (1985).

[10] 80 BR at 882, citing Thomas, 105 S.Ct. 3325, 3334-35. *See also* Commodity Futures Trading Com'n v. Schor, 106 S.Ct. 3245 (1986).

[11] *Id.*

[12] *Id.*

the interest of comity with state courts or respect for state law, from abstaining[13] from hearing a particular proceeding arising under or in chapter 11 or related to a case under chapter 11. In addition, §1334(c)(2)[14] mandates that the district court abstain from hearing certain proceedings based upon a state law or claim. Each district court may provide that any and all cases and proceedings arising under chapter 11 or arising in or related to a case under chapter 11, are to be referred to the bankruptcy court."[15]

Importance—BAFJA

The reader will appreciate this short interlude with BAFJA, as necessary not only for the understanding of the *Commercial Heat* case, but as still playing an important role in other cases. Now, the reader will remember that the defendant also filed a separate motion to dismiss the complaint. The argument of the respective parties did not involve the merits of their positions, namely, whether plaintiff was entitled to be paid for the services and goods, but addressed only the court's jurisdiction.[16] Plaintiff argued that a number of bankruptcy courts[17] had held that collections of prepetition accounts receivable (or similar contract claims) were within the jurisdiction of the bankruptcy court as core proceedings.

---

[13] *See* 28 USC §1334(c)(2) for conditions restricting abstention. *See also* §305 (Abstention). *See also, supra* Chapter 5, this handbook, Involuntary Petition subtitle "Abstention of Chapter 11."

[14] Additional restrictions are posed in §1334(c)(2): Any decision to abstain is not reviewable "by appeal or otherwise. . . . This subsection shall not be construed to limit the applicability of the stay provided for by section 362 . . . as such section applies to an action affecting the property of the estate in bankruptcy." Subsection 1334(d) grants the district court in a case pending under chapter 11 exclusive jurisdiction of all property of the estate wherever located at the time of commencement of the case.

[15] *See* 28 USC §157(a).

[16] *See* 28 USC §1334 and 28 USC §157(b)(2).

[17] 80 BR at 884. *See, e.g.,* Baldwin-United Corp. v. Thompson, 48 BR 49 (B. SD Ohio 1985); *In re* Perry, Adams, & Lewis Securities Inc., 30 BR 845 (B. WD Mo. 1983); *In re* All American of Ashburn, 49 BR 926 (B. ND Ga. 1985).

Core Proceedings

Supporting its position, the plaintiff cited various combinations of a list contained in §157(b)(2) as core proceedings, but the section clearly indicated that "[c]ore[18] proceedings include, but are not limited to - [this listing]."[19] In connection with the latter contention, plaintiff argued that the court was the proper venue[20] for the proceeding since the section deals with property of the estate, which in nature is a turnover proceeding, and the presence of state law contract issues does not determine whether this proceeding is core or non-core.

In opposition, defendant argued that the proceeding was not a turnover proceeding but rather a breach of contract, and as such, it was a noncore proceeding for which no jurisdiction under §1334 existed in the district court and accordingly no jurisdiction in the bankruptcy court;[21] and in the absence of federal jurisdiction under §1334, the proper jurisdiction and venue was at its place of business in the state Court of Common Pleas, Ohio.

Lack of Jurisdiction

The court stated that the threshold issue raised by the defendant's motion to dismiss was the court's lack of jurisdiction to hear the plaintiff's complaint. Referring to this motion the court drew a clear distinction of the jurisdiction of the bankruptcy court as having a dual position in core and noncore cases. The exercise of jurisdiction by a bankruptcy court rested on "a limited and circumscribed reference of derivative authority from the district court to the bankruptcy

---

[18] *Id.* (citing §§157(b)(2)(A), (E) and (O)).

[19] *Id.* citing §157: "(A) matters concerning the administration of the estate; . . . (E) orders to turn over property of the estate; . . . (O) other proceedings affecting the liquidation of assets of the estate . . . except personal injury tort. . . ."

[20] *See infra* Chapter 8, this handbook, Venue.

[21] *See supra* note 2, Commercial Heat, 80 BR at 884 (citing Northern Pipeline, 102 S.Ct. at 2882, White Motor Corp. v. Citibank N.A., 704 F2d 254, 266 (6th Cir. 1983)).

court over most, but not all, proceedings that are connected to a bankruptcy case."[22]

Referring to §157(b)[23] the bankruptcy court cited the *Salem* case.[24] In that case, the bankruptcy judge's proposed order approving the class certification and the settlement of a class action suit was reversed by the district court for lack of jurisdiction. In reversing the district court's decision and reinstating the bankruptcy judge's order, the Sixth Circuit in *Salem* made evident that the jurisdictional grant contained in BAFJA was to be construed in the broadest constitutionally permissible manner [in 28 U.S.C. §1334]. . . ."[25]

The court then concluded that this broad grant of jurisdiction to the district court over all matters connected to a bankruptcy case or proceeding and approving the reference of that broad jurisdiction to the bankruptcy judge, left no doubt that jurisdiction to hear and determine the trustee's action to collect the prepetition account receivable existed in the district court and had been properly referred to the bankruptcy court. To the extent that the defendant's motion to dismiss rested on the proposition that jurisdiction to hear the trustee's complaint did not exist in the bankruptcy court, the defendant's motion was denied.

Definition "Under or Arising In," "Core," "Related To," and "Noncore"

"The more difficult issue presented in this proceeding concerns the manner in which this existing jurisdiction should

---

[22] *Id.* (citing *In re* Arkansas Communities, Inc., 827 F2d 1219 (8th Cir. 1987)) ("This broad grant of authority establishing the existence of jurisdiction in the district court has been recognized repeatedly in various circuit opinions.").

[23] 28 USC §157. Procedures and 28 USC §157(b) "(1) Bankruptcy judges may hear and determine all cases under title 11 and all core proceedings arising under title 11 . . . (2) Core proceedings include, but are not limited to—. . ." *See also* §157(c)(1): a bankruptcy judge may hear a proceeding that is not a core proceeding. . . . In such proceeding, the bankruptcy judge shall submit proposed findings of fact and conclusions of law to the district court, . . ."

[24] *In re* Salem Mortg. Co. ("Salem"), 783 F2d 626 (6th Cir. 1986).

[25] *See supra* note 2 Commercial Heat, 80 BR at 885 citing Salem.

be exercised by the bankruptcy court."[26] The exercise of this jurisdiction required the court to turn to §157 for a determination of whether the debtor in possession could maintain an action in the bankruptcy court to collect a prepetition account receivable. Referring to the *Wood* case,[27] the court clarified the meanings of core and noncore cases with simple examples of the meanings of the statutory phrases:

> [T]he phrases arising "under" and "arising in" are helpful indicators of the meaning of core proceedings. If the proceeding involves a right created by the federal bankruptcy law, it is a core proceeding; for example, an action by a trustee to avoid a preference.[28] If the proceeding is one that would arise only in bankruptcy, it is also a core proceeding; for example, the filing of a proof of claim or an objection to the discharge of a particular debt. If the proceeding does not invoke a substantive right created by the federal bankruptcy law and is one that could exist outside of bankruptcy it is not a core proceeding; it may be *related* to the bankruptcy because of its potential effect, but under §157(c)(1) it is an "otherwise related" or non-core proceeding.[29]

The court concluded that nothing in §157(b)(2) outlining core proceedings would justify a finding that collection of a prepetition account receivable was a core proceeding. However, "a discussion of §157(b)(2)(E)—orders to turn over property of the estate; . . . contains language that would appear to include a proceeding in the bankruptcy court to collect a prepetition account receivable as a core proceeding. A prepetition account

---

[26] 80 BR at 887.

[27] *Id.* at 889 (citing *In re* Wood, 825 F2d 90 (5th Cir. 1987) where a "similar analysis was recently employed. . . ." [of an identification of non-core cases]).

[28] *Id. See also* §547.

[29] *Id.* at 889 quoting *In re* Wood, 825 F2d at 96–97.

receivable becomes property of the estate upon the filing of the case."[30]

Notwithstanding such holding, the court turned to a collection of bankruptcy cases containing contrary holdings in core/non-core determinations concerning the collection of accounts receivable under §157(b) together with the cogent reasoning supporting a determination that such proceedings are noncore.

Effect of Bona Fide Dispute

Addressing the *Acolyte*[31] case, the court reasoned: "To the extent that a BONA FIDE[32] dispute exists with regard to the existence of an identifiable fund or *res,* a proceeding to recover that res is not a turnover within the meaning of BAFJA unless and until the existence, magnitude and identity of the res are first established. The jurisdiction to establish this existence, magnitude and identity is precisely what [*Northern Pipeline v.*] *Marathon* prohibits Congress from granting to the bankruptcy court. In order to protect the constitutional integrity of BAFJA, it must therefore be read so as not to include contested collection suits to be core proceedings."[33]

Enunciating the four characteristics set forth in *Northern Pipeline v. Marathon*, the court held that a proceeding to collect a prepetition account receivable that is subject to a bona fide dispute such as the case at bar, was a noncore proceeding. The court stated that its conclusion was reached "aware of the various express and inherent arguments and concerns that surround this issue—Congress could (or should) have enacted a better legislative response to Northern Pipeline. . . ."

---

[30] *Id.* at 890 citing §§542(b): "[A]n entity that owes a debt that is property of the estate and that is matured, payable on demand, or payable on order, shall pay such debt to, or on the order of, the trustee. . . ." *See also* United States v. Whiting Pools, Inc., 103 S.Ct. 2309 (1983).

[31] *Id.* citing Acolyte Elec. Corp. v. City of New York, 69 BR 155, 167-75 (B. EDNY 1986), *aff'd,* 1987 WL 47763 (EDNY 1987).

[32] *Id.* (emphasis in original).

[33] *Id.* Commercial 890.

[I]t is as anomalous that a bankruptcy court can enter a final judgment ordering millions of dollars paid to or from an estate in a core proceeding, but must only recommend findings of fact and conclusions of law in a non-core proceeding involving the smallest amount; an obvious result of this conclusion will be an increased expenditure of time and money by litigants, counsel and various state and federal courts. . . ."[34]

The court, nonetheless, denied the defendant's motion to dismiss and entered an order setting a trial date and requiring counsel to advise the court of their decision concerning their joint consent to a trial by the bankruptcy court.[35] As to venue, the court opined: "Venue is proper in this bankruptcy court where the action was commenced".[36]

Observation

The bankruptcy judge opined he was reluctant to render a decision that a DIP could not collect a $7,250.20 claim concerning which there was a bona fide dispute. However, the judge had no choice even though there appeared to be wide latitude in the wording of §157(b)(2)(A)-(O), for fear, as other courts had opined, that the ghost of *Northern Pipeline* would reappear: "In order to protect the constitutional integrity of BAFJA, it must therefore be read so as not to include contested collection suits [or for that matter any bona fide contested litigation] to be core proceedings."[37]

A simpler procedure would be Congressional legislation conferring "Article III status upon bankruptcy judges [which] would ensure the reestablishment of pervasive jurisdiction and

---

[34] *Id.* at 890.

[35] *See* 28 USC §157(c)(2). *See also infra* Chapter 8, this handbook, Venue subtitle "Choice of Venue."

[36] Commercial Heat, 80 BR at 891 citing *In re* Robert's Furniture, Inc., 70 BR 29, 31 (B. SD Ohio 1987).

[37] *Id.* at 890 (emphasis in original) (citing Acolyte Elec. Corp. v. City of New York, 69 BR at 171).

would provide operational authority comparable to the district courts in the Federal System."[38]

The bankruptcy court did not hesitate to observe that "constitutional issues continue to be implicated in the present jurisdictional scheme, and BAFJA has not been specifically examined by the United States Supreme Court,...[and] while circuit courts continue to acknowledge these constitutional concerns, there is no circuit court decision holding unconstitutional the present congressional enactments governing jurisdiction and jurisdictional procedures in bankruptcy cases and proceedings."[39]

Awaiting a further decision by the Supreme Court or a Congressional Amendment, we turn to appellate jurisdiction.

Appellate Jurisdiction

In 1984, O'Sullivan's Fuel Oil Co.[40] filed a chapter 11 petition that was converted to chapter 7 in 1986. Thomas M. Germain was the trustee in bankruptcy. In 1987, Germain sued Connecticut National Bank ("CNB"), a successor to one of O'Sullivan's creditors, in Connecticut state court, seeking to hold the bank liable for various torts and breaches of contract. CNB removed the suit to the federal district court of Connecticut, "which, pursuant to local rule, automatically referred the proceeding to the Bankruptcy Court, ..."

Interlocutory Orders

Germain then filed a demand for a jury trial. CNB moved to strike Germain's demand. The Bankruptcy Court denied CNB's motion and the district court affirmed. CNB then tried to appeal to the Second Circuit, but the court dismissed for lack of jurisdiction. The Second Circuit held that a court of appeals may exercise jurisdiction over interlocutory orders in bankruptcy only when a district court issues the order after

---

[38] *See* article Howard Schwartzberg, Bankruptcy Judge SDNY, *The Retreat from Pervasive Jurisdiction in Bankruptcy Court,* 7 BANKR. DEV. J. #1 (1990).

[39] Commercial Heat, 80 BR at 883.

[40] *In re* O'Sullivan's Fuel Oil Co., 88 BR 17 (D. Conn. 1988).

having withdrawn a proceeding or case from a bankruptcy court, and not when the district court acts in its capacity as a bankruptcy court of appeals.

To resolve the problem, the Supreme Court considered the jurisdiction of the courts of appeals over interlocutory orders as reflected in two statutes. "Courts of appeals have jurisdiction over '[i]nterlocutory orders of the district courts of the United States' under 28 USC §1292."[41] CNB contended that §1292(b) applied by its terms in this case and the court of appeals should have exercised discretionary jurisdiction over its appeal. Germain argued to the contrary contending Congress limited §1292 through 28 USC §158(d) which deals with bankruptcy jurisdiction. CNB responded that nothing in §158(d) limited §1292.[42]

"Subsection (d), which is pivotal in this case, provides: 'The courts of appeals shall have jurisdiction of appeals from all final decisions, judgments, orders, and decrees entered under subsections (a) and (b) of this section.'" The Court stated that neither subsection 158(d) nor any part of §158 mentions interlocutory orders entered by the district courts in bankruptcy. "The parties agree, as they must, that §158 did not confer jurisdiction on the Courts of Appeals."[43]

Germain reasoned that although 28 USC §§1291 and 1292 appeared to "cover the universe of decisions issued by the district courts—with §1291 conferring jurisdiction over appeals from final decisions of the district courts, and §1292 conferring jurisdiction over certain interlocutory ones—that cannot in fact be so. If §1291 did cover all final decisions by a district court, he argues, that section would render §158(d) superfluous, since a final decision issued by a district court sitting as a bankruptcy appellate court is still a final decision

---

[41] Connecticut National Bank v. Germain ("Germain"), 112 S.Ct. 1146 (1992).

[42] *Id.* at 1148 citing 28 USC §1292: "(a) . . . [T]he courts of appeals shall have jurisdiction of appeals from: (1) Interlocutory orders of the district courts of the United States. . . . (b) When a district judge, in making in a civil action an order not otherwise appealable under this section . . . may materially advance the ultimate termination of the litigation . . . [t]he Court of Appeals . . . may thereupon, in its discretion, permit an appeal. . . ."

[43] *Id.* at 1148–49.

of a district court.[44] If §158(d) is to have effect, Germain contends, then that section must be exclusive within its own domain, which he defines as the universe of orders issued by district courts sitting pursuant to §158(a) as courts of appeals in bankruptcy. . . ."[45]

Decision of Supreme Court

The Court observed that redundancies across statutes were not unusual events in drafting, "and so long as there is no 'positive repugnancy' between two laws. . .,[46] a court must give effect to both. Because giving effect to both §§1291 and 158(d) would not render one or the other wholly superfluous, we do not have to read §158(d) as precluding courts of appeals, by negative implication, from exercising jurisdiction under §1291 over district courts sitting in bankruptcy."[47]

The final words of the Supreme Court make it obvious that §158(d) contains all the provisions of §1292: "So long as a party to a proceeding or case in bankruptcy meets the conditions imposed by §1292, a court of appeals may rely on that statute as a basis for jurisdiction." Reversed and remanded "for proceedings consistent with this opinion."[48]

Observation

Section 158(d) is now enlarged with the statutory contents of §1292. Of course, Germain doesn't answer the problem of what is a final decree or interlocutory order but §1292(b) grants a helpful hand to the district judge: "When a district judge, in making in a civil action an order not otherwise

---

[44] *Id.* at 1149.

[45] *Id.* The paragraph concludes: "Germain claims to find support for his view in his reading of the legislative history of §158(d)."

[46] *Id.* citing Wood v. United States 16 Pet. 342, 363, 10 L.Ed. 987 (1842).

[47] *Id.*

[48] *Id.* at 1150. *See, e.g., In re* Johns-Manville Corp., 824 F2d 176, 179 (2d Cir. 1987), holding that in bankruptcy cases, orders are final, if they "finally dispose of discrete disputes within the larger case." *See also, In re* Chateaugay Corp., 80 BR 279 (SDNY 1987), containing a summary of factors to consider in determining an order as "final," and decisions of other circuits.

appealable under this section, shall be of the opinion that such order involves a controlling question of law as to which there is substantial ground for difference of opinion and that an immediate appeal from the order may materially advance the ultimate termination of the litigation, he shall so state in writing such order. The Court of Appeals . . . may thereupon, in its discretion, permit an appeal to be taken from such order, ...[49]

Chapter 8, Venue, discusses the importance of the location of the district court in which the proceedings under chapter 11 shall be commenced—importance to the debtor, creditors, and substantial parties in interest.

---

[49] *Id.* at 1148 citing 28 USC §1292(b).

Chapter 8
Venue

Distinguished From Jurisdiction

Venue is to be distinguished from jurisdiction.[1] In the *Pinehaven* case[2] the court opined: "The term 'venue' refers to locality, *i.e.,* the place where a lawsuit should be heard. Unlike the term jurisdiction which implicates the power of a court to adjudicate, venue denotes only the place of adjudication. . . . The purpose of any venue statute is to provide a judicial forum locus that meets the legitimate needs of litigants or parties. . . ."[3]

---

[1] *See supra* Chapter 7, this handbook, Jurisdiction of Bankruptcy Court.

[2] *In re* Pinehaven Associates ("Pinehaven" or "Debtor"), 132 BR 982 (B. EDNY 1991).

[3] *Id.* at 987.

Choice of Venue

The court then proceeded to discuss "[t]he venue statute[4] governing bankruptcy cases . . . [which] gives wide latitude to a prospective Debtor. Under 28 USC §1408 there are four alternative, broad-based predicates upon which a person or entity can select the district of a bankruptcy filing, (1) domicile, (2) residence, (3) location of principal place of business [in the United States],[5] or (4) location of principal assets [in the United States]; or a chapter 11 may be commenced in the district court for the district "in which there is pending a case under title 11 concerning such person's affiliate, general partner, or partnership."[6] Section 1409 contains provisions for proper venue for proceedings arising in chapter 11 and §1410 for "Venue of cases ancillary to foreign proceedings. The overall change of venue or proceeding is §1412, wherein . . . [a] district court may transfer a case or a proceeding under title 11 to a district court for another district, in the interest of justice or for the convenience of the parties."[7]

"Implementing this statute is Bankruptcy Rule 1014(a) which Rule, in relevant part, provides as follows: (1) If a petition is filed in a proper district, on timely motion of a party in interest, and after hearing on notice to the petitioners, . . . the case may be transferred to any other district if the court determines that the transfer is in the interest of justice or for the convenience of the parties."[8] However, if filed in an improper district it may be transferred for the same reasons or dismissed, but dismissal is only upon a timely motion.[9]

Pinehaven, a New York limited partnership, consisted of a New York corporate general partner, *The Phynn Group, Inc.* ("Phynn"), and 25 limited partners. Pinehaven was formed for the purpose of owning and managing real estate. Its only business consisted of the ownership and operation of a 96 room Best Western franchise motel in Southhaven, Mississippi.

---

[4] 28 USC §1408.

[5] 132 BR at 987.

[6] *Id.* 28 USC §1408(2).

[7] *Id.*

[8] *Id.*

[9] *Id.*

Business offices were located in Nassau County, in the Eastern District of New York. Alan Wolpert ("Wolpert") and Melvin Schreiber ("Schreiber") were each 50% owners of Phynn. Each performed personal services at the Nassau location. Major decisions and overall supervision of Pinehaven's affairs were made through the Debtor's offices in the Nassau County office. Pinehaven and Phynn had no employees. "The business affairs of Pinehaven, to the extent they are conducted in the Eastern District of New York, are *de facto* carried on, in the main, by *Wolpert* and Wolpert Associates . . . who perform booking services."[10]

Sunburst Bank ("Sunburst") was a Mississippi state bank, with branches in Southhaven, Mississippi. The Motel and Pinehaven's interest in the ground lease were encumbered by a 1987 deed of trust, constituting a first mortgage position in favor of Sunburst that secured a 1987 loan in the amount of $2 million made by Sunburst to Western Inns, Inc., a Texas corporation from which Pinehaven earlier acquired the Motel. The last payment on the loan was received on September 1, 1990. Sunburst instituted a foreclosure proceeding and a sale was scheduled for April 18, 1991. The Debtor filed its chapter 11 on April 16, staying the foreclosure.[11]

Court's Discretion: Transfer of Venue

Sunburst, the largest creditor, moved the court to transfer the chapter 11 case from the Eastern District of New York to the Bankruptcy Court for the Northern District of Mississippi. Sunburst was supported by all creditors who made their positions known to the court. The Debtor opposed the motion supported by its limited partners. In its discussion of the law the court opined that under 28 USC §1412 and B.Rule 1014(a)(1), a properly venued bankruptcy case may be transferred in the interest of justice or the convenience of the parties and "[t]hat venue of Pinehaven's Chapter 11 case in the Eastern District of New York is technically proper under

---

[10] *Id.* at 984. *Compare supra* Chapter 11, this handbook, Prepackaged Chapter 11 subtitle "De Facto Plans."

[11] *Id.* at 983. *See supra* Chapter 6, this handbook, Automatic Stay subtitle "Foreclosure."

28 U.S.C. §1408, as Sunburst readily concedes, does not preclude transfer to another district."[12] Furthermore, a transfer under §1412 "lies within the sound discretion of the bankruptcy court."[13]

Burden of Proof on Moving Party

In considering such transfer under §1412, the court emphasized that "[t]he party moving for change of venue has the burden of proof and that burden must be carried by a preponderance of the evidence."[14] In addition, the court indicated the difficulty of citing cases to support such discretion under §1412: "There is no litmus test or hard and fast rule offering precise guidance for transfer of venue and the bankruptcy courts are left to a case by case determination based upon all relevant factors."[15]

Convenience of Parties to Courts

The court then turned to the convenience of the parties and cited five factors to be determined,[16] namely, the proximity to the court of (1) creditors, (2) Debtor, (3) witnesses, (4) location of assets, and (5) economic administration of the estate. The court found that the only factor that possibly supported the retention of venue in the district was the location of the Debtor in New York. Although the business revolved around Mississippi property, it was managed by people located in Southhaven.

Convenience of Parties

The problems involving the status of the Motel signified factors that would warrant transfer. "An appraisal will be

---

[12] *Id.* at 987.

[13] *Id.* at 988 citing *In re* Pavilion Place Assocs., 88 BR 32, 35 (B. SDNY 1988); *In re* Eleven Oak Tower Ltd. Partnership, 59 BR 626, 628 (B. ND Ill. 1986).

[14] *Id.* citing Gulf States Exploration Co. v. Manville Forest Prods. Corp. (*In re* Forest Prods. Corp.), 896 F2d 1384, 1390 (2d Cir. 1990).

[15] *Id.* at 988 citing *supra* note 14.

[16] *Id.* citing *In re* Commonwealth Oil Refining Co., 596 F2d 1239, 1247 (5th Cir. 1979), *cert. denied,* 100 S.Ct. 732 (1980).

required to establish the Motel's value. Such valuation may arise in the context of adequate protection[17] aspects of a lift stay motion,[18] a sale of the Motel or fixing the amount of Sunburst's secured claim under 11 U.S.C. §506(a) . . .[19] Mississippi appraisers will be selected. . . . [T]o value the Motel, the testimony of local appraisers, brokers, sales agents . . . will be highly probative. . . . [I]n the event [of] a sale of the Motel . . . title searches will have to be conducted in Mississippi."[20]

In the event the Debtor should propose a plan of reorganization, the Debtor would be confronted with maintaining the Motel. Since the Motel is the Debtor's only asset, "major issue will be whether cash flows from the Motel will be adequate to pay debt service to Sunburst and other lenders. . . .[21] [C]ompetition in the area will be highly probative." The court, having discussed the five factors that determined the basis of a transfer which amounted to a finding that Mississippi was the venue most suitable for the convenience of the parties, turned to the alternative of §1412: Was the transfer "in the interests of justice?" Analyzing the problem the court opined: "The state of title to and interests in the Motel, and the property of which the Motel forms a part, involve documents which are voluminous, complex, unclear and subject to significant questions. . . . Further, the Mississippi bankruptcy court is in a better position to render accurate and proper decisions on these questions. . . ."[22]

The court observed that: "The interest of justice component of §1412 is an elusive term not easily amenable to definition.

---

[17] *See supra* Chapter 3, Use, Sale or Lease of Property.

[18] *See supra* Chapter 6, this handbook, Automatic Stay subtitle "Foreclosure."

[19] *See* Pinehaven, 132 BR at 988 note 9: "11 U.S.C. §506(a). . . ." *See also* Dewsnup v. Timm, 1128 S.Ct. 773 (1992) where the court denied a Debtor's request to strip down a secured creditor's lien by eliminating the unsecured portion of the lien having no secured value.

[20] *Id.* at 987–88.

[21] *Id.* at 988. 11 U.S.C. §1129(a)(11) contains a requirement that confirmation is not likely to be followed by the Debtor's liquidation, or the Debtor's need for further financial rehabilitation.

[22] *Id.* at 990 citing *In re* Developers of Caguas, Inc., 26 BR 977, 980 (B. EDNY 1983).

The Congress provided no compass for the meaning to be ascribed to 'interest of justice,' which phrase is more easily felt than precisely defined. It is so in this case. An interest of justice venue transfer encompasses, among other things, inquiry as to the forum which facilitates the efficient, proper and expeditious functioning of the courts. Although vague, this inquiry would include looking into the desirability of having a judge familiar with applicable law hear and determine issues arising in the case."[23]

The court continued emphasizing that in transferring venue to Mississippi, the state of title to and interests in the Motel and the property of which the Motel encompasses were: (1) a single asset located in Southhaven; (2) Debtor has no employees; (3) staffed and managed locally in Southhaven - Memphis area; (4) venue chosen for personal preference and convenience of one man, Wolpert; (5) purpose to make the chapter 11 more burdensome to creditors and Sunburst; (6) accommodating Wolpert's personal convenience "at the expense of creditors and other interested parties does not advance the 'interest of justice;' and (7) having chosen to buy a Motel in Mississippi, Debtor "cannot be heard to complain that its chapter 11 effort is being transferred to that location."[24]

Forum Group Inc.
Involuntary Petition

The transfer issue may be confronted in the context of an involuntary proceeding. Such was the situation in the *Forum Group* case[25] where an alleged Debtor in an involuntary case was able to successfully transfer venue. The petitioning creditors alleged venue was proper in the Northern District of

---

[23] *Id.* citing Heller Financial, Inc. v. Midwhey Powder Co., Inc., 883 F2d 1286, 1293 (7th Cir. 1989).

[24] *Id.* at 991.

[25] *In re* Forum Group, Inc. ("Forum Group"), Case No. 391-31268-RCM-11 (Involuntary Case) (B. ND Tex. 1991) "Memorandum of Law in Support of Emergency Motion For Order Dismissing or Transferring Venue of the Involuntary Case." *See also, supra* Chapter 2, this handbook, Lender's Participation subtitle "Forum Case—Current Lending."

Texas because "[t]he Debtor's principal assets have been within this district for the 180 days preceding the filing of this Petition. . . ."[26] In support of this assertion, the creditors identified two facilities located in Dallas.

The alleged Debtor argued that a transfer of venue to the Southern District of Indiana was warranted as venue was improperly laid in the Northern District of Texas. In support of its argument the alleged Debtor observed that "Forum's domicile . . . is Indiana. . . . [T]he Debtor's residence is Indiana. . . . [T]he Debtor maintains its principal place of business, in the form of its headquarters and "nerve center" [in] . . . Indiana."[27]

In further support of its argument, the alleged Debtor also noted that only six percent of the alleged Debtor's total assets were located in the Northern District of Texas and that only five percent of its annual net revenues were derived from operations in that district. In its Unofficial Transcript granting the motion to transfer venue the court stated that: "[t]ransfer of venue to the Indiana bankruptcy court will facilitate the effective administration in *Forum's* Chapter 11 case, will be most convenient to all parties concerned, and will be in the interest of justice."[28]

Dismissal Venue

Bad Faith

We go a step further than "transfer of venue" and consider the alternative of "dismissal" of the *Bayoutree*[29] case filed in the wrong venue as not being in the interest of justice. On March 5, 1990 Bayoutree filed a petition under chapter 11 in the District of Arizona, Tucson division. An apartment complex located in Houston, Texas was Bayoutree's principal asset.

---

[26] *Id.* "Memorandum of Law in Support of Emergency Motion For Order Dismissing or Transferring Venue of the Involuntary Case" at 6.

[27] *Id.* at 9–10.

[28] *See* 28 USC §1412.

[29] *In re* Hall, Bayoutree Associates, Ltd., ("Bayoutree" or "Debtor"), 939 F2d 802 (9th Cir. 1991).

Two lien creditors, Oaks and RTC[30] moved the bankruptcy court to transfer venue or in the alternative to dismiss for improper venue. On July 5, the court took the motion under consideration and thereafter issued an order denying the motion with leave to renew at the hearing on confirmation of the plan of reorganization. On August 3, 1990, the court entered a final order denying the motion to transfer venue or dismiss for improper venue, but the August 3rd order did not refer to the motion to dismiss for bad-faith filing, nor did it contain any findings of fact or conclusions of law.

Oaks appealed the August 3rd order to the district court and RTC joined in the appeal. Although the designation of issues on appeal and the parties' briefing were limited the question of venue, the record on appeal also included the motion of bad-faith filing that had been before the bankruptcy court. On January 8, 1991 the district court entered an order holding that venue in Arizona was improper and finding that the bankruptcy case had been filed in bad faith and, therefore, dismissed the case with prejudice.

Dismissal with Prejudice Improper

Bayoutree appealed to the court of appeals, not on the court's holding that venue was improper in Arizona, but its appeal was limited to the question of whether the district court erred by dismissing the case with prejudice because of bad-faith filing. "Although it was within the district court's discretion to either dismiss the case or transfer it 'in the interest of justice,' it was an error for the district court to dismiss the case with prejudice. A determination of improper venue does not go to the merits of the case and therefore must be without prejudice."[31] Referring to Rule 41(b),[32] the court observed that "although a dismissal normally operates as an

---

[30] *Id.* at 803: The Oaks of Woodlake Phase III, Ltd. ("Oaks") and the Resolution Trust Co. as conservator for Brookside Federal Savings and Loan Association ("RTC").

[31] *Id.* Costello v. United States, 81 S.Ct. 534, 544–45 (1961).

[32] Federal Rules of Civil Procedure Rule 41(b).

adjudication on the merits, one exception to this rule is a dismissal for improper venue. . . ."[33]

> A dismissal for improper venue is specifically excluded from the types of dismissals that operate as an adjudication on the merits. Fed. R. Civ. P. 41(b). We hold that the discretion given to the district court under Bankruptcy Rule 1014(a)(2) and 28 U.S.C. §1406(a) to dismiss a case for improper venue does not include the power to dismiss a case with prejudice.[34]

Review on Appeal to District Court

Considering whether the issue of bad-faith filing was proper before the district court, the court of appeals observed that the designation of issues on appeal was limited to venue. The record on appeal, however, included the motion to appeal for bad faith. "A district court, reviewing a bankruptcy appeal, can decide an issue that is not raised on appeal, if that issue is purely legal and is fully supported by the record. . . .[35] If the bankruptcy court's factual findings are silent or ambiguous as to a material factual question, the district court must remand the case to the bankruptcy court for the necessary factual determination, . . ."

Status of Appeal
District Court: Limited Fact Finder

Since the question of whether a bankruptcy case was filed in bad faith is a factual question, the district court was not free to make its own determination of bad faith. "The district court should have remanded the case to the bankruptcy court for factual findings on that question."[36] Another alternative "was

---

[33] Bayoutree, 939 F2d 804.

[34] Bayoutree, 939 F2d at 804.

[35] *Id.* citing *In re* Pizza of Hawaii, Inc., 761 F2d 1374, 1377 (9th Cir. 1985).

[36] *Id.* at 805.

clear that under §157(d), a district court may withdraw reference at any time, for cause shown, but it is unclear whether it can withdraw reference by implication. . . . Moreover, we have approved a district court's withdrawing reference *nunc pro tunc*[37] to justify deciding a non-core matter." Having some doubt on the issue, but "even if withdrawal can be found by implication, there still must be some 'cause shown' for the withdrawal. . . ."[38] The district court did not declare any cause for a withdrawal of the reference in this case. The district court was not faced with a decision on a non-core matter.[39] The question whether a bankruptcy case was filed in bad faith 'is a matter for the bankruptcy court's discretion.'"[40]

The court of appeals held that the district court should have remanded the matter to the bankruptcy court for actual findings. "Its decision to reach the issue of bad faith was not a withdrawal by implication but rather an incorrect attempt by an appellate court to assume the role of a fact finder."[41]

The final issue was whether the district court abused its discretion by dismissing the case rather than transferring it to Texas. As the court had discussed, Bankruptcy Rule 1014(a)(2), just as 28 U.S.C. §1406(a) "provides that a court may dismiss a case filed in an improper district unless transferring the case to a proper district is in the 'interest of justice.' We review a determination of whether to transfer or dismiss for abuse of discretion."[42]

"A review of the record revealed that the district court did not abuse its discretion in dismissing the case. Although dismissal of an action for improper venue is a harsh penalty, dismissal is proper where filing in an improper forum

---

[37] *Id.* citing Barona Group of Captain Grande Band of Mission Indians v. American Management & Amusement, Inc., 840 F2d 1394, 1399 (9th Cir. 1988), *cert. denied*, 109 S.Ct. 7 (1988).

[38] *Id.* citing §157(d).

[39] *Id. See, supra* Chapter 7, this handbook, Jurisdiction of Bankruptcy Court subtitle "Core Proceedings." *See also* Chapter 9, this handbook, Jury Trials subtitle "Core or Non-Core Proceeding."

[40] *Id.* citing *In re* Stolrow's Inc., 84 BR 167, 170 (B. 9th Cir. 1988).

[41] *Id.*

[42] *Id. cf.* Central Valley Typographical Union No. 46 v. McClatchy Newspapers, 762 F2d 741, 745 (9th Cir. 1985).

evidences bad faith.[43] . . . We therefore affirm the district court's dismissal of the case." However, the court remanded the order for further proceedings consistent with its opinion. Those proceedings include a dismissal without prejudice for improper venue, but may include "a return of the case to the bankruptcy court for further proceedings (including the issuance of findings of fact) regarding the bad faith motion, or a determination of whether the case should be withdrawn from the bankruptcy court in accordance with 28 USC §157(d)."[44]

Consequences of Dismissal

As the *Monterey* case[45] held, a consequence of dismissal, even without prejudice to the Debtor, may be harmful to creditors. Where venue is improper, dismissal of the case is held to be improper as a remedy. "Dismissal may result in preference recoveries being lost.[46] It may result in a valuable asset being lost to foreclosure.[47] These and other consequences[48] should lead to an interpretation of Section 1412 which precludes the power to dismiss."[49]

Observation

The provision of §1412 to allow the court to transfer a case to another district in the interest of justice, or for the convenience of parties, helps considerably in the reorganization process. The discretion the section grants the court is an opportunity to evaluate the testimony and determine what objectives are advanced by either party in maintaining the *status quo* or seeking a transfer. *Pinehaven*

---

[43] *Id.* at 806 citing 1. J. Moore, A Vestal & P. Kurland, MOORE'S MANUAL, FEDERAL PRACTICE AND PROCEDURE, §7.13[1] (1990); *cf.* Phillips v. Illinois Central Gulf R.R., 874 F2d, 984, 986 (5th Cir. 1989).

[44] *Id.*

[45] *In re* Monterey Equities-Hillside, 73 BR 749, 753-54 (B. ND Cal. 1987).

[46] *See infra* Chapter 15, this handbook, Preferences.

[47] *See infra* Chapter 16, this handbook, Fraudulent Transfers and Obligations subtitle "Good Faith—Shareholders Protected."

[48] *See infra* Chapter 14, this handbook, Trustee's Strong Arm Power.

[49] *Id.* citing 1 COLLIER ON BANKRUPTCY ¶3.02(d)(ii).

goes to the extent of analyzing whether the Debtor's venue can be sustained by its absence of a sound cash flow necessary for two contingencies: (1) the failure to pay the Bank's installments, which may result in a foreclosure; or (2) endeavoring reorganization without the necessary funds to sustain a solvent business. The transfer of venue to Southhaven, Mississippi was sound.

The *Forum Group* case emphasizes that a Debtor can obtain a speedy order for a transfer of venue in an involuntary case and during the time it is necessary to obtain a transfer of venue. The Code[50] provides a "gap" claim superior to all unsecured claims as an administrative expense for payment of current debt pending grant of a transfer. The result is to keep the Debtor operating until such time as the transfer, if at all, occurs.

Bayoutree delves into the dangers of dismissal, a hardship to creditors in the loss of the recovery of funds improperly or illegally transferred. *Bayoutree* also presents a strong objection to any dismissal with prejudice. Absent bad faith in filing, both positions are sound.

With chapters on Jurisdiction and Venue completed, we turn to Chapter 9, Jury Trials.

---

[50] *See* §§502(f) and 507(a)(2). *See also, supra* Chapter 5, this handbook, subtitle "Gap Period."

Chapter 9
Jury Trials

I n a brief section, "28 U.S.C. §1411. Jury trials,"[1] we read:
"(a) Except as provided in subsection (b) of this section, this chapter and title 11 do not affect any right to trial by jury that an individual has under nonbankruptcy law with regard to a personal injury or wrongful death tort claim."[2] Discretion is given to the court in subsection (b): "The district court may order the issues arising under section 303 of title 11 to be tried without a jury." With two references to obligatory jury trials and discretionary authority, the statutes remain silent as to what other proceedings in bankruptcy are available for jury trials. Recent cases, however, appear for and against such trials in adversary proceedings.

---

[1] See §303. Involuntary cases.
[2] See also supra Chapter 5, this handbook, subtitle "Involuntary Chapter 11."

One of the current cases to tackle the problem of an allowable jury trial in an adversary case, was the *Granfinanciera*[3] case, a chapter 11 case decided by the Supreme Court. A chapter 11 trustee instituted an action against defendants who allegedly had received fraudulent transfers. In the bankruptcy court, the defendants moved for a jury trial and for dismissal of the case on grounds of lack of jurisdiction. The bankruptcy court denied the motions, which were also denied on successive appeals to the district court and the court of appeals. Granting *certiorari*, the Supreme Court held that the defendant, who had not filed a claim against the bankruptcy estate, had a right to a jury trial when sued by a trustee to recover an alleged fraudulent monetary transfer. "We hold that the Seventh Amendment[4] entitles such a person to a trial by jury, notwithstanding Congress' designation of fraudulent conveyance actions as 'core proceedings'. . . ."[5]

Private Versus Public Rights

After analyzing a number of cases at common law involving legal rights entitling a party to a jury trial, private versus public rights in comparison with equitable rights,[6] and observing that bankruptcy courts were not in essence courts of equity, the Court concluded that the defendant was entitled to a jury trial; but it left a caveat:

---

[3] *See* Granfinanciera, S.A. ("Granfinanciera") v. Nordberg, 109 S.Ct. 2782, 2789 note 3 (1989): "The current statutory provision for jury trials in bankruptcy proceedings—28 U.S.C. §1411 . . . is notoriously ambiguous. . . . The confused legislative history of these provisions has further puzzled commentators. . . ."

[4] 109 S.Ct. at 2790: "The Seventh Amendment provides: 'In Suits at common law, where the value in controversy shall exceed twenty dollars, the right of trial by jury shall be preserved. . . .'"

[5] *Id.* citing 28 USC §157(b)(2)(HH)(1982 ed., Supp. IV). *See, supra* Chapter 7, this handbook, Jurisdiction of Bankruptcy Court subtitle "Core Proceedings."

[6] *See* Langencamp v. Culp, 111 S.Ct. 330 (1990) (Actions to recover preferences involve private rights and a party is entitled to a jury trial provided no proof of claim has been filed).

We do not decide today whether the current jury trial provision—28 U.S.C. §1411 . . . permits bankruptcy courts to conduct jury trials in fraudulent conveyance actions like the one respondent initiated. Nor do we express any view as to whether the Seventh Amendment or Article III allows jury trials in such actions to be held before non-Article III bankruptcy judges. . . . We leave those issues for future decisions.[7] We do hold, however, that whatever the answer to these questions, the Seventh Amendment entitles petitioners to the jury trial they requested. Accordingly, the judgment of the Court of Appeals is reversed and the case is remanded for further proceedings consistent with this opinion.[8]

Dissent: Katchen v. Landy

The Court's decision was a close call—five to four. Justice White in dissenting considered "the question of the precedent that the Court most disregards today, *Katchen v. Landy.* . . .[9] Though the court professes not to overrule this decision, and curiously to be acting in reliance on it . . . there is simply no way to reconcile our decision in *Katchen* with what the court holds today."

In *Katchen*, the petitioner filed a claim to recover funds that were allegedly due him from the bankruptcy estate and requested a jury trial. The trustee resisted paying the claims based on §57(g) of the former Bankruptcy Act "which forbade payments to creditors holding void or voidable preferences. Petitioner claimed, much as petitioners here do, that the question whether prior payments to him were preferences was a matter that could not be adjudicated without the benefit of a jury trial. We rejected this claim holding that 'there is no Seventh Amendment right to a jury trial' on claims such as Katchen's. . . . [L]ike the petitioner in *Katchen*, petitioners in

---

[7] *See* 109 S.Ct. at 2802 note 19 referring to opinion of Justice White.

[8] *Id.* at 2802.

[9] *Id.* at 2806 citing Katchen ("Katchen") v. Landy, 86 S.Ct. 467 (1966).

this case have no Seventh Amendment right to a jury trial when respondent trustee seeks to avoid the fraudulent transfers they received."[10]

Bankruptcy Court
A Court of Equity

Moreover, Justice White indicated that under the 1984 Act[11] an action to recover fraudulently transferred property has been classified as a "core" bankruptcy proceeding.[12] "[T]he forum in which a claim is to be heard plays a substantial role in determining the extent to which a Seventh Amendment jury trial right exists."[13] Justice White referred to *Katchen,* which opined that in cases of bankruptcy "many incidental questions arise in the course of administering the bankruptcy estate, which would ordinarily be pure cases at law, and in respect of their facts triable by jury, but, as belonging to bankruptcy proceedings, they become cases over which the bankruptcy court, which acts as a court of equity, exercises exclusive control. Thus, a claim of debt or damages against the bankrupt is investigated by chancery methods."[14]

Ben Cooper Case

It was not too long before the Second Circuit endeavored to pierce the indecision of granting a jury trial by a bankruptcy

---

[10] *Id.*

[11] *See, supra* Chapter 7, this handbook, Jurisdiction of Bankruptcy Court.

[12] *See* 28 USC §157(b)(2)(H).

[13] 109 S.Ct. at 2807.

[14] *Id.* citing Katchen v. Landy, 86 S.Ct. at 477. *See also, In re* J.T. Moran Financial Corp., 124 BR 931 (SDNY 1991), where in an adversary proceeding conducted by Debtor to recover money, the defendants interposed counterclaims, but did not file claims. The court held that counterclaims by creditors constitute in effect objections constituting non-core claims as against Debtor's claims since the latter are property of the estate.

court presiding over a core case. *Ben Cooper,*[15] a toy and costume manufacturer, filed a chapter 11. Provisions in the reorganization plan required the Debtor to adequately insure its properties against damage by fire and other hazards. In fulfillment of its obligation, the Debtor retained its current insurance broker to obtain coverage for various facilities. Subsequent to confirmation of the plan, one of the facilities caught fire resulting in damages of approximately $2 million. After an investigation, the insurance company determined it was not liable for the claim because of misrepresentations in the policy's application and the Debtor's exaggerated claim. Consequently, the insurance company canceled its policy with the Debtor and instituted an action against the Debtor in state court claiming that the insurance policy was void due to the Debtor's misrepresentations.

Debtor's Injunction

The Debtor thereupon obtained a stay of the state court action and a preliminary injunction requiring the insurance company to maintain the insurance policy. The Debtor also commenced an adversary proceeding in the bankruptcy court requesting that: (1) the policy remain in effect; (2) the insurance company be held liable for all losses sustained in the fire; and (3) in the event the insurance company was not found liable for the loss, that the insurance broker be held liable due to its allegedly negligent conduct in obtaining the insurance.

Core or Non-Core Proceeding

The insurance company opposed the bankruptcy court's jurisdiction and moved the district court for withdrawal of reference. Further, the company moved to have the state court stay removed and the preliminary injunction lifted. The district court did not reach the merits of the case but remanded to have the bankruptcy court determine whether

---

[15] *In re* Ben Cooper, Inc., 896 F2d 1394 (2d Cir. 1990) judgment vacated and remanded, 111 S.Ct. 425. On remand the circuit court reinstated its prior decision, 924 F2d 36 (2d Cir. 1991), but the Supreme Court denied *certiorari,* 111 S.Ct. 2041 (1991).

the adversary proceeding was a "core" or "non-core" proceeding. The bankruptcy court determined that the proceeding was core and retained jurisdiction. In an oral ruling the district court reversed the bankruptcy court and held that the insurance companies were entitled to a jury trial by the bankruptcy court.

Abstention

The case was first heard by the Second Circuit on appeal from the district court's order withdrawing the reference of the bankruptcy court, abstaining from exercising jurisdiction and lifting the stay of proceedings in the state court without stating whether its abstention was permissive or mandatory. The issues before the circuit court were whether the adversary proceeding was a core proceeding, and secondly, whether the appellees were entitled to a jury trial.

Adversary Proceeding
Core

As to the first issue, the court determined that the adversary proceeding was a core proceeding. The court characterized the insurance agreement as a postpetition contract, thus distinguishing it from the prepetition contract considered by the Supreme Court in *Northern Pipeline Const. Co. v. Marathon Pipe Line Co.*[16] Furthermore, the court reasoned that: (1) postpetition contracts were integral to the administration of the estate; (2) the insured facility was an asset of the estate; (3) the reorganization plan itself required adequate insurance for the asset; (4) confirmation of the plan was premised on such adequate insurance; and (5) the insurance company was fully aware that it was dealing with a DIP. In totality, the property covered by the policy was an asset of the estate.

---

[16] 102 S.Ct. 2858 (1982). *See, supra* Chapter 7, this handbook, Jurisdiction of Bankruptcy Court subtitle "Northern Pipeline Decision."

Court of Appeals Approves Jury Trial by Bankruptcy Court

The court of appeals then turned its attention to the second issue, namely, whether the litigants were entitled to a jury trial. The court answered in the affirmative, reasoning that the claims on appeal were inherently legal. The court then decided the question ancillary to the jury issue, whether the bankruptcy court could conduct a jury trial in a core proceeding.

Recognizing that a paucity of specific statutory guidance existed, nevertheless, the court opined that if bankruptcy courts have the power to enter final judgments in core proceedings without violating Article III, then it follows that jury verdicts in bankruptcy courts do not violate Article III.

No Mandatory Abstention
Core or Non-Core

After the Second Circuit rendered its opinion, a petition for *certiorari* was filed in the Supreme Court. The Supreme Court vacated and remanded for a determination of the appellate court's jurisdiction and consequently Supreme Court jurisdiction. Essentially, if the Second Circuit determined that the instant case was a core proceeding, i.e., "arising in or under title 11," then mandatory abstention was unauthorized and no jurisdictional obstacle barred appellate court review. However, if it were determined that the proceeding was "non-core," but merely "related to" a case under title 11, then the prerequisite for mandatory abstention had been met and the district court's decision was not reviewable, "by appeal or otherwise," in the court of appeals and therefore review in the Supreme Court would be equally impermissible.

On remand, the Second Circuit determined the proceeding to be "core"; it could not be a candidate for mandatory abstention, and therefore abstention was permissible and reviewable by an appellate court. Even though the Second Circuit reinstated its prior decision, thus paving the way for the Supreme Court to determine whether bankruptcy courts may conduct jury trials for core proceedings, the Court denied *certiorari,*[17] leaving the *Ben Cooper* case as authority for the bankruptcy court to conduct a jury trial in a core case in the Second Circuit.

Contrasting Decisions: Jury Trial, Availability Bankruptcy Court

Time flies: three years after *Granfinanciera* and just one year after *Ben Cooper,* the Seventh Circuit, in the *Grabill*[18] case, had for consideration whether the bankruptcy court had jurisdiction to conduct a jury trial. The opening paragraph cannot be omitted:

> This appeal presents an issue the Supreme Court has twice saved for another day: [1] whether bankruptcy courts possess the statutory (and if so, the constitutional) authority to conduct jury trials in core proceedings.[19]

The defendant in the *Grabill* case, National Bank of North Carolina (NBNC), petitioned the district court to withdraw the reference to the bankruptcy court. "Although the claims involved are 'core' proceedings, . . . which normally fall within the bankruptcy court's jurisdiction, NBNC demanded a jury trial, to which the parties agree it is entitled under the Seventh Amendment, . . . [T]he parties dispute whether the bankruptcy court has the statutory and constitutional authority to conduct such a proceeding. . . ."[20]

The district court denied NBNC's petition and concluded that bankruptcy courts may conduct jury trials. "NBNC brought this interlocutory appeal. . . . The sole issue before us is whether the bankruptcy court has authority to conduct a jury trial in this core proceeding."[21] Assuming familiarity of

---

[17] *See, supra* note 14.

[18] *In re* Grabill ("Grabill"), 967 F2d 1152 (7th Cir. 1992).

[19] *Id.*

[20] *Id.*

[21] *Id.* at 1152–53 citing 28 USC §1292(b) and *In re* Jartran, Inc., 886 F2d 859, 865 (7th Cir. 1989) et al.

the history, legal arguments and law review articles on the subject, the court of appeals limited "discussion primarily to the rationales upon which we ground our decision."[22]

At the outset, we note that the circuits are divided three to one on the issue.[23] The Second Circuit (the first to address the issue) [Ben Cooper] held that bankruptcy courts may conduct jury trials. . . . The Sixth, Eighth and Tenth Circuits held otherwise. . . . There is no express statutory authority in the Bankruptcy Amendments And Federal Judgeship Act of 1984 ("BAFJA") granting bankruptcy courts the power to conduct jury trials; even the Second Circuit recognizes this. . . . The issue, then, is whether such power may be implied. Discerning any intent here is no easy task."[24] However, the BAFJA[25] sections indicated the right to a jury trial in personal injury and wrongful death cases as well as the bankruptcy court's discretion in involuntary bankruptcy. Nonetheless, the cases threw little light as to whether all other trials were excluded.

Continuing with other provisions of BAFJA giving bankruptcy judges the authority to "'hear and determine' all core proceedings, 28 USC §157(b)(1), likewise is readily susceptible to differing interpretations. . . ."[26] The court found that legislative history was not enlightening starting with the "Emergency Rules adopted in response to *Northern Pipe Line*. . . ."[27] In addition, the trustee argued "that if 'a judge is not empowered to conduct a jury trial unless Congress expressly says so . . . then even district courts could not conduct such trials. . . .' In our view, however, this overlaps a relevant distinction between the two: bankruptcy courts and other Article I tribunals are ordinary creatures of statute . . . and

---

[22] *Id.* at 1153.

[23] *Id.* citing cases of circuit courts: Baker & Getty Fin. Servs., Inc., 954 F2d 1169 (6th Cir. 1992); *In re* United Missouri Bank, N.A., 901 F2d 1449 (8th Cir. 1990); and *In re* Kaiser Steel Corp., 911 F2d 380 (10th Cir. 1990).

[24] *Id.*

[25] *See, supra* Chapter 7, this handbook, Jurisdiction of Bankruptcy Court subtitle "Importance—BAFJA."

[26] *Id.* at 1154. *See* Kaiser Steel Corp., 911 F2d at 391.

[27] *Id. See, supra* Chapter 7, this handbook, Jurisdiction of Bankruptcy Court subtitle "Interpreting Northern Pipeline."

derive their authority solely from Congress, while district courts are accorded their inherent powers in Article III. . . ."[28]

Congressional Action

The court also stated that it was significant that subsequent to Northern Pipeline Congress had twice declined to elevate the bankruptcy courts to Article III status. Non-Article III tribunals granted authority to conduct trials, have either been given explicit authority (magistrate judges) or "play particularly unique roles in the federal scheme. District of Columbia courts, for example,. . ."[29] The court's conclusion was influenced by the constitutional issue, i.e., "'avoid an interpretation of a federal statute that engenders constitutional issues if a reasonable alternative poses no constitutional question.'"[30]

In its final holding, the court of appeals stated that it was unpersuaded by pragmatic arguments, such as: (1) "policy of efficient judicial administration" (citing the responsive number of bankruptcy cases pending in the courts); (2) "strategic behavior by requesting a jury trial in the district court in order to delay proceedings" (response, same activity would be possible in bankruptcy court);[31] (3) "[a]s to systemic efficiency concerns . . . retaining jury trials with bankruptcy courts . . . could actually impede efficiency," (response, "[t]he rapid pace of bankruptcy cases and proceedings do not mesh with jury procedures").

In conclusion, the circuit court held:

> In our view, it would be venturesome to hold that bankruptcy courts are impliedly empowered by BAFJA to conduct jury trials in

---

[28] *Id.* at 1156 citing Northern Pipeline, 102 S.Ct. at 2858, 2868.

[29] *Id.* at 1157 citing: "*See* Vern Countryman, Scrambling to Define Bankruptcy Jurisdiction: The Chief Justice, the Judicial Conference, and the Legislative Process, 22 HARV. J. ON LEGIS. 1, 29–32 (1985)."

[30] *Id. See* United Missouri Bank, 901 F2d at 1456–57 (quoting Gomez v. United States, 109 S.Ct. 2237, 2241 (1989)).

[31] *Id.* at 1158 citing Baird, Jury Trials After Granfinanciera, 65 AM. BANKR. L.J. 1, 11 (1991).

core proceedings. Although our determination may be "a choice between uncertainties" . . .[32] given the factors militating against finding implied authority—significantly, the textual ambiguity and the sparse legislative history—we choose that which requires the lesser reach. Accordingly, for the reasons expressed above, as well as those delineated by the Sixth, Eighth, and Tenth Circuits, we hold that the Bankruptcy Code, as amended by the 1984 Act, does not authorize bankruptcy judges to conduct jury trials. Where a jury trial is required by the Seventh Amendment, that trial must be held in the district court, sitting in its original jurisdiction in bankruptcy.[33]

Dissenting Opinion

The circuit court reversed the district court's order and remanded with directions to withdraw the reference and to conduct a jury trial with respect to those issues for which a timely demand for jury trial was made. In a dissenting opinion Judge Posner observed: "The intricate interpretive maneuvers that lawyers use to answer questions of statutory meaning lead nowhere in this case, . . . On the one hand the statute [§157(b)(1)] says that 'bankruptcy judges [not juries] may hear and determine. . . all core proceedings', but on the other hand this can be read as 'bankruptcy judges may hear and determine . . . all core proceedings [whether they are jury or nonjury cases].' It is all a matter of emphasis. . . . The majority opinion, with refreshing candor, reports the parries as well as the thrusts, but insists that the statute has a meaning and that the court has found it."[34]

Practical Considerations

Judge Posner opined that since the diverse opinions in the circuit courts find no assistance in statutory text, legislative

---

[32] *Id.* citing Cheng Fan Kwok v. Ins., 88 S.Ct. 1970, 1975–76 (1968).

[33] *Id.*

[34] *Id.* at 1159.

history, precedent or other sources of guidance to statutory meaning, "[W]e ought in these circumstances to base our decision on practical considerations, and they all line up on the side of allowing bankruptcy judges to conduct jury trials. The main advantage is that it avoids shifting a case, or rather part of a case, from one tribunal and one judge—the bankruptcy court and bankruptcy judge—to another—the district court and the district judge."[35]

Referring to the bankruptcy judges' stature and abilities as judges, Judge Posner commented: "Very few state trial judges have life tenure either, yet the vast majority of jury cases in this country are tried in state courts and we do not hear howls of protest."[36] Again turning to rules of evidence: "Since the same rules of evidence apply in bench and in jury trials, the biggest differences between the two sorts of trials from the judges standpoint are jury voir dire and jury instructions. Any competent judicial officer can voir dire or instruct a jury. . . . Many district judges now use magistrate judges routinely to voir dire the jury. . . ."[37]

"We should be realistic. The question whether to allow bankruptcy judges to conduct jury trials has not been answered for us by Congress. It has been left to us. We should decide it . . . without concern that Article I judicial officers may appear to be encroaching on the turf usurping the prerogatives . . . of Article III judges. We should answer the question 'yes.'"[38]

Filing Claim
Effect of Bar Date

A difficult situation arises when a party withholds the filing of a proof of claim and is subsequently confronted with notice of a bar order setting the date for filing before the party

---

[35] *Id.*

[36] *Id.* at 1160.

[37] *Id. See* BLACK'S LAW DICTIONARY (1990) at p. 1575: "Voir dire (L. Fr. To speak the truth). This phrase denotes the preliminary examination which the court and attorneys make of prospective jurors to determine their qualification and suitability to serve as jurors. . . ."

[38] *Id.* at 1161.

can make its decision to file a jury demand. This scenario was illustrated in *Hooker Investments*,[39] where a chapter 11 Debtor filed various adversary proceedings. Among these proceedings were avoidance of fraudulent transfers and recovery of real estate property against two banks, its largest creditors, who requested a jury trial in the adversary proceedings.

Subsequent to the request, the Debtor moved the bankruptcy court to issue a bar date. The banks objected, arguing that if they complied with the bar date prior to the resolution of the adversary proceedings they might very well be denied their rights to a jury trial. The bankruptcy court, nonetheless, issued the bar date rejecting the bank's contention by characterizing the choice as a matter of litigation strategy faced by every secured creditor in a bankruptcy case. The bankruptcy court's determination is particularly relevant because a bar date is not considered a final order and consequently, the banks cannot appeal to the district court subsequent to the bar date.

Observation

Granfinanciera provided for a jury trial of any cause of action for the recovery of a sum of money in a core action under §157. The decision, however, left open whether a jury trial could be held before the bankruptcy judge: "We do not decide today. . . ."[40]

Ben Cooper went a step further and decided that a non-core proceeding involving a DIP's transaction with a creditor was a core proceeding and the creditor was entitled to a jury trial by the bankruptcy court as the claim constituted a core proceeding. *Certiorari* was granted. The case was remanded and then upon remand, the court of appeals adhered to its opinion granting jury trials in core actions and the Supreme Court denied *certiorari*. The Second Circuit at this time remains the only circuit granting jury trials.

Hooker held that a bar date set by the bankruptcy court for filing a proof of claim was obligatory upon all claimants who

---

[39] *In re* Hooker Investments, Inc. ("Hooker Investments"), 122 BR 659 (SDNY 1991).

[40] *See, supra* note 8.

contested the amount due from the Debtor. Those claimants who had to comply by filing a claim before the bar date and failed to comply, would not participate as creditors in the estate. Filing, of course, meant submitting to the jurisdiction of the court and failing to obtain a jury trial.

Moran's district court affirmed findings of fact and conclusions of law submitted by the bankruptcy court, which held that collection of debt cannot be held to be a core proceeding in every case where the Debtor's right to the unpaid funds is disputed until the Debtor prevails at the trial. In addition, counterclaims by the defendants in an adversary proceeding by the Debtor, where no proof of claim was filed, do not create a core proceeding. Further, the summons and complaint in any adversary proceeding can be served anywhere in the United States.[41]

Grabill raised the count of the number of circuit courts holding that the bankruptcy court could not conduct a jury trial in a core case. We agree, however, with Judge Posner's opinion and conclusion and therefore, call attention to the court's mathematics: adding *Grabill* to the number of dissents, we should include Judge Posner's affirmative vote in the count. Should the tally then be corrected from 4–1 to 3½–1½?

In Chapter 10 of this handbook, we turn to discuss committees whose functions play an important role, not only in guiding and overlooking the Debtor's operations, but in developing the reorganization plan.

---

[41] *See* B.Rule 7004. Process; Service of Summons, Complaint.

Chapter 10
Committees of Creditors and Equity Security Holders

The reader will recall that in the *Southland* case, a prepackaged bankruptcy,[1] the Committee of Bondholders, assisted by its attorneys, accountants and investment bankers, were the principal participants in developing a plan of reorganization. Furthermore, after the petition was filed, the same Unofficial Committee was appointed by the U.S. trustee as the Official Committee retaining the same professionals in the chapter 11 case. The number of creditors, as well as equity security holders[2] and the variety of their interests or class affiliation, determine the necessity of requiring one or more committees.

---

[1] *See, supra* Chapter 1, this handbook, Prepackaged Bankruptcy.

[2] *See* 11 USC §101(16): "'equity security' means—(A) share in a corporation whether or not transferable or denominated 'stock' or similar security; (B) interest of a limited partner in a limited partnership; (C) warrant or right. . . ." *See also* §101(17) regarding equity security holder.

It is not surprising therefore, that §1102(a)(1) provides an early start for the DIP presenting the section with "Creditors' and equity security holders' committees," and commencing with the sentence: "As soon as practicable after the order for relief under chapter 11 of this title, the United States trustee shall appoint a committee of creditors holding unsecured claims and may appoint additional committees of creditors or equity security holders as the United States trustee deems appropriate."[3] The U.S. trustee has only to examine the Debtor's schedules filed with its bankruptcy petition to find a list of the twenty[4] largest unsecured creditors with names and addresses of each. This list must be filed by the Debtor with the voluntary petition as well as with a list of all the Debtor's other creditors. These lists give the U.S. trustee an opportunity to operate speedily; and depending on the size or nature of the case, the U.S. trustee may decide as to the number and classification of the committee.

Supplementing this section is subsection 1102(a)(2) allowing the court to appoint additional committees, at the request of a party in interest, if necessary to assure adequate representation of the creditors or equity security holders. Even though the court orders the appointment, it is the U.S. trustee that is required to select such committee.[5]

The selection of members of the Committee "shall ordinarily consist of the persons, willing to serve, that hold the seven largest claims[6] against the Debtor, of the kinds represented on such committee, or of the members of a committee organized by creditors before the commencement of

---

[3] 11 USC §1102(a)(1).

[4] *See* B.Rule 1007(d): "In addition to the list required by subdivision (a) of this rule . . . a Debtor in a . . . voluntary chapter 11 reorganization case shall file with the petition a list containing the name, address and claim of the creditors that hold the 20 largest unsecured claims, excluding insiders, as prescribed by the appropriate Official Form [#4]."

[5] *See* 11 USC §1107(a)(2): "In an involuntary case, the Debtor shall file within 15 days after the entry of the order for relief, a list containing the name and address of each creditor unless a schedule of liabilities has been filed."

[6] *See* §1102(b)(1). *See also, In re* Salant Corporation, 53 BR 158 (B. SDNY 1987) *infra* note 21 where the Committee of Unsecured Creditors consisted of 27 members.

the case under this chapter,[7] if such committee was fairly chosen and is representative of the different kinds of claims to be represented."[8] The same requirement of "willing to serve" is provided for a committee of equity security holders appointed pursuant to subsection (a)(2), but they are required to consist of holders of the seven largest dollar amounts of equity securities of the Debtor of the kinds represented on this committee. The phrase "fairly chosen" is generally applicable to prepackaged chapter 11 since these committees are formed without approval of the U.S. trustee until their members seek appointment after filing of the petition. Then the U.S. trustee has the duty of determining whether they were fairly chosen.[9]

Prepackaged Committee

As we mentioned previously, the *Southland* case involved a prepackaged chapter 11, in which a committee of creditors was elected. Rule 2007 applies to a motion seeking to review such appointment by the United States trustee after the chapter 11 has been filed to determine whether the appointment of the committee satisfies the requirements of § 1102(b)(1).[10] "The court may find that a committee organized by unsecured creditors before the commencement of a . . . chapter 11 case was fairly chosen if: (1) it was selected by a majority in number and amount of claims of unsecured creditors . . . [who] were present in person or represented at a meeting . . . and written minutes were kept and are available for inspection; (2) all proxies [that] voted . . . have been submitted to the United States trustee; and (3) the organization of the committee was in all other respects fair and proper."[11] Subsection (c) authorizes the court to direct the U.S. trustee to vacate the appointment of the Committee and take such other appropriate action if the court finds that the

---

[7] *See, supra, e.g.,* Chapter 1, this handbook, Prepackaged Chapter 11.

[8] *See* 11 USC §1102(b)(1).

[9] *See* B.Rule 2007. "Review of Appointment of Creditors' Committee Organized Before Commencement of Case."

[10] *See* B.Rule 2007(a). Motion To Review Appointment.

[11] *See* B.Rule 2007(b)(1),(2), and (3) (Selection of Members of Committee).

appointment failed to satisfy the requirements of section 1102(b)(1).[12]

The Advisory Committee's Note to Rule 2007 as amended on August 1, 1991 is helpful. The Note specifically refers to Section 1102(b)(1), explaining that the subsection permits the court "to appoint as the unsecured creditors' committee, the committee that was selected by creditors before the order for relief. This provision recognizes the propriety of continuing a 'prepetition' committee in an official capacity. Such a committee, however, must be found to have been fairly chosen and representative of the different kinds of claims to be represented." The Advisory Committee Note—1991 Amendment states: "A finding that a prepetition committee has not been fairly chosen does not prohibit the appointment of some or all of its members to the creditors' committee. . . . [This] rule. . . does not preclude judicial review under Rule 2020 regarding the appointment of other committees."[13]

Seeking Additional Committee Members

The *McLean Industries*[14] case involved four jointly administered cases concerning related corporate Debtors. While the cases were procedurally consolidated for ease of administration, the cases were not substantively consolidated.[15] Since there was no substantive consolidation, the assets of the individual corporate Debtors remained separate and distinct. On December 11, 1986, the U.S. trustee appointed a single committee, consisting of unsecured and secured creditors, trade debt and debenture holders. During

---

[12] *See* B.Rule 2007(c), Failure To Comply With Requirements for Appointment.

[13] *See* B.Rule 2007. *See also* Advisory Committee Note–1991 Amendment to B.Rule 2007.

[14] 70 BR 832 (B. SDNY 1987).

[15] *See* B.Rule 1015, Consolidation Or Joint Administration Of Cases Pending In The Same Court. *See also* Advisory Committee Note: "Consolidation, as distinguished from joint administration, is neither authorized nor prohibited by this rule since the propriety of consolidation depends on substantive considerations and affects the substantive rights of creditors of the different estates. . . ." *See also, infra* Chapter 14, this handbook, Trustee's Strong Arm Powers Marshaling of Assets.

the course of the case, a group of debenture holders requested the appointment of an additional creditors' committee to represent their separate interests.

Debenture Holder's Position

Several arguments were presented in support of their motion. First, it was noted that the debentures constituted virtually all of McLean's debt. Second, relying predominantly on the statutory requirement for adequate representation of creditors' interests,[16] the debenture holders asserted that as a matter of law, adequate representation of their particular interests could only be satisfied by the "appointment of a committee to represent public debt where jointly administered cases include a parent whose significant assets consist only of the stock of its subsidiaries and whose liabilities consist principally or almost exclusively of widespread publicly held debt."[17]

Generally, the debenture holders identified the joint administration of the related corporate entities as a major structural impediment to the adequate representation of all interests by a single creditors' committee. Specifically, they alleged a conflict between themselves and other members of the creditors' committee who were creditors of the subsidiaries. The conflict primarily arose "from the notion that payment to [the debenture holders], absent substantive consolidation, depends on satisfying creditors of those Debtor subsidiaries having the real assets of the enterprise."[18]

Even though the court ultimately determined that an evidentiary hearing would be necessary to flesh out the concerns raised by the debenture holders, the court did not wholly embrace the movants' arguments related to the alleged existence of a conflict among creditors. The court recognized that conflicts among creditors were not unusual in reorganization proceedings:

---

[16] *See* 11 USC §§1102(a)(2), (b)(1).

[17] *See also* 70 BR at 855.

[18] *Id.*

> [T]he presence of potential conflict may not always require separate committees for representation to be adequate. . . . [C]reditors' committees often contain creditors having a variety of viewpoints. Debentures, for example, are often subordinate to senior institutional indebtedness but not to trade debt. Maximization of return to debenture holders may lead to different views from those of senior indebtedness. In the usual case, [conflicts] might not require a separate committee unless they impair the ability of the unsecured creditors' committee to reach a consensus.[19]

Notwithstanding the court's reluctance towards accepting the movants' conflict argument, it did explicitly note that the appointment of a single creditors' committee in a jointly administered case raised concerns involving adequate representation and that "[t]hese matters generally should be fleshed out in an evidentiary hearing."[20]

Union Seeks Another Committee

Even though the court required an evidentiary hearing in the McLean case, to determine whether another committee should be appointed, the court in the *Salant* case,[21] in an almost identical situation, resolved the request for another committee without a hearing. "The three Chapter 11 Cases have been procedurally, but not substantively consolidated." The U.S. trustee had appointed a single Committee of 27 creditors consisting of members of each of the three Debtors.

Amalgamated Clothing and Textile Workers Union (ACTWU), AFL-CIO sought to have the court appoint an Official Employees Creditors' Committee consisting of the representatives of nonmanagement employee wage and benefit claims, including health, welfare and pension plans. ACTWU argued that the interests of nonmanagement employees were

---

[19] 70 BR at 852 (citations omitted).

[20] *Id.* at 862.

[21] *In re* Salant Corporation, 53 BR 158 (B. SDNY 1985).

too diverse from the interests of general trade and institutional creditors to be adequately represented by a single creditors' committee.

In opposition to the request, the Debtors argued that the creation of another creditors' committee would result in substantial and unnecessary administrative expenses. Further, the creditors' committee argued that the scope of the employees' claims were limited to certain pension payments and therefore, the appointment of an additional committee was simply not warranted. The bankruptcy court agreed:

> Under the circumstances of this case, a separate employees' committee is not warranted. The employees' claims are not large enough to justify a separate committee. Nor is the interest in continued employment one which gives rise to a creditor claim sufficient in itself to justify appointment of an employees' committee.[22]

Although the court denied the appointment of an additional creditors' committee, the court did appoint three additional members as it was of the view that the present committee was not representative of the claims of nonmanagement employees since it had "no member having a claim of that kind."[23]

Johns-Manville
Necessity Delays Stockholders Meeting

When more than one creditors' committee is appointed, the road to plan confirmation is not always a smooth one. The Johns-Manville[24] bankruptcy is a case in point. Several committees were appointed in an attempt to facilitate the orderly administration of the Debtor but the Equity Committee emerged ultimately delaying the formulation of a plan. The friction arose when Manville and several of its

---

[22] 53 BR at 161.

[23] *Id.*

[24] *In re* Johns-Manville Corp. ("Manville"), 801 F2d 60 (2d Cir. 1986).

committees finally came to terms in "formulating a plan that would earmark billions of dollars for payment to present and future asbestosis victims as well as to others damaged by the asbestos products that Manville once manufactured and sold."[25]

"[O]n the eve of their submission of the plan to the bankruptcy court for confirmation," the equity committee brought an action in Delaware state court seeking to compel Manville to hold a shareholders' meeting.[26] The equity committee pursued this course of conduct because it objected to the proposed plan that had been approved by the board of directors and by all the other committees. Manville, however, had sought an injunction "prohibiting the Equity Committee from pursuing the Delaware action arguing that the holding of a shareholders' meeting would obstruct Manville's reorganization."[27] The bankruptcy court granted the injunction and further granted Manville summary judgment *sua sponte*. The district court affirmed. The court of appeals reversed the summary judgment award to Manville and remanded for a more elaborate inquiry at an evidentiary hearing to ascertain whether there was clear abuse and irreparable harm. Notwithstanding such approval of the plan by the board of directors and all the committees, the majority of the court of appeals held:

> The Debtor is given the power to propose a plan of reorganization. No reason is advanced why stockholders, if they feel that the present board of directors is not acting in their interest, or has caused an unsatisfactory plan to be filed on behalf of the Debtor, should not cause a new board to be elected which will act in conformance with the stockholders' wishes.[28]

Circuit Court Judge Oakes dissented, and, in addition to emphasizing the danger involved in the rehabilitation of the

---

[25] 801 F2d at 62.

[26] *Id.*

[27] *Id.* at 63.

[28] *Id.* at 65.

Debtor in calling a meeting of stockholders after more than three years of negotiations conducted by the parties in chapter 11, the judge cited the holding in the *Potter* case:[29]

> [T]he court has a duty to refuse to order a shareholder's meeting upon a showing of clear abuse which would probably jeopardize both [the Debtor's rehabilitation] and the rights of creditors and stockholders. . . .

Upon an evidentiary hearing on remand before the bankruptcy court, the bankruptcy judge again enjoined the stockholders' committee, and no further appeal was taken. The plan of reorganization was ultimately confirmed.

Unofficial Committee

Right To Be Heard

Committees that we have just discussed are often referred to as Official Committees when elected in chapter 7 by a vote of the creditors, or when appointed by the U.S. trustee. Unofficial Committees are those generally referred to as having no official standing in court, and of course, have neither the duties nor the powers set forth in the Bankruptcy Code. No official terminology, however, restricts an informal committee often bearing the terminology of "ad hoc" committee, as well as any person who has an interest in a chapter 11 case, or an adversary proceeding from participating in either a case or proceeding. Such right is contained in §1109 of the Code designated by the section as the "Right to be heard."

Section 1109(a) provides that the Securities and Exchange Commission[30] "may raise and may appear and be heard on any issue in a case under this chapter, but . . . may not appeal from any judgment, order, or decree entered in the case." Section 1109(b) is wide in scope: "A party in interest, including the

---

[29] *Id.* at 70. *See In re* Potter Instrument Co., 598 F2d 470, 475 (2d Cir. 1979).

[30] *See, supra* Chapter 1, this handbook, Prepackaged Chapter 11 subtitle "SEC Compliance."

Debtor, a creditors' committee, an equity security holders committee, a creditor, an equity security holder, or any indenture trustee, may raise and may appear and be heard on any issue in a case under this chapter."

Flexibility

The flexibility of the statute with reference to the number or kinds of committees is indicated by the discretion of the bankruptcy judge to extend the number of members of the committees beyond the "seven largest number of claims" mentioned in §1102(b)(1) depending on the kinds of claims represented on the committee. In addition, claims of the same kind may have one committee even though they consist of several jointly administered corporations in comparison to a corporation that has been substantively consolidated.[31] The number of committees to be appointed and size of membership depend on the need to protect the interests of creditors and equity security holders, but should, at the same time, recognize, Debtor requirements to deal with them.

Powers and Duties of Committees

Since Committees represent all types of creditors, unsecured, security interests, and bondholders, all of whom have a vital interest in the estate, one can easily understand the broad powers with which the Bankruptcy Code provides them under "§1103. Powers and duties of committees." At a scheduled meeting of a committee appointed under §1102 . . . with the court's approval . . . such committee may select and authorize the employment by such committee of one or more attorneys, accountants, or other agents, to represent or perform services for such committee."[32] It is not unusual that

---

[31] *See* B.Rule 1015, Consolidation Or Joint Administration Of Cases Pending In Same Court. *See, infra* Chapter 13, this handbook, Assumption or Rejection of Executory Contracts and Unexpired Leases of Real Property.

[32] *See* §1103(a). *See also* §1103(b): "An attorney or accountant employed by such committee represents a committee appointed under §1102, may not represent any other entity having an adverse interest in the case. Representation of one or more creditors of the same class as represented by

such "agents" include investment bankers, or experts in reorganization matters, known as "turnaround" experts.[33]

With such assistance at hand, a committee is given broad powers. A committee may: (1) consult with the trustee or DIP concerning the administration of the case;[34] (2) investigate the acts, conduct, assets, liabilities and financial condition of the Debtor, the operation and desirability of its business and of its continuance, and any other matter relevant to the case or the formulation of a plan; (3) participate in the formulation of a plan and advise those represented of the committee's determinations as to any plan formulated, and collect and file with the court acceptances or rejections of a plan; (4) request the appointment of a trustee or examiner under §1104; and (5) "perform such other services as are in the interest of those represented."[35]

Crowthers
Debtor's Limitation of Authority

In some situations the performance of services in the interest of those represented may include the initiation of an adversary proceeding by an unsecured creditors' committee. In *Crowthers McCall Pattern*[36] the Debtor and the committee began an investigation of some prepetition transactions. Upon

---

the committee shall not per se constitute the representation of an adverse interest." (*See* BLACK'S LAW DICTIONARY (1990) at p. 1142: "Per se (Lat.) By itself; in itself; taken along . . . in its own nature without reference to its relation. . . .")

[33] *See also, infra* Chapter 11, this handbook, subtitle "Appointment Turnaround Manager." *See* B.Rule 2014. Employment of Professional Persons: (a) Application for an Order of Employment; and (b) Services Rendered by Members or Associates of Firm of Attorneys or Accountants. *See also* §327, Employment of professional persons; §328, Limitation on compensation of professional persons; §329, Debtor's transactions with attorney; §330, Compensation of officers; and §331, Interim compensation. *See also* Chapter 5, this handbook, subtitle "Necessity of Experienced Counsel."

[34] *See* §1103(c)(1)–(5).

[35] *See* §1103(c)(5).

[36] Crowthers McCall Pattern, Inc. v. Lewis ("Debtor"), 114 BR 407 (SDNY 1990).

Debtor's counsel perceiving a possible conflict of interest, Debtor and the committee stipulated that discovery proceedings and possible actions be conducted in Debtor's name by the committee. The stipulation was approved by the bankruptcy judge.

It is not unusual for the committee to institute such actions with the consent of the court, and upon notice, where such conflicts exist. In the *Noyes'* case,[37] a creditors' committee initiated an adversary proceeding in the name of the Debtor "only when the Debtor 'unjustifiably failed to bring suit or abused its discretion in not suing to avoid a preferential transfer.'"

Even though the district court was uncertain whether the Noyes standard would be implicated where the Debtor authorized the committee's actions, it still remanded for a determination since "compliance with the Noyes procedure will eliminate the possibility that the case may be fully tried and the outcome found to have been invalid for failure to comply with the rule."[38]

Observation

The comment of the district court is relevant: "As a *sine qua non* to approving commencement of an action by a creditor's committee, [the Noyes Court] held that the bankruptcy court was obligated to determine: (1) whether the creditor's committee presented a colorable claim for relief . . . and (2) whether an action asserting such claim(s) would be likely to benefit the estate. . . ."

The following chapter leads on to officers of the court, including the U.S. trustee, some of whose functions we have already discussed.

---

[37] 114 BR at 408 (quoting Unsecured Creditors Committee of Debtor STN Enters. v. Noyes, 779 F2d 901, 904 (2d Cir. 1985)).
[38] *Id.* at 409.

Chapter 11
Trustees, Examiners, and Officers of the Court

It is important to note the significant role the U.S. trustee plays in the administration of bankruptcy proceedings.

Twenty-one regions of the United States were created and each region is served by a U.S. trustee[1] who is appointed by the Attorney General. In addition, the U.S. trustee is aided by such number of assistants as the district may require. If the court orders the appointment of a trustee or examiner, and the officer dies or resigns or fails to qualify "then the U.S. trustee, after consultation, with parties in interest, shall appoint, . . . one disinterested party . . . to serve as examiner or trustee."[2]

---

[1] 28 U.S.C. §581. Alabama and Georgia have until year 2002 to opt into the system and presently a bankruptcy administrator performs many of the functions of a U.S. trustee.

[2] See §1104(c).

Requirements Of Operating Guidelines by DIP

28 U.S.C. §586 contains a list of the duties to be performed by the U.S. trustee and the supervision to be exercised by the Attorney General. As for the U.S. trustee, not only is there a requirement to "establish, maintain and supervise a panel of private trustees . . ." in cases under chapters 7, 11, and 13, but to "monitor applications for allowance and reimbursement filed under section 330 of title 11. . . ." Many other duties, to name a few, are required, including monitoring plans and disclosure statements under chapters 11, 12, and 13, and monitoring creditors' committees appointed under chapter 11.

In compliance with the foregoing duties, in 1992 the U.S. trustee[3] for judicial district (2)[4] issued practical business data, "Operating Guidelines and Financial Reporting Requirements Required in all Cases under Chapter 11, . . .," for trustees and debtors in possession.[5] An Introduction provides that Debtors in bankruptcy cases and operating trustees have a "fiduciary obligation and a legal duty to account for their operations of a business." This duty is met substantially by: (1) the use of new bank accounts, (2) obtaining and maintaining insurance, and (3) filing monthly and annual reports. "The failure to comply with these duties is a general indication that the Debtor is not operating properly and should either be liquidated or denied the protection of the Bankruptcy Code."

Notwithstanding this warning,[6] sound and orderly operation of a business requires such compliance. For example, this U.S. trustee's Guidelines indicate specific procedures that are helpful in the operation of a business: (1) opening a DIP bank account, and separate tax accounts, making remittances within a week; (2) insurance coverage, including fire, theft, business interruption, workmen's compensation, etc.; (3) monthly financial statements, which include balance sheets prepared in accordance with generally accepted accounting principles ("GAAP"); (4) disclosure requirements; (5) annual

---

[3] U.S. trustee Harold D. Jones.

[4] *See also* §581(a)(2), one of the 21 districts of the United States and its statutory affiliations.

[5] Issued by former U.S. trustee Harold D. Jones.

[6] *See* 28 U.S.C. §581(a) listing 21 Federal judicial districts.

financial statements; (6) waiver or modification of reporting requirements; and (7) conclusion, which contains an "illustrative financial statement."[7]

U.S. Trustee's Powers

The U.S. trustee is required to supervise the administration of cases by DIP and all trustees appointed in bankruptcy cases. In those instances where additional services are needed, the U.S. trustee is authorized to hire others to assist in the performance of the duties as trustee. Trustees who are appointed by the court serve in a case or elected in a chapter 7 case are likewise supervised by the U.S. trustee.

The duties, rights, and powers of the trustee are reviewed and subject to appeal to the bankruptcy judge. Some of the principal powers accorded the U.S. trustee in reorganization cases, in addition to those discussed, are: (1) the power to raise and appear on any issue in any case or proceeding under the Code; (2) to appoint trustees and examiners;[8] (3) to convene and preside at any meeting of creditors; and (4) may convene a meeting of equity security holders.[9]

> These broad duties and powers of the U.S. trustee are subject to review by the bankruptcy court: "A proceeding to contest any act or failure to act by the United States trustee is governed by Rule 9014."[10]

---

[7] *See* B.Rule 2015 (Duty to Keep Records, Make Reports, and Give Notice of Case).

[8] *See* §§303(g) and 1104(c).

[9] *See* §341.

[10] *See* B.Rule 9014. Contested Matters: "In a contested matter in a case under the Code, not otherwise governed by these rules, relief shall be granted by motion. . . ." *See also In re* Revco D.S., Inc., 898 F2d 498 (6th Cir. 1990) (U.S. trustee has standing under 11 USC §307 to appeal decision of bankruptcy court refusing to appoint examiner).

U.S. Trustee Calls Meeting of Creditors

Speaking of the U.S. trustee, we cannot let some of the activities of Harold D. Jones,[11] a former U.S. Trustee who (with his assistants) was chief administrator of all bankruptcy cases in New York, Connecticut and Vermont, elude our discussion. The *New York Times* reported a little of his activities dealing with committee meetings:[12]

> On a recent Monday, Mr. Jones, . . . brought creditors of the Daily News together at the Vista Hotel in Manhattan to select a committee that would monitor the newspaper's recovery efforts.
>
> Four days later he led another meeting at the hotel, this time for the creditors of the Orion Pictures Corporation. The group was a mixture of advertising and insurance representatives, as well as the lawyer for [actors].
>
> Orion's creditors, at their recent meeting did not seem pleased to learn there would be one 19 person committee. Why, they buzzed, had the bondholders won only one-fifth of the seats, when they were owed more than any other group?

Appointment of Examiner

Trustee Jones of the Second District is to be credited for providing operating guidelines and financial reporting requirements under all cases under chapter 11. The appointment of an examiner is dependent upon whether the court appoints a trustee under §1104(a). Section 1104(b) then provides ". . . the court (a) shall appoint an examiner to conduct such an investigation of the debtor as is appropriate . . . if—(1) such appointment is in the interests of creditors,

---

[11] *See* N.Y. TIMES, January 2, 1992 at LDI.

[12] *See supra* Chapter 10, this handbook, subtitle "U.S. Trustee."

any equity security holders and other interests of the estate; or (2) the debtors fixed, liquidated, unsecured debts, other than debts for goods, services or taxes, or owing to an insider, exceed $5,000,000."

Limited Duties of Examiner

As we stated, the U.S. trustee appoints the examiner on order of the court. The Code specifies that the examiner's duties shall include, *inter alia*, two of the trustee's duties, i.e., (1) investigating the acts, conduct and financial condition of the Debtor and (2) the operation of the Debtor's business, as well as "any other duties of the trustee that the court orders the debtor in possession not to perform."[13] These are precisely the functions to be performed by a committee. This latter duty, although not akin in verbiage is similar to the duty of the creditors'committee to "perform such other services as are in the interest of those represented."

Notwithstanding these limited powers, the court has discretionary power to appoint a trustee. In the *Table Talk* case[14] the U.S. trustee moved for the appointment of an examiner. He alleged, *inter alia*, that there were continuing operating losses by the DIP, that no plan had been presented by the Debtor for consideration, and that there was a need for an investigation of the acts, conduct, and financial condition of the Debtor, as well as the operation of the Debtor's business. After taking testimony, the court observed: "There is no question that the trustee has sufficiently supported his allegations that the Debtor has consistently not met its projections. But that still leaves me with the question of what protection an examiner would provide."

Answering his rhetorical question, the bankruptcy judge replied that what the trustee and the creditors wanted the examiner to do was "to make an impartial assessment as to the Debtor's ability to effect a turn-around." To accomplish this objective, the judge indicated that the creditors'committee had asked for the appointment of Price Waterhouse & Co. so that the committee "would not have to rely exclusively on the

---

[13] §1106(b) incorporating §1106(a) subsections (3) and (4).

[14] *In re* Table Talk, Inc., 22 BR 706 (B. Mass. 1982).

Debtor's numbers." Furthermore, he added: "It is not clear to me precisely what it is that the creditors'committee wants an examiner to ascertain that Price is not capable of doing."[15] The court concluded that although there was evidence that prior management showed poor judgment, there was no evidence of lack of integrity or ability and accordingly denied the application.

Examiner's Function Duplicated

The duplication of work in the *Table Talk* case with the additional expense and cost is obvious. With two national accounting firms to perform the necessary accounting services, the examiner would have to retain a third for assistance as well as attorneys for representation unless the examiner was a member of either profession. However, the Code does not authorize the examiner to retain any professional and this leaves the examiner without the aid required to perform adequately.

This handicap, however, has not deterred several bankruptcy courts in appointing examiners with rights and powers unauthorized by the Code. In the *Harmon* case[16] the order appointing the examiner furnished him with "the sole right, power, and duty to operate the business of the estate" and added that he "shall have all other powers granted to a trustee or examiner under the Bankruptcy Code."

Examiner's Extended Powers

In the *White Motor* case,[17] the court stated that it "had no choice but to appoint an examiner as requested" by several nonunion salaried employees and indicated it would expand the examiner's duties if the Debtor failed to file a plan within a specified period. The dichotomy existing between examiner and trustee was further blurred in the *Curlew Valley*

---

[15] Additionally, Main Hurdman & Cranston represented the Debtor and two secured creditors had their own accountants.

[16] Bankruptcy Case No. Bk 2-79-133 (B. ND Tex. 1979).

[17] Bankruptcy Case No. B-280-3360 (B. ND Ohio 1980).

Associates case[18] where a special examiner was appointed with authority to employ accountants, attorneys, and/or other agents or representatives to assist in the performance of his duties "just as if he were a trustee."

The chameleon cloak of the examiner was further expanded to include the office of "Responsible Officer" in the *FSC* case.[19] Since the Debtor had no board of directors, the court appointed an individual in such capacity as the person required to perform the duties of the DIP. Subsequently, when he was authorized to vote the shares of the Debtor's wholly-owned subsidiaries to elect a board of directors, the equity security holder's committee objected. In overruling the objection, the court found authority in the Delaware Corporation Law, as well as in §1107(a) of the Bankruptcy Code granting the DIP all the rights of a trustee in bankruptcy and, finally, in §105 of the Code,[20] which empowered the court to issue any order necessary to carry out the provisions of the Code.

Without delving into the soundness of the court's decision, of which there is much to be said, the designation of a person as a "Responsible Officer" that gives him the duties of a DIP creates another instance of confusion in the designation of officers who are not specified in chapter 11. Moreover, the Delaware statute provides for a receiver or custodian, but since no such officer is authorized under the Code the logical procedure would have been to direct the equity security holders'committee to arrange for the calling of a stockholders'meeting to elect a new board, which would have appointed qualified responsible officers.

In the recent *Shelter* case,[21] the issue of the mandatory or discretionary appointment of an examiner under §104(b)(2) was squarely joined. In denying the joint application of the Securities and Exchange Commission and an indenture

---

[18] Bankruptcy Case No. 80-00876 (B. Utah 1980).

[19] *In re* FSC Corporation, 11 BCD 886 (B. WD Penn. 1983).

[20] *See, infra* Chapter 14, this handbook, Trustee's Strong Arm Powers Marshalling of Assets.

[21] *See* Decision NKFW Partners v. Saxon Industries, Inc., Civil Action No. 7468, Court of Chancery, Del. 1984 where Equity Committee of chapter 11 Debtor sued to compel holding of shareholders' meeting.

trustee, the court observed that the appointment would result in incurring unnecessary costs and expenses, that there was a Debenture Holders Committee with powers under §1103(c) that could do the work: "[T]o slavishly and blindly follow the dictates of Section 1104(b)(2) is needless, costly and non-productive. . . ." The court found that the appointment of the examiner "would serve no useful or beneficial purpose."

Use of Name Trustee

As we indicated in the subtitle of the U.S. Trustee's Powers,[22] the nomenclature "trustee" is used as a general term in the Code, including a use for a DIP. A fine distinction is drawn between the duties of a trustee and a DIP.[23] The trustee's duties include an investigation of "the acts, conduct, assets, liabilities and the financial condition of the Debtor, [as well as the] operation of the Debtor's business and the desirability of the continuance of such business, and any other matter relevant to the case or the formulation of a plan. . . ."[24]

Debtor in Possession
Rights and Powers

Section 1107 dealing with the "Rights, powers and duties of debtor in possession," clearly articulates that a DIP shall have all the rights of a trustee subject to such rights or limitations that the court may prescribe and "shall perform all the functions and duties, except the duties specified in section 1106(a)(2), (3) and (4) of this title, of a trustee serving in a case under this chapter."[25]

---

[22] *See, supra* subtitle "U.S. Trustee's Powers."

[23] *See* §1106(a): "A trustee shall (1) perform the duties of a trustee specified in sections 704(2); (5), (7), (8) and (9) of this title. . . ."

[24] *See* §1106(a)(2), (3) and (4).

[25] *See* §1107. *See also* §1108 (Authorization to operate business).

Appointment of Turnaround Manager

Applications for the appointment of a trustee often take into consideration whether a DIP's wrong-doing can be rectified, without the necessity for such appointment. In the *General Oil Distributors* case,[26] the creditors' committee considered the issue of the appointment of a trustee and concluded that "the appointment of a trustee would create a stigma and discourage the company's suppliers from continuing to do business with [the DIP]," and would add more costs and expense than would arise from the appointment of professionals. In lieu of the appointment of a trustee, the DIP agreed to the appointment of a manager who would exercise control of the Debtor with the powers of an operating trustee.[27] The committee approved the retention of a managing company with broad experience to provide management services. Moreover, when the Debtor and the committee completed their negotiations, the management services were suspended.[28]

The refusal to appoint a trustee notwithstanding findings that bordered on malfeasance was counterbalanced by the position occupied by the creditors' committee. "The findings show numerous instances of conduct approaching gross mismanagement, violations of fiduciary obligations, incompetence and dishonesty. . . . Under the watchful eye of G.O.D's creditors, the court is convinced that their interests are better served by permitting [the Debtor] to lead G.O.D. into reorganization, rather than by saddling the estate with the expense of a trustee and additional counsel."[29]

---

[26] *In re* General Oil Distributors, Inc. ("DIP" or "G.O.D."), 42 BR 402 (B. EDNY 1984).

[27] *See In re* Johns-Manville Corp., 36 BR 743 (B. SDNY), aff'd, 39 BR 234 (SDNY 1984) (appointing a representative for future claimants). *See In re* Revco D.S. Inc., 898 F2d 498 (6th Cir. 1990) (U.S. Trustee granted power to appoint examiner over objection of creditors' committee).

[28] *Compare* with §1105 (Termination of trustee's appointment).

[29] 42 BR at 410.

Observation

There is so much to gain in keeping an entity alive in reorganization that it is rarely that creditors seek the appointment of a trustee. To substitute a new operator for the DIP raises a problem of a possible discontinuance of the business by rejecting the principals who have organized the business and are familiar with its operations and control. Indeed, if there exist preferences or fraudulent conveyances, actions to recover such transfers are generally left to the attorneys and the accountants for the creditors' committees before a plan is being confirmed or becomes part of a plan. Cases such as *Ionosphere*[30] required the appointment of a trustee because the enterprise lost its power to operate profitably after having been given an opportunity to continue operations for thirteen months, suffering losses and having no prospects for a future profit.

The U.S. trustee performs an important administrative function. Although the U.S. trustee keeps a watchful eye on operations and reports, the ultimate goal is to assist in the DIP's reorganization. If the DIP follows the Operating Guidelines with his attorneys, accountants, and financial advisors, the DIP will find that compliance with the Operating Guidelines is essential to reorganization.[31]

Examiners should be limited to the powers set forth in the Code. Most committees have competent certified public accountants who aid them in performing essentially the same duties performed by the examiner. Every entity is interested in finding the correctness of the balance sheet and the operating statements. Indeed, at times it becomes necessary for a Debtor to retain a business consultant to assist the Debtor "to fully identify and implement the actions needed to improve [its] near-term and long-term business operations."[32]

The services of a turnaround are used to operate the DIP's business in instances such as General Oil Distribution where

---

[30] *See In re* Ionosphere Clubs, Inc., 113 BR 164 (B. SDNY 1990).

[31] *See supra* this chapter, note 9.

[32] *See* DAILY BANKR. REV., Mar. 6, 1992, p. 2, "Zale Corp. Seeks O.K. To Retain Business Consultant" (published by Federal Filings, Inc.–A Dow Jones Company).

the debtor was found inept in its conduct of operating the business. Of course, the creditors could have asked the court to appoint a trustee, but their reasons seemed adequate, when added to their problems were a "managing company with broad experience to provide management service."

We turn now to Chapter 12 of this handbook, which deals with a problem confronting Debtors upon filing a chapter 11: A seller's right to reclaim goods that the seller has sold in the ordinary course of business within 10 days prior to the time the Debtor has filed its petition.

Chapter 12
Reclamation of Goods

Conditions of Reclaiming Goods

The quiet and restrictive status of the automatic stay is oftentimes interrupted, but not violated,[1] by sellers' demand for a return of goods. Again, Congress indulges in a nomenclature for a proceeding and this one is known as "Reclamation." Yet, §546 bears the title of "Limitation on avoiding powers. . . ." Correctly so, because reclamation of goods would ordinarily be avoided by these powers unless §546(c) limited the powers to the trustee.

Limitation of Reclamation

Code §546(c) limits the avoiding rights and powers of the trustee,[2] ". . . subject to any statutory or common law right of

---

[1] *See, In re* Production Steel, 21 BR 951 (B. MD Tenn. 1982) (demand not a violation of the stay).

[2] *See* §546 Limitation on avoiding powers. *See also* §546(c): "Except as provided in subsection (d) of this section, the rights and powers of a trustee under sections 544(a), 545, 547 and 549 are subject to any statutory or common law right of a seller of goods that has sold goods to the Debtor, . . ." *See, infra* Chapter 14, this handbook, Strong Arm Powers including Marshaling of Assets.

a seller of goods that has sold goods to the Debtor, in the ordinary course of such seller's business, to reclaim such goods, if the Debtor has received such goods while insolvent[3] but—. . .

"(1) such a seller may not reclaim any such goods unless such seller demands in writing reclamation of such goods before ten days after receipt of such goods by the Debtor; and (2) such right may be denied to a seller who makes a demand only if the court grants the seller either: (A) a priority claim of a kind specified in §503(b); or (B) secures such claim by a lien."

Reclamation in Action

Now let us observe how the section works when applied to an ordinary business transaction. In September 1982, *Shamonah Golf Club*[4] purchased golf carts and dumpsters for $75,930 from *Highland Golf Cars*.[5] The transaction was unsecured and Shamonah paid $8,500 on account of the transaction. The balance of the purchase price was never paid. The golf carts were delivered approximately on September 13, 1982. No written demand for reclamation was made by Highland within ten days after delivery. In January 1983 Shamonah filed a chapter 11 petition.

Creditor Asserts UCC Provision for Reclamation

An action[6] was commenced by Highland seeking to reclaim a number of golf carts from Shamonah. Highland's complaint was "predicated upon I.C. 28-2-702 entitled, 'Seller's remedies upon discovery of buyer's insolvency,'. . . ." This section part of the Uniform Commercial Code, provides that "where the seller discovers the buyer has received goods on credit while insolvent, the seller may reclaim the goods upon demand made

---

[3] *See* "11 USC §101. Definitions (32) 'insolvent means'—(A) with reference to an entity other than a partnership and a municipality, financial condition such that the sum of such entity's debts are greater than all of such entity's property, at a fair valuation, exclusive of—. . . ."

[4] *In re* L.T.S., Inc., dba Shamonah Golf Club ("Shamonah" or "Debtor"), 32 BR 907 (B. Ohio 1983).

[5] Highland Golf Cars of Idaho ("Highland").

[6] Idaho ("Highland").

within ten days after receipt, but if misrepresentation of solvency has been made to the seller in writing within three months before delivery, the ten-day limitation does not apply. . . ."[7]

§546 Preempts Common Law and UCC §2-702

The Debtor contended that the right of a seller of goods such as plaintiff to reclaim such goods upon the buyer's insolvency was controlled exclusively by §546(c), when the buyer has filed for relief under the Bankruptcy Code. A motion for summary judgment was before the bankruptcy court by Highland seeking to reclaim a number of golf carts from Shamonah. Addressing §546(c), the court noted that the section had generated a great deal of discussion among the courts and commentators and was also reflected in the legislative history of the section: "'The purpose of the provision is to recognize *in part*, the validity of section 2-702 of the Uniform Commercial Code which has generated much litigation, confusion and divergent decisions in different circuits.' (Emphasis supplied.)"[8]

The court commented that "the issue addressed by most courts was whether that 'partial' recognition of §2-702 was limited to those situations, where a *written* demand for reclamation is made within the ten day period, *i.e.,* whether §546(c) adds an additional requirement and is exclusive. . . ." If so, a seller who failed to make a written, timely demand was barred from asserting the §2-702 right from a bankrupt buyer on the ground that an oral demand had been made or a misrepresentation of insolvency had occurred within three months preceding delivery of the goods.

A review of the case law indicates that virtually every court considering the question has

---

[7] L.T.S., Inc., 32 BR 908. The section further provides: "Except as provided in this section the seller may not base a right to reclaim goods on the buyer's fraudulent or misrepresentation of insolvency or intent to pay."

[8] *See* Sen. Rep. No. 95-989, 95th Cong. 2d Sess. 86-7 (1978). *See also* Weintraub and Edelman, *Seller's Right to Reclaim Property Under Section 2-702 of the Code Under Bankruptcy Act: Fact or Fancy*, 32 Bus. Law. 1165 (1977).

concluded that §546(c) is the sole means for a seller to successfully assert a right to reclaim goods sold to an insolvent buyer when that buyer has filed for relief under the Code and, thus, that a written demand under the section is mandatory.[9]

Shamonah relied upon the *A.G.S.* case[10] for the proposition that §546(c) was not exclusive and the requirement of written demand was not binding. In that case, a timely oral demand under §2-702 was made but a written demand within the same time was not made. The creditor instituted an adversary proceeding to reclaim the goods against the trustee. In A.G.S., the court held that the trustee (defendant) misconceived the function and application of §546(c): "Section 546(c) recognizes a seller's right to reclaim goods under §2-702 of the Uniform Commercial Code. If the seller meets the requirements of §546(c), the seller's right to reclaim is insulated from attack by the trustee under the avoiding powers set forth in §546(c). In the event the seller fails to meet the requirements of §546(c), the seller loses the benefit of the shield afforded by that section and the trustee can attack the reclamation under the indicated avoiding powers. . . ."[11]

Necessity of Demand

In effect, the court in A.G.S. opined that if a creditor did not comply with §546(c), and obviously Shamonah did not, and the Debtor returned the goods, the creditor lost the protection

---

[9] 32 BR 908, citing ". . . Any common law or statutory right to reclaim goods in the ordinary course of business is contingent upon (the seller) making a written demand [before] ten days of the Debtor's receipt of the goods. . . ."

[10] *Id.* at 909. *In re* A.G.S. Food Systems, Inc. ("A.G.S."), 14 BR 27 (B. SC. 1980).

[11] *Id. See, supra* note 2 restricting the rights and powers of a trustee to set aside any reclamation of goods granted in accordance with the provisions of §546(c). *See also* §546 "Limitation on avoiding powers" including §546(a): "An action or proceeding under section 544, 545, 547, 548 or 553 . . . may not be commenced after the earlier of—(1) two years after the appointment of a trustee under §702, 1104f; . . . or (2) the time a case is closed or dismissed."

of all the sections designed to protect creditors against the trustee's powers to set aside voidable transactions.[12] "The failure to make a demand in writing does not preclude the seller from reclaiming the goods. Rather, it merely opens the reclamation to an attack by the trustee under the specified avoiding powers including the 'strong-arm clause' of §544(a).[13] In order for the trustee to prevail over the seller the trustee must establish that his rights, as a judicial lien creditor on the date of the commencement of the case, are superior to the seller's right to reclaim."[14]

The bankruptcy court observed that at the time of the decision, no court[15] had appeared to have followed the line of analysis set forth in A.G.S., and were that position adopted in the present case, the Debtor would have to litigate the issue of whether its rights as a lien creditor defeated the interests of the plaintiff. This determination would assume that "an oral demand was made within ten days [of the] September 13 delivery (a fact which does not appear of record) or assuming that the execution by defendant of a bill of sale or invoice . . . constitutes a misrepresentation of solvency under §28-2-702(2).[16]

"I find it unnecessary, however, to engage in this latter analysis since I conclude that, under the clear language of §546(c) the weight of authority, compliance with the requirement of a timely written demand is essential for a seller to claim property of the bankrupt estate through the vehicle of statutory reclamation. Though harsh, Congress has established the 'equities' of the situation and has determined

---

[12] *See infra* Chapter 14, this handbook, Trustee's Strong Arm Powers Marshaling of Assets; and Chapter 15, this handbook, Preferences.

[13] *Id.* at 909. *Compare In re* Griffen Retreading Company 795 F.2d 676 (8th Cir. 1986) where Debtor had plans to sell goods immediately after filing petition and when demand was made within 10 days, no goods were in Debtor's possession. The court of appeals held that creditor was entitled to either alternative because of Debtor's deceit.

[14] *Id. See supra* note 2.

[15] *Id.*

[16] *Id.* at 909. *See* UCC §1-201(23): "A person is insolvent who either has ceased to pay his debts in the ordinary course of its business or cannot pay his debts as they become due or is insolvent within the meaning of the federal bankruptcy law."

that such goods remain in the estate and that the seller be treated as a general creditor."[17] The Debtor's motion for summary judgment was granted.

Telex Within Ten Days
Timely Notice

The *Marin* case,[18] considered as one of its issues dealing with reclamation, was the type of demand that was required under §546(c). The creditor had sent a written demand of reclamation by telex through Western Union to Marin, the Debtor, on April 21, 1981 at 11:04 p.m. This was the tenth day after the receipt of the goods by Debtor. The telex was physically received by the Debtor at 9:04 a.m. on April 22 when it opened for business and turned on its telex machine. In delineating the history of §546(c), the court indicated its interrelationship with §2-702:

> The solution of the drafters of the Bankruptcy Code was essentially to adopt §2-702(a) as part of the federal bankruptcy law, but to modify that section by requiring that the seller had to make a *written* demand for reclamation.[19]

The court of appeals stated that neither §546(c) nor the UCC defined what constituted a demand. The court, therefore, looked to the policy behind §546(c) for determination. "Congress favored certainty . . . minimizing the number and difficulty of disputes that will arise between the parties. . . . Under a dispatch rule there will be very few disputes concerning whether the seller made a timely dispatch. . . . [F]or example the court can simply look at the postmark date on the envelope or the electronically recorded date and time that a telex was sent. . . ."[20]

---

[17] *Id.*

[18] *In re* Marin Motor Oil, Inc., 740 F2d 220 (7th Cir. 1984), *cert. denied* 103 S.Ct. 1196 (1985).

[19] *Id.* at 223.

[20] *Id.* at 228.

Denial
Equivalent Protection For Creditor

As we have indicated in the previous chapters, rehabilitation of a Debtor is a primary concern of the Bankruptcy Code and that concern is not only present in §546(c), but in its amendments in §546(1) and (2) denying reclamation where the court finds Debtor's need for use of the goods by giving the creditor equivalent protection.[21]

Classification
Reclamation Creditors

The *Marin* case asserted the dichotomy between the Bankruptcy Code and the UCC reclamation statutes. Marin soundly disagreed with the *A.G.S.* decision. A creditor must send a timely written demand for reclamation. Indeed, reclamation has become so important a business transaction that it is not unusual to find a financial report that discusses its cooperative feature between the Debtor and its creditors who seek reclamation in a reorganization under chapter 11. In a current report of *The Daily Bankruptcy Review*:

Circle K Reviews Bid To Settle Reclamation Claims

Circle K's proposed plan of reorganization which set a separate class of major reclamation creditors to choose immediate payment on their claims in exchange for entering into a credit agreement to provide unsecured trade credit which would receive a super-priority administrative claim status, or in the alternative to receive monthly payments on such claim over a two-year period.[22]

The cooperation between the Debtor, the reclamation creditors, and the other classes of creditors in approving such priority in a plan of reorganization is sound for business and helpful to all parties.

---

[21] *See* §546(c)(2)(A), and (B).

[22] *See* issue of February 26, 1991 (published by Federal Filings Inc.—A Dow Jones Company).

Observation

In the *A.G.S.* case[23] the court held that §546(a) recognized the right to reclaim goods under §2-702 of the UCC. Thus, if the seller met the requirements of §546(c) the seller's right to reclaim would be free from attack by insulating the DIP's powers and rights under the Bankruptcy Code's avoiding powers. However, if the seller failed to meet the requirements of §546(c), the seller lost the benefit of the shield afforded by the section and the DIP could attack the claim for reclamation under the indicated avoiding powers of §546(c).

With a light spirit, A.G.S. seems to indicate that a failure to comply is not to be of any concern to the DIP. It is only a piffle for the DIP to assert its "'strong arm clause' of §544(a)," establish its "rights, as a judicial lien creditor . . . [as being] superior to the seller's right to reclaim." Quite a simple proceeding for a DIP that may have dozens of reclamations! Simply stated, it is like putting the cart before the horse. Might just as well approve the common law method of reclamation, oral misrepresentation without demand. Clearly, §546(c) preempts "any statutory or common-law right of a seller of goods. . . ."

An early area where both the Debtor and creditors should consider the benefits or harm that result to either, is the next chapter, "Assumption or Rejection of Executory Contracts and Unexpired Leases."

---

[23] *See* note 11.

Chapter 13
Assumption or Rejection of Executory Contracts and Unexpired Leases of Real Property

The workshop of setting the house in order has hardly been completed, when the debtor is confronted with problems dealing with executory contracts and unexpired leases of nonresidential real property. Fortunately, as we have indicated in the previous chapters, additional support for rehabilitation is provided by §365 of the Code[1] that gives the Debtor the right, with the court's approval, to assume or reject an executory contract including an unexpired lease of nonresidential real property which in essence is an executory contract.

---

[1] *See* 11 USC §§365(a)–(o) Executory contracts and unexpired leases.

Countryman Definition

Executory Contract

Let us consider the meaning of "executory" as applied to §365 and its application to the assumption or rejection of contracts and leases. The standard definition of executory contracts, lacking one provided by the Bankruptcy Code, which most courts have adopted, is the Countryman[2] definition. However, as we shall read shortly, the elimination of "executoriness"[3] has appeared in law review articles that have been partially absorbed in the *Drexel Burnham* case and followed by *In re Walnut Associates*.[4] First, the Countryman definition as derived by the Walnut Court: "The Bankruptcy Code does not define the term 'executory contract.' Courts addressing this issue have generally relied upon the definition set forth in V. Countryman. . . :

> [A] contract under which the obligation of both
> the bankrupt and the other party to the contract
> are so far unperformed that the failure of either
> to complete the performance would constitute a
> material breach excusing the performance by
> the other.[5]

Such assumption or rejection by a Debtor, however, is conditioned upon the application of the business judgment test, a determination test as to not only whether the contract benefits the estate, but that it does not damage the non-debtor unfairly:

---

[2] *See* Countryman, *Executory Contracts in Bankruptcy, Part I,* 57 MINN. L. REV. 439, 460 (1973); and *Executory Contracts in Bankruptcy, Part II,* 58 MINN. L. REV. 479 (1974).

[3] *See infra* ,this chapter, subtitle Executoriness "Rejected."

[4] *See* Walnut Associates, 145 BR *infra* 489, note 116. *See also infra* this chapter, subtitle "Drexel Burnham Executory Contracts and In *re* Walnut Associates" (following the authorities and reasoning of Drexel Burnham).

[5] *In re* Walnut Assoc., 145 BR 489, 496 (B. ED Pa. 1992).

> The primary issue under the business judgment test is whether rejection of the contract would benefit general unsecured creditors. This question may well involve a balancing of interests and rejection may be disallowed where the party whose contract is to be rejected would be damaged disproportionately to any benefit to be derived by general creditors.[6]

Under §365(a), the Debtor has the power with court approval to assume the contract if it is beneficial to the Debtor and its creditors or to reject the contract if it is not beneficial. Assumption of the contract requires both parties to conform to the provisions of the contract. Rejection of the contract, because it is onerous or burdensome, frees the Debtor from any obligation under the contract, but allows the non-debtor to file an unsecured claim for damages for the breach. However, if the DIP assumes the contract with the court's permission any breach by the Debtor thereafter will constitute an expense of administration.[7]

Distinction

Payment of Debt

An executory contract is not to be confused with a promise to pay money, or a note, or a guaranty of an obligation at a future date. In the *Grayson*[8] case, the court of appeals held: "[A]n agreement of guaranty of the lease is not an executory contract which the guarantor can reject." The Code's lack of a definition for "executory" has prompted the courts generally to

---

[6] *See In re* Huang, 23 BR 798, 801 (B. 9th Cir. 1982); *see also In re* Minges, 602 F2d 38, 43 (2d Cir. 1979). (The court of appeals rejected a rigid test which "might work a substantial injustice where it can be shown that the nondebtor contracting party will reap substantial benefits under the contract while the debtor's creditors are forced to make substantial compromises of their claims.")

[7] *See* §501. Filing of proof of claims or interests; §502. Allowance of claims or interests; §503. Allowance of administrative expenses; and §507. Priorities.

[8] *In re* Grayson-Robinson Stores, Inc. ("Grayson"), 321 F2d 500, 502 (2d Cir. 1963).

adopt the Countryman definition: "[W]e believe that Congress intended §365 to apply to contracts where significant unperformed obligations remain on both sides."[9]

Assumption Requirements
Exclusion of Insolvency Provisions

Assumption of an executory contract or lease[10] requires the DIP to provide adequate assurance that it will promptly[11] cure such default and that the DIP will compensate the other party for any actual pecuniary loss resulting from such default.[12] Furthermore, adequate assurance of future performance must be provided under such contract or lease. Curing the default or performance of the other requirements does not apply to a default that is a breach of a provision relating to the insolvency or financial condition of the Debtor or the commencement of a case or appointment of a trustee under the Bankruptcy Code or of the appointment of a custodian (assignee for the benefit of creditors or general receiver) before the commencement of the case.[13] We leave for the moment our discussion of executory contracts. Before we return to a challenge of the *Countryman* definition in the *Drexel Burnham* and *Walnut* cases, we will discuss the specific details of §365

---

[9] *In re* Streets & Beard Farm Partnership, 882 F2d 233, 235 (7th Cir. 1989). *See infra,* this chapter, subtitle "Security Agreement Not Executory Contract."

[10] *See* 11 USC §365(a): "[T]he trustee, subject to the court's approval, may assume or reject any executory contract or unexpired lease of the debtor." *See* B.Rule 6006(a): "Proceeding To Assume, Reject, or Assign." *See also* B.Rule 6006(b) governed by Rule 9014, "reasonable notice and opportunity for hearing," and 6006(c) "Hearing." *See also* Local B. Rule 44 (B. SDNY 1990): "Relief from Automatic Stay; Motion to Assume Executory Contract or Unexpired Lease."

[11] *See In re* Lafayette Radio Electrics Corp., 9 BR 993 (B. EDNY 1981), giving a flexible interpretation to "prompt" as depending upon the circumstances of the case.

[12] *See* 11 USC §365(b)(1)–(4).

[13] 11 USC §365(b)(2). *See* T.S. Industries, Inc., 117 BR 682, 685 (B. D. Utah 1990) ("that section invalidates 'ipso facto' clauses that terminate a contract or modify its terms in the event of a bankruptcy").

and its application to particular settings, such as in nonresidential leases.

Nonrestrictive Provisions

Other provisions with respect to executory contracts or unexpired leases prohibit a trustee from assuming or assigning such contracts, whether or not such contract or lease prohibits assignment, where applicable law excuses a party other than the debtor from accepting or rendering performance to the DIP or an assignee, and such party does not consent to such assumption or assignment, or the contract is a contract to make a loan or extend other debt financing for the debtor.[14] Moreover, the assignment by the DIP of a contract or lease that the DIP assumed, relieves the DIP and the estate from any liability for any breach occurring after such assignment. However, a provision in an executory contract or lease that it cannot be assigned may, nevertheless, be assigned if the trustee assumes said contract or lease and the assignee gives adequate assurance of future performance whether or not there has been a default.[15]

Shopping Center Leases

Additional requirements must be met when adequate assurance affects assumption or assignment of a lease of real property in a shopping center, such as the source of rent, the percentage of rent and noninterference with other restrictive covenants. However, if there has been a default under any lease, the DIP may not require the lessor to provide services or supplies incidental to such lease before the assumption unless the lessor is compensated before the assumption.[16] However, before we continue the discussion of the shopping center leases, it is helpful to consider as a foundation damages which accrue as a result of rejection or breach of a lease. In addition, we need to ascertain whether an agreement to purchase real

---

[14] 11 USC §365(c)(1)(A), (B), (c)(2), and (c)(3).

[15] *See* 11 USC §365(k) and 11 USC §365(f)(1), (2)(A), and (2)(B).

[16] 11 USC §365(b)(3) and (4).

estate by installment payments constitutes an executory contract.[17]

Damages Upon Rejection of Lease

Section 502(b)(6) of the Code[18] provides that such claim resulting from the termination of a lease of real property shall not exceed the rent reserved by such lease, without acceleration, for the greater of one year, or 15%, not to exceed three years of the remaining term of the lease following the earlier of the date of the filing of the petition and the date on which the premises are surrendered. Added to this sum is any unpaid rent due under the lease prior to the commencement of the case. Both constitute general unsecured claims, but the lessor has an administrative claim for use and occupancy of the premises by the DIP.

Damages

Breach of Lease

There is more to be said about damages accruing to a lessor upon a lessee's breach of a lease. In *Bob's Sea Ray Boats*[19] a chapter 11 trustee objected to the claim of Henry A. Albers ("Albers") filed in the sum of $265,722 arising from the Debtor's breach of a commercial real estate lease, the breach of a related consulting agreement and repair damages occasioned by the destruction or removal of certain items of property. Albers was the owner of commercial property in Bismarck, North Dakota, where he had, for some time, operated a retail boat sales and service business.

In April 1989, the Debtor entered into two separate agreements with Albers: (1) a lease by which Debtor agreed to lease the retail boat facility for a term of three years commencing May 1, 1989, and terminating on May 1, 1992 at

---

[17] *See infra,* this chapter, subtitle "Shopping Center Lease Dissected Goldblatt."

[18] 11 USC §502(b)(6).

[19] *In re* Bob's Sea Ray Boats, Inc. ("Debtor"), 143 BR 229 (B. ND. 1992).

a rate of $5,500 per month with Debtor responsible for all taxes; and (2) a consulting agreement by which Debtor, acknowledging the need of Albers' boating expertise, agreed to pay him $2,527 per month for 36 months for his advice concerning the business of retail boats and related items. "The Debtor paid Albers the consulting fee for the months of June through November 1989 but failed to pay for the month of May 1989 or for December 1989 and thereafter."[20]

The boat business faltered and Albers recovered possession of the leasehold in December 1989. In January 1990, he had relet the premises to Hank Albers Leasing which was paying rent of $4,000 per month and which commenced operating under the name, Hanks Boat Sales. Hank Albers Leasing also began to pay Albers a salary of $3,000 per month. Upon recovering the premises Albers discovered damages to the carpeting, and other equipment that needed replacement at a cost of $1,614. In addition, the Debtor had removed light fixtures, which would cost $10,395 to replace. Lastly, the Debtor failed to pay real estate taxes during the term of occupancy.

Calculation of Damages

Although in his proof of claim Albers sought recovery for the 29 months remaining on the lease, both he and the trustee agreed that §502(b)(6) was applicable to the calculation of the damages resulting from the lease termination but disagreed on the manner of making that calculation and what costs and expenses were covered by the section. After referring to §502(b)(6) limiting a claim for damages, the court stated:

> Section 502(b)(6) was designed to compensate a landlord for the loss suffered upon termination but at the same time limit the recovery to a reasonable amount that would not prevent other creditors from recovering from the estate.[21]

---

[20] *Id.* at 230.

[21] *Id.* at 231 citing H.R.Rep. No. 95-595, 95th Cong., 1st Sess. 353 (1977), U.S. CODE CONG. & ADMIN. NEWS 1978, pp. 5787, 6309.

Disagreeing with the trustee, the court stated that "[a]lthough some courts take the position, and the trustee so argues, that the damages spoken of in section 502(b)(6) encompass virtually any cost or expense arising in consequence of a breach, others take a more measured view opining that the section is intended to limit only those damages which a lessor would have avoided but for the lease termination. . . . It does not address damages wholly collateral to the termination event—such things as waste, destruction or removal of leasehold property."[22]

Damages Subject to Mitigation

Turning now to the problem of mitigation of the damages after determining the arithmetical formula set forth in §502(b)(6) the court opined: "As with any claim for damages arising out of the breach of a lease, a claim for damages under section 502(b)(6) is subject to mitigation including an obligation on the part of the landlord to attempt the reletting of the premises. . . ."[23] The formula for application of §502(b)(6) is first to deduct the rent resulting from re-letting against "the statutory calculations, . . . before the section 502(b)(6) cap is applied."[24]

The court's estimation for damages began with a calculation of unpaid rent due from the Debtor if the lease had not been breached plus ongoing tax obligations bringing "the total due over the remaining lease term to $171,000. This figure is then reduced by the sums received by Albers in consequence of his successful mitigation effort leading to the re-letting of the premises . . . leaving total damages of $59,100. We now apply the section 502(b)(6) cap rate, . . . [f]ifteen percent. . . and the value of one year of the remaining term is approximately $70,800. . . . This sum is greater than 15% of

---

[22] *Id.* approving *In re* Atlantic Container Corp., 133 BR 980, 987 (B. ND. Ill. 1991); *contra, In re* Storage Technology Corp., 77 BR 824 (B. D. Colo. 1986).

[23] *Id.*

[24] *Id.* citing *In re* Goldblatt Bros., Inc., 66 BR 337 (B. ND. Ill. 1986). *See infra,* this chapter, subtitle "Shopping Center Lease Dissected Goldblatt Case."

the remaining term and is less than 3 years of rent, thus Albers is entitled to a claim of $70,800 for post-termination damages arising from the breach. He is also entitled to all accrued but unpaid taxes accruing pre-termination. . . ."[25]

Harm to Premises
Separate Obligation

The court held that damages due to misusage of the premises had nothing to do with §502(b)(6). However, under the terms of the lease, the "Debtor was to quit and surrender the premises in as good condition as when received. Nothing therein gave the Debtor the right to remove property or destroy it. Other courts have held that damages caused by a tenant's failure to properly repair and maintain the premises are not subject to section 502(b)(6) since that is a separate obligation imposed on a tenant which under applicable non-bankruptcy laws are regarded as separate items of damage unrelated to the breach itself. . . . [T]he North Dakota Supreme Court held that the cost of repair and reconstruction is the proper measure of damages for injury caused to property. The court accepts Albers' evidence on the costs to restore the premises as reasonably certain and accordingly allows him a claim of $12,036.70."[26]

Consulting Agreement
Mitigation of Damages

Finally, the court considered the consulting agreement as a separate agreement. "Damages arising in consequence of its breach are, however, subject to mitigation.[27] . . . He has not lost any income as a result of the post-termination brief and accordingly his claim for damages arising therefrom is disallowed."[28] The court, however, observed that the Debtor

---

[25] *Id.* at 231–32.

[26] *Id.* at 232 *In re* Atlantic Container Corp., *supra* and Swain v. Harvest States Cooperatives, 469 N.W.2d 571 (ND 1991).

[27] *Id.* citing Vallejo v. Jamestown College, 244 N.W.2d 753 (ND 1976)."

[28] *Id.*

failed to pay consulting fees for a month and allowed him such fees. "In sum, . . . the claim of Henry A. Albers is allowed in the total aggregate amount of $87,714.78."[29]

Security Agreement
Not Executory Contract

In the *Streets* case[30] the question presented to the court was whether an installment contract for the sale of real estate between the vendors and the Debtor was an executory contract within the meaning of §365 of the Bankruptcy Code. The contract provided that upon completion of all installment payments, the vendor was required to deliver legal title to the Debtor. The Debtor complied with all the requirements of the contract but defaulted on its annual payment, and the vendor instituted forfeiture proceedings under the Illinois Mortgage Foreclosure Law.

The Debtor thereupon filed a petition under chapter 12[31] and listed the farmland as an asset and the vendor as a secured creditor. In response, the vendor argued that the installment land agreement was an executory contract and requested that a time be set for the DIP to accept or reject the contract under §365.[32] The bankruptcy judge dismissed vendor's petition holding that the agreement between vendor and Debtor was not an executory contract and this decision was affirmed by the district court.

Conflict of Courts

The court of appeals examined many bankruptcy cases that were divided on this issue: "The seemingly straightforward issue presented by this case has in fact provoked a division

---

[29] *Id.*

[30] *In re* Streets & Beard Farm Partnership ("Streets"), 882 F2d 233 (7th Cir. 1989).

[31] *See* §103(a): ". . . chapters 1, 3, and 5 of this title apply in a case under chapters 7, 11, 12, or 13 of this title."

[32] *See* §365(a): "Except. . . the trustee, subject to the court's approval, may assume or reject any executory contract or unexpired lease of the debtor."

among the bankruptcy courts in this circuit."[33] Referring to this division, the court cited *Bertelsen*[34] holding that an installment contract for the sale of real estate was in substance a security agreement and not an executory contract within the meaning of §365. In contrast *Buchert* reached the opposite conclusion.[35] Moreover, "[t]his division between our own bankruptcy courts on this issue reflects a split that exists throughout the nation. . . ."[36] citing a number of cases for comparison.[37]

Such diversity, of course, still requires the court of appeals to make a choice and again we hear the accustomed observation:

> The Bankruptcy Code does not contain a precise definition of the term executory contract. The legislative history to §365, however, provides that *an executory contract is a contract on which performance remains due to some extent on both sides*[38]. . . . Taken literally, this definition would render almost all agreements executory since it is the rare agreement that does not involve unperformed obligations on either side. . . .[39]

Application of State Law

The court, however, rejected this viewpoint as not affecting Congress' intent that §365 apply to contracts where significant unperformed obligations remain on both sides.[40] In

---

[33] Streets, 882 F2d at 234.

[34] *In re* Bertelsen, 65 BR 654 (B. CD. Ill. 1986).

[35] *In re* Buchert, 69 BR 816 (B. ND. Ill. 1987) *aff'd* 1987 WL 16019 (ND. Ill. 1987).

[36] Streets, 882 F2d at 234.

[37] *Id.* "compare *In re* Speck, 798 F2d 279 (8th Cir. 1986) . . . (all treating the contract as a security device)."

[38] *Id.* at 235 citing S.Rep. No. 989, 95th Cong. 2d Sess. 58 and H.Rep. No. 595, 95th Cong., 1st Sess. 347.

[39] *Id.* (emphasis added).

[40] *Id.* citing V. Countryman, E*xecutory Contracts In Bankruptcy: Part I*, 57 MINN. L. REV. 439, 460 (1974). "Defining an executory contract. . . ."

determining the significance of the remaining obligations under an executory contract, the court must examine relevant state law which in this case was Illinois. The "determination of property rights in assets of a bankrupt's estate [is] left to state law."[41]

The court of appeals concluded that the district court was correct in holding that the installment land contract was not executory because under Illinois law the Debtor became the equitable owner of the property and the delivery of legal title was "a mere formality and does not represent the kind of significant legal obligation that would render the contract executory. Rather, we believe the arrangement in this case is merely a security agreement where the vendor holds legal title in trust solely as security for the payment of the purchase price. . . . As security agreements are not executory contracts within the meaning of §365 of the Bankruptcy Code, . . . we affirm the district court's decision denying the appellants' motion to set a time certain to accept or reject the contract."[42]

Shopping Center Lease Dissected
Goldblatt Case

Having considered the definition of an executory contract and unexpired lease and their relevance to state law, we shall examine their application to shopping center problems. In *Goldblatt*[43] the question before the court of appeals was whether the district court properly affirmed the bankruptcy court's order that approved a Debtor's assumption of an unexpired lease over the landlord's objection.

Goldblatt rented a store from American[44] under a lease executed in 1957. On June 15, 1981 Goldblatt filed for chapter 11. American thereupon filed a petition to have Goldblatt assume or reject the lease. After Goldblatt notified American of its intention to assume the lease, American objected on the grounds that Goldblatt had not met the conditions that were

---

[41] *Id.* at 235 citing Butner v. United States, 99 S.Ct. 914, 918, (1979).

[42] *Id.* citing *In re* Pacific Exp., Inc., 780 F2d 1482, 1487 (9th Cir. 1986).

[43] *In re* Goldblatt Bros., Inc. ("Goldblatt"), 766 F2d 1136 (7th Cir. 1985). *See also* §365(b) (assumption conditioned on curing defaults).

[44] American National Bank & Trust Company of Chicago ("American").

precedent to assumption of the lease by curing the default and compensating American for damages as well as providing adequate assurance of future performance.[45] In addition, American argued that the store was part of a shopping center.[46] The bankruptcy court overruled American's objections and approved Goldblatt's assumption of the lease, and this order was affirmed by the district court.

Curing Default of Lease

In the court of appeals, American objected to the assumption of the lease claiming that Goldblatt had defaulted in several respects and could not assume the lease unless Goldblatt "cures or provides adequate assurance that [Goldblatt] will promptly cure, such default. . . ."[47] The principal objection raised by American was that Goldblatt defaulted under the lease by failing to use the second floor as a retail store and to operate its business during all business hours without interruption, both causing a drop in payable percentage rental that would have accrued to American.

Measuring Loss

Weighing the loss from the Debtor's actions as against the total rental paid for the premises, the court stated: "[A]s long as the tenant does not violate the explicit requirements of the lease, we think it is entitled to some discretion to exercise its business judgment in deciding how best to achieve its goal."[48] In a footnote, the court of appeals emphasized that the lease did not include any provision requiring that a specified portion

---

[45] *See* §365(b)(1).

[46] *See* §365(b)(3).

[47] *See* 11 USC §365(b)(1). Goldblatt, 766 F2d 1136 (7th Cir. 1985). *See also In re* Currivan's Chapel of the Sunset, 51 BR 217 (ND. Cal. 1985) (Condition of assumption of lease by paying security deposit did not violate any specific statutory provision and was within court's equitable power of §105(a)); *In re* H.M. Bowness, Inc., 89 BR 238 (B. MD. Fla. 1988) (rejection denied since it would not benefit the estate and would result in a large damage claim). *See also infra* Chapter 14, this handbook, subtitle "Trustee's Strong-Arm Powers."

[48] 766 F2d at 1139.

of the retail area be used for actual "sales," as distinguished from ancillary functions such as storage or administration, or "complete use" for actual sales.[49]

The court of appeals agreed with the bankruptcy court that the lease did not require that all rented space be used for sales. The court noted that the base rent was substantial and was paid in addition to, rather than in lieu of, the percentage rent, which was comparatively minor. In addition, Goldblatt stopped using the second floor because of the discontinuance of certain product lines. The court noted that Goldblatt's failure to use the second floor was not in bad faith to reduce sales volume, but rather "to streamline its sales efforts as part of the reorganization."[50]

Shopping Center Lease
A Definition

American contends that Goldblatt was a shopping center since it was one of eight stores, known as the *"Belmont Stores"*; commonly owned, located on the same block, and seven of which were contiguous. Characterizing Goldblatt as a "shopping center" would enable American to invoke the special protections available to shopping center landlords. "The term 'shopping center' is not defined [in §365(b)(3)], but is left to case by case interpretation."[51]

American's expert witness testified that the Belmont stores formed "a strip shopping center, basing his opinion on the satisfaction of three criteria: common ownership of contiguous parcels, the existence of an 'anchor tenant' [Goldblatt] and joint off-street parking adjacent to all stores."[52] The bankruptcy court rejected this definition. The court of appeals agreed that although the criteria urged by American certainly were significant, the court believed that they were not of themselves determinative:

---

[49] *Id.* at note 3 citing Fox v. Fox Valley Trotting Club, 8 Ill.2d 571 (Ill. 1956).

[50] *Id.* at 1140.

[51] *Id.*

[52] *Id.*

> As the bankruptcy court stressed, there is no evidence whatsoever that the stores were developed to be a shopping center. Moreover, typical indicia of shopping centers, such as a master lease, fixed hours during which the stores are all open, common areas or joint advertising, are noticeably absent.[53]

For these reasons the court found no error in the bankruptcy court's holding. In addition, the court held as irrelevant American's argument that damages were due as a result of the nonuse of the second floor since no default had occurred.

Sixty-Day Period
American Case

Having discussed the debtor's power to assume an executory contract or an unexpired lease, we now consider the time within which a debtor must act to assume or reject an unexpired nonresidential lease of real property. "Sixty Days" seems to be the keynote. The *American* case[54] decided by the Fifth Circuit brought to the forefront the problem of computing when the 60-day period commenced and at what date the 60-day period terminated. The issue was whether several adjournments that were contiguously granted within the 60-day extension constituted a proper extension as provided in §365(d). The bankruptcy court's decision that the motion to assume was timely and should be granted, was affirmed by the district court. The court of appeals considered the Debtor's argument as being based on the language of §365(d)(4) requiring a lessee to assume or reject leases "within 60 days after the date of the order for relief, or within such additional time as the court, for cause, *within such 60-day period*, fixes."[55]

The court of appeals finally held: "[Debtor's] contention is unpersuasive. Rule 6006(a) is clearly intended to provide

---

[53] *Id.* at 1141.

[54] *In re* American Healthcare Management, Inc. ("American" or "Debtor"), 900 F2d 827 (5th Cir. 1990).

[55] *Id.* at 829, citing 11 USC §365(d)(4) (emphasis in original).

lessors with notice and a hearing when a lessee has actually filed a motion to assume or reject. . . . The district court properly concluded that neither section 365(d)(4) nor Rules 6006(a) and 9014 require notice and a hearing before a bankruptcy court grants an extension of time in which a lessee may assume or reject its leases."[56]

Antiwaiver

Acceptance of Rent

We come again to §365(d)(4)[57] in the case of *T.F.P. Resources*,[58] where the Lessor sought an order declaring a lease with the debtor to be rejected and directing the debtor to deliver possession of the premises; and, alternatively, the Lessor sought an order pursuant to §365(d)(3)[59] requiring the Debtor to pay administrative rent due and owing. The Debtor contended that the Lessor waived its rights under §365(d)(4) by acceptance of payments for rent due and owing and postpetition rent.

The Debtor rented commercial office space pursuant to a five-year lease dated May 27, 1983. On December 19, 1984, the Debtor-Lessee filed a chapter 11 petition. Since the filing date, the Debtor had not moved to assume or reject the lease, or to extend its time to do so. Subsequent to the filing date, the Debtor had tendered to the managing agent for the Lessor several rent payments for the period from January 1985 to June 1985. Two checks, however, which were tendered were dishonored for insufficient funds. A certified check tendered for rent due in November was returned to the Debtor with a notation that the rent was in default in the sum of $61,236.41, and demanded that it be cured in three days while the Lessor reserved its rights under §365(d)(4).

---

[56] *Id.* at 832–33. *See* §365(d)(4) dealing with automatic default upon debtor's failure to assume or reject within 60 days and *see also, supra,* note 9 discussing B. Rules 6006(b) and (c) and 9014.

[57] *See supra,* this chapter, subtitle "Amendment of Lubizol: §365(n)."

[58] *In re* T.F.P. Resources, Inc. ("Lessor" or "Debtor"), 56 BR 112 (B. SDNY 1985).

[59] *See supra,* this chapter, subtitle "Assumption Requirements."

Acceptance
Nonwaiver

As we indicated, under §365(d)(4) a debtor as lessee is given 60 days to assume or reject an unexpired lease, but failure to act within 60 days without an extension results in a rejection of the lease. Section 365(d)(3) requires timely performance by a DIP of all the obligations arising from the lease after the entry of an order for relief until the lease is assumed or rejected. However, the section specifically adds that "[a]cceptance of any such performance [rent payments in the present case] does not constitute waiver or relinquishment of the lessor's rights under such lease or under this title."[60]

The Debtor claimed that the Lessor waived §365(d)(4)'s requirement of assumption of the lease within 60 days by acceptance of rental payments during the 60-day period that expired on February 18, 1985, by the statute's express language. The court stated that the express language of the statute "gives substance to the Debtor's claim that the antiwaiver provision of §365(d)(3) does not bar waiver by acceptance of rental payments after the expiration of the 60-day period. In requiring that postpetition rent be paid '*until* such lease is assumed or rejected,' and barring waiver through '[a]cceptance of any *such* performance,'. . .(emphasis added), §365(d)(3) is expressly limited to payments made prior to assumption or rejection. . . ."[61]

Waiver
Intent

Reading §365(d)(3) with its companion section 365(d)(4) that provides for rejection if not assumed within 60 days or an extended period, the court held "that all the non-waiver clause expressly covers is acceptance of rental payments during that period: By its terms, therefore, the statute does not address the issue presented here, i.e., whether acceptance of rent by a

---

[60] T.F.P. Resources, 56 BR at 114.

[61] *Id.* (emphasis in original).

lessor after expiration of the period would constitute a waiver of the automatic rejection afforded by §365(d)(4). . . ."[62]

The words of the statute being sufficiently plain, they control and further inquiry as to their meaning is unnecessary.[63] The court went on to explain that: "[W]hether or not there was in fact a waiver should be a question of intent as manifested by the lessor's acts. Such a test applies to a lessor's alleged waiver of a forfeiture clause contained in a lease."[64]

Intellectual Property

Executory Property

Subsection 365(n) was enacted[65] to overcome the decision in the *Lubrizol* case.[66] Richmond, a licensor, sought to reject as executory a technology licensing agreement with Lubrizol, a licensee. The bankruptcy court approved the rejection pursuant to §365(a), but the district court reversed, holding that the contract was not executory and alternatively, rejection could not reasonably be expected to benefit the debtor substantially. The court of appeals reversed.

In July 1982, Richmond entered into a contract with Lubrizol that granted Lubrizol a nonexclusive license to utilize a metal coating process technology owned by Richmond. Under the agreement Richmond owed several duties to Lubrizol: (1) to notify Lubrizol of a patent infringement and to defend such suit; (2) to notify Lubrizol of any other use or licensing of the

---

[62] *Id.*

[63] *Id.* at 114–15 citing "United States v. Bass, 92 S.Ct. 515, 518 (1971). We turn, nevertheless, to the legislative history to see if a contrary interpretation forcefully appears. . . . The little that there is confirms the conclusion that the waiver clause pertains only to rental payments required by §365(d)(3) and not others accepted by lessor. . . ."

[64] *Id.* at 116 citing *In re* Duplan Corp., 473 F.Supp. 1089, 1093 (SDNY 1979); *In re* Fifth Ave. Originals, 32 BR 648, 656 (B. SDNY 1983).

[65] *See* Amendment by Pub.L. 100-506 effective Oct. 18, 1988, but not retroactive.

[66] Lubrizol Enterprises Inc. ("Lubrizol") v. Richmond Metal Finishers, Inc. ("Richmond"), 756 F2d 1043 (4th Cir. 1985), *cert. denied,* Lubrizol Enterprises, Inc. v. Canfield, 106 S.Ct. 1285 (1986).

process and to reduce royalty payments if a lower royalty rate was reached with another licensee; and (3) to indemnify Lubrizol for losses arising out of any misrepresentation or breach of warranty by Richmond.[67]

Lubrizol owed Richmond reciprocal duties of accounting for and paying royalties for the use of the process and of canceling certain indebtedness. Although the contract provided that Lubrizol would defer use of the process until May 1, 1983, Lubrizol never used the technology.

On August 16, 1983 Richmond filed for chapter 11. As part of its plan to emerge from bankruptcy, Richmond sought to reject its contract with Lubrizol pursuant to §365(a) in order to facilitate sale or licensing of the technology unhindered by the restrictions of the agreement.

Contents of Executory Contract
Performance

The court of appeals held initially that for a contract to be executory within the contemplation of §365(a) required that performance was due to some extent by both parties. "This court has recently adopted Professor Countryman's more specific test. . . ."[68] Applying the test the court concluded that the licensing agreement was at the critical time executory since Richmond owed Lubrizol the continuing duties of notifying Lubrizol of further licensing of the process and of reducing Lubrizol's royalty rate. Moreover, contingent duties rendered unperformed until the term of the contract expired left open the possibility that an event triggering a contingent duty might occur.

Observing that the contract had to be executory as to both parties, the court turned to Lubrizol, which owed Richmond the duty of accounting for and paying royalties, for the life of the agreement. Lubrizol owed Richmond more than an

---

[67] *Id.* at 1045.

[68] *Id.* citing NLRB v. Bildisco & Bildisco, 104 S.Ct. 1188 (1984). *See also, supra,* this chapter, subtitle "Countryman Definition Executory Contract." *See also, infra,* this chapter, subtitle "Drexel Burnham-Executory Contracts."

obligation to make payments of money;[69] it owed a promise to account for and pay royalties, that required Lubrizol to deliver written quarterly sales reports and keep books of account subject to inspection by an independent Certified Public Accountant. "This promise goes beyond a mere debt, or promise to pay money, and was at the critical time executory."[70]

Debtor's Rejection

Finding the contract executory as to both parties, there remained the question of whether rejection of the executory contract would be advantageous for the Debtor. "Courts addressing that question must start with the proposition that the bankrupt's decision upon it is to be accorded the deference mandated by the sound business judgment rule as generally applied by courts to discretionary actions or decisions of corporate directors."[71]

Transposing the discretion of corporate directors to bankruptcy litigation the court stated that the "issue is one of fact to be decided as such by the bankruptcy court by the normal process of fact adjudication. . . ."[72]

Addressing the evidence before the bankruptcy court, the court of appeals observed that the metal coating process subject to the licensing agreement was Debtor's principal asset and that the sale or licensing of the technology represented its primary source of funds by which the debtor might emerge from bankruptcy.[73] The testimony of *Richmond*'s president, which was factually uncontested by *Lubrizol*, also indicated the benefits of further licensing by stripping *Lubrizol* of its contract rights. On the basis of this evidence the court of appeals approved the bankruptcy court's determination that the debtor's decision to reject was based on sound business judgment but rejected as clearly erroneous the district court's

---

[69] *Id.* at 1046 citing *In re* Smith Jones, Inc. 26 BR 289, 292 (B.D. Minn. 1982); H. Rep. No. 95-595, 95th Cong. 2d Sess. 347 (1978).

[70] *Id.* citing *In re* Select-A-Seat Corp., 625 F2d 290, 292 (9th Cir. 1980).

[71] *Id.* citing NLRB v. Bildisco & Bildisco, 104 S.Ct. at 1195.

[72] *Id.* at 1047 citing *In re* Minges, 602 F2d 38, 43 (2d Cir. 1979).

[73] *Id.*

findings that relief from the contingent obligations was not a substantial benefit.

A second point asserted by the district court was that by rejecting the agreement, the Debtor could not deprive Lubrizol of all right to the process. Referring to §365(g),[74] the court of appeals held that Lubrizol would be entitled to treat rejection as a breach and seek a money damages remedy. "[H]owever, it could not seek to retain its contract rights in the technology by specific performance even if that remedy would ordinarily be available upon breach of this type of contract. . . . For the same reason, Lubrizol cannot rely on provisions within its agreement with [Richmond] for continued use of the technology by Lubrizol upon breach by [Richmond]. Here again, the statutory 'breach' contemplated by §365(g) controls, and provides only a money damages remedy for the non-bankrupt party. . . ."[75]

Lubrizol strongly urged policy concerns in support of the district court's decision refusing to defer to the Debtor's decision to reject or, to treat the contract as executory for §365(a) purposes. The court of appeals commented that allowing rejection of such contracts as executory imposed serious burdens upon contracting parties such as Lubrizol and comparable cases and "could have a general chilling effect upon the willingness of such parties to contract at all with businesses in possible financial difficulty."[76]

Amendment of Lubrizol: §365(n)

What is the response to a socioeconomic problem presented to the courts? The court of appeals presented the answer succinctly, indicating once again the constitutional division between the law makers and the judiciary:

> Congress has plainly provided for the rejection
> of executory contracts, notwithstanding the

---

[74] *See* 11 USC §365(g): "Except . . . the rejection of an executory contract or unexpired lease of the debtor constitutes a breach of such contract or lease—. . . ."

[75] Lubrizol, 756 F2d at 1048.

[76] *Id.*

obvious adverse consequences for contracting parties thereby made inevitable. Awareness by Congress of those consequences is indeed specifically reflected in the special treatment accorded to union members under collective bargaining contracts,. . .[77] and to lessees of real property[78]. . . . But no comparable special treatment is provided for technology licensees such as Lubrizol. . . .[79]

Congress did hear the message. It was loud and clear and resulted in a new subsection (n) to §365 and its objective was to protect a licensee's rights in the use of intellectual property, notwithstanding the rejection of the licensing agreement as an executory contract.[80] Subdivision (n)(1) starts: "If the trustee rejects an executory contract under which the debtor is a licensor of a right to intellectual property, the licensee under such contract may elect—. . . ." The options for the debtor as licensor of intellectual property present choices for the debtor licensor and the nondebtor licensee. If the debtor rejects the contract, the licensee may treat the rejection as terminating the license or retain its rights, or if the licensee elects to retain its rights, the debtor must allow the licensee to exercise such rights and on the written request of the licensee, the debtor is required to provide the licensee with any intellectual property held by the debtor and not to interfere with the rights of the licensee as provided in such contract. Finally, the licensee is required to pay to the trustee all royalties due under the contract.

El Intern Under §365(n)

We now come to a current case that amplifies the holding of Congress' intent in overcoming the hardship of Lubrizol. In

---

[77] *Id.* citing NLRB v. Bildisco & Bildisco, 104 S.Ct. at 1193–96. *See also,* 11 USC §1113. Rejection of collective bargaining agreements.

[78] *Id.* citing 11 USC 365(h).

[79] *Id.*

[80] *See* this chapter, subtitle "Countryman Definition–Executory Contract" as applicable to intellectual property.

El Intern,[81] a creator of customized computer software had agreed to supply its software system to one of Ontario Hydro's plants that generated electricity. After filing the petition, the executory contract was rejected by the Debtor under 11 U.S.C. §365(n). Ontario Hydro filed a claim against the Debtor, which was acknowledged, but a dispute arose as to the difference involving a setoff that the Debtor asserted. "Section 365(n) was enacted by Congress in 1988 (Public Law 100-506), to treat contracts involving licenses to rights in intellectual properties, entitled 'An Act to Keep Secure the Rights of Intellectual Property Licensors and Licensees Which Come Under the Protection of Title 11 of the United States Code, The Bankruptcy Code.'"[82] Stated generally, §365(n) "affords the licensee of an intellectual property an option if the licensor elects to reject the executory contract. . . . If the licensee elects to retain its rights under the agreement, the licensee must make all royalty payments. . . ."[83]

The court held that "[w]hile questioning the right of El [Intern] to a setoff, the assertion of such right may have an effect upon the extent of El [Intern's] admission of the Ontario Hydro claim. . . ."[84] Accordingly, the Debtor will have the option of accepting an allowable amount without the setoff or request a hearing to present further evidence to support its position. Of interest is the court's observation of the enactment of §365(n) to protect the interests of both parties without utilizing the harsh effect of the Lubrizol case. The Lubrizol case is a good example of the constituents of an executory contract, which notwithstanding the benefits to the Debtor of intellectual property, nevertheless rendered harm to the non-debtor and required Congressional protection.

---

[81] *In re* El International, 123 BR 64 (B.D. Idaho 1991) ("El Intern" or "Debtor").

[82] *Id.* at 66, note 1.

[83] *Id.* at 66.

[84] *Id.* at 69.

Drexel Challenge

Executory Contract

Now that we have explored the Countryman definition of executory contract in §365, along comes the *Drexel* case[85] contending that "executory" should be eliminated from any such definition and suggesting a new procedure for the section. So powerful an effect was the Drexel case that it has won over an advocate in the *Walnut* case.[86] The Drexel court in commencing its opinion stated: "We rely heavily on the careful scholarship of the above-quoted law school professors . . .[87] and abandon the traditional focus on the 'executoriness' of contracts in bankruptcy in favor of a more practical, functional approach, which we believe is faithful to the historical purposes that gave birth to the 'assume-or-reject' election now codified at §11 U.S.C. §365 . . . of the Bankruptcy Code." Several other cases are then analyzed, leading us to our "observation" relative to the Countryman definition.

We turn now to the background of the case. Drexel and DBL were core companies of a number of related business entities that transacted a worldwide business in securities, commodities, and other financial products. During the 1980s the Drexel empire was subject to a series of massive investigations by the SEC arising from allegations of insider trading.

Guilty pleas to felony charges by Debtor and DBL resulted in a consent agreement with the SEC under which a Final Judgment was entered in the SEC's suit. Among other conditions of the Final Judgment, Drexel and DBL continued operations upon compliance with an extensive set of internal

---

[85] *In re* Drexel Burnham Lambert Group, Inc., ("Drexel" or "Debtor"), 138 BR 687 (B. SDNY 1992); and its subsidiary, Drexel Burnham Lambert, Inc. ("DBL").

[86] *In re* Walnut Associates ("Walnut" or "Debtor"), 145 BR 489 (B. ED. Pa. 1992).

[87] Drexel, 138 BR at 690 citing Andrew, *Executory Contracts Revisited: A Reply to Professor Westbrook,* 62 U. COLO. L. REV. 1, 1 (1991) and *id.* citing Westbrook, *A Functional Analysis of Executory Contracts,* 74 MINN. L. REV. 227, 228 (1989). *See also, id.* at 696 Andrew, *Executory Contracts in Bankruptcy: Understanding 'Rejection,'* 59 U. COLO. L. REV. 845, 884 (1988).

reforms. One paragraph provided for the employment of individuals acceptable to the SEC in the positions of general counsel and director of compliance. Among their duties were "the authority to cancel or revoke securities transactions executed or effected by other Drexel or (Debtor) personnel."[88] *Saul Cohen, Esq.* ("Cohen") was recommended by the SEC as General Counsel, Chief Legal Officer and Corporate Secretary for Drexel and its wholly-owned subsidiary, DBL.

In compliance with the Final Judgment, Cohen was approved to the position and two documents were signed, an Employment Agreement among Cohen, Debtor and DBL, and an Escrow Agreement for bond portfolios being held for Cohen. Cohen's employment commenced on April 17, 1989, and was to have been for a period of four years. However, in the months thereafter business shrank and Debtor filed a chapter 11 petition on February 13, 1990. Its far flung financial empire had now narrowed to Drexel's developing a plan of reorganization.

Claims for Discharge of Employment

On or about April 25, 1990, Cohen was advised by the president who had executed both agreements on behalf of the Debtor, that he "would be terminated as of May 12, 1990, because, with the change in the nature of Drexel's operations, Cohen was no longer needed to perform the functions contemplated by the Employment Agreement."[89] Cohen's employment with the Debtors did in fact terminate as of May 12, 1990, one year and 25 days after he began work, and 83 days after Debtor filed its petition. Cohen thereafter filed proofs of claim against the Debtor for the "unpaid portion of the total compensation due him over the course of the four-year contract"[90] and an immediate turnover of portfolios held under the Escrow Agreement.

The various elements of the compensation package in the Employment Agreement totaled $8 million payable over the four years. The component parts consisted of a $1 million

---

[88] *Id.* at 691.
[89] *Id.*
[90] *Id.*

bonus payable upon execution and delivery of the Employment Agreement and paid; and payment of a base salary of $250,000 per year over the four-year contract of which payment was made for the first year and a prorated portion for the second year's salary. Payment was also sought of the $732,734.83 balance due for the two years and 11 months remaining under the contract and an annual $1 million bonus payable upon the conclusion of each year Cohen worked. Payment was received for the first year and was sought for each remaining year. In addition to the monetary payments, there were four stock portfolios purchased by Cohen from the Debtor for $100 each, which when assembled by the Debtor, had a value of about $500,000 each at the time of purchase. These three remained in escrow, the fourth having been released to Cohen.[91]

Parties Legal Arguments

Another point that had to be considered was "[t]he language of the Employment Agreement that clearly disclosed that it was made with the prospect in full view that the Debtor might subsequently become insolvent or a debtor in bankruptcy. The language used by the parties also evidenced a clear intention that, if Cohen's employment was terminated as a result of bankruptcy or insolvency, he would be entitled to the Special Severance Payment," even if he, in such event, terminated his own employment.[92] This Severance Payment was defined in the Employment Agreement to include both Cohen's rights to the escrowed bond portfolios and a lump sum payment equal to the total cash.

Cohen timely filed proofs of claim against both Debtors in this proceeding since DBL[93] subsequently filed chapter 11 for itself and its subsidiaries.[94] Cohen then instituted a motion for

---

[91] *Id.* at 693.

[92] *Id.*

[93] *Id.* at 690. *See* case note 1 asserting subject matter jurisdiction under 28 USC §1334(b) as a core matter under §28 USC §§157(b)(2)(A) and (B). *See also, supra,* Chapter 10, this handbook, Jurisdiction.

[94] *Id. See* case note 3. "Cohen does not claim administrative expense status against DBL, because his employment was terminated prior to DBL's ... Chapter 11 filing, which makes his claim against DBL a plain-vanilla, prepetition claim."

summary judgment seeking in his complaint findings that: the termination of his employment entitled him to payment of $5,232,784.83 as an administrative priority claim under §503(b); immediate turnover of the three escrowed bond portfolios; and an order requiring Debtor to pay immediately his administrative claim under §503(a). Debtor responded with a motion for summary judgment to reject its contract with Cohen that strips Cohen of all his rights in the escrowed interests, and also sought to limit the amount of Cohen's claim to the cap provided by §502(b)(7).

The court, in examining the Employment Agreement, noted that it also provided that if "Debtor or DBL terminated Cohen's employment other than due to Disability or for Cause, then [Cohen] shall be entitled to receive, promptly following the date of such termination, all accrued but unpaid amounts of Base Salary and Annual Bonuses to the date of such termination, and [Debtor] shall pay to [Cohen] . . . the Special Severance Payment."[95] The parties agreed that Cohen's termination was not for cause, nor due to disability.

Delivery of the portfolios to Cohen was "governed solely by the Escrow Agreement. The Escrow Agent is directed by Article 3 of the Escrow Agreement to successively transfer one of the bond portfolios to Cohen on each anniversary of the Commencement Date while he was employed. . . . [I]n the event Cohen's employment was terminated by reason of death, disability, or under circumstances entitling him to receive the Special Severance Payment provided under the Employment Agreement, to transfer all remaining portfolios to Cohen and register them in his name."[96] The Escrow Agent had refused to deliver the remaining portfolios to Cohen, because of the Debtor's representation that to do so would be a violation of the automatic stay,[97] despite the fact that the Employment Agreement authorized the Escrow Agent to conclusively rely on Cohen's written statement that he was entitled to transfer the bonds notwithstanding written notice from the Debtor or DBL to the contrary.

---

[95] *Id.* at 692, 693.

[96] *Id.*

[97] *Id. See* §362. Automatic Stay. *See also supra* Chapter 6, this handbook, Automatic Stay.

Summary of Parties' Positions

The court's task was to determine the extent to which the parties prepetition intentions, as expressed in their written agreements, survived postpetition. Cohen's initial argument was that by terminating him postpetition, after accepting his services for a period of time, Debtor breached his Employment Agreement postpetition and therefore the balance of his salary constituted a postpetition administrative expense.[98] Debtor's response was a motion under §365(a) to reject the Employment Agreement. Simultaneously, the Debtor moved for summary judgment, asserting that Cohen's claims were not entitled to administrative expense status as a matter of law and partial summary judgment only as to the allowed amount of Cohen's claims.

Rejection of Countryman Definition

The arguments led the court to comment that a confusion existed in the area of executory contracts. In order to overcome this problem, the court referred to the writings of Professors Westbrook and Andrew. "Each of the two conflicting, variegated visions of the law nipped from the welter of cases which is composed of bits and pieces have focused on the 'executoriness' *vel non* of the particular executory contract at issue as the key to deciding whether it can be assumed or rejected under §365(a)."[99] Finding it "hardpressed to choose between them, based on the traditional analyses Courts have applied in the area of executory contracts,. . . [o]ur review of a large sample of the larger body of precedent persuades us that Prof. Westbrook is correct, arguing that 'the threshold requirement of 'executoriness' is not merely unnecessary but leads to error.'" The court then continued: "After grappling with the issues presented by the parties, we believe that we could, using existing 'executoriness' precedent, plausibly justify any number of results, from affording either party the complete relief it seeks, to deciding the case as we actually do.

---

[98] *Id.* at 693–94 note 8. *See* 11 USC §503(b).

[99] *Id.* at 696, citing Westbrook, 74 MINN. L. REV. at 287. *See also supra* note 86.

While 'executoriness' analysis can provide a reason for any result we might reach, we find it useless as a tool for reaching a reasoned result. Accordingly, we proceed by outlining the parties' arguments, describing the history and limitations of 'executoriness,' and then decide the matter on what we believe to be the appropriate bankruptcy principles."[100]

The court opined that the current, generally accepted test for executoriness was the material breach test articulated by Harvard Law School Professor Vern Countryman.[101] After much discussion of the Countryman definition and analyses of cases submitted by both parties as well as the "Historical Background of 'Executoriness,'" the court indicated that "[b]oth arguments illustrate how the 'very simple, uncontroversial principle' that gave rise to the assume-or-reject election in the first place has been lost in the last century of jousting between creditors and trustees over whether the obligations of particular contracts can be declined. The 'chronic uncertainty and constant litigation' that characterize the present state of the law of executory contracts, . . . result directly from a focus on 'executoriness' as a precondition to the election. Ironically, the present test for determining whether a contract can be assumed or rejected, the 'Countryman test,' was itself an attempt to cut through the confusion and turn to the basics."[102]

With the observation that the Countryman definition was only a step in history and that history must continue on its growth, the court opined: "Whether or not 'deemed rejection' is now a feature of reorganization cases, we believe that the plain language of §365[;] . . . when read, . . . changes in the structure of modern bankruptcy law . . . compels the conclusion that a rejected contract is actually breached . . . immediately preceding the bankruptcy filing. Accordingly, it is in this light that we determine Cohen's claim to the escrowed bonds."[103]

---

[100] *Id.*

[101] *Id.* at 696.

[102] *Id.* at 703.

[103] *Id.* at 707.

Escrow Agreement Valid
New York State Law

Resolving the issues of title to the portfolios and the claim for administrative expense payment for the employment funds, the court first analyzed the portfolios. "'Property interests are created and defined by state law.'[104] . . . Accordingly, we must look to New York law to determine the legal effect of the parties' respective interests in the escrowed portfolios."[105] Under New York law: "[F]or an escrow to be valid the delivery of the property must be irrevocable. . . ."[106] Second, [U]nder New York law legal title to property placed in escrow remains with the grantor until the occurrence of the condition specified in the escrow agreement. . . ." Moreover, the court continued: "Even legal title to escrow would not help the Debtor, however, because. . . the deposit of property placed in escrow 'creates in the grantee such an equitable interest in the property that upon full performance of the conditions according to the escrow agreement, title will vest at once in him.'"[107] Accordingly, the court held that all restrictions on the bonds were removed pursuant to the terms of the Employment Agreement and Cohen was entitled to immediate possession.

The court observed, however, that "[w]hether or not the transfer of the bond portfolios to Cohen is subject to one of the Code's avoiding powers has not been placed in issue.[108] In either case, however, the estate clearly benefits . . . because rejection 'constitutes a breach of such contract . . . immediately before the date of the filing of the petition.' §365(g). Thus, the $3,732,734.83 balance owed Cohen after the deduction of the value of the bond portfolios becomes a general unsecured claim

---

[104] *Id.* at 710 citing Butner v. United States, 99 S.Ct. 914, 918–919 (1979).

[105] *Id.*

[106] *Id.* citing *In re* O.P.M. Leasing Services, Inc., 46 BR 661, 667 (B. SDNY 1985).

[107] *In re* OPM Leasing Service, Inc., 46 BR 661, 667 quoting 28 AM. JUR. 2D, Escrow, §10 (1964).

[108] 138 BR at 711. *See also, infra,* Chapter 14, this handbook, Trustees Strong-Arm Powers; Chapter 15, this handbook, Preferences; and Chapter 16, this handbook, Fraudulent Transfers and Obligations.

that can be paid in 'tiny Bankruptcy dollars,' . . . instead of real United States dollars.[109] Accordingly, we grant the Debtor's motion to reject the contracts."

Assume-or-Reject Test

The court then continued: "Accordingly, we reject the Countryman test, and adopt instead an understanding of the 'assume-or-reject' election of §365 gleaned from the carefully reasoned articles of Professors Andrew and Westbrook."[110] After analyzing Professors Andrew's and Westbrook's analyses of "assume-or-reject," the court continued: "This understanding of the nature of the trustee's assume or reject option results in a simple four step analysis": (1) a determination by the trustee as to whether the contract gives the non-Debtor party an enforceable interest that has passed to the estate, such as Cohen's interest in the escrowed bonds; (2) trustee's consideration whether any such interest of the non-Debtor is avoidable under the Code's avoiding powers; (3) if there is no such interest or if it is avoidable, the trustee must determine whether the estate will benefit more from breach and payment of the dividend to creditors, or by performance; (4) finally, if the non-Debtor has a nonavoidable interest the trustee must determine whether the estate will benefit most from breach or performance.[111]

Prepetition Employment Subject to §502(b)(7) ("Cap")

Turning now to Cohen's claimed entitlement to be paid the Special Service Payment as an administrative expense despite the rejection of the contract, the court observed: "His argument teeters precariously on inapt analogy to unsound precedent, and ultimately depends for its success on our ruling that his contract is not executory, which we refuse to do."[112] After reviewing several cases presented by Cohen, the court

---

[109] *Id.* citing Westbrook 74 MINN. L. REV. at 253.

[110] *Id.* at 708 citing Professors Andrew and Westbrook.

[111] *Id.* at 709.

[112] *Id.*

analyzed distinctions as against the present case law or the facts.

"Finally, we address Cohen's claim that he is not subject to the claims' allowance cap of §502(b)(7): 'If . . . objection to a claim is made, the court . . . shall determine the amount of such claim . . . as of the date of the filing of the petition and shall allow such claim in such amount, except to the extent that—(7) if such claim is the claim of an employee for damages resulting from the termination of an employment contract, such claim exceeds—(A) the compensation provided by such contract, without acceleration, for one year. . . .'"[113]

Cohen's argument however, was that the claim was not for damages resulting from termination of an employment contract, but "payment of the Special Severance Payment. . . it was not his employment contract that was terminated, but his employment. . . The line Cohen attempts to draw between termination of employment and termination of an employment contract cannot be plausibly maintained. While §502(b)(7) does speak of 'termination of an employment contract,' §502(b)(7)(ii) indicates that it is the termination of employment that matters. By rejecting the contract, the Debtor has breached it. . . . The Debtor's motion for summary judgment as to this issue [is] granted."[114]

Court's Decision

Recapitulating its findings, the court granted Cohen's motion for summary judgment with respect to the bonds with a caveat: "This holding does not preclude Debtor from attacking Cohen's right to the bonds under the Code's avoiding powers.[115] Debtor's motion for summary judgment will be granted in the following respects: Its motion to reject the contract with Cohen is granted. Cohen's claim to administrative priority for Special Severance Payment will be disallowed, without prejudice to his right to file an amended proof of claim for (a) the reasonable value of any uncompensated services provided postpetition as an

---

[113] *Id.* at 713 citing 11 USC §502(b)(7).

[114] *Id.*

[115] *Id. See, supra,* note 107.

administrative expense, and (b) an unsecured claim for damages suffered as a result of the termination of his employment. The damages limitation cap of §502(b)(7) applies to his damage claim."[116]

Observation

All cases analyzing §365 agree that the Bankruptcy Code supplies no definition of an executory contract. Professor Countryman has supplied the void, which most courts have adopted. Yet we have only to turn several volumes of the Bankruptcy Reporter in the same year to meet the *Walnut Associates*[117] case, which follows in the footsteps of the *Drexel* case[118] by agreeing with its approval of Professors Andrew and Westbrook's law review articles as a basis for its holdings. Indeed, the *Walnut*[119] case went so far as to comment that the "matter considered herein presents an excellent vehicle to explain why this Court should no longer accept the assumption implicit in several of its previous decisions,[120] notably . . . that rejection of an executory contract necessarily voids or eliminates the underlying contract. Rather, we adopt the analysis presented in several recent law review articles and synthesized in *In re Drexel Burnham* . . . which concludes that rejection of an executory contract constitutes merely a refusal of a debtor's estate to assume a contract and accord administrative status to the claims of the non-debtor party to the contract."[121]

At about the same period of *Drexel* and *Walnut*, the Ninth Circuit Court of Appeals in the *Qintex*[122] case had for

---

[116] *Id.* at 714.

[117] *In re* Walnut Associates ("Walnut" or "Debtor") 145 BR 489 (B. ED. Pa. 1992).

[118] *In re* Drexel Burnham Lambert Group, Inc., 138 BR 687 (B. SDNY 1992) ("Drexel" or "Debtor").

[119] 145 BR 489.

[120] *Id.* at 491 citing *In re* W&L Associates, Inc., 71 BR 962 (B. ED. Pa. 1987).

[121] *Id.*

[122] *In re* Qintex Entertainment, Inc. ("Qintex"), 950 F2d 1492 (9th Cir. 1991).

consideration whether the district court erred in finding whether both or either of the two agreements with the debtor's licensors, Scott and Preminger, were executory contracts before the court would allow a sale of the assets covered by the agreements pursuant to §363(b)(1).[123] Qintex, without discussing the articles of either Professors Andrew or Westbrook or the opinion of Drexel arrives at several legal conclusions that are definitely contrary to those reached by Drexel Burnham: [1] "An executory contract does not become an asset of the estate until it is assumed pursuant to §365 of the Code...."[124] [2] Whether a contract is executory for a party in bankruptcy is a question of federal law...."[125] [3] Although the Code does not specifically define the term 'executory contract', the Supreme Court has defined it as a contract on which performance remains due to some extent on both sides...." The court then continued: "Thus, we will only consider a contract executory if material unperformed obligations remain for *both* parties." [4] Executory contracts contain "obligations of both parties that are so far unperformed that the failure of either party to complete performance would constitute a material breach and thus excuse performance of the other...." [5] Finally, the court stated: "We review applicable state law to help determine the status of a contract. State law controls both the question of breach and construction of a contract...."[126]

Observation

Does Countryman hold firmer ground than Drexel? The answer rests with Congressional legislation. In the meantime, the Countryman definition seems to be tumbling. One cannot overlook several current treatises that require consideration

---

[123] *Id.* at 1495. *See supra* Chapter 3, this handbook, Use, Sale, or Lease of Property.

[124] *Id.* at 1495 citing §365(a); *In re* Tleel, 876 F2d 769, 770 (9th Cir. 1989). ("Unless and until rights under an executory contract are timely and entirely assumed by the trustee, they do not become property of the estate.")

[125] *Id.* citing *In re* Wegner, 839 F2d 533, 536 (9th Cir. 1988).

[126] *Id.* at 1496–97 citing *In re* Aslan 909 F2d 367, 369 (9th Cir. 1990).

such as the ALI-ABA Conference.[127] "This report addresses executory contracts and focuses primarily on section 365. This is one of the few areas in the Bankruptcy Code in which the basic conception of the section has not always been well understood. More reworking is required here than in other places in the Code."[128] *See also*, Shanker, "A Proposed New Executory Contract Statute."[129] *See also* Mark E. Mac Donald, Esq., et al., "Chapter 11 As a Dynamic Evolutionary Learning Process In a Market with Fuzzy Values, Norton Annual Survey of Bankruptcy Law 1993–1994."

Not to be overlooked is S.540, Bankruptcy Reform Legislation introduced in the Senate in 1993 and containing among its provisions: (1) Section 204, Unexpired Leases of Personal Property In Chapter 11 Cases, consisting of three subdivisions; (2) Section 205, "Protection Of Assignees of Executory Contracts And Unexpired Leases Approved By Court Order In Cases Reversed On Appeal; and (3) Section 206, Protection of Security Interest in Post-Petition Rents." With all that we have observed, it may be possible that the Supreme Court or congressional amendments may resolve the conflicting problems raised among the cases and the law review articles. We await such development. Until such

---

[127] *See* "Bankruptcy Reform Circa 1993: A Presentation of the National Bankruptcy Conference's Bankruptcy Code Review Project," June 10–12, 1993, Atlanta, Ga.; "Executory Contracts," 179–204.

[128] *Id.* at 179.

Table of Contents

[129] Morris G. Shanker, John Homer Kapp, Professor of Law at Case Western Reserve University School of Law, article published in *Annual Survey of Bankruptcy Law* 1993–4.

development the courts of appeal of each circuit, will make their views followed.

From here we turn to three succeeding avoidance chapters designed to provide equality of distribution to all creditors and the estate.

Chapter 14
Trustee's Strong-Arm Powers

S ection 544 of the Code is best known by its synonym, the "strong-arm clause." The title indicates its powers: "Trustee as lien creditor and as successor to certain creditors and purchasers." The power of the section is in the creation of hypothetical powers, which are designed to avoid transfers of property that would be voidable by a simple creditor who is clothed under state law[1] as a creditor with the highest status such creditor could reach by litigation, *i.e.,* a judicial lien, an execution returned unsatisfied, a perfected lien on real property and a bona fide purchaser of real property. Such power is granted at the commencement of the case to a simple creditor. The section is designed to extend the

---

[1] *See* Uniform Commercial Code §9-301:37. Insolvency representative. The category of insolvency representatives embraces an assignee for benefit of creditors, from the date of assignment; a trustee in bankruptcy, from the date of filing of the petition; and a receiver in equity, from the time of appointment. These, in turn, are classified by the Code as "lien creditors."

recoveries set forth in our next two chapters "Preferences" and "Fraudulent Conveyances and Transfers." In addition, the trustee uses powers as a judicial lien creditor to assume a status in the principle of "Marshaling of Assets."

Background Adversary Proceeding

The *Mc Elwaney*[2] case brings us to an exploration of §544. On February 3, 1983, a chapter 7 petition was filed by the Debtor and shortly thereafter the *Federal Land Bank*[3] instituted an adversary proceeding to determine the validity, priority, or extent of its lien. The complaint requested that the Bank be allowed to apply Debtor's stock in the Bank against the Bank's claim. The other defendants were the trustee in bankruptcy and the Farmers Home Administration of the U.S. Department of Agriculture ("FmHA"). On October 24, 1983, the FmHA filed a cross claim against the trustee, and thereafter the parties filed a stipulation of facts and the FmHA and the Bank both moved for summary judgment.

The findings of fact indicated that on October 4, 1977, the Debtor purchased approximately 475 acres of farmland in Putnam County, Georgia,[4] assuming an obligation with the Bank that was secured by a first lien on the farmland which, at the time of the adversary proceeding, was worth more than the debt owed to the Bank. In assuming the obligation, the Debtor was required to purchase stock in the Bank that was valued at $11,780. The parties stipulated that the Bank had a lien on the stock and the FmHA had no lien. The Putnam County farmland, however, was encumbered by a second lien in favor of the FmHA, and it was undisputed that the Bank's claim was fully secured and the FmHA's claim was only partially secured.

---

[2] *In re* Mc Aloin ("Debtor"), 40 BR 66 (B. MD. Ga. 1984).

[3] Federal Land Bank of Columbia ("Bank").

[4] *See supra*, note 1. Most states, including Georgia, have adopted UCC §9-301:37.

Issue Presented
Abandonment of Property

The issue presented to the court was whether the Bank's stock issued to the Debtor could be first applied by the Bank against its claim, even though the claim was fully secured by the farmland. The Bank argued that the court should order the Bank's stock abandoned[5] as burdensome or of inconsequential value, so that the Bank could dispose of the stock and use the proceeds to reduce the Bank's claim. The FmHA concurred in the Bank's request to first apply the Bank's stock against its claim. The trustee, however, argued that should the Bank satisfy its claim solely from the farmland, that the FmHA then would be entitled to the remaining proceeds from the farmland, and that the trustee would be entitled to the stock for the benefit of Debtor's unsecured creditors.

The court, in analyzing the Farm Credit Act,[6] found that a Federal Land Bank issuing shares under §2034(a) "shall have a first lien on the stock."[7] The court, after reviewing several cases, held that the Bank had "a right to apply the stock to reduce Debtor's debt with it and even may be under a duty to do so if it is in the best interests of Debtor's other creditors."[8] Although the Bank consented to first apply the stock in question to reduce its claim, the Trustee argued that the court should marshal assets so that the Bank must satisfy its claim in full from the farmland.

Requirements for Marshaling

The court then opined that the objective of marshaling was to prevent a creditor who had two funds from which to satisfy its debt from not defeating the claim of another creditor who could resort only to one of those funds.[9] The court opined that

---

[5] *See* 11 USC §554(b): "On request of a party in interest and after notice and a hearing, the court may order the trustee to abandon any property of the estate that is burdensome to the estate or that is of inconsequential value and benefit to the estate."

[6] The Farm Credit Act of 1971, 12 USC §2034 (1984).

[7] *See* Mc Aloin, 40 BR at 68.

[8] *Id.* at 69.

[9] *Id.* citing Meyer v. United States, 84 S.Ct. 318, 320 (1963).

since marshaling is an equitable remedy, three elements must be satisfied. The court then cited the requirements set forth in *United States v. Friend*:[10]

> (1) The existence of two creditors with a common Debtor; (2) the existence of two funds belonging to the Debtor; (3) the legal right of one creditor to satisfy his demand from either or both of the funds, while the other may resort to only one fund.

The court continued: "In this adversary proceeding,[11] the Trustee seeks to invoke the doctrine of marshaling on the ground that he is a lien creditor of Debtor under §544 (the "strong-arm" provision) of the Bankruptcy Code. . . ."[12]

Trustee's Power as Lien Creditor

After setting forth the contents of §544, the court opined that the strong-arm provision was directed to protect general unsecured creditors against secret unperfected liens,[13] otherwise the Bankruptcy Code did not vest the trustee with better rights than belonged to the Debtor.[14] Although in the instant case there were no secret liens, nonetheless, the trustee was attempting to use his status as a lien creditor under §544 to compel the marshaling of assets for the benefit of Debtor's unsecured creditors and to the detriment of a perfected junior secured creditor of Debtor, the FmHA.[15]

---

[10] *Id.* citing *In re* A.E.I. Corp. 11 BR 97 (B. ED. Pa.) (1981). *See also In re* The Computer Room, Inc., 24 BR 732 (B. ND. Ala. 1982).

[11] *Id. See* Adversary Proceedings. B.Rule 7003. Commencement of Adversary Proceeding and B.Rule 7004. Process Service of Summons, Complaint.

[12] *Id.*

[13] *Id.* at 70 citing *In re* Weiman, 22 BR 49 (B. 9th Cir. 1982).

[14] *Id.* citing *In re* Forester, 529 F2d 310 (9th Cir. 1976).

[15] *Id. See In re* Spectra Prism Industries, Inc., 28 BR 397, 400 (B. AP. Cal. 1983) (Volinn, B.J., dissenting).

Equitable Doctrine Applicable to §544

The court cited *Meyer v. United States*,[16] a Supreme Court decision often cited by the courts: "Marshaling is an equitable doctrine, and it should not be applied to frustrate the policies of the Bankruptcy Code."[17] Thus, outside bankruptcy, secured creditors hold a position superior to unsecured creditors and in a chapter 7 case have the same standard, and are entitled to a return of their collateral or through distribution receive the value of their collateral. If marshaling were allowed, the Trustee would recover the stock for Debtor's unsecured creditors and Bank would be paid its secured claim in full from the proceeds of the farmland, but the *FmHA* would not receive as much as it would if the Bank first looked to the stock to reduce its claim. The trustee therefore, sought to use marshaling to benefit unsecured creditors at the expense of the FmHA, a junior secured creditor of Debtor.

Strong-Arm
Effect of Date of Filing Petition

The court referred to the history of marshaling by citing the Supreme Court case of *Lewis v. Manufacturers*.[18] In that case, the Court held that "under section 70c of the Bankruptcy Act, the former strong-arm provision, the rights of the hypothetical lien creditor were to be determined at the time of the bankruptcy filing rather than at an earlier date. To hold otherwise, said the Court, would enrich unsecured creditors at the expense of secured creditors, creating a windfall merely by the happenstance of bankruptcy."[19]

Trustee's Lien Under §544

Several cases were then analyzed by the court to sustain the position that a trustee's lien under §544 did not supersede

---

[16] 84 S.Ct. 318 (1963).

[17] *Id.* at 70.

[18] *Id. See* Lewis v. Manufacturers National Bank 81 S.Ct. 347 (1961).

[19] *Id.* citing 81 S.Ct. at 350.

that of a secured creditor's priority. In *Caplinger*, "the Eighth Circuit held that section 70c of the Bankruptcy Act granted the trustee a lien on all property of the bankrupt, but the court also noted that Caplinger had no lien on personal property due to his failure to perfect it.[20] However, the court concluded that the trustee could not require the marshaling of assets to deprive Caplinger of his interest in the real estate. The court observed that. . . '[N]o cases have been called to our attention or found which would support giving the bankruptcy Trustee's lien, based upon the strong-arm and voidable preference provisions of the Bankruptcy Act, a superior equitable position over Caplinger's valid preexisting lien on the real estate under the circumstances of this case, . . .'"[21]

Trustee Cites Jack Green's

Having discussed cases that supported the Bank's and FmHA's position, the court then considered cases that supported the trustee. In *Jack Green*'s case[22] the court held that since the unsecured creditors of a corporate bankrupt would receive no dividend if the bank were allowed to exhaust the business assets of the corporation without first looking to the real estate pledged by the shareholders of the corporation, the trustee was entitled to have the assets marshaled so that the bank must proceed against the real estate first.[23] "In Jack

---

[20] *Id.* at 71 citing Caplinger v. Patty, 398 F2d 471 (8th Cir. 1968).

[21] *Id.* citing 398 F2d at 476.

[22] Berman v. Green (*In re* Jack Green's Fashions for Men-Big & Tall, Inc.), 597 F2d 130 (8th Cir. 1979) ("Jack Green's").

[23] 40 BR at 71. *See* note 10: "Most courts have held that marshaling would be denied in the Berman situation because to marshal assets, the two funds must belong to a common debtor and, unless the corporate veil is pierced, the corporate assets and personal assets are separately and distinguishably owned. *In re* Harrold's Hatchery and Poultry Farms, Inc., 17 B.R. 712, (B. MD.Ga. 1982); *In re* A.E.I. Corp., 11 BR 97, (B. ED. Pa. 1981); Farmers & Merchants Bank v. Gibson, 7 BR 437 (B. ND. Fla. 1980)." The decision in Berman was criticized by several courts. *See In re* The Computer Room, Inc., 24 BR 732 (B. ND. Ala. 1982); *In re* United Medical Research, Inc., 12 BR 941 (B. CD. Cal. 1981).

Green's, however, it was unclear whether the marshaling by the trustee would harm a secured creditor."[24]

"Also in Spectra Prism,[25] the appellate panel held that a trustee is given the status of a lien creditor to protect assets and that, as such lien creditor, the Trustee has standing to block the marshaling of assets. . . ." In the *Spectra Prism* case, Judge Volinn dissented and argued that the trustee should not be benefitted by the marshaling doctrine.

Rejecting Jack Green's and Spectra Prism

"To the extent that *Berman* [Jack Green's] and *Spectra Prism* suggest that the Trustee can employ the marshaling doctrine to his benefit and to the detriment of a junior secured creditor, the court is persuaded that the cases holding to the contrary are the better reasoned. . . . [T]he Trustee's request for marshaling must be denied."[26]

Since the court found that there was no genuine issue of material fact and the FmHA and the Bank having demonstrated that they were entitled to judgment as a matter of law, the court granted their motions for summary judgment. The court thereupon ordered the Federal Land Bank's stock abandoned so that the Federal Land Bank could apply the stock against its claim.[27]

San Jacinto
Rejecting Jack Green's

Since *Jack Green's* case has been the subject of much diversity and is the keystone of the establishment of the "two fund" principle in marshaling of assets, we consider first the opinion of the Eighth Circuit in *Jack Green's*[28] and then both

---

[24] *Id.* at 72. (*See infra,* this chapter, subtitle "San Jacinto Rejecting Jack Green's Case," leaving no doubt that the secured creditor was harmed.)

[25] 28 BR 397 (B. 9th Cir. 1983).

[26] *Id.*

[27] *See* §554. Abandonment of property of the estate.

[28] 597 F2d 130 (8th Cir. 1979).

sides of marshaling of assets by the trustee in the *San Jacinto* case.[29]

The Eighth Circuit had for consideration appeals by a corporate bankrupt and John F.B. Green and John F. Green,[30] controlling stockholders, who were individual bankrupts. The district court had upheld an order allowing the marshaling of assets in the bankruptcy litigation. At the time of the bankruptcies in 1977, the bank,[31] a secured creditor, held a lien on the business assets of the corporation and an additional lien on three parcels of real estate, which were owned by Messrs. Green and their respective wives.

Trustee Seeks Marshaling of Assets

After discussing the previous business activities of the Greens, which ultimately led to bankruptcy, the court of appeals observed that voluntary petitions in bankruptcy were filed by the corporations and Messrs. Green. Adjudication[32] of the parties as bankrupts followed. A trustee was appointed of all three of the bankrupt estates and he liquidated the business assets of the corporation, which realized $28,000. The balance due the Bank at that time was $65,000, and the value of the real estate subject to the lien of the Bank was about $135,000. The court stated: "The Bank filed a secured claim for the amount of its debt, and it is obvious that if that claim is satisfied in part out of the assets of the corporate bankrupt, the general creditors of the corporation will get nothing."[33] The trustee, therefore, filed an application with the bankruptcy court for an order requiring a marshaling of assets that would require the Bank to proceed against the parcels of real estate before proceeding against the business assets of the corporation.

The application was opposed by the Greens and their wives, but not the Bank. The bankruptcy judge granted the

---

[29] *See infra,* this chapter, subtitle "San Jacinto." *In re* San Jacinto Glass Industries, Inc., 93 BR 934 (B. SD Tex. 1988).

[30] 597 F2d at 132 (collectively, the "Greens").

[31] Centenial Bank & Trust of Mission, Kansas ("Bank").

[32] *See* Chapter 7 of the Code: Liquidation, and Subchapter I: Officers and Administration.

[33] 597 F2d 132.

petition and dismissed the claim of the Bank and directed that the Bank proceed against the real estate, but without prejudice to renewal "should the Bank be unable to obtain satisfaction of its claim from its real estate security."[34] The Greens, husbands and wives, appealed to the district judge who sustained the holding of the bankruptcy judge. All four Greens then appealed to the circuit court; the Bank did not appeal.[35]

Agreeing with the bankruptcy court that the debt to the Bank was contracted as a debt of an old partnership, which was succeeded by the corporation, the court held that "it became a corporate debt when the corporation was formed and assumed the debts of the partnership."[36] The bankruptcy judge and the district court had ordered marshaling "by reference to general principles of equity." The court of appeals defined the effect of marshaling as follows:

> If a senior lienor has a lien that extends to and covers two funds or potential funds, and if a junior lienor has recourse to only one of those funds to satisfy the debt due to him, the senior lienor may be required to exhaust the fund available to him exclusively before proceeding against the fund that is also available to the junior lienor.[37]

Bankruptcy Court
Court of Equity

The court then proceeded to state that "Federal courts of bankruptcy are courts of equity and may apply the doctrine of marshaling in proper cases. . . ."[38] In this case it would be in the highest degree inequitable to allow the Bank to exhaust the business assets of the corporate bankrupt without first looking

---

[34] *Id.*

[35] *Id.*

[36] *Id.*

[37] *Id.* citing Meyer v. United States (or "Meyer"), 84 S.Ct. 318 (1963).

[38] *Id.* at 133, citing Caplinger v. Patty, 398 F2d 471, 474 (8th Cir. 1968) and cases cited. *See supra,* subtitle "Trustee's Lien Under §544."

to the real estate mortgaged to it. To permit such a course would leave the general creditors of the business with nothing."[39] In addition, the court noted that appellants cited "the Supreme Court in 'Meyer', supra, that assets are not available in a marshaling process if they are exempt under state law from seizure in satisfaction of the senior creditor's claim. And appellants rely on the Missouri rule of law that a creditor holding a lien on real estate owned by a husband as tenants by the entirety cannot foreclose his lien if one of the spouses has obtained a discharge in bankruptcy even though both of the spouses may have been parties to the obligation. . . ."[40]

The court of appeals rejected the argument noting that as yet none of the bankrupts had obtained discharges of their personal obligations[41] and it was doubtful that the Missouri rule had any application to the case, at least as of the time of the decision. "In any event under the order of the district court, the Greens may advance the contention in question in any foreclosure proceedings commenced by the Bank in the courts, and if the contention is upheld by those courts, the Bank will still have recourse to the funds presently in the hands of the trustee. The order of the district court is affirmed."[42]

---

[39] 597 F2d at 133.

[40] *Id.* citing Farmington Prod. Credit Assn. v. Estes, 504 SW2d 149 (Mo. App. 1974).

[41] *Id.* at 133. *See* §727. Discharge; subsection (b): ". . . [A] discharge under subsection (a) of this section discharges the Debtor from all debts that arose before the date of the order for relief under this chapter, . . ." *See also,* B. Rule 4004. Grant or Denial of Discharge.

[42] *Id.*

San Jacinto Marshaling
Rights of Secured Creditors

We turn now to the *San Jacinto* case[43] where the court had for consideration a motion by the Debtor to sell personal property pursuant to §363.[44] A discussion of the case finds itself in this chapter in lieu of Chapter 3, this handbook, "Use, Sale, or Lease of Property," because of an interesting discussion on marshaling of property. The *Jack Green's* case also comes in for discussion and dwells heavily on the doubt left with the *McElwaney* Court,[45] i.e., harm to the guarantor as a secured creditor. Indeed, we could have joined this section with Chapter 18, this handbook, "Confirmation of Consensual Plan," since we discuss a sale that the trustee also argued in essence constituted a consent "to plan," before the proper procedure for confirmation had taken place.[46]

Involuntary Petition
Chapter 11 Liquidation

San Jacinto was a chapter 11 Debtor by virtue of an involuntary chapter 7 petition filed on June 30, 1988, and a conversion to chapter 11 on August 1, 1988.[47] Prior to filing of the involuntary, the Debtor had entered into security agreements with First City National Bank of Houston ("First City") and Westinghouse Credit Corporation ("WCC"). As security for the note, First City was given a priority interest in Debtor's accounts, chattel paper, instruments, general intangibles, and current and after acquired inventory. Its proof

---

[43] *In re* San Jacinto Glass Industries, Inc. ("San Jacinto" or "Debtor"), 93 BR 934 (B. SD. Tex. 1988).

[44] *See* §363(b)(1). "The trustee, after notice and a hearing, may use, sell, or lease, other than in the ordinary course of business, property of the estate." *See also supra* Chapter 3, this handbook, subtitle "Sale of Property Not In Ordinary Course [Of Business]."

[45] *See supra* subtitle "Trustee Cites Jack Green's."

[46] *See infra* Chapter 18, this handbook, Confirmation of Consensual Plan.

[47] *See supra* Chapter 5, this handbook, Involuntary Petition.

of claim showed a balance of $661,024, which First City stipulated was less than fully secured.

As for WCC, it made two purchase money loans to Debtor to finance the acquisition of certain specified production line equipment. WCC had a senior preferred security interest in this equipment that secured a deficiency of $217,695, and in another transaction Debtor guaranteed a loan by WCC to a sister company on which there was a balance due of $7,128. The three debts were later cross-collateralized.[48] "Additionally to secure payment of its purchase money loans, WCC required Debtor to obtain an irrevocable standby letter of credit for $100,000. By its terms, the letter of credit could be drawn on by WCC if WCC presented proof of Debtor's default on loan repayments."[49]

The letter of credit was personally guaranteed by Debtor's chairman of the board and his wife ("Galtneys"). The issuer of the letter of credit, Allied Bank, received as security from the Galtneys municipal bond units worth $100,000. WCC had not drawn on the letter of credit even though the Debtor had not made a loan payment since April 1988, over two months since the involuntary petition had been filed.

First City's Request for Marshaling

Since the filing of the petition, Debtor had sought and obtained court approval to sell substantial portions of its assets on three different occasions. The second and third sales consisted exclusively of equipment subject to WCC's purchase money security interest. However, only the proceeds of the second sale were paid to WCC without dispute. While it was without question that WCC had a priority claim to the $214,000 in proceeds from the third sale, First City requested that the court "order a marshaling of assets to compel WCC to proceed first against the letter of credit to satisfy its claim. The proceeds of the equipment sale would then be used only to the extent needed to cover any remaining deficiency owed to WCC. If WCC were to proceed in this manner, approximately $90,000

---

[48] *Id.* at 936. *See* note 2. *See also supra* Chapter 2, this handbook, Lender's Participation subtitle "Cross-Collateralization."

[49] 93 BR at 936.

would be made available to unsecured creditors," which would include First City to the extent its claim was undersecured.[50]

History of Marshaling

Needless to say, examining the principles of law underlying the historical growth of marshaling is extremely helpful to its understanding: "Marshaling of assets originated as a common law doctrine and enjoys continued vitality in state and federal case law. The doctrine is founded in equity, . . ."[51] As in the *McElwaney* case, it approves the equitable procedure that in fairness to the junior lienor, the senior should satisfy its claim from assets not encumbered by the junior. By exercising such choice there are more funds available for distribution to other creditors of the common debtor. In addition, the court cites the three traditional threshold requirements of marshaling: "(1) the contesting claimants both have secured claims against a common debtor; (2) the assets or funds subject to marshaling belong *solely* to the common debtor; and (3) one of the lienholders, alone, has the right to resort to more than one fund or asset of the debtor."[52]

In *San Jacinto*, First City, the party invoking the marshaling doctrine, was an undersecured creditor of the Debtor with outstanding claims totaling $661,024. However, in regard to the equipment, First City was an unsecured creditor due to WCC's priority position as purchase money security interest holder. "Both parties have stipulated to the validity and seniority of WCC's lien. In addition, First City does not claim and does not hold any enforceable interest in the letter of credit, or in any other collateral of Debtor to which WCC may look for satisfaction of its claim. First City, then,

---

[50] *Id.* at 936.

[51] *Id.* at 937, citing 28 USC §1481 added by Pub.L. 95-598. *See, e.g., In re* Dealer Support Services International, Inc., 73 BR 763, 764 (B. ED. Mich. 1987): "Traditionally, the equitable doctrine of marshaling has been used by secured creditors, but has not been available to unsecured creditors. 'The Edith' 94 U.S. [4 Otto] 518 (1877); *In re* Francis Construction Co., 54 BR 13, 14 (B. DSC 1985)."

[52] *Id.*

holds unsecured status with regard to all assets which might be the subject of a marshaling order against WCC."[53]

Status of Letter of Credit

The court first discussed the status of the letter of credit holding that it was "well established that [neither] credit extended by a third party on behalf of a debtor via a letter of credit nor the proceeds distributed pursuant to a letter of credit, are considered property of the bankruptcy estate."[54] "This view, however, does not hold for the party who is entitled to receive payment via a letter of credit. Such right to payment is deemed the property of the beneficiary, even if not exercised until after bankruptcy. . . ."[55] The facts of this case indicate that WCC is entitled to draw on the letter of credit as the beneficiary of the contract made between the issuer, Allied Bank, and the Debtor. . . . While WCC's reliance on the letter of credit might be viewed as contingent, WCC nonetheless, holds an undisputed legal right to receive payment from the letter of credit. Therefore, the letter of credit and its proceeds are to be considered the property of WCC, and not that of the Debtor."[56]

"The hallmark of the marshaling doctrine is contained in the requirement that one creditor alone have access to more than one of the Debtor's assets in order to realize its claim. In equity, the paramount creditor's power to make discretionary choices regarding sources of repayment should be tempered but only to the extent necessary to insure that other deserving creditors be spared needless adverse effects. . . ."[57] No equitable remedy can encumber the paramount creditor, or otherwise jeopardize his right to fully realize his claims."[58]

---

[53] *Id.*

[54] *Id.* citing *In re* Compton Corp., 831 F2d 586, 589 (5th Cir. 1987).

[55] *Id.* citing *In re* Swift Aire Lines, Inc., 20 BR 286, 288 (B. CD. Cal. 1982), *rev'd* 30 BR 490 (BAP 9th Cir. 1983).

[56] *Id.*

[57] *Id.* at 938, citing Meyer v. United States, 84 S.Ct. at 321.

[58] *Id.* citing 2 J. Story, COMMENTARIES ON EQUITY JURISPRUDENCE §869 at 247 (14th ed. 1918). *See also In re* Computer Room, Inc., 24 BR 732, 736 (B. ND. Ala. WD 1982).

The court observed that it had already been shown that WCC had the right to draw against the letter of credit if it chose to do so. The payment was not deemed one in violation of the automatic stay. There were no legal impediments, such as fraud. With respect to the equipment encumbered by WCC's purchase money security interest, all monies resulting from the sale of such equipment were being held in escrow. As to WCC demanding access to these funds, the court stated that it need only obtain court authorization based on a favorable disposition of the chapter 11. However, as to First City, an unsecured creditor, it did not have access to either fund, which was the subject of its marshaling request.

Unsecured Creditor Seeks Marshaling

First City argued that its unsecured status and the fact that one of the funds is not property of the Debtor should not prevent marshaling. In support of its position, First City relied upon *Jack Green's* case[59] "and the line of cases following this controversial Eighth Circuit decision. WCC contests application of this line of cases, noting that other circuits and commentators have severely criticized the extension of such equitable remedy to unsecured creditors."[60] The court's response was that: "bankruptcy courts have broad equitable powers. . . .[61] However, equitable remedies such as marshaling should be administered with temperance to prevent established commercial standards from being undermined in the process. . . .[62] So while the marshaling doctrine should be invoked to effect an equitable result, it should, to the extent possible, uphold the rights and duties that parties contract for when undertaking business transactions."[63]

---

[59] *See supra* this chapter, *McElwaney* case subtitle "Trustee Cites Jack Green's."

[60] 93 BR at 938.

[61] *Id. See supra* note 47.

[62] *Id.* citing *In re* Samuels & Co., Inc., 526 F2d 1238 (5th Cir. 1976), *cert. denied sub nom* Stowers v. Mahon, 97 S.Ct. 98 (1976).

[63] *Id.*

Application on Jack Green's Hypothetical Lien Creditor: §544(a)

The court noted that traditional requirements for marshaling have been strictly construed. However, "in light of the new, broadened applications of the doctrine, a study of commercial and bankruptcy ramifications is in order to test the strictness of the marshaling requirements and their suitability to this case."

"The marshaling elements that the Jack Green's line of cases tries to soften are (1) the lack of standing of an unsecured creditor, and (2) the property-of-the-estate requirement. The courts have found a means to 'end-run' these requirements in the name of equity. To satisfy the standing issue, courts have granted to the bankruptcy trustee (or the debtor in possession) the status of a hypothetical judgment lien creditor as defined in 11 U.S.C. §544(a).[64] As for the property requirement, courts have sought a means to either reclassify a particular fund or asset as that of the bankruptcy Debtor (the 'two fund' theory) or alternatively, to view the actions of a Debtor's guarantor in such a way as to characterize the guarantor as an alter-ego of that Debtor, i.e., piercing the corporate veil (the 'common Debtor' theory)."[65]

Reliance Theory

Following the precedent established by Jack Green's, the court in the *Gibson* case[66] "attempted an exceptional application of marshaling by using §544(a) to grant standing to the trustee and using 'a reliance theory' so as to deem the proceeds of a guaranteed loan a capital contribution to the debtor's estate. In that case, a working capital loan was personally guaranteed by the debtor corporation's president

---

[64] *Id.* at 939. *See* this chapter, note 1. *See* House and Senate Reports (Reform Act of 1978) following Section 544 (trustee has rights of a creditor on a simple contract with judicial lien on debtor's property or a creditor with an unsatisfied writ of execution, as of petition date).

[65] *Id.* at 938–39.

[66] Farmers and Merchants Bank v. Gibson ("Gibson"), 7 BR 437 (B. ND. Fla. 1980).

and principal stockholder and also by his spouse. Security for the loan included real and personal assets of the guarantors and a second mortgage on their personal residence. A loan note covering the guarantee was co-signed by the corporation and the individuals. . . ."[67]

Loan Guarantee
Contribution to Capital

The *Gibson* court acknowledged sound reasoning for otherwise upholding the three traditional marshaling requirements. Nonetheless, the court observed that the "working capital loan could have induced suppliers and service providers to extend credit to the debtor. In that light, the loan guarantee could be construed as a "'contribution' to capital. Accordingly, the general creditors were to be given greater equitable considerations than the loan guarantors would enjoy and marshaling was ordered. The court chose to marshal by directing the creditor—bank to proceed first against the guarantor's assets. The trustee was then subrogated to the bank's right to any surplus from these liquidations. . . ."[68]

After appeals to the district court that remanded the case, the bankruptcy court found no material error in its previous findings and therefore reasserted that "marshaling was not applicable to the exempted property in the case." In essence, the bankruptcy court didn't need to reach the marshaling issue in this case. "However, the reasoning of the case makes clear that the court would entertain a possible exception to the common debtor requirement under a contribution to capital theory. . . ."[69]

Inequitable Conduct of Guarantors

The San Jacinto Court distinguished two cases that reached opposite results in having guarantors considered as

---

[67] 93 BR at 939.

[68] *Id.*

[69] *Id.* at 940 citing Gibson v. Farmers and Merchants Bank, 81 BR 84, 87 (ND. Fla. 1986).

common Debtors. In *Tampa Chain*,[70] the trustee succeeded in obtaining common Debtor status applied to shareholder guarantors. The court found that "the creditor-bank loaned working capital funds in large part on the strength of the guarantee which was collateralized with the personal assets of the guarantors."[71] The court in the *Tampa Chain* case also found inequitable conduct used by the guarantors through both their receipt of a significant portion of the corporate borrowings and their use of corporate funds to pay for expenses of a personal nature. This inequitable conduct along with lenders' reliance on the guarantor's collateral, against that of the corporation, supported the court's finding of "two fund" and "common Debtor" theories.

Turning now to the *Multiple Services*[72] case, the San Jacinto Court reviewed another guarantor dressed in the mantle of a "common Debtor." The Multiple Services Court ordered a creditor bank to marshal assets and to look first to the guarantors on a corporate debt before claiming the assets of the corporation. "The guarantor, an officer and shareholder of the Debtor, had secured his guarantee with a second mortgage on his personal residence."[73] The court ordered marshaling on the request of the trustee "under a contribution to capital theory, even though there was no other mitigating evidence with which to support a common Debtor exception."[74] Furthermore, the court gave little thought to the fact that the Bank "was having to suffer the extra expense, delay and risk of foreclosing and paying off the first mortgage on the residence rather than proceeding directly against the Debtor's assets. The court noted plainly that marshaling will not always be denied because there is a delay in enforcing one's rights as a secured creditor."[75]

---

[70] *In re* Tampa Chain Company, Inc., 53 BR 772 (B. SDNY 1985).

[71] 93 BR at 940.

[72] *In re* Multiple Services Industries, Inc., 18 BR 635 (B. ED. Wis. 1982).

[73] 93 BR at 940.

[74] *Id.*

[75] *Id.*

Common Debtor
Guarantor's Position

In its "Discussion," the San Jacinto Court alluded to the cases it analyzed, and agreed "in principle with the notion that bankruptcy courts should allow marshaling even when, at times, strict adherence to the common Debtor requirement has not been met. . . ."[76] What seems to be lacking from the above decisions, however, is a set of standards by which courts and those privy to commercial transactions may test guarantor behavior for primary liability under a marshaling order. As [another] commentator has noted, the obligation to which the guarantor submits is the contingent claim of the secured creditor with whom he contracts. . . ."[77] In other words, if a creditor has a right to resort to two persons who are its Debtors jointly and severally, the creditor is not "compellable to yield up his remedy against either, since he has a right to stand upon the letter and spirit of his contract *unless some supervening equity changes or modifies his rights.*"[78]

Referring to the *United*[79] case, the bankruptcy court commented: "The concern for non-justified interference with the regularity of commercial transactions was aptly described in [United] . . . where the court refused to allow marshaling of a guarantor's assets without a strong showing of inequitable conduct with which to justify piercing the corporate veil."

> It is poor policy for courts to upset legitimate business transactions because of some vague concept of equity. We tend to forget that these decisions affect future commercial transactions.[80]

---

[76] *Id.*

[77] *Id.* at 941. *See* Lachman, *Marshaling Assets in Bankruptcy: Recent Innovations in the Doctrine,* 6 CARDOZO L. REV. 671, 677 (1985).

[78] *Id.* citing 2. J. Story, COMMENTARIES ON EQUITY JURISPRUDENCE §866 at 245 (14th ed. 1918) (emphasis added).

[79] *In re* United Med. Research, Inc., 12 BR 941 (B. SD. Cal. 1981).

[80] 93 BR at 941 citing 12 BR at 943.

Approval of Equitable Exception

"In the spirit of the foregoing, I endorse the approach to marshaling in . . . [the *Vermont* case[81]]. . . . That court ruled that exceptions to marshaling should be applied only when the moving party presents clear and convincing evidence of (1) the basis of the marshaling exception and (2) inequitable conduct by the person(s) or entity whose assets are subject to marshaling."[82]

Continuing its discussion of the *Vermont* case, the court commented on its recognition of a "common debtor" exception when sufficient evidence of inequitable guarantee conduct by supporting an alter-ego relationship between corporate Debtor and guarantor. "However, while many courts recognize the exception, it has been rarely applied because of 'lack of proper allegation or evidence.'"[83]

> Putting this standard of proof to the facts of the cases it is seen that First City falls short of carrying its burden of pleading and proof. First City does little more than reason that the unsecured creditor's estate would be benefitted by a marshaling of assets in this case. At no point does First City allege inequitable conduct by the guarantor, Walter Galtney. Neither does it put forth grounds on which to find an alter-ego relationship between the debtor company and its president/guarantor.[84]

The court continued, "[n]either does [First City] allege an inducement to extend credit to the debtor based on the receipt by the debtor of working capital loan proceeds as a result of the Galtney's guarantee. . . . In short, there is insufficient evidence in the record with which to justify an equitable exception to the rules governing the commercial transaction at

---

[81] *In re* Vermont Toy Works, Inc. ("Vermont"), 82 BR 258 (B D.Vt. 1987), *rev'd,* 135 BR 762 (D. Vt. 1991).

[82] 93 BR at 941 citing Vermont, 82 BR at 314.

[83] 93 BR at 941.

[84] *Id.*

issue here. Without such an exception, First City's motion for marshaling cannot be granted."[85]

First City's "cases used to support its position, Green's, Farmers, and Tampa Chain, are cited only for the notion that secured creditors can be required to first look to the property of a shareholder/guarantor before proceeding against the corporate debtor's assets."[86] The court commented that while 'Tampa Chain's reasoning and result support First City's position, nonetheless First City had not shouldered its burden of proof, namely, there was insufficient evidence to justify an equitable exception to the rules governing the commercial transaction at issue.

> The spirit of the Code protects the value of the debtor's estate while it tries to minimize detrimental effects to creditors. In this vein, this court is required to review the competing equities and legal rights of all parties-in-interest. Where as here, the unsecured creditor has failed to plead and present evidence of conduct or circumstances that would justify elevating its rights over those who have taken steps to protect their claim, there are no supervening equitable rights to be recognized. The law of commercial transactions will not be modified by the Bankruptcy Court unless and until a claimant establishes that his equitable rights are at least equal to those who have otherwise waived the protections of their legal rights through wrong doing or overreaching. There is no evidence of such conduct here, nor has First City so plead.

"For the reasons stated, First City's motion to compel WCC to draw against its letter of credit with Allied Bank is therefore denied."[87]

---

[85] *Id.* at 941–42.

[86] *Id.* at 942.

[87] *Id.*

Liquidating Plan
Sub Rosa

We have, of course, not completed the San Jacinto Court's decision on the effect that marshaling of the Debtor's assets has upon the confirmation of the plan. "First City's contention that the sale of equipment to Viracon is a *sub rosa*[88] plan of reorganization is partially mooted by this court's authorization to sell the assets given at the hearing held September 19, 1988. Further, the decision to disallow First City's motion to order marshaling of assets clears the way for WCC to obtain the proceeds of said sale."[89]

In addition, the court found no merit in First City's contention that the three sales constituted sales being conducted outside a plan of (liquidating) reorganization. First City raised no objection to the second sale. In fact, prior to the filing of the involuntary petition, the Debtor had already undertaken a program of controlled liquidation of the business. The Debtor had also proposed a plan of reorganization that called for full satisfaction of all allowed secured claims. Under the terms of the plan WCC, as well as other secured claims, would be paid from sales of all other equipment and inventory. "Given that WCC's priority claim to the proceeds is undisputed, and since marshaling will not be ordered in this case, I do not see that anything will be gained by making WCC wait for the funds that, by all accounts, will eventually be paid to them."[90]

Observation

What has happened to this common law doctrine? Section 544 of the Code has bestowed additional powers to the trustee by granting the trustee the status of a lien creditor. As such, every case with a senior secured creditor has a junior resulting in: (1) the existence [which the courts create] of two creditors

---

[88] *Id. See also supra* Chapter 1, this handbook, Prepackaged Chapter 11 subtitle "De Facto Plans."

[89] *Id.*

[90] *Id.* at 942–43.

with a common Debtor; (2) the existence of two funds belonging to the Debtor [which the courts create]; and (3) the legal right of one creditor to satisfy the demand from either or both funds while the other may resort to only one fund [which the courts are now creating]. As the Supreme Court stated in *Meyer v. United States*: "Marshaling is an equitable doctrine, and it should not be applied to frustrate the policies of the Bankruptcy Code."[91] Assumption of the doctrine is a far distance from the common law, to the extent of allowing the existence of the trustee as one of the "two creditors." Certainly, a creditor loses nothing if the second fund constitutes part of the estate, such as the assets resulting from piercing of the corporate veil. However, when the guarantor of the Debtor's senior creditor's debt constitutes the second fund, a problem arises.

The problem presented: can the senior utilize the second fund to satisfy its claim so that the junior's claim by subordination receives compensation from the first fund? In the "two fund" theory the cases are divided on what constitutes an "equitable" doctrine. In the first case, Jack Green's, the court of appeals held that a guarantor's home could be reached when no inequitable conduct was indicated on the guarantor's part. Some cases seemed to approve such opinion as equitable.

Several other cases seemed to find the second fund under potential recoveries such as "a reliance fund," which considered the proceeds of a guaranteed loan as a capital contribution to the debtor's estate, the "piercing of a corporate veil," or the interference with "the regularity of commercial transactions."

The problem must be resolved by the overall doctrine of an equitable transaction. It may be difficult to determine with cases like Jack Green's which is held to be equitable, but the same problem is involved with every bankruptcy case and for every Jack Green's there appears to be more than one San Jacinto.

A word as to the holding that the Greens had not as yet been granted their discharge. We consider the holding a lame defense. No urgency was indicated. The court applying

---

[91] *See supra,* this chapter, subtitle "Equitable Doctrine Applicable to §544."

equitable principles could have deferred the marshaling until such hearing had taken place. Bankruptcy Rule 4004, "Grant or Denial of Discharge," provides: "In a chapter 7 liquidation case a complaint objecting to a Debtor's discharge under §727(a) of the Code shall be filed no later than 60 days following the first date set for the meeting of creditors held pursuant to §341(a)."[92]

Furthermore, it is questionable that in extending credit, the general creditors rely upon the debtor's personal secured assets, which have been guaranteed to the secured creditor as an additional asset to be utilized by marshaling in the event of debtor's inability to pay its debt. At any rate, the requirement that the guarantor's assets should be utilized as a second fund belonging to a Debtor for the purposes of marshaling by the trustee as a lien creditor under §544(a) should be subject only to the existence of inequitable business conduct by the Debtor.

---

[92] *See also* "B. Rule 4004(b). Extension of Time, . . . the court may extend for cause the time for filing a complaint objecting to discharge."

Chapter 15
Preferences

From the trustee's strong-arm powers we turn to §547(b), the elements of Preferences,[1] not quite as strong a power, but designed for the same reason of recovering transfers of property of the estate that violate the basic principle of equality of distribution of the Debtor's property to all creditors.[2] Exceptions to the preference power, designed to protect commercial transactions for the benefit of the creditor, are contained in §547(c). Before proceeding with the elements of a preference and its corresponding exceptions, an explanation of the objective of a preference is helpful for our understanding. The Supreme Court in the *Begier* case stated:[3]

---

[1] *See* 11 USC §547. "Preferences."

[2] *See* 11 USC §726. "Distribution of property of the estate." *See also* §547(a) for meaning in this section of "inventory," "new value," "receivable," and "debt for a tax."

[3] Begier v. I.R.S. ("Begier"), 110 S.Ct. 2258, 2262–63 (1990).

> Equality of distribution among creditors is a central policy of the Bankruptcy Code. According to that policy, creditors of equal priority should receive pro rata shares of the Debtor's property.[4]

The Court further discussed how §547(b) enforces this policy by permitting a trustee in bankruptcy to avoid certain preferential payments made by the debtor within 90 days before the debtor files a bankruptcy petition. The purpose of §547(b) is to prevent the debtor from

> favoring one creditor over others by transferring property shortly before filing for bankruptcy. . . . The reach of §547(b)'s avoidance power is therefore limited to transfers of "property of the debtor."[5]

Property of the debtor is defined in §541[6] and "serves as the postpetition analog to §547(b)'s 'property of the debtor.'"[7]

Exploring Elements of a Preference

The spirit of §547, the Preference section, is contained in Section 547(b): "except as provided in subsection (c) of this section, the trustee may avoid any transfer of an interest of the debtor in property . . ." (1) made to or for the benefit of a creditor;[8] (2) for or on account of an antecedent debt owed by the Debtor before such transfer was made; (3) made while

---

[4] *Id.* at 2263 citing 11 USC §726(b) ("Distribution of property of the estate").

[5] *Id.* at 2263. *See also* §547(a) which consists of definitions applicable to §547: "inventory," "new value," "receivables," and when "debt for tax is incurred."

[6] 11 USC §541. "Property of the estate." *See* §541(a)(1): "[A]ll legal or equitable interests of the debtor in property as of the commencement of the case. . . ."

[7] *See* Begier v. I.R.S., *supra* note 3 at 2263.

[8] *See In re* Spada, 903 F2d 971 (3d Cir. 1990) (Creditors may also enforce §547 for the benefit of the estate).

Debtor was insolvent;[9] (4) made on or within 90 days before date of filing of the petition; or between 90 days and one year before the date of filing of the petition, if such creditor at the time of such transfer was an insider;[10] and (5) creditor received more than such creditor would receive if (A) the case were under chapter 7 of this title; (B) the transfer had not been made; (C) and such creditor received payment of such debt to the extent provided by the provisions of this title.

Seven Exceptions to §547(b)

There are seven exceptions[11] to §547(b) available to creditors, which are delineated in §547(c): for example, as in subsection (c)(1)(A), a contemporaneous exchange for new value given the debtor and "(B) in fact a substantially contemporaneous exchange." A current exception involving transfer in the ordinary course of business according to the nature of the industry's business is an essential feature of many cases.[12] In the meantime, the reader will note, as we continue, that exceptions may have various interpretations as to their allowances.

Presumptions
Debtor—Creditor

Furthermore, presumptions applying to §547(b) are not to be overlooked: (1) §547(f) provides that the debtor is presumed

---

[9] *See* §547(f).

[10] *See infra* note 15 for definition of insider.

[11] *See* additional exceptions in subsections 547(c):

> (2) transfers in the ordinary course of business between the debtor and creditor and in the industry; (3) acquisition of security interest; (4) new value not secured by unavoidable security interest; (5) creating perfected security interest in inventory or a receivable to prejudice of unsecured creditors; (6) fixing a statutory lien that is not avoidable under section 545 [*see supra* Chapter 12, this handbook]: and (7) consumer debts.

[12] *See infra In re* Tolona Pizza Products Corporation under subtitle "Circuits Divided §547(c)(2)(C)."

to have been insolvent on and during the 90 days immediately preceding the filing of the petition; (2) the trustee has the burden under §547(g) of proving the avoidability of a transfer under subsection (b); and (3) the party or creditor against whom recovery or avoidance is sought "has the burden of proving nonavoidability of a transfer under subsection (c) of this section."

Insider–Outsider

Beyond 90 Days

The *Cartage* case[13] brings us back to §§547(b)(4) and (5): (1) the officers of Cartage were held to be creditors; (2) payments to Bank in satisfaction of obligation to debtor's two officers were avoidable as preferences; and (3) Bank was initial transferee of payment made directly to Bank from debtor in discharge of Cartage's obligation to debtor's obligation to the officers. We turn then to the facts.

In March, 1983, the bank made two personal loans totalling $50,000 to the Fosters, officers of Cartage, the debtor. The Fosters then transferred the funds to Cartage to finance its business operations. On March 2, 1984, Cartage filed for chapter 11, which was later converted to chapter 7, and a trustee appointed. Within the year preceding the filing of the petition, Cartage made nine payments of $1,399.31 to the Bank each on the first Foster loan. Six were made by checks payable directly to the Bank, while three were made by checks payable to Della Foster who in turn endorsed them over to the Bank. Two of the nine payments were within 90 days preceding bankruptcy. On the second Foster loan, Cartage paid $957.45 directly to the Bank, within 90 days of the filing of the petition.

---

[13] *In re* C-L Cartage Co., Inc. ("Cartage") v. City Bank and Trust Company ("Bank"), 899 F2d 1490 (6th Cir. 1990).

Transfer Loan Proceeds
Foster and Creditors

The parties stipulated: (1) that Cartage was insolvent[14] when the loan payments were made, and (2) that the Fosters were insiders[15] within the meaning of §547(b)(4)(B). The bankruptcy and district courts agreed that the Fosters were creditors of Cartage because they had an existing or contingent claim against the company.[16] The district court rejected the Fosters' argument that the transfer of the loan proceeds to Cartage was a capital contribution since the Fosters were creditors. The bankruptcy and district courts concluded that the payments to the Bank were "to or for the benefit of creditors within §547(b)(1)"[17] and were therefore, voidable preferences.

Insider's Arguments

The court of appeals had for consideration two provisions constituting preferences: (1) The Bank's contention that Cartage's payments do not meet §547 requirements for voidable preferences; and (2) the trustee's cross-appeal that

---

[14] *See* 11 USC §101 (32): "insolvent means—with reference to an entity other than a partnership and a municipality, financial condition such that the sum of such entity's debts is greater than all of such entity's property, at a fair valuation, exclusive of— . . . ." *See also,* §547(f): "Debtor is presumed to have been insolvent on and during the 90 days. . . ."

[15] *See* §101 (31)(B) "insider includes— . . . if the Debtor is a corporation—(i) director of the Debtor; (ii) officer of the Debtor; (iii) person in control of the Debtor; (iv) partnership in which the Debtor is a general partner; (v) general partner of the Debtor; or (vi) relative of a general partner, director, officer, or person in control of the Debtor. . . ."

[16] Cartage, 899 F2d at 1492; see definition of creditor, §101(10)(A): "'Creditor' means—(A) entity that had a claim against the debtor that arose at the time of or before the order for relief concerning the debtor; . . ." *See also,* Covey v. Commercial National Bank of Peoria, 960 F2d 657 (7th Cir. 1992).

[17] *Id. See also,* §101(5); "claim means—(A) right to payment, . . . (B) right to an equitable remedy. . . ."

§550(a)(1)[18] permits recovery of payment from the bank during the extended preference period of one year when such payments benefitted insider creditors.

In analyzing the problem as to whether the Fosters were creditors, since no promissory notes were signed and delivered to Cartage, the Bank argued that the transfer of the loan proceeds was a capital contribution and not a debt. The court of appeals stated that the "[f]ixed periodic repayments each month to the Bank to discharge its obligations to the Fosters suggests that the Fosters had a debt rather than an equity relationship with Cartage."[19]

Creditor
One Holding Claim

The court observed further that whether viewed as creditors or guarantors, the Fosters fall within the broad definition of "creditor" in section 101(10)(A) since they had a real "claim" against Cartage.[20] This left the court with one remaining statutory requirement to classifiy these payments as voidable preferences, specifically §547(b)(5), which is directed at determining whether the transfers enabled creditors to receive more of a dividend if the estate had been liquidated under chapter 7 and the disputed transfer had not been made. The court found that §547(b)(5) was satisfied.

---

[18] *See* "§550(a)(1). Liability of trustee of avoided transfer: (a) Except as otherwise provided in this section to the extent that a transfer is avoided under §544, 545, 547, 548 . . . the trustee may recover, for the benefit of the estate, the property transferred, or if the court so orders, the value of the property from— . . . (1) the initial transferee . . . or the entity for whose benefit such transfer was made; or (2) any immediate or mediate transferee of such initial transferee;" . . . but (b): may not recover under §(a)(2) from "(1) a transferee that takes for value . . . or (2) any immediate or mediate good faith transferee of the transferee."

[19] *Id.* at 1493.

[20] *Id.* "Accordingly, the finding that the Fosters were creditors of Cartage within the meaning of section 547(b)(1) was not clearly erroneous [and therefore, as creditors,] Cartage's payments to the Bank discharging its own liability to the Fosters were 'to or for the benefit of a creditor' within the meaning of section 547(b)(1)." *See also,* B. Rule 9033(d)—Standard of Review.

Liability
Initial Transferee or Beneficial Transferee

Having determined that the transfer was preferential, the court next needed to address from whom the preference was recoverable. The court turned to §550(a)(1)[21] to determine whether the Bank was a transferee. While conceding it was a transferee, the Bank contended that it was not the initial transferee and therefore recovery should be limited to the Fosters. The court, however, opined: "a literal reading of section 550(a)(1) together with sections 547(b)(1) and (b)(4)(B) permits recovery from an outsider transferee for transfers made during the extended preference period when the beneficiary of the transfers is an insider creditor or an insider guarantor. . . ."[22] Section 550, unlike section 547, makes no distinction on its face between insiders and outsiders."[23] The court of appeals held that the trustee could recover from the Bank.

Cartage and Deprizio
Rejecting Two Transfer Theory

The *Cartage* case cited the *Deprizio* case[24] with approval in rejecting the "two transfer" theory. In Cartage the court opined: "other courts have adopted what has been dubbed as the 'two transfer' theory, which treats the single payment as two separate and independent transfers since both the insider and the outsider separately benefit from the single payment.[25] . . . Under the two-transfer theory, section 547(b) gives the trustee the power to avoid the extended preference period

---

[21] *Id.* citing Section 550(a)(1). *See supra,* note 18.

[22] *Id.* at 1494.

[23] *Id.*

[24] Levit v. Ingersoll Rand Financing Corp. ("Deprizio" or "Debtor") 874 F2d 1186 (7th Cir. 1989).

[25] 899 F2d 1404, citing Goldberger v. Davis Jay Corrugated Box Corp. (*In re* Mercon Industries, 37 B.R. 549 (Bankr. ED Pa. 1984); Levit v. Melrose Park Nat'l Bank (*In re* V.N. Deprizio), 58 B.R. 478, 481 (B. ND Ill. 1986), *rev'd* sub nom. Levit v. Ingersoll Rand Financial Corp., 874 F2d 1186 (7th Cir. 1989).

under 'transfer' but not the separate and independent benefit or transfer to the outsider. The approach incorrectly equates 'transfer' with 'benefit received.' The Code, however, equates transfer with payments made. . . ."[26]

> Sections 547 and 550 both speak of a transfer being avoided; avoidability is an attribute of the transfer [debtor's payment] rather than of the creditor. While the lenders want to define transfer from the recipients' perspectives, the Code consistently defines it from the debtor's. A single payment therefore is one transfer, no matter how many persons gain thereby.

Referring to a law review article following the previous Deprizio observation, the court of appeals commented: "by creating two transfers from a single payment the two-transfer theory adopts a 'tortured construction of the statute.'"[27]

Deprizio Insiders
Status of U.S. Code Trusts and Taxes

The Cartage Court's conclusion followed Deprizio's opening: "[W]e prefer a literal reading of the statute permitting recovery from non-insider transferees for payments made during the extended preference period which benefit insider creditors or guarantors. . . . Favoring certain creditors over others similarly situated is precisely what sections 547 and 550 seek to prevent. . . ."[28] The Deprizio case's opening was significant: "we must decide a question no other appellate court has addressed:[29] whether payments to creditors who dealt at arms' length with a debtor are subject to the year-long preference-recovery period that 11 U.S.C. §547(b)(4)(B)

---

[26] *Id.* at 1495 citing Levit 874 F2d at 1195.

[27] *Id.* at 1495 citing Levit 874 F2d at 1195 and Note, The Interplay Between Sections 547(b) and 550 of the Bankruptcy Code, 89 COLUMBIA L. REV. 530, 540 (1989).

[28] *Id.* citing Cartage at 1495. Levit v. Ingersoll Rand Financial Corp. ("Deprizio"), 874 F2d 1186 (7th Cir. 1989).

[29] Cartage was decided April 3, 1990 and Deprizio May 12, 1989.

provides for 'inside' creditors when the payments are for the 'benefit of insiders', §547(b)(1). The bankruptcy court in this case answered 'no' . . . and the district court 'yes'. . . . We agree with the district court for the most part, although we conclude that payments satisfying pension obligations ordinarily are not for the benefit of inside creditors, and payment of tax obligations never are."[30]

In 1980 Deprizio Construction Co. was awarded contracts by the City of Chicago to do $13.4 million of work on the extension of Chicago's subway system to O'Hare airport. The company also borrowed from other sources. By 1983 the company was in trouble and filed a petition under chapter 7. "The trustee instituted adversary proceedings to recover payments against the lenders, the pension and welfare funds, and the United States—none of them insiders—seeking to recover payments made more than 90 days but within the year before the filing. The Trustee reasoned that the payments, made to these outside creditors were 'for the benefit' of inside co-signers and guarantors, because every dollar paid to the outside creditor reduced the insider's exposure by the same amount."[31]

Bankruptcy Court's Two Transfers Theory

The bankruptcy judge without deciding whether any of the payments were preferential or worked to the benefit of any insiders, denied the trustee's request. The judge "concluded that any transfer to an outside creditor for the benefit of an insider should be treated as two transfers: one being the money and the other the benefit. A transfer may be recovered under §550(a)[32] only to the extent it is avoidable under §547. The monetary transfer to the outsider is not avoidable . . . when made more than 90 days before the filing. Thus it may not be recovered from the outsider, even though the benefit to the insider may be recovered from the insider."[33]

---

[30] Deprizio at 1187.

[31] *Id.* at 1188.

[32] *Id. See supra* note 18 and text defining and describing §550(a).

[33] *Id.*

District Court
One Transfer

The district court reversed holding that the payment was only one transfer although a transfer may create benefits for many persons. If the insider receives a benefit, then the transfer is avoidable under §547(b)(4)(B) if made within a year of bankruptcy and does not qualify for the exclusions of §547(c).[34] "Section 550(a) as the [district court] read it, allows the trustee to recover the transfer from either the recipient or the indirect beneficiary, at the Trustee's option. . . ."[35] The court of appeals then cited the relevant sections dealing with the recovery of a preference namely §547(b), §101(4) defining "claim, and §101(9) defining 'creditor,'[36] and 'insider,'[37] and §101(32) defining 'insolvency.'"[38]

Insiders—Outsiders
"Yes" or "No" Affecting Outsiders

"Many bankruptcy and district judges have addressed the question we confront[39] as have commentators. A majority of judges have concluded that insiders' guarantees do not expose outside lenders to an extended preference-recovery period, frequently because they feel that recovery would be inequitable when ordinarily outside creditors need restore only preferences received within 90 days before bankruptcy. The

---

[34] *See infra*, this chapter, subtitle "Circuits Divided §547(c)(2)(C)."

[35] *Id.*

[36] *Id. See supra*, note 16.

[37] *Id. See supra*, note 15.

[38] *Id. See supra*, note 14.

[39] *Id.* at 1189. *See* note 2. "Five cases answer, 'yes': . . . ." the district court's decision here [citing them] plus *In re* Robinson Bros. Drilling, Inc., 97 BR 77 (WD Ohio 1988) . . . [Other] cases answer 'no' on the ground that extended preference recovery would be inequitable. . . . Two answer 'no' on the ground that insider and outsider receive different 'transfers' only one of which may be recovered: the bankruptcy judges opinion in our case and *In re* Marcon Industries, Inc., 37 BR 549 (B. ED Pa. 1984). . . ."

commentators are evenly divided."[40] As we can observe from the Cartage case, the courts are still divided. Indeed, the Senate passed a bill that is designed to overrule the choice for the trustee to determine whether to eliminate the outsider from liability and leave recovery only against the insider.[41]

Outside Creditors
Adversary Proceedings

Let us turn now to the adversary[42] proceedings instituted by the trustee against the lenders, the pension and welfare funds, and the United States—none of them insiders—seeking to recover payments made more than 90 days but within the year before the filing.

First, the court of appeals discussed the various definitions of §547 and §550 and stated: "The Trustee's argument for extended recovery from outside creditors flows directly from the interlocked provisions. . . . Section 547(b)(4) distinguishes according [to whether a Guarantor is an 'insider'] but §550 does not. . . . So Lender may have to repay transfers received during the year before filing though Lender is not an insider. Viewing each payment as two transfers—one to Lender another to guarantor—they [i.e., the creditors] insist that the only transfer avoidable under §547 is the one to Guarantor. Second, several of the Lenders say that the insiders are not 'creditors' for particular debts. Third, CIT submits that a payment of a non-guaranteed loan backed by a senior security

---

[40] *Id. See* note 3. "Compare Lawrence P. King, 4 COLLIER ON BANKRUPTCY ¶550.02 at 550-8 (15th ed. 1987) and Vern Countryman, *The Trustee's Recovery in Preference Actions,* 3 BANKRUPTCY DEVELOPMENTS p. 449, 464 (1986) both saying "no" on grounds of equity with Isaac Natoric, *The Bankruptcy Preference Laws Interpreting Code Sections 547(c)(2), 550(a)(1) and 546(a)(1),* 41 BUS. LAW. 175, 186–189 . . . both answering 'yes'. . . ."

[41] *See* Senate Bill S. 1985 (1992). *See also infra* Chapter 16, this handbook, Fraudulent Transfers.

[42] *Id.* at 1188.

interest does not produce a 'benefit' for an inside guarantor of a junior secured creditor. . . ."[43]

After intensive analysis of both arguments, the court held: (1) ". . . Payments to the tax collector, although to the benefit of the responsible person, are not to his benefit *as creditor*, and the Trustee may not recover funds from the United States for transfers more than 90 days before the filing,"[44] and "Pension Funds look to the employer for payment. Section 515 of the Employee Retirement Income Security Act (ERISA). Nothing in ERISA requires insiders of the firm to stand behind its pension commitments. . . ."[45]

Principal Question
Which Transfer May Be Avoided

"Now for the principal question: whether the trustee may recover from an outside creditor under §550(a)(1) a transfer more than 90 days before the filing that is avoided under §547(b) because of a benefit for an inside creditor. . . . No one doubts that a transfer to Lender produces a benefit for Guarantor. After §547 defines which transfers may be avoided, §550(a) identifies who is responsible for payment: 'the initial transferee of such transfer or the entity for whose benefit such transfer was made' (emphasis added). This gives the trustee the option to collect from Lender, Guarantor, or both, subject only to the provision in §550(c) that there can be but one satisfaction. . . ."[46]

Conclusion
Deprizio Court of Appeals

"To sum up: . . . [1] [I]nsiders who may be liable on account of the firm's failure to pay taxes are not 'creditors' because

---

[43] *Id.* at 1191. The court stated that the district court did not consider this argument and it should be resolved in the first instance by the bankruptcy court and accordingly the court would discuss it briefly at the close of its opinion.

[44] *Id.* at 1192.

[45] *Id.*

[46] *Id.* at 1194. *See also* 1197.

they do not hold 'claims' against their firms. Accordingly, delinquent taxes paid more than 90 days before the filing may not be covered under §550(a). We conclude . . . that pension and welfare trusts may recover from insiders only to the extent state law allows that under rules for disregarding the corporate form, or the insiders make contractual commitments enforceable under §515 of ERISA. When state law supports 'veil piercing' it does so on the ground that the investor and the firm are a single entity, which precludes the insider from holding 'a claim' against the firm. The Trustee therefore may not recover payments to pension and welfare trusts made more than 90 days before the filing unless. . . . [3] We hold . . . that the preference recovery period for outside creditors is one year when the payment produces a benefit for an inside creditor, including a guarantor.

"The judgments of the district court are affirmed in part and reversed in part. The cases are remanded for further proceedings consistent with this opinion."[47]

Waiver of Guarantee Strikes at §547(c)(2)(C)

The recent case of *XTI Xonics Technology, Inc.*[48] discussed the "Deprizio doctrine." The case held that inside guarantors' waiver of subrogation rights in guarantee removed alleged preferential transfers from the extended one-year insider preference period. "Finally, the guarantor has a right of subrogation which permits him to be substituted to the position of the creditor whom he has paid. . . . These rights will be enforced by the court as a court of equity whether or not they are the subject of a specific contractual agreement between the parties. . . . If these equitable rights are specifically recognized by the terms of a contract, to the extent that they are not waived or modified the contract terms are simply a reaffirmance of preexisting equitable rights."[49] Result: (1) guarantors surrendered their rights of indemnity, continuation, and exoneration; (2) right of subrogation was a claim under Bankruptcy Code; and (3) anti-Deprizio waiver

---

[47] *Id.* at 827.

[48] XTI Xonics Technology, 156 B.R. 821 (B. D. Or. 1993).

[49] *Id.* at 827.

provisions in guarantee were not inequitable and against public policy. Query whether citation of waiver and equitable policy's applicability are not methods designed to overcome recovery against noninsiders as well?

Timing Importance

A Day In or Out

Several Supreme Court cases indicate the method by which a debtor or creditor may lose or gain a day, which results in a preference against the creditor or is excepted from §547(b).

1. In the *Barnhill* case[50] the Supreme Court held that the transfer of a check resulted in a preference within the 90-day period, since the 90-day period occurred when the check was honored by the drawee bank and not when delivered to the payee.

2. In the *Dewey Barefoot* case, the Supreme Court held that a wire transfer of a check by a creditor to a debtor for the purpose of making good a bounced check was delivered outside the 90 days.[51]

3. In the *Union Bank v. Wolas* case, the Supreme Court held that a long-term monthly installment debt was payable just as a short-term debt was, namely, within the ordinary course of business as defined in §547(c)(2)(A), (B), and (C).[52]

---

[50] Barnhill v. Johnson, 112 S.Ct. 1386 (1992).

[51] *In re* Dewey Barefoot, d/b/a D&M Mobile Homes ("Dewey") and Champion Credit Corporation ("Champion"), 952 F2d 795 (4th Cir. 1991).

[52] Union Bank ("Bank") v. Wolas, 112 S.Ct. 527 (1991).

Circuits Divided
§547(c)(2)(C)

Union Bank v. Wolas brings for our consideration the recent case of *Tolona Pizza*[53] decided by the Seventh Circuit dealing with the same problem involving the interpretation of §547(c)(2)(C). The theme of the case is set forth very clearly in the court of appeals' opening: "but what does the third requirement—that the payment[s] have been 'made according to ordinary course of business terms'—add? And in particular does it refer to what is 'ordinary' between this debtor and this creditor or what is ordinary in the market or industry in which they operate? The circuits are divided in the market or industry in which they operate, compare. . . ."[54]

The court did compare and proceeded to analyze the facts in Tolona, a maker of pizza. Tolona issued eight checks to Rose, its sausage supplier, "within 90 days before being thrown into bankruptcy by its creditors."[55] The checks, which totalled $46,000, cleared and as a result all debts to Rose were paid in full. Tolona's other trade creditors would receive only $0.13 on the dollar under the plan approved by the bankruptcy court if the preferential treatment was allowed to stand. Accordingly, Tolona, as DIP, brought an adversary[56] proceeding against Rose to recover the eight payments as voidable preferences.

Conflict: Invoice and Late Payments

The bankruptcy judge entered judgment for Tolona. The district judge reversed: "he thought that Rose did not, in order to comply with section 547(c)(2)(C) have to prove the terms on which it had extended credit to Tolona were standard terms in

---

[53] *In re* Tolona Pizza Products Corporation ("Tolona"), —F2d— (7th Cir. 1993) Lexis 21169. The footnotes are temporarily those used by Lexis, pages 2–7.

[54] *Id.* at 2. *See supra* Deprizio case subtitle "Circuits Divided."

[55] *Id.* at 2. *See* "Chapter 5. Involuntary Petition," subtitled "Debtor's Option—7 or 11 (Farley)" (pp. 84–86).

[56] *Id. See* Chapter 14, this handbook, Trustee's Strong-Arm Powers, subtitle "Adversary Proceeding."

the industry, but if this was wrong the testimony of Rose's executive vice-president, Stiehl, did prove it. The parties agree that the other requirements of section 547(c)(2)[(A) and (B)] were satisfied."[57]

Now turning to §547(c)(3)(C) the court of appeals observed that Rose's invoices recited "net 7 days" meaning that payment was due within seven days. For years preceding the preference period, however, Tolona rarely paid within seven days; nor did Rose's other customers. Most paid within 21 days, and if they paid later than 28 or 30 days Rose would usually withhold future shipments until payment was received. Rose was a favored customer and for 34 months prior to the 90-day period that Rose's invoices were outstanding, payment was made in 26 days and the longest time was 46 days. "Rose consistently . . . made Tolona . . . one of a 'sort of exceptional group of customers of Rose . . . falling outside the common industry practice and standards.'"[58]

The Court of Appeals was concerned as to the late payments: "It may seem odd that paying a debt late would ever be regarded as a preference to the creditor thus paid belatedly. But it is all relative. . . . If [debtor] pays one and not the others, as happened here, the payment though late is still a preference to that creditor and is avoidable unless the conditions of section 547(c)(2) are met. . . . A late payment normally will not be. It will therefore be an avoidable preference."[59] The purpose of the preference statute is to prevent the debtor during his slide toward bankruptcy from trying to stave off the evil day by giving preferential treatment to his most importunate creditors, who may sometimes be those who have been waiting longest to be paid. Unless the favoring of particular creditors is outlawed, the mass of creditors of a shaky firm will be nervous, fearing that one or a few of their number are going to walk away with all the firm's assets; and this fear may precipitate debtors into bankruptcy earlier than is socially desirable."[60]

---

[57] *Id.* at 3, —F2d— (7th Cir. 1993).

[58] *Id.*

[59] *Id.*

[60] *Id.* at 4 citing *In re* Xonics Imaging, Inc., 837 F2d 763, 765; *In re* Fred Halves Organization, Inc., 957 F2d 239 at 243 n. 5.

Debtor and Creditor Establishing Own Norm in §547(c)(2)(C)

The court, however, from this standpoint, did not consider the dealings between the debtor and the allegedly favored creditor to "conform to some industry norm, but that they conform to the norm established by the debtor and creditor, in the period before, preferably well before, the preference period. That condition is satisfied here—if anything, Rose treated Tolona more favorably (and hence Tolona treated Rose less preferentially) before the preference period than during it."[61]

Again the court observed that if all the third subsection of §547(c)(2) required, "it might seem to add nothing to the first two subsections which require that both the debt and the payment be within the ordinary course of business of both the debtor and the creditor."[62] In that event a "'late payment' really isn't late if the parties have established a practice that . . . deviates from the strict terms of their written contract. But we hesitate to conclude that the third subsection, requiring conformity to 'ordinary business terms' has no function in the statute.

"We can think of two functions that it might have. One is evidentiary.[63] If debtor and creditor dealt on terms that the creditor testifies were normal for them but that are wholly unknown in the industry, this casts some doubt on his (self-serving) testimony. Preferences are disfavored, and subsection (C) makes them more difficult to prove. . . . As to the second possible function is to allay concerns of creditors that one or more of their number may have worked out a special deal with the debtor, before the preference period, designed to put that creditor before the preference period, ahead of the others in the event of bankruptcy. . . . But such a creditor does have an advantage during the preference period, because he can

---

[61] *Id.* at 4.

[62] *Id.*

[63] *Id.* citing *In re* Lottery Winery, Ltd., 107 BR 707, 710 (9th Cir. BAP 1989); *In re* Morren Meat and Poultry Co., 92 BR 737, 740–41 (WD Mich. 1988); David J. DeSimone, *Section 547(c)(2) of the Bankruptcy Code: The Ordinary Course of Business Exception Without the 45 Day Rule*, 20 AKRON L. REV. 95, 123–28 (1986).

receive late payments then, and they will still be in the ordinary course of business for him and his debtor."[64]

Necessity for Maintenance §547(c)(2)(C)

The court continued with the two functions it had identified: "a natural reluctance to cut out and throw away one-third of an important provision of the Bankruptcy Code, persuade us that the creditor must show that the payment he received was made in accordance with the ordinary terms in the industry.... This does not mean establishing the existence of some uniform set of business terms as the Debtor argued. . . ."[65]

The problem presented the court was the nature of the debtor's business, which constituted participation in business with a number of industries. "Not only is it difficult to identify the industry whose norm shall govern (is it, here, the sale of sausages to makers of pizza? The sale of sausages to anyone? The sale of anything to makers of pizza, but there can be great variance in billing practice within an industry. . . . The average period between Rose's invoice and Tolona's payment during the preference period was only 22 days, which seems well within the industry norm, whatever exactly it is. The law should not push businessmen to agree upon a single set of billing practices; . . ."[66]

Court of Appeals' Definition of Ordinary Course of Business (§547(c)(2)(C))

In conclusion, the Seventh Circuit opined that "'ordinary business terms' [§547(c)(2)(C)] refers to the range of terms that encompasses the practices in which terms similar in some general way to the creditor in question engage, and only dealings so idiosyncratic as to fall outside that broad range

---

[64] Id.

[65] Id. citing David DeSimone, *Section 547(c)(2) of the Bankruptcy Code: The Ordinary Course of Business Exception Without the 45 Day Rule*, 20 AKRON L. REV. 95, 123–28 (1986).

[66] Id. at 5.

should be deemed extraordinary and therefore outside the scope of subsection C. . . ."[67] Although the court of appeals arrived at its decision that the business dealing between the parties did not comply with a transaction within the ordinary course of business in an industry, the court considered an argument that "Tolona might have argued that the district judge gave insufficient deference to the bankruptcy judge's contrary finding. The district judge, and we, are required to accept the bankruptcy findings on questions of fact as long as they are not clearly erroneous. . . ."[68]

"But since Tolona did not argue that the district judge had not applied an incorrect standard of review . . . 'clear error,' he may well have believed that the record as a whole left no doubt that Tolona's dealings with Rose were within the broad band of accepted practices in the industry. . . . But the undisputed evidence concerning those dealings and the practice of the industry demonstrates that payment within 30 days is within the outer limits of normal industry practices, and the payments at issue in this case were made on average in a significantly shorter time. . . . The judgment reversing the bankruptcy judge and dismissing the adversary proceeding is AFFIRMED."[69]

Dissenting Opinion

The dissenting judge nonetheless agreed with the majority that under 11 U.S.C. §547(c)(2)(C) Rose was required to show that Tolona's payments had been made in accordance with the ordinary business terms of the industry in order to defeat the inference that the payments were preferential. "I respectfully dissent, because I cannot conclude that Rose in fact made the requisite showing."[70]

---

[67] *Id.* citing *In re* SPW Corp., 96 BR 676, 681–82 (B. ND Texas 1989); *In re* White, 64 B. 843, 850 (B. ED Tenn. 1686); *In re* Economy Milling Co., 37 B. 914, 922 (D.S.C. 1983).

[68] *Id.* at 5 citing Fed. R. Bankr. p. 8013, *In re* Bonnett, 895 F2d 1155, 1157 (7th Cir. 1989).

[69] *Id.*

[70] *Id.* referring to note at page 5: "Contrary to the position of the majority, I believe that Tolona did raise this issue on appeal . . . [in his] brief. . . . While admittedly Tolona did not invoke the words 'clear error,' it

Observations

1. In the Tolona case, the court found it "difficult to identify the industry whose norm shall govern. . . ."[71] From the facts, it would appear to be the sausage industry, although the Debtor had several suppliers from whom merchandise was purchased, and Rose was the one seeking the exception. Referring to the two functions that the third exception required, the court mentioned "evidence" and allaying "the concerns of creditors that one may have worked out a special deal with the debtor. . . ."[72] The non-existence of the sausage supplier's testimony might very well have indicated, there was no provision that the industry utilized §547(c)(2)(C). Furthermore, the facts on its face, sounded very much as a preferential transfer.

2. Time and again we will hear the courts opining that one of the principal objectives of the Code is to provide for equal distribution of the debtor's property among all parties having claims or equity interests in the estate. The Preference section, as does the previous Chapter 14 of this handbook discussing §544, endeavors to preserve that objective. Modifying §547(b) containing the basic elements that constitute such preference, the Code hastily follows with seven exceptions of subsection (c)(1) to (c)(7), which would seem to diminish the equal distribution formula. Quite to the contrary: Congress has considered that problem and realized that without such exceptions normal business relations between debtor and creditors, particularly credit extension, would hasten a debtor to chapter 11.

3. Cartage, Deprizio, and Tolona bring for consideration the outsider (financier) and the insider (Debtor). The financier at times extends credit to a debtor whose status is somewhat financially tenuous, but upon condition that a person of substantial financial resources, that is a director, officer or stockholder of the Debtor or a subsidiary, guarantees payment. Section 547(b) allows a recovery against an outside creditor within 90 days and against an insider within one year.

---

indicated that the district court paid them insufficient deference."

[71] *Id.*

[72] *Id.* at 4.

However, cases starting with court of appeals cases such as Deprizio, and followed by C-L Cartage, hold that the provisions of §550 are to be considered as they affect the guarantor, inasmuch as §550 is applicable to §547 and provides for a recovery "for the benefit of the estate, the property transferred . . . from (1) the initial transferee . . . or (2) any immediate or mediate transferee of such initial transferee."

4. What about the "two-transfer" theory? The Cartage case approved the Deprizio case rejecting such theory. "A single payment therefore is one transfer, no matter how many persons gain thereby. . . . By creating two transfers from a single payment, the two transfer theory adopts 'a tortured construction of the statute.'"[73] The result may be that lenders are left with the commercial concern that loans with a guarantor may not be considered creditworthy. Of course, the position of Deprizio is that such situations must stand up against the law. On this issue we await the Supreme Court's determination on whether to approve cases following Deprizio and Cartage, the "no" group or the "yes" group, or the "non-Deprizio" group, or will Congress win the race? A continuance of equality of distribution of the estate for creditors would necessitate the soundness of Deprizio and Cartage.

We turn now to Fraudulent Transfers, another one of the trio helpful in the aid for monetary equality among creditors by avoidance and recovery of such transfers.

---

[73] *Cartage* at 1495.

Chapter 16
Fraudulent Transfers
and Obligations

I n addition to the avoiding powers the trustee has exhibited in the Strong Arm Powers and Preference sections of the Code, we find a third section of the Code which aids in recovery of fraudulent transfers.[1] As we shall see, it is not unusual to find several of these sections linked together with each other. Indeed, the linkage carries over to the Uniform Fraudulent Transfer or Conveyance Acts in complaints served by the trustee or the creditor's committees. As has often been stated by the courts, the objective of these actions has been to maintain the Debtor's estate in such status that all its creditors will receive equal distribution of property of the

---

[1] 11 USC §548. Fraudulent transfers and obligations.

estate.[2] It is not unusual therefore, to find cases which contain actions by the trustee or debtor in possession (DIP), or a creditor's committee acting on behalf of the DIP, instituting an avoidance action in which two or more of the family participate.

We turn now to the *Bigelow*[3] case which discusses a transfer not only from the actual and constructive provisions of §548 but also from the provisions of §547, and whether the transfer constituted a preference.

Tripartite Involvement

In September 1985, Donatelli & Klein[4] acquired 50% of the Debtor's stock in exchange for a cash payment and the arrangement with First American Bank of Baltimore ("First American") for a line of credit for the benefit of the Debtor. This line of credit was personally guaranteed by Ann and Louis Donatelli. The line of credit was rolled over many times and eventually reached $1 million. Although D&K was the maker of the line of credit, only the Debtor received the draws and all payments were made directly from the Debtor to First American. Subsequently the Debtor executed a note for $1 million to D&K with substantially the same terms as the line of credit between First American and D&K. Throughout 1986 and 1987, the Debtor drew upon the lines of credit and sent the payments directly to First American.

> Technically, a tripartite relationship exists, where Donatelli & Klein is a creditor of the Debtor and First American is a creditor of Donatelli & Klein. The Debtor, in making its

---

[2] 11 USC §541. Property of the estate. "(a) The commencement of a case under section 301, 302, or 303 of this title creates an estate. Such estate is comprised of all the following property wherever located and by whomever held: . . . [property in which the trustee recovers under its avoiding powers]."

[3] *In re* Jeffrey Bigelow Design Group, Inc. ("Bigelow Design" or "Debtor"), 956 F2d 479 (4th Cir. 1992). For the purposes of this chapter we do not consider other issues decided by the court, namely the court's discretion in denying trustee's third amendment to the complaint and Debtor's payments on preference theory.

[4] Donatelli & Klein, Inc. ("D&K").

payments, in effect skips its true creditor and sends the money to First American, to whom it has no direct obligation.[5]

On December 22, 1987, Bigelow Design filed a chapter 7 petition. In August 1988, the trustee added a cause of action seeking to recover payments from the Debtor to First American as voidable preferences. First American then joined D&K, Ann Donatelli, and Louis Donatelli as parties. After twice amending the complaint, the trustee stated a cause of action for fraudulent conveyances. Arguments were heard before the bankruptcy judge and at the hearing the trustee requested a third amendment to the complaint in order to state an additional cause of action alleging preferences to insiders.[6] The bankruptcy judge denied the request and determined that the payments were not fraudulent conveyances but, rather, constituted preferences. The district court upheld the denial of the request to amend and held that the payments were neither fraudulent transfers nor preferences. The court of appeals affirmed the decision of the district court in its entirety.[7]

Definitions
Actual and Constructive Fraud

In its analysis of the law of the case, the court of appeals cited §548, "Fraudulent transfers and obligations." These

---

[5] *Id.* at 481.

[6] *See Id.* at 483 note 2 where the circuit court found justification in denying the third motion to modify the complaint stating that "the trustee should have known of . . . [t]he 'insider preference' theory [which] was formulated by the Seventh Circuit in the so called Deprizio case . . . and [which] has become very controversial. *See* generally . . . *In re* Arundel Housing Components, Inc., 126 BR 216 (B. D. Md. 1991) (rejecting theory)." The court declined to comment on the viability of the theory. *See also* Senate Bill S.1985 (1992), passed by the Senate, which would legislatively overrule Deprizio. *See also, supra,* Chapter 15, this handbook, Preferences subtitle "Deprizio-Preference Against Guarantor."

[7] *Id.* at 488.

transfers consist of two general[8] types of fraudulent transfers, specifically §548(a)(1) with actual intent to defraud any entity[9] and §548(a)(2) as constructive fraud:

> (a) The trustee may avoid any transfer of an interest of the Debtor in property, or any obligation incurred by the Debtor . . . on or within one year before the date of the filing of the petition, if the Debtor voluntarily or involuntarily—
>
> (1) made such transfer or incurred such obligation with actual intent to hinder, delay or defraud any entity to which the Debtor was or became, on or after the date that such transfer was made or such obligation incurred, indebted; or
>
> (2)(A) received less than a reasonably equivalent value in exchange for such transfer or obligation; and (B)(i) was insolvent. . . ; (ii) . . . [had] unreasonably small capital; or (iii) . . . would incur, debts that would be beyond the Debtor's ability to pay as such debts matured.[10]

Actual Fraud

The trustee argued that the bankruptcy court erred in finding that under §548(a) no actual intent to hinder, delay, or defraud existed. In response the court held that "[w]hile each fact does not have to demonstrate actual fraud, the facts taken

---

[8] *See also* subsections: (b) power of trustee of partnership; (c) except to the extent that a transfer voidable under this section is voidable under §§544, 545 or 547, transferee that takes for value and in good faith has lien or retains interest transferred; (d)(1) transfer made when transfer so perfected that bona fide purchaser from Debtor against whom applicable law permits transfer to be perfected cannot acquire a superior interest; "(2) In this section—(A) 'value' means property, or satisfaction or securing of a present or antecedent debt . . . ; (B) a commodity broker . . . ; (C) a repo participant, . . . and (D) a swap participant. . . ."

[9] *See* 11 USC §101(15): "'entity' includes person, estate, trust, governmental unit. . . ; and United States Trustee. . . ."

[10] 11 USC §548 (a)(1) and (a)(2) (1992).

together must lead to the conclusion that actual fraud existed.[11] . . . [C]ourts, however, are aware that there is a difference between actual and constructive fraudulent intent. Regardless of the ability of the courts to infer actual fraudulent intent from the presence of 'badges of fraud,'[12] . . . actual fraudulent intent requires a subjective evaluation of the Debtor's motive. Certainly, an objective determination has bearing on whether constructive fraudulent intent exists, but is not conclusive for actual fraudulent intent."

As proof of the evaluation of the elements of actual fraud the trustee noted that the books of the Debtor had not listed any obligation payable directly to D&K but payable to First American. The trustee argued that "this concealment is an indicium of fraud and drew an analogy to a case which found that fraud existed where individuals were misappropriating property of the corporation for their personal use."[13] The court noted, however, that while transactions involving insiders should be closely scrutinized,[14] the facts did not suggest that the insider gained personally from this transaction. In fact, only the Debtor drew on the lines of credit.

Further arguments that fraud existed were to the effect that the Debtor paid First American regularly while falling into debt with creditors. However, the financial manager for the Debtor stated that he did not intend payments to First American to be different from payments to other creditors. The final conclusion on actual fraud was to the effect that the Debtor had not acted negligently or recklessly. The books did not list D&K because, as the parties agreed, the Debtor, not D&K, was responsible for the payments to First American. "The books reflected the economic reality of the situation."[15]

---

[11] Bigelow, 956 F2d at 483–84.

[12] *Id.* at 484 citing Boston Trading Group, Inc. v. Burnazos, 835 F2d 1504, 1509 (1st Cir. 1987). *See also, infra,* this chapter, subtitle "Actual Fraud (Badges) or Constructive Fraud."

[13] *Id.* citing *In re* Rockaway Soda Water Mfg. Co., 226 F2d 520 (EDNY 1915).

[14] *See* EEE Commercial Corp. v. Holmes (*In re* ASI Reactivation, Inc.), 934 F2d 1315, 1323 & n. 3 (4th Cir. 1991).

[15] Bigelow, 956 F2d at 484.

Constructive Transfer
Indirect Benefit

Addressing whether the facts indicated a constructive transfer the court of appeals held: "For the constructive fraudulent transfer count to succeed, the trustee must show that the Debtor received less than reasonably equivalent value in exchange for its payments and that the Debtor was insolvent at the time. . . .[16] Because it is uncontested that the Debtor was insolvent during the period one year prior to the bankruptcy, the issue was whether reasonably equivalent value was given in exchange for the payments. . . ." In response the court held: "It is well settled that reasonably equivalent value can come from one other than the recipient of the payments, a rule which has become known as the 'indirect benefit' rule."[17] The court then held that as long as the unsecured creditors were no worse off because the Debtor, and consequently the estate, had received an amount reasonably equivalent to what it paid, no fraudulent transfer had occurred. The corporation had served merely as a conduit.[18] The primary focus was whether the net effect of the transfer had depleted the estate.[19] In summation, the court of appeals concluded that (1) no abuse of discretion occurred in refusing to allow the trustee to amend the "complaint a third time; (2) no actual fraudulent transfer occurred; (3) no constructive fraudulent transfer occurred; and (4) the payments met the requirements of the ordinary course of business exception to voidable preferences."[20]

---

[16] *Id. See* 11 USC §548(a)(2).

[17] *Id.* at 485 citing Rubin v. Manufacturers Hanover Trust Co., 661 F2d 979 (2d Cir. 1981).

[18] *Id. See also* Coral Petroleum Inc. v. Banque Paribas-London, 797 F2d 1351, 1356 (5th Cir. 1986), and *In re* Bohlen Enterprises, Ltd., 859 F2d 561 (8th Cir. 1988), for cases discussing "earmarking" of funds to a Debtor.

[19] *Id.*

[20] *Id.* at 488. *See, supra,* Chapter 15, this handbook, Preferences subtitle "Payment Made—No Preference—Ordinary Course of Business."

The Uniform Fraudulent Conveyance and Transfer Acts

We turn now to the Uniform Fraudulent Conveyance Act (UFCA) and the Uniform Fraudulent Transfer Act (UFTA) to examine what influence the Statute of Elizabeth and English common law cases have exerted on modern state law and federal bankruptcy law.[21] In 1918 the Commissioners who drafted the UFCA stated in a Prefatory Note that uniformity in the law of fraudulent conveyances was highly desirable because business largely disregards state lines and it is important for a creditor extending credit to know the degree to which he can rely on the property of his Debtor which is situated in another state. Confusion and uncertainties were due to three legal oversights: (1) the absence of a well-recognized definition of insolvency; (2) the failure to clarify the persons legally harmed by a fraudulent conveyance; and (3) the attempt to make the Statute of Elizabeth cover all conveyances which wrong creditors, even where actual intent to defraud does not exist.

To overcome these deficiencies, there was incorporated in the UFCA section 7.[22] The language of that section was described in one case as "having no broader meaning than the same expression in Statute of Elizabeth and [does] not embrace mere preferences."[23] Another snatch of law from the Statute of Elizabeth appears in the amendments to the UFCA by New York State which provide that: "Every conveyance made without fair consideration, *when the person making it is a defendant in an action for money judgment* damages or a judgment in such action has been docketed against him, is fraudulent as to the plaintiff. . . ."[24]

---

[21] *See* Baird & Jackson, 38 VAND. L. REV. 829 (1985). "In 1571 Parliament passed a statute making illegal and void any transfer made for the purpose of hindering, delaying, or defrauding creditors. This law commonly known as the Statute of Elizabeth was intended to curb what was intended to be a widespread abuse." *See* note 1 at 829, "13 Eliz., ch. 5 (1571)."

[22] *See* 7A U.L.A. at 513, annotating cases to UFCA §7.

[23] *Id.* citing Irving Trust Co. v. Kaminsky, 19 F. Supp. 816 (SDNY 1937).

[24] *See* Commissioner's Report 7A U.L.A. at 429 (1985) (emphasis added).

Uniform Fraudulent Transfer Act ("UFTA")

The UFTA is the successor to the UFCA in 26 states. The UFCA still remains in several states, including New York. Sections of the UFCA were adopted in the sections of the Bankruptcy Act of 1938. However, the UFTA followed the Bankruptcy Code of 1978 in adopting sections dealing with fraudulent transfers and obligations. Moreover, realizing the necessity for uniformity, the UFTA has modelled many of its definitions to conform to the Bankruptcy Code. As for the Statute of Elizabeth, the UFCA and the UFTA were "a codification of 'better' decisions applying the Statute of Elizabeth. . . ."[25]

Actual Fraud (Badges) or Constructive Fraud

A further observation of the Commissioners of the UFTA was that although the Statute of Elizabeth was enacted in some form in many states, nonetheless, the avoidability of fraudulent transfers is part of the law of every American jurisdiction. Disconcerting, however, was that the section to hinder, delay, or defraud was seldom susceptible of direct proof, leading the courts to rely on badges of fraud based on the Statute of Elizabeth. However, these badges varied greatly in each jurisdiction and the Conference sought to minimize or eliminate the diversity. This could be accomplished "by providing that proof of certain fact combinations would conclusively establish fraud. The absence of evidence of the existence of such facts, left proof of a fraudulent transfer to depend on evidence of actual intent."[26]

---

[25] *See* WEST UNIFORM LAWS ANNOTATED (West) Vol. 7A at 427 (UFCA) and (UFTA) at 639. *See* Supplement at 133. New York has not adopted the UFTA. The UFCA is contained in MCKINNEY'S CONSOLIDATED LAWS OF NEW YORK, DEBTOR AND CREDITOR LAW §270. California among other states adopted the UFTA.

[26] *See* Uniform Fraudulent Transfer Act § 4(a)(1), 7A U.L.A. at 653 (1985): "(a) A transfer . . . is fraudulent . . . if the Debtor made the transfer . . . (1) with actual intent to hinder, delay, or defraud any creditor of the Debtor; . . . (b) In determining actual intent under subsection (a)(1), consideration may be given, among other factors to, whether: (1) the transfer or obligation was to an insider. . ." (*See* subsections 1–11 for all factors.) *See*

Observation

The Statute of Elizabeth has served a useful guide to the clarification of fraudulent transfers. Badges of fraud will be helpful in ascertaining actual fraud; helpful also in such search are the factors set forth in UFTA, even though the complaint may be instituted under §548. Moreover, even without actual fraud present, the definition of constructive fraud has been expanded to clarify a fraudulent transfer law. Added to the accomplishment of UFTA, have been its efforts to follow the provisions of the Bankruptcy Code, specifically in §§544, 548, and 550.

Leveraged Buyout

The field of fraudulent conveyances has added to its family the leveraged buyout, but instead of using the common terminology of "Debtor," "Creditor," and "Transferee," it has acquired a nomenclature of its own: a shell corporation ("Acquirer"); Debtor ("Target"); and financial institution ("Lender"). The *Wieboldt* case[27] not only deals with the factual elements constituting an LBO, but discusses many areas of the law applicable to a leveraged buyout we have discussed in previous chapters. In addition, it includes the responsibility of directors under state corporate law for damage caused to the Debtor.

---

also §4(a)(2) as to receipt of "reasonably equivalent value" when about to engage in business or a transaction with unreasonably small capital or intended to incur debt beyond ability to pay.

[27] Wieboldt Stores, Inc. v. Schottenstein ("Wieboldt" or "Debtor"), 94 BR 488 (ND Ill. 1988), *appeal certified,* 1989 WL 51068 (ND Ill. 1989).

What is a Leveraged Buyout "LBO"?

Wieboldt filed for chapter 11 on September 8, 1987, and instituted an action as debtor in possession in the district court under §548, as well as under the fraudulent conveyance laws of Illinois[28] and the Illinois Business Corporation Act.[29] As an "Introduction," the court summarized the fraudulent transfers which constituted the LBO:

> Wieboldt's complaint against the defendants concerns the events and transactions surrounding a leveraged buyout ("LBO") of Wieboldt by WSI Acquisition Corporation ("WSI"). WSI, a corporation formed solely for the purpose of acquiring Wieboldt, borrowed funds from third-party lenders and delivered the proceeds to the shareholders in return for their shares. Wieboldt thereafter pledged certain of its assets to the LBO lenders to secure repayment of the loan.[30]

Wieboldt, as debtor in possession, alleged in its complaint that the LBO reduced the assets available to its creditors, liabilities were increased by millions, and the proceeds made available by the LBO Lenders were paid out to Wieboldt's then existing shareholders and did not accrue to the benefit of the corporation. Wieboldt further alleged that the Corporation became insolvent after the LBO, thereby leaving Wieboldt with insufficient unencumbered assets to sustain its business and ensure payment to its creditors. "Wieboldt therefore commenced this action on behalf of itself and its unsecured creditors, seeking to avoid the transactions constituting the LBO on the grounds that they are fraudulent under federal and state fraudulent conveyance laws."[31]

---

[28] *See* Ill. Rev. Stat. ch. 59 §4. Adopted UFTA effective January 1, 1990.

[29] *See* Business Corporation Act §9.10(c)(1).

[30] Wieboldt, 94 BR at 493.

[31] *Id.*

Reason for LBO

After a small operation as a dry goods store in 1883, William A. Wieboldt's business prospered and diversified and later incorporated under Illinois law. In 1982, business was done by twelve stores and a distribution center. At that time Wieboldt employed approximately 4,000 persons and had annual sales of approximately $190 million. Its stock was publicly traded on the New York Stock Exchange. After 1979, business started to decline and Wieboldt was able to continue its operations only by periodically selling its assets to generate working capital.

In this action Wieboldt sued 119 defendants whom the court grouped into three non-exclusive categories: (1) controlling shareholders, officers and directors ("Acquirers"); (2) other shareholders of Wieboldt's common stock who owned and tendered more than 1,000 shares in response to the tender offer ("Schedule A Shareholders"); and (3) entities which loaned money to fund the tender offer ("Lenders"). "The individuals and entities who controlled Wieboldt in 1982 became 'Controlling Shareholders' as a . . . result of [the] 1982 'takeover effort.'"[32]

Motion To Dismiss Complaint

On a motion to dismiss the complaint[33] the court held that it must accept the allegations of the complaint as true and must view the allegations in the light most favorable to the plaintiff. "'A complaint should be dismissed for failure to state a claim only if it appears beyond doubt that the plaintiff is unable to prove any set of facts that would entitle the plaintiff to relief. . . .'"[34]

---

[32] *Id.*

[33] *Id.* at 498. Motions were also made by several defendants to dismiss under Federal Rule of Civil Procedure 12(b)(2) for lack of personal jurisdiction, but the court held Bankruptcy Rule 7004(d) applied and Fed. R. Civ. P. 9(b) which provides that amendments of fraud are to be stated with particularity. The court dismissed both motions.

[34] *Id.* at 499, citing Doe v. St. Joseph's Hospital, 788 F2d 411, 414 (7th Cir. 1986).

Applicability of UFTA to Queen Elizabeth Statute

The *Weiboldt* court indicated that under §§544, 548, and 550 of the Bankruptcy Code and state law (Illinois) creditors are "protect[ed] . . . from transfers of property that are intended to impair a creditor's ability to enforce its rights to payment or that deplete a Debtor's assets at a time when its financial condition is precarious."[35] The *Wieboldt* court traced its authority, as did the *Kupetz* case,[36] back to the Queen Elizabeth Statute, "the substance of which has been either enacted in American statutes prohibiting such transactions or has been incorporated into American law as part of the English common law heritage."[37]

Defendants' Objections

The court overruled the objections of the defendants who contended that fraudulent conveyances were not applicable to LBO's because (1) applying them to public tender offers effectively allows creditors to insure themselves against subsequent mismanagement of the company; (2) rendering LBO's void severely restricts their usefulness and results in great unfairness; and (3) fraudulent conveyance laws were never intended to be used to prohibit or restrict public tenders.

The court responded by stating that although some support existed for the defendants' arguments,[38] the court could not upon a motion to dismiss hold that this LBO was entirely exempt from fraudulent conveyance laws. "Neither Section 548 of the Code nor the Illinois statute exempt such transactions from their statutory coverage."[39] In addition, the court listed a string of opinions of other courts "which have addressed this

---

[35] *Id.*

[36] *See infra,* this chapter, subtitle "Kupetz—No Fraudulent Conveyance."

[37] *Id.* citing Sherwin, *Creditors' Rights Against Participants in a Leveraged Buyout,* 72 MINN. L. REV. 449, 465–66 (1988).

[38] *Id.* citing Baird & Jackson, *Fraudulent Conveyance Law and its Proper Dominion,* 38 VAND. L. REV. 829 (1985).

[39] *Id.*

issue [and] have concluded that LBO's in some circumstances may constitute a fraudulent conveyance."[40]

Collapsing Interrelated Transactions

Certain defendants argued that they were protected by the literal language of §548 and the "good faith transferee for value" rule in §550. They contended that they did not receive Wieboldt property during the tender offer and if they did they were protected by the good faith rule in §550 and without knowledge of the voidability of the transfer.[41]

The court observed that the merit of the assertion turned on the court's interpretation of the tender offer and the LBO transactions. Defendants contended that the tender offer and LBO were composed of a series of interrelated but independent transactions.

> Wieboldt, on the other hand, urges the court to collapse the interrelated transactions into one aggregate transaction which had the overall effect of conveying Wieboldt property to the tendering shareholders and LBO lenders. This approach requires the court to find that the persons and entities receiving the conveyance were direct transferees who received an interest of the Debtor in property during the tender offer/buyout, and that WSI and any other parties to the transactions were mere conduits of Wieboldt's property. If the court finds that all

---

[40] *Id.* "*See, e.g.,* Kupetz v. Continental Illinois National Bank and Trust, 77 BR 754 (CD Cal. 1987), *aff'd sub nom* Kupetz v. Wolf, 845 F2d 842 (9th Cir. 1988) (applying section 548 and the California statute, West's Ann. Cal. Civ. Code ¶¶3439–3439.12); ... United States v. Gleneagles Investment Co., Inc., 565 F. Supp. 556 (MD Pa. 1983), *aff'd in part and remanded in part,* United States v. Tabor Court Realty, 803 F2d 1288 (3d Cir. 1986), *cert. denied,* McClellan Realty Co. v. United States, 107 S.Ct. 3229 (1987) (applying the Pennsylvania Uniform Fraudulent Conveyance Act, 39 P.S. §351). ..."

[41] *Id.* at 500. *See* §550(a) and (b) (Liability of transferee of avoided transfer). *See also* §551 (Automatic preservation of avoided transfer); §552 (Postpetiton effect of security interest); and §553 (Setoff).

the transfers constituted one transaction, then defendants received property from Wieboldt and Wieboldt has stated a claim against them.[42]

Kupetz—No Fraudulent Conveyance

The court responded that few courts have considered whether complicated fraudulent conveyances should be valued separately or collapsed into one integrated transaction. However, the court turned to the *Kupetz* and *Tabor* cases whose "opinions provide some illumination on this issue."[43] In *Kupetz,* the Ninth Circuit declined to strike down an LBO on fraudulent conveyance grounds holding that the trustee could not avoid the transfer to the shareholders because (1) they did not sell their shares in order to defraud Debtor's creditors; (2) they did not know that the Acquirer intended to leverage the company's assets to finance the purchase of shares; and (3) the LBO had the indicia of a straight sale of shares and was not the Debtor's attempt to redeem its own shares.[44]

The *Wieboldt* court, however, noted that the Ninth Circuit did state that "In an LBO, the lender, by taking a security interest in the company's assets, reduces the assets available to creditors in the event of failure of the business. The form of the LBO, while not unimportant, does not alter this reality. Thus, where the parties in an LBO fully intend to hinder the general creditors and benefit the selling shareholders, the conveyance is fraudulent under [the fraudulent conveyance laws]."[45]

---

[42] *Id.* at 500.

[43] *Id. See supra* note 40.

[44] *Id.* at 501.

[45] *Id. See* note 18: "The court decided *Tabor Court* on the basis of Pennsylvania's version of the Uniform Fraudulent Conveyances Act ("UFCA"), 39 Pa. Stat. §§354–357, 803 F2d at 1291. However, the basic principles in the case are equally applicable to cases decided under the Code."

Tabor—Fraudulent Conveyance

In *Tabor,* the Third Circuit discussed the liability of an LBO Lender, whereas in *Kupetz* the Ninth Circuit discussed shareholder liability under the fraudulent conveyance laws. In *Tabor,* the controlling shareholders of the Debtor corporation solicited a purchaser for the company. The purchaser formed a holding company to purchase the Debtor's outstanding shares. The holding company then acquired the controlling shares of the Debtor by borrowing funds from a third party Lender and securing the loan with first and second mortgages on Debtor's assets.[46]

After the company failed and many of its assets had been sold, the United States sought to recover judgment on certain tax liens against the Debtor's property and satisfy the judgments out of assets which the company owned before it mortgaged those assets to secure LBO funds. The Third Circuit affirmed the district court's conclusion that the mortgages Debtor gave to the Lender "were fraudulent conveyances within the meaning of the constructive and intentional fraud sections of the Pennsylvania UFCA. . . . In affirming the district court, the Third Circuit noted that all three parties—the lender, the Debtor and the purchaser—participated in the loan negotiations, and that the [Lender] therefore knew of the purpose to which [the Acquirer] intended to put the loan proceeds. . . . The Court held that the district court, in interpreting the LBO, correctly integrated the series of transactions because the [Acquirer] merely served as a conduit for a transfer between [the controlling stockholders] and [Lender] (and ultimately to the shareholders) and did not receive the funds as any form of consideration."[47]

Although neither of the foregoing cases involved transactions which were identical to the *Wieboldt* buyout, their opinions were "nonetheless, significant because the courts in both cases expressed the view that an LBO transfer—in whatever form—was a fraudulent conveyance if the circumstances of the transfer were not 'above board.'"[48] Thus, even

---

[46] *Id.*

[47] *Id.* at 502 citing Tabor, 803 F2d at 1296 and 1302.

[48] *Id.* citing Kupetz, 845 F2d at 847.

though the court in *Kupetz* declined to hold the selling shareholders liable, "there was no showing in *Kupetz* that the shareholders intended to defraud [the company's] creditors nor even knew that the purchaser intended to finance the takeover by leveraging the company's assets."[49]

In contrast, "the court in *Tabor Court* found the LBO lender liable because it participated in the negotiations surrounding the LBO transactions and knew that the proceeds of its loan to [Acquirer] would deplete the Debtor's assets to the point at which it was functionally insolvent under the fraudulent conveyance and bankruptcy laws. These cases indicate that a court should focus not on the formal structure of a transaction but rather on the knowledge or intent of the parties involved in the transaction."[50]

Parties Liable By Fraudulent LBO

Applying the foregoing principle to defendants' assertion the district court concluded: "[I]t is clear that, at least as regards the liability of the controlling shareholders, the LBO lenders, and the insider shareholders, the LBO transfers must be collapsed into one transaction. The complaint alleges clearly that these participants in the LBO negotiations attempted to structure the LBO with the requisite knowledge and contemplation that the full transaction, tender offer and LBO, be completed."[51] In addition, the complaint alleged that the board and insider-shareholders knew that the Acquirer "intended to finance its acquisition of Wieboldt through an LBO . . . and not with any of its own funds . . . they knew that Wieboldt was insolvent before the LBO and that the LBO would result in further encumbrance of Wieboldt's already encumbered assets. . . ; [A]ttorneys . . . apprised the Board of the fraudulent conveyance laws and suggested that they structure the LBO so as to avoid liability . . .," and, moreover, the insider shareholders nonetheless, recommended that

---

[49] *Id.*

[50] *Id.*

[51] *Id.*

Wieboldt accept the tender offer and tendered their own shares to WSI (Acquirer).[52]

Good Faith Shareholders Protected

> [This] court, however, is not willing to "collapse"[53] the transaction in order to find that the Schedule A shareholders also received the Debtor's property in the transfer. . . . Wieboldt does not allege that the Schedule A shareholders were aware . . . that the consideration they received for their tendered shares was Wieboldt property. . . . In fact, the complaint does not suggest that the Schedule A shareholders had any part in the LBO except as innocent pawns in the scheme. They were aware only that WSI made a public tender offer for shares of Wieboldt stock.[54]

The court stated that its conclusion was in accordance with the fraudulent conveyance laws: "The drafters of the Code, while attempting to protect parties harmed by fraudulent conveyances, also intended to shield innocent recipients of fraudulent conveyed property from liability."[55] Indicating that while §550(a) permits a trustee to avoid a transfer to an initial transferee or its subsequent transferee, subsection (b) limits recovery from a subsequent transferee by providing that a trustee may not recover fraudulently conveyed property from a transferee who takes property in good faith, for value, and without knowledge that the original transfer was voidable.[56]

As for the LBO lenders and the controlling and insider shareholders of Wieboldt, they were direct transferees of Wieboldt property. Although WSI participated in effecting the transactions, it served mainly as a conduit for the exchange of assets and loan proceeds between LBO lenders and Wieboldt

---

[52] *Id.*

[53] *Id.* at 503.

[54] *Id.*

[55] *Id.*

[56] *Id. See* §550.

and shares of stock between LBO lenders and insider and controlling shareholders. The Schedule A shareholders, however, were not direct transferees of Wieboldt property.

The court continued by observing that the formal structure of the transaction alone could not shield the LBO lenders or the controlling and insider shareholders from Wieboldt's fraudulent conveyance claims. The contrary was true with respect to Schedule A shareholders who were apparently unaware of the financing transactions and participated only to the extent that they exchanged their shares for funds from WSI. Therefore, based on the allegations of the complaint the court concluded: "1. the motions to dismiss filed by the LBO lenders, inside shareholders, and controlling shareholders are denied at this point because these parties received Wieboldt property through a series of integrated LBO transactions; and 2. the Schedule A shareholders' motions to dismiss are granted because these defendants did not receive Wieboldt property through the separate exchange of shares for cash."[57]

Actual Fraud by Defendants

Having determined that the LBO lenders, the insider shareholders, and controlling shareholders remain parties to the action, the court turned to whether the complaint stated sufficient facts to constitute a fraudulent conveyance under the provisions of §548(a)(1) and Illinois law. Section 548(a)(1) of the Bankruptcy Code requires a trustee to allege that the transfer was made within one year before the filing of the petition and the transfer was made with actual fraud.

In finding actual fraud, inferences can be drawn from a course of conduct, such as a scheme or general plan to strip the Debtor of its assets without regards to the needs of its creditors and, in addition, "badges of fraud" may constitute an indication of actual fraud. Applying the law to the allegations of the complaint, several of the defendants received Wieboldt's interest in real property with actual intent. Specifically, the "LBO Lenders and the controlling and insider shareholders structured the LBO transfers in such a way as to attempt to

---

[57] *Id.* at 504.

evade fraudulent conveyance liability."[58] The allegations were a sufficient assertion of actual fraud and defendants' motions to dismiss these counts were denied.

Constructive Fraudulent Counts

No definition of actual fraud is supplied by §548(a)(1), but help may be obtained by §§4(a) and 4(b) of UFTA. Section 4(b) suggests eleven factors which may be considered in proving actual intent, but if difficulty exists in proving those factors, then §548(a)(2) requires a plaintiff to allege only constructive fraud. In the *Wieboldt* case, the trustee joined both actual and constructive intent as separate counts in the complaint.

The basic allegation in constructive fraudulent conveyances is insolvency. As to "insolvency," the court discussed §101(31)(A) of the Code as "a condition which occurs when the sum of an entity's debts exceeds the sum of its property 'at a fair valuation'. . . ."[59] Wieboldt's complaint alleged that the corporation was insolvent in November, 1985 'in that the fair saleable value of its assets was exceeded by its liabilities when the liquidity of those assets is taken into account.'" The court held that Wieboldt's "insolvency" requirement was satisfied.[60]

Finally, defendants claimed that Wieboldt could not state a claim under §548(a)(2) because it received "reasonably equivalent value" in the transfer to the shareholders and the conveyance of certain real property.

> Wieboldt granted a security interest in substantially all of its real estate assets to Household Commercial Finance Services and received from the shareholders in return 99% of its outstanding shares of stock. . . . This stock

---

[58] *Id.*

[59] *Id.* at 505.

[60] *Id. See* §548(a)(2)(A): "received less than a reasonably equivalent value in exchange for such transfer"; (a)(2)(B)(i): "was insolvent on the date that such transfer was made . . . or became insolvent. . ."; (and) (B)(ii): "was engaged in business . . . for which any property remaining with the Debtor was an unreasonably small capital; or (B)(iii) intended to incur . . . debts that would be beyond the Debtor's ability to pay as such debts matured."

was virtually worthless to Wieboldt[61]. . . .
Wieboldt received less than a reasonably
equivalent value in exchange for an encumbrance on virtually all of its non-inventory
assets, and therefore, has stated a claim against
the controlling and insider shareholders.[62]

Another fraudulent transfer diagnosed by the court to
indicate that Wieboldt did not receive reasonably equivalent
value involved "State Street Property." The effect and
intention of the parties was to generate funds to purchase
outstanding shares of Wieboldt stock. The property was sold
to One North State Street Limited Partnership for $30 million
and the proceeds used to pay off part of the $35 million owed
to another creditor. "Wieboldt did not receive a benefit from
this transfer."[63] The motion to dismiss these counts was
denied.

Fraudulent Conveyance Under State Law

The court then turned to §544(b)[64] of the Bankruptcy Code.
A trustee may avoid transfers that are avoidable under state
law if there is at least one creditor at the time who has
standing under state law to challenge the transfer. Turning to
the Illinois fraudulent conveyance statute,[65] the court observed
its similarity to §548 of the Bankruptcy Code. "Illinois courts
divide fraudulent conveyances into two categories: fraud in law
and fraud in fact. . . . In fraud in fact cases, a court must find
a specific intent to defraud creditors; in fraud in law cases,
fraud is presumed from the circumstances."[66] Analyzing the
facts and the law, the court held that it could not dismiss
Wieboldt's claim under section 4 of the Illinois statute.

---

[61] *Id.* citing *In re* Roco Corp., 701 F2d 978, 982 (1st Cir. 1983), et al.

[62] *Id.*

[63] *Id.* at 506 citing Tabor Court, 803 F2d at 1330.

[64] *Id. See supra* Chapter 14, this handbook, subtitle "Trustee's Strong-Arm section 544."

[65] *Id.* citing Ill. Rev. Stat. ch. 59 §4 (1976).

[66] *Id.* citing Tcherepnin v. Franz, 475 F. Supp. 92, 96 (ND Ill. 1979).

Directors' Breach of Fiduciary Duty
State Law

The complaint also contained a claim for relief against Wieboldt's former directors for breach of fiduciary duty alleging that the directors owed Wieboldt a fiduciary duty of "utmost good faith, care and loyalty"[67] when dealing with the corporation and the board was required to investigate thoroughly corporate transactions such as the LBO. A similar duty was owed to Wieboldt's unsecured creditors. Overruling defendants' argument that Wieboldt did not have standing to bring an action against the directors for breach of fiduciary duty, the district court held that Wieboldt in its capacity as "a trustee in bankruptcy, has the right to bring any action in which the Debtor has an interest, including actions against the Debtor's officers and directors for breach of duty or misconduct. . . ."[68] 'In that capacity, the trustee acts to benefit the Debtor's estate, which ultimately will benefit the Debtor's creditors upon distribution.'"[69]

The directors contended that the principles the Supreme Court enunciated in the *Bangor Punta* case[70] precluded Wieboldt from asserting such claim. The court distinguished *Bangor* from the facts in Wieboldt. In *Bangor*, the Supreme Court held that "principles of equity precluded a corporation's new majority shareholder from maintaining an action against the company's former owners for corporate waste and mismanagement. The court reasoned that, although the suit was purportedly brought on behalf of the corporation, the principal beneficiary of a recovery from the former owners was the new majority shareholder. . . ."[71]

To the contrary, Wieboldt argued that it filed its action against the directors, not on behalf of WSI's equity interest, but on behalf of its unsecured creditors. The court of appeals

---

[67] *Id.* at 507.

[68] *Id.* citing Koch Refining v. Farmers Union Cent. Exchange, Inc., 831 F2d 1339, 1348 (7th Cir. 1987), *cert. denied,* 108 S.Ct. 1077 (1988); et al.

[69] *Id.* citing Koch, 831 F2d at 1348.

[70] Bangor Punta Operations, Inc. v. Bangor Aroostook Railroad Co. ("Bangor Punta" or "Bangor"), 94 S.Ct. 2578 (1974).

[71] 94 BR at 507.

noted that the *Bangor Punta* decision did not require the court to dismiss in their entirety Wieboldt's claims for breach of fiduciary duty. "The creditors cannot receive a 'windfall' recovery, but may recover only to the extent of their claims. By contrast, the Bangor Punta Court specifically noted that the plaintiff brought its cause of action on its own behalf, not on behalf of its creditors. . . ."[72]

Taking each of the directors' arguments step by step, following the *Bangor Punta* case, the district court rejected the other directors' arguments: First, this was not an action by Wieboldt asserting personal claims of particular creditors, but "[t]he complaint alleges that Wieboldt is the corporate victim of the Board's poor management and that consequently its unsecured creditors have suffered harm as well . . . [that] the Board's action resulted in a depletion of the assets available to repay the claims of its unsecured creditors. The complaint does not identify any specific loss to a creditor in its individual capacity. . . . Wieboldt, as Debtor-in-possession of its bankrupt estate, clearly may assert a claim for breach of fiduciary duty on behalf of its group of unsecured creditors."[73]

Equitable Subordination of Post-LBO Creditors

The directors further argued that Wieboldt may not represent the interest of any *post-transaction* creditor who should have known of the Debtor's financial condition when entering into its credit transaction. Such creditor "who is allowed to recover in a subsequent law suit would receive more than the value of the bargain it freely entered into and would be unjustly enriched."[74] Observing that the current lawsuit was collateral to Wieboldt's chapter 11 proceeding, the court stated that the claims of each creditor would be adjudicated in the reorganization. "The trustee and the bankruptcy court can subordinate the claims of any creditors who are not entitled to reimbursement from the Chapter 11 estate pursuant to Section 510(c) of the Code at the time of distribution. Consequently, the court need not exclude any group of

---

[72] 94 BR at 508.

[73] *Id.* at 508–09.

[74] *Id.* at 509.

creditors from participating in a recovery on this stage of this proceeding."[75]

Directors' Degree of Care
Business Judgment Rule

No duty was owed to the corporation at the time of the LBO the directors argued, but rather the directors owed a duty only to "shareholders who were of record on or before December 19, 1985 [the date on which the directors resigned or were replaced]. Because no such shareholder claims to have been injured by the buyout, the directors argue, Wieboldt has no claim."[76]

The court responded that directors "must exercise the degree of care that a reasonably prudent director of a similar corporation would use under the circumstances. . . . However, Illinois law also provides for a 'business judgment rule.' Under the business judgment rule, directors who perform diligently and carefully and have not acted fraudulently, illegally, or otherwise in bad faith will not be liable for honest errors or mistakes of judgment."[77] Rejecting the directors' argument that they did not owe a duty to the corporation during the formulation and execution of the LBO, the court stated: "A corporate board of directors has a fundamental duty to protect the corporate enterprise from 'harm reasonably perceived irrespective of its source.'"[78]

Holding that the complaint alleged sufficient facts to support a cause of action against the directors for breach of their fiduciary duty to the corporation, the court turned to the Illinois Business Corporation Act.[79] Section 9.10(c) prohibits a

---

[75] *Id.* citing §510(c) Equitable Subordination.

[76] *Id.*

[77] *Id. See also* Treco, Inc., v. Land of Lincoln Savings & Loan, 749 F2d 374, 377 (7th Cir. 1984).

[78] *Id.* citing Unocal Corp. v. Mesa Petroleum, 493 A2d 946, 954 (Del. Supr. 1985). *See also* at 509 note 29: "Illinois courts have often looked to Delaware law for guidance in deciding previously undecided corporate law issues. *See, e.g.,* Treco 749 F2d at 379. . . ."

[79] *Id.* at 510. Illinois Business Corporation Act of 1983, Ill. Rev. Stat. ch. 32, ¶¶865(a)(1) and 9.10(c)(1) ("IBCA").

board of directors from authorizing a distribution to shareholders that would have the effect of rendering the corporation insolvent. Section 8.65(a)(1) provides that directors who assent to a distribution prohibited by §9.10 are jointly and severally liable to the corporation for the amount of the distribution. The court noted that:

> Neither Section 9.10 nor any other section of the IBCA defines the term "distribution" as it is used in the Act. . . . Section 1.40(6) provides that the term "distribution" encompasses: a direct or indirect transfer of money or other property (except [a corporation's] own shares) or incurrence of indebtedness by a corporation to or for the benefit of its shareholders in respect to any of its shares. A distribution may be in the form of a declaration or payment of a dividend; a purchase, redemption or other acquisition of shares; a distribution of indebtedness; or otherwise.[80]

Necessary Parties to Action

The court then held that in the absence of contrary authority, it appeared likely that the Illinois legislature contemplated a broad range of transfers, including indirect transfers such as the exchange of cash and shares between a lender and the shareholders. The directors' motion to dismiss this count was likewise denied. This left a motion by certain of the defendants to dismiss the complaint under "Fed. R. Civ. P. 12(b)(7) on the grounds that Wieboldt has failed to join parties who are necessary for just adjudication under F[ed]. R. C[iv]. P. 19 . . . [namely the] absence of (1) all those persons who held and tendered fewer than 1,000 shares during the tender offer ('Absent Shareholders'), and (2) WSI Sub, Inc., WSI Acquisition Corp., and their principals ('WSI Parties')."[81]

---

[80] *Id.* at 511.

[81] *Id.* at 512. "Fed. R. Civ. P. 19(a) states in part: '(a) Persons to be joined if feasible. . . . A person who is subject to service of process and whose joinder will not deprive the court of jurisdiction over the subject matter of the action

The court held that the Absent Shareholders were not necessary parties to the action. The court dismissed the count against the Schedule A shareholders because they did not receive Wieboldt's property during the LBO transactions and therefore could not be liable as a transferee of fraudulently conveyed property. "The court's reasoning applies equally well to the Absent Shareholders. Wieboldt does not allege in its complaint that the absent shareholders were aware of the insider and controlling shareholders' and LBO Lenders' alleged scheme to defraud Wieboldt's creditors. Like the Schedule A shareholders, the Absent Shareholders participated in the scheme only to the extent that they exchanged their shares for funds from WSI. The Absent Shareholders are not necessary parties to this litigation."[82]

The finality of the opinion dealt with the necessity of the WSI Parties to a just adjudication of the dispute. "The absence of the WSI Parties does not create the possibility that defendants will incur inconsistent obligations because the WSI Parties could not obtain the relief that Wieboldt requests in its complaint from these defendants in a subsequent lawsuit. . . . Only a trustee in bankruptcy or Debtor-in-possession can request relief under the fraudulent conveyance provisions in the Bankruptcy Code. . . . As this court has previously discussed, equity precludes WSI, as Wieboldt's new majority shareholder, from bringing an action against Wieboldt's former managers for mismanagement and breach of their fiduciary duty."[83]

Defendant's Rule 19 motion to dismiss was denied. The Schedule A shareholder defendants' motion to dismiss Count VIII against them was granted. The other defendants' motions to dismiss the remaining counts of the complaint were denied.

---

shall be joined as a party in the action if (1) in the person's absence complete relief cannot be accorded. . . .'"

[82] *Id.*

[83] *Id.*

Observation

This chapter on fraudulent conveyance cases may almost be likened to a historical novel dating as it does by common law to the Statute of Queen Elizabeth (1571) to *Wieboldt* (1988) and back again. But undoubtedly, there will be more history written as time advances. The *Wieboldt* case indicates that there are several ramifications of a complaint alleging a fraudulent conveyance, not only as to the allegations dealing with the Bankruptcy Code, but also as to those which support the trustee under state law by virtue of §544.[84]

As the district court indicated, the allegations in the complaint are to be taken as they are written. A ruling against a motion to dismiss a count in the complaint is not to be taken as a final determination by the court that that particular count has been decided by the court. What the court has done is to hold that upon a trial the plaintiff will prove the elements set forth in the count, so that judgment will be granted or the plaintiff will fail to prove the necessary elements, in which case judgment of the count will be denied.

The *Wieboldt* case is a comprehensive case transaction which holds a flashlight to merchants concerning what problems of law have to be considered in supporting the validity of an LBO from start to finish. The case commences with actual fraudulent conveyances, defined by badges of fraud described by the U.C.C., or with constructive fraud under the Code. Also discussed were state laws having similar fraudulent transfer statutes extending beyond the Code's provisions but which are applicable by §544, the trustee's strong-arm powers. Thus, the trustee's powers as a judgment creditor authorize the trustee to institute additional actions such as breach of fiduciary duties, against former members of a board of directors, claiming damages for breach of corporate duties.

---

[84] *See* 94 BR 488, 499: "Modern fraudulent conveyance law derives from the English Statute, . . . the substance of which has been enacted either in American statutes prohibiting such transactions or has been incorporated into American law as part of the English common law heritage."

The pervasiveness of these problems as they extend from the Code to the laws of every state illustrate the dangers which should be avoided when contemplating an LBO.

Foreclosure of Real Property
Fraudulent Transfer Analyzed

Another area of the law which the courts have attempted to regulate so as to avoid a fraudulent transfer is the foreclosure of real property. Several circuit courts have taken contrary opinions in deciding whether a procedure in foreclosing a sale of real property constitutes a fraudulent transfer. We start with the most recent decision, *In re BFP, A Partnership Debtor,*[85] which analyzed three cases that preceded it. First, the *Durrett*[86] case, which held that a prepetition foreclosure sale constituted a fraudulent sale because the sale brought less than 70% of the fair market value of the property. Second, the *Madrid*[87] case, which arrived at a contrary opinion establishing the "irrebuttable presumption" rule, namely, that a foreclosure sale would not be set aside as a fraudulent transfer although less than 70% of the fair market value had been received. However, the secured creditor had to demonstrate that the consideration was received at a non-collusive and regularly conducted nonjudicial foreclosure sale. Such sale satisfied the reasonably equivalent value of §548(a)(2)(A) as a matter of law and the sale could not be set aside.

In the third case, *Bundles,*[88] the court focused on reasonably equivalent value, holding that the bankruptcy court should neither grant a conclusive presumption in favor of a purchaser at a regularly conducted, non-collusive foreclosure sale, nor limit its inquiry to a simple comparison of the sale price to the fair market value. Reasonable equivalence should depend on all the facts of each case. In addition, the

---

[85] 974 F2d 1144 (9th Cir. 1992) ("BFP" or "Debtor").

[86] Durrett v. Washington National Insurance Co. ("Durrett"), 621 F2d 201 (5th Cir. 1980).

[87] *In re* Madrid ("Madrid"), 21 BR 424 (BAP 9th Cir. 1982), *aff'd on other grounds,* 725 F2d 1197 (9th Cir.), *cert. denied,* 105 S.Ct. 125 (1984).

[88] *In re* Bundles ("Bundles"), 856 F2d 815 (7th Cir. 1988).

bankruptcy court while determining whether the foreclosure meets with the federal standard of reasonable equivalent value, must accord respect to the state foreclosure proceeding. While the state law is not conclusive with respect to the issue of federal law before the bankruptcy court, it is an important element in analysis of that question.

Having completed its observation on *Durrett* (5th Cir.), *Madrid* (6th Cir.), and *Bundles* (7th Cir.), the court of appeals, in the *BFP* case (9th Cir.), observed that in a published decision[89] the Bankruptcy Appellate Panel applied its earlier decision in *Madrid* and held that the price received at a noncollusive, regularly conducted foreclosure sale establishes as a matter of law reasonably equivalent value under 11 U.S.C. §548(a)(2)(A). "Although the issue is a close one we agree that the *Madrid* rule is the appropriate interpretation of the Bankruptcy Code. As the Sixth Circuit has stated, '[T]he better view is that reasonable equivalence for the purposes of a foreclosure sale under §548(a)(2)(A) should be consonant with the state law of fraudulent conveyances.'"[90]

Taking such position the court stated: "We necessarily part from the position taken by the Fifth Circuit in *Durrett v. Washington Nat'l. Ins. Co.* . . .[91] and the Seventh Circuit in *Bundles.*"[92] Summarizing, the Ninth Circuit stated that "[the] *Bundles* analysis (and implicitly that of the *Durrett* approach) rests on a plain language interpretation of §548(a)(2). Granting an *irrebuttable* presumption of reasonable equivalence under a noncollusive foreclosure sale, the *Bundles* court argued, effectively creates a judicial exception to the trustee's avoiding powers under §548. . . . In turn, an irrebuttable presumption undermines the ability of the trustee or Debtor to recover lost equity, which is the purpose of the

---

[89] *In re* BFP, 132 BR 748 (BAP 9th Cir. 1991).

[90] *In re* BFP, 974 F2d at 1148 citing *In re* Winshall Settlor's Trust, 758 F2d 1136, 1139 (6th Cir. 1985) (citing Madrid).

[91] *Id. See also* 974 F2d at 1148 n. 4 (discussing Durrett's "70% floor rule").

[92] *Id. See* 974 F2d at 1148 n. 5 objecting to the middle ground taken by Bundles between Durrett and Madrid.

§548 avoiding powers. The position is persuasive, but we think that broader considerations require a different result."[93]

The court opined that one of the problems involved in requiring the bankruptcy court to undo a foreclosure, carries with it the strong potential to destabilize state mortgage transactions. "[T]he prospect that trial courts will determine reasonable equivalence on a case-by-case basis is untenable from both federal and state perspectives. From a state viewpoint, an *ad hoc* approach produces intolerable uncertainty regarding the finality of any purchase at a foreclosure sale even if the price paid at the sale is close to, but not equal to, the retail market value. From a federal perspective this uncertainty undermines the price-maximizing objectives of section 548(a)(2)(A) because potential buyers will discount their assessment of the true market value of the property to reflect this uncertainty."[94]

Observation

With sound advice, which prompts us to agree, the court concluded that following the *"Madrid* formulation," a more reasonable meaning will be given to §548 "without unduly upsetting local real estate markets or state law. Unlike the *Bundles* court, we see the issue as *both* one of statutory interpretation *and* the growing tension between preemption and the requirements of a vigorous federal system. . . . Thus, by interpreting §548 in accordance with the *Madrid* formulation, we are able to balance bankruptcy policy and comity concerns."[95] Of additional importance is the statement of the court "that the *Madrid* formulation has been adopted by the National Conference of Commissioners on Uniform State

---

[93] *Id.* (emphasis in original).

[94] *Id.* citing Ehrlich, *Avoidance of Foreclosure Sales As Fraudulent Conveyances: Accommodating State and Federal Objectives,* 71 VA. L. REV. 933, 963–64 (1985).

[95] *Id.* at 1149 (emphasis in original). *See* Cipollone v. Liggett Group, Inc., 112 S.Ct. 2608, 2617–18 (1992).

Laws . . . and has been recommended by the American Bar Association. . . ."[96]

Fraudulent Transfers
Racketeering Influenced Corrupt Organizations (RICO)

Having previously discussed a group of three sections as a close family designed to recover prepetition transfers by a trustee, we awaited the arrival of an in-law, the Racketeering Influenced Corrupt Organizations Act ("RICO").[97] In the *Sattler* case,[98] the trustee instituted an action against defendants alleging eight claims for relief, including one under RICO, and another for "state fraudulent transfers; . . ."[99] Thus, again, we see that §544 also finds itself utilizing the UFCA.

Under RICO, a private right of action is expressly granted if the plaintiff sufficiently pleads economic injury. The requisite economic harm must arise from either of the following prohibited activities: (1) the use of income derived from a pattern of racketeering activity to acquire a financial interest in an enterprise; (2) the acquisition or maintenance of an interest in an enterprise through a pattern of racketeering activity; (3) conducting the affairs of an enterprise through a pattern of racketeering activity; and (4) a conspiracy to commit any of the above activities. Although originally designed to target organized criminal activity, the broad civil provisions of the Act also reach activity not associated with organized crime.

Bankruptcy Procedure

The RICO statute meets the Bankruptcy Code when a business which has engaged in alleged violations of the RICO statute, subsequently files for bankruptcy relief or an involuntary petition is filed against it, and the trustee or

---

[96] *Id.* at n. 6: "[S]ee Unif. Fraudulent Transfer Act §3(b) 1984 . . . see 1983 A.B.A. Sec. of Real Prop. Rep. 106(B)."

[97] *See* 18 USC §1962(c).

[98] *In re* Sattler's, Inc. ("Sattler"), 73 BR 780 (B. SDNY 1987).

[99] *Id.* at 784.

debtor in possession attempts to avoid the suspect prepetition transfers as fraudulent conveyances. A vivid illustration of the manner in which RICO violations are subject to fraudulent conveyance attack appears in the *Ahead by A Length* case[100] in which a chapter 7 trustee alleged that certain prepetition transactions of the Debtor violated the RICO statute and constituted fraudulent conveyances under applicable federal bankruptcy and state fraudulent conveyance law. Specifically, the trustee alleged that two principals of the corporation caused fraudulent invoices totalling approximately $25 million to be paid by the Debtor. The trustee also alleged that corporations owned by two individuals affiliated with the Debtor submitted the fraudulent invoices and that the Debtor did not receive any goods or services in return for the payments.

Actual and Constructive Intent

Not only does actual and constructive fraudulent intent constitute the fundamental components of a fraudulent transfer under the Bankruptcy Code, but the identical components also exist under state law. This similarity emerges from the court's discussion of the trustee's claims: "[T]he defendants advance one further argument for dismissing the state law constructive fraud claim—that they provided fair consideration for the transfers. . . . The concepts of fair consideration [are found] under section 272 of the New York Debtor and Creditor Law. . . ."[101] The "defendants assert a meritorious challenge to the actual fraud claims which the trustee apparently intended to plead under federal and state law. The seventh claim for relief is alleged to be brought under Code section 548 without reference to any particular subsection thereof, and the eighth claim for relief is alleged to be brought under Debtor and Creditor Law section 270 and the sections following, without reference to any particular section of that article."[102]

---

[100] *In re* Ahead By A Length, Inc., 100 BR 157 (B. SDNY 1989).

[101] *Id.* at 169.

[102] *Id.*

Considering whether the trustee's claims would withstand the defendants' motion to dismiss the fraudulent conveyance claims, the court concluded that the facts constituting the fraudulent scheme had been laid out in sufficient detail to fairly apprise defendants of the nature of the conduct, transactions, and occurrences of which the trustee complained. The trustee alleged that the transferees prevented the Debtor from timely paying the legitimate debts, forced the Debtor into insolvency and resulted and precipitated the filing of the involuntary bankruptcy petition against the Debtor.

> The trustee undeniably has standing to assert a RICO claim on behalf of the Debtor for harm done to the corporation itself. But she may not raise a creditor's claim directly, even though in a bankruptcy, a recovery for the corporation is a recovery for its creditors.[103]

The court noted, however, that if the claim sued upon is personal to the creditors, it does not become property of the estate under §541 and is not enforceable under §704,[104] and the trustee could not recover under §544. "This is because the trustee, unless she is exercising her statutory avoidance powers, stands in the shoes of the Debtor and may only institute whatever actions the Debtor could have brought itself. . . . [However,] [a]lthough inartfully pleaded, the Amended Complaint seems to be referring to a cognizable injury to the Debtor. Accordingly, the standing challenge must be rejected."[105]

Observation

When courts speak of the common law in relationship with the statutory law, the basic principles seem to be incorporated. An actual fraudulent transfer at common law marked by the

---

[103] *Id.* at 172. *See* Mixon v. Anderson (*In re* Ozark Restaurant Equipment Co., Inc.), 816 F2d 1222, 1225 (8th Cir. 1987) *cert. denied sub nom.* Jacoway v. Anderson, 108 S.Ct. 147 (1987).

[104] 11 USC §704. Duties of trustee.

[105] 100 BR at 173.

badges of fraud was no different than what today is considered constructive fraud pleaded by enumerating the very factors that amounted to a traditional fraudulent transfer. Moreover, the Bankruptcy Code's §544, which unites bankruptcy law with state law, the UFCA, the UFTA, and these other state and federal statutes, invites separate, common counts in a complaint.

We now turn to Consolidation of Multi-Tiered Corporations and their necessity in considering a plan of reorganization.

Chapter 17
Substantive Consolidation of Multi-Tiered Corporations

Substantive Consolidation and Joint Administration

Consolidation of cases is to be distinguished from joint administration.[1] The Code provides no definition for either but Rule 1015[2] is entitled: "Consolidation or Joint Administration of Cases Pending in Same Court." Section 1015(b) provides for example, that in cases involving two or more related debtors, such as husband and wife or a partnership with one or more of its general partners, or a

---

[1] *See* B. Rule 1015 (Consolidation or Joint Administration of Cases Pending in Same Court).

[2] *See also* Advisory Committee Note: "Consolidation, as distinguished from joint administration, is neither authorized or prohibited by this rule since the propriety of consolidation depends on substantive consideration and affects the substantive rights of the creditors of the different estates. . . ."

debtor and an affiliate, the court may order a joint administration of the estates.

Bankruptcy Rule 1015(c), entitled "Expediting And Protective Orders," goes a step further, and with reference to an order for consolidation or joint administration of two or more cases the court, while protecting the rights of the parties under the Code, may enter orders as may tend to avoid unnecessary costs and delay. These proceedings will generally include a single docket for administrative purposes. The joint cases continue to maintain their own identity as to assets and liabilities. Consolidation, *inter alia,* involves cases of a parent and subsidiaries, corporation, or partnership, which are united into one or more entities in order to mingle the assets and creditor liabilities: The objective, as we shall see, is to constitute a plan of reorganization which is equitable to all parties. In essence, consolidation of cases is generally a prelude to reorganization.[3]

Chemical Case

Consolidation

Even though Thomas Wolfe's sagacious advice was that you can't go home again, nevertheless, we do pay another visit to the early case of the *Chemical Bank New York Trust Co. v. Kheel*[4] to explore to what extent current bankruptcy cases have followed the *Chemical* principle of substantive consolidation in reorganization cases. The reader will note that the *Chemical* case is a Bankruptcy Act[5] case but it is cited in virtually every case in the Bankruptcy Code dealing with substantive consolidation.

In the *Chemical* case, Seatrade Corporation ("Seatrade") and seven corporations were engaged in the shipping trade and all were Debtors seeking reorganization under Chapter X

---

[3] *See, infra,* this chapter, "Applicability of Consolidation at Confirmation or Exigency."

[4] Chemical Bank New York Trust Co. ("Bank") v. Kheel ("trustee"), 369 F2d 845 (2d Cir. 1966).

[5] *See* United States Realty and Improvement Co., 60 S.Ct. 1044 (1940) and SEC v. Liberty Baking Corporation, 240 F2d (2d Cir.), *cert. denied,* 77 S.Ct. 719 (1957).

of the Bankruptcy Act.[6] A plan of Reorganization having failed, all were in liquidation. The United States, a major creditor, moved for consolidation of the proceeding. The bankruptcy trustee joined in the motion. The Bank, however, trustee for bondholders under a mortgage and indenture of Seatrade covering one of the vessels, and others opposed the motion for consolidation.

On reference to a Referee[7] as Special Master, consolidation was recommended. The district court and the court of appeals affirmed. "The Referee found that the debtor corporations were operated as a single unit with little or no attention paid to the formalities usually observed in independent corporations, that the officers and directors of all, so far as ascertainable, were substantially the same and acted as figureheads for [Manuel E.] Kulukundis, that funds were shifted back and forth between the corporations in an extremely complex pattern and in fact pooled together, loans were made back and forth, borrowings were made by some to pay obligations of others . . . and withdrawals and payments made from and to corporate accounts by Kulukundis personally [were] not sufficiently recorded on the books."[8] Observing the foregoing facts and others, the court of appeals held that the Referee's conclusion that auditing of the corporations' financial condition and "especially the intercompany relationships would entail great expenditure of time and expense without assurance that a fair reflection of the conditions of the debtor corporations would in the end be possible."[9]

Cases Distinguished

The court of appeals observed that the Bank's mortgage was under attack in the courts of Boston, the East Hampton

---

[6] Chapter X of the Bankruptcy Act Corporate Reorganization, 11 U.S.C. Title 11, Chapter X, §§501–676. *See* §129. "If a corporation be a subsidiary, an original petition by or against it may be filed either as provided in section 128 of this Act or in the court which has approved the petition by or against its parent corporation."

[7] 369 F2d at 846. *See, supra,* note 6 (now Judge of the Bankruptcy Court).

[8] *Id.*

[9] *Id.*

having been sold in proceedings in admiralty. The proceeds were sufficient to satisfy the secured debt if the mortgage was held to be good. The Bank was concerned, however, that "the mortgage may be defeated, and the claim become an unsecured one in which case it bears a lower eventual realization. . . . It contends . . . that consolidation of the assets and liabilities as to appellant is beyond the court's power absent a showing that it knowingly dealt with the group as a unit and relied on the group for payment."[10]

The court of appeals held that no such limitation on the power of the reorganization court existed, citing the *Soviero*[11] and *Stone*[12] cases. In the former case, the trustee in bankruptcy pierced the veil of corporate separateness of parent and affiliates by showing a unity of interest and ownership between the affiliates and the bankrupt. In the latter case, the court's reasoning was predicated upon the well known equitable doctrine of subordinating a parent's claim against a subsidiary where the "subsidiary has been allowed to transact business as an independent corporation and credit has been extended to it as such on the faith of its ownership of the assets in its possession."[13]

Equality—Piercing Corporate Veil

It was only a stone's throw away from that principle of equitable subordination to arrive at the equitable principle of piercing the corporate veil and consolidating the companies.

> Only by entirely ignoring the separate corporate entity of the Virginia corporation and consolidating the proceedings here with those of the parent corporation in New Jersey can all the creditors receive the equality of treatment

---

[10] *Id.* at 847.

[11] Soviero v. Franklin Nat'l. Bank of Long Island, 328 F2d 446 (2d Cir. 1964) and Stone v. Eacho 127 F2d 284 (4th Cir.) *rehearing den.* 128 F2d 16, *cert. denied*, 317 U.S. 635 (1942).

[12] Stone v. Eacho, 127 F2d 284 (4th Cir. 1942).

[13] 127 F2d at 288.

which it is the purpose of the Bankruptcy Act to afford.[14]

Thus, the principle of piercing the corporate veil, which shields a corporation against liability for another's debt, is enforced to preserve the doctrine that "bankruptcy is equality." The beneficial effect of consolidation is important to creditors as well as Debtors because of the "equality" syndrome of distribution. It is important also for the reorganization process since it has the effect of eliminating intercompany claims, combining assets of all Debtors, which become common assets, and eliminating duplicative claims and cross guarantees.

Applicability of Consolidation at Confirmation or Exigency

As a preliminary question the court of appeals considered whether consolidation of assets and liabilities should "not await the court's action on a plan of liquidation and be submitted as part of such a plan."[15] Although the court of appeals considered this to be the normal course where feasible,[16] it was conceded "that there were some cases, such as the instant case where a determination to consolidate prior to the plan is required by the exigencies of the situation."[17]

The Bank's resistance to consolidation was not difficult to understand; it had a mortgage on a vessel of the Seatrade Corporation ("Seatrade"), covering the vessel East Hampton. Presumably, if the cash value of this mortgage was assimilated with the general assets, the Bank would be an unsecured creditor sharing with other unsecured creditors of all the entities. This would be to the Bank's disadvantage because of the potential for a higher return if the Seatrade were not consolidated with the other cases.

---

[14] *Id.*

[15] 369 F2d at 846.

[16] *See, infra,* this chapter, subtitle "Continental Vending Follows Chemical." *See also In re* Continental Vending Machine Corp., 517 F2d 997 (2d Cir. 1975), *cert. denied sub nom.* James Talcott, Inc. v. Wharton, 424 U.S. 913 (1976).

[17] 369 F2d 847 (citing several cases for comparison).

Power to Consolidate

The Bank's argument, therefore, was that consolidation should be denied unless the trustee could prove that the Bank relied on the group of Debtors as a unit. The court of appeals, however, concluded that such reliance was unnecessary for the Bank's striking a caveat to eliminate consolidation:

> The power to consolidate should be used sparingly because of the possibility of unfair treatment of creditors of a corporate debtor who have dealt solely with that debtor without knowledge of its interrelationship with others. Yet in the rare case such as this, where the interrelationships of the groups are hopelessly obscured and the time and expense necessary even to attempt to unscramble them so substantial as to threaten the realization of any net assets for all the creditors, equity is not helpless to reach a rough approximation of justice to some rather than deny any to all.[18]

Rejecting the Bank's argument which was based on the *Soviero*[19] case where the facts indicated that creditors dealt with the Debtor and its affiliates as one, the court of appeals proceeded to follow its precept of using the power to consolidate "sparingly." The court then turned from "sparingly" to "usefulness," explaining the need for consolidation:

> By the order of consolidation, in effect the intercompany claims of the debtor companies are eliminated, the assets of all debtors are treated as common assets and claims of outside creditors against any of the debtors are treated as against the common fund, eliminating a large number of duplicative claims filed against

---

[18] 369 F2d 847.

[19] *See, infra,* note 11 and text. *See, supra,* note 12 and text.

several debtors by creditors uncertain as to
which debtor was eventually liable.[20]

Concurring Opinion

However, the concurring opinion of Judge Friendly
presented a more practical solution for consolidation than
solely a confusion of books and records, in contrast to those
cases where the books and records reflect a true demarcation
of assets and liabilities of each entity. Tackling the *Stone*[21]
case, he observed that consolidation was based on the fact that
the subsidiary carried on "no separate corporate activity of any
sort" and accordingly, "no creditor could possibly have done
business with it in reliance on its credit—a demonstration not
at all made in this case." Thus, because of the Bank's failure
to "come forward with something more," all creditors should be
treated alike.[22]

Reliance on Single Entity

Moreover, Judge Friendly disagreed with the majority in
not following the opinion of the *Stone*[23] case where it was held
that:

> If any creditors should prove such reliance [on
> the credit of one entity]—an extraordinary
> unlikely possibility on the facts—they would be
> sufficiently protected by the statement in the
> original opinion that their claims should be
> heard in the consolidated proceedings, a
> reservation conspicuously lacking here.

In other words, why not allow consolidation if the
circumstances warrant such consolidation preserving such
rights as any creditor had in reliance upon a particular entity.

---

[20] 369 F2d 847.

[21] *See also, supra,* this chapter, subtitle "Cases Distinguishing
Chemical."

[22] *Id.* at 848.

[23] *Id. See, supra,* note 12 and text.

Such rights would not defeat consolidation but could be asserted in the consolidation proceeding.

One of Twelve Refused Consolidation

Four years later we meet Judge Friendly again in the *Flora Mir* case,[24] but this time writing the unanimous opinion for the court of appeals which refused to consolidate one of twelve subsidiaries with the others since it had substantial rights in a recovery of moneys in a pending lawsuit not available to the others. Although citing the *Chemical* case with approval, the court found consolidation was not appropriate because it would result in unfair treatment of the creditors of Meadors, Inc., one of the group. However, it was not bothered by the fact that the books and records were in good condition since "the accountants in relatively short order had managed to come up with financial statements of each of the debtors."[25]

Consolidation, therefore, was allowed as to eleven of the twelve Debtors excluding only Meadors, Inc., since the Debtors' testimony in this connection indicated: (1) a multitude of intercompany transactions, many without apparent business purpose; (2) the difficulty of disentangling them;[26] and (3) the consideration by the trade of all the Debtors as a group. Consolidation, therefore, was rejected as to Meadors, Inc., but allowed as to the others even though financial statements of each of the Debtors existed thereby destroying the necessity for a showing of an inability to "reconstruct the financial records of the Debtors."[27]

Continental Vending Follows Chemical

In the *Continental Vending* case,[28] a plan of reorganization, again under the former Bankruptcy Act Chapter X Reorganization, provided for a consolidation of the unsecured debt of a parent and its subsidiary but refused to elevate the

---

[24] *In re* Flora Mir Candy Corp., 432 F2d 1060 (2d Cir. 1970).

[25] *Id.* at 1063.

[26] *Id.* at 1061.

[27] *Id.*

[28] *In re* Continental Vending Machine Corp., 517 F2d 997 (2d Cir. 1975).

secured creditor's claim. Aside from the "fair and equitable" principle followed by the court, the dissent again indicated the court's reliance on *Chemical* as a basis for consolidation:

> Moreover, as noted by the court in [*Chemical*] and by the trustee in the instant case, consolidation was properly ordered in this case because it was virtually impossible to reconstruct claims, transactions, liabilities and ownership of assets.[29]

Gulfco Overcomes Accounting

In the *Gulfco* case,[30] the Tenth Circuit considered an appeal from an interlocutory order in a Bankruptcy Act Chapter X case and affirmed an order denying consolidation. Referring to the *Chemical* case, the court observed that *Chemical* "considered the difficulty of accounting as a factor. Unlike here, the interrelationships were so strong that great expense [in order to bring about an unscrambling] threatened any recovery."[31] The Tenth Circuit, however, was willing to go so far as to do without detailed certified audits and remanded the case before it would order consolidation.

Bankruptcy Courts have been careful to walk gingerly with the *Chemical* court's admonitions for consolidation to be "used sparingly because of the possibility of unfair treatment of creditors of a corporate Debtor who have dealt solely with that Debtor without knowledge of its relationship with others. Yet in the rare cases such as this where the interrelationships of the group are hopelessly obscured and the time and expense necessary to unscramble them is so substantial as to threaten the realization of any net assets for all creditors, equity is not helpless to reach a rough approximation of justice to some rather than deny any to all."[32]

---

[29] *Id.* at 1005.

[30] *In re* Gulfco Inv. Corp., 593 F2d 921 (10th Cir. 1979).

[31] *Id.* at 930.

[32] Chemical Bank, 369 F2d at 817.

Interstate and Toys "R" Us

The prevalence of the multi-tiered companies in reorganization cases and the court's application for a dual consolidation of subsidiaries is seen in the *Interstate Stores, Inc.* case.[33] The two principal Debtors were Interstate, which operated a chain of department stores and through a subsidiary, and Toys "R" Us, Inc. ("Toys"), which operated a chain of retail stores. The Chapter X trustee proposed a partial consolidation, namely, consolidating Interstate with all its department store subsidiaries and Toys with all its toy shops. Creditors of Interstate, seeing greater returns in a complete consolidation with Toys, objected. In overruling the objections to full consolidation the court followed *In re Flora Mir*:

> Neither the Interstate creditors nor the debenture holders did business with the Toys "R" Us Debtors. They hold no obligations of those Debtors nor do they hold any of their guarantees. . . . [C]omplete consolidation is unjustified . . . and will obviously result in permitting those creditors . . . to resort to these assets in the first instance to the detriment of those creditors who hold the obligations of Toys "R" Us Debtors. *In re* Flora Mir, *supra*, forbids such a result.[34]

Such consolidation of two separate and distinct entities is not the general run of the mill case, but the partial consolidation of each principal, Interstate and Toys, is a sound holding requiring consolidation only of those entities which had a common enterprise with common creditors. For Toys' creditors, the operations of its Debtors seemed to represent higher business returns. Likewise, Interstate glanced at a complete consolidation for the same reason.

---

[33] *In re* Interstate Stores, Inc., et al. ("Interstate"), 15 C.B.C. 634 (B. SDNY 1980).

[34] *Id.* at 642. *See supra*, this chapter, subtitle "Refusal Confirmation One of Twelve Subsidiaries."

Thus, addressing the problem of consolidation of the Interstate group and the Toys group *inter se*, the court stated:

"The necessity for Courts to fashion the equitable remedy has become more frequent with the increasing appearance before the bankruptcy courts of large public parent companies[35] with their multi-tiered subsidiaries. The *need* for some form of substantive consolidation is readily apparent in the case involving as it does a parent and 188 separate corporate Debtors. Separate plans of reorganization would not be *feasible*." (Emphasis added.)

Observation

We emphasized two words, "need" and "feasible." Both should also be the hallmarks of consolidation. However, the Interstate Court issued the caveat of *Flora Mir* and *Chemical*, namely, "used sparingly." In an effort to reconcile this concept with the "needs" concept, it may be helpful to categorize the basis for the court's opinion. The uncontroverted evidence supported the proposed substantive consolidation of all Toys and its subsidiaries in one group and Interstate and its subsidiaries into another group. The facts which supported consolidation in Toys were (1) operation of entities as a single unit; (2) different officers than Interstate; (3) trade creditors independent from Interstate; (4) issued own forms of purchase orders and financial statements; and (5) Toys' subsidiaries operated as a single entity to the trade. These facts were evidently sufficient to warrant consolidation for the Toy Group.

As for the Interstate Group, it had (1) common management, centralized accounting; (2) payment procedures, parent guarantees for obligations; (3) one buying corporation, (4) receipts centralized in one paying corporation; and (5)

---

[35] *See* Memorandum and Order, *In re* Food Fair, Inc., No. 78-B-1768 (B. SDNY 1981) where consolidation was granted to a parent having a seven page list of related companies engaged in a variety of operations.

"most importantly, it would not be possible to ascertain which Debtor is the obligor with respect to the debt owed to any particular trade creditor since the account for such transactions was, in effect, done on a consolidated basis. In the language of *Continental* and *Chemical,* the relationship of these Debtors is 'hopelessly obscured.' These are the classic factors supporting substantive consolidation."

Consolidation Disallowed

In *Augie/Restivo*[36] the Second Circuit had for consideration the consolidation of two chapter 11 cases and reversed the consolidation. Prior to 1985, Augie and Restivo were two unrelated family-run wholesale bakeries. Augie was a borrower of the Union Saving's Bank ("Union") and Restivo a borrower of Manufacturers Hanover Trust Company (MHTC).

Augie's Deal With Restivo

Between July 1983 and September 1984, Union loaned Augie $2.1 million secured by a mortgage on Augie's real property located in Central Islip, Long Island, to finance an expansion. In November 1984, Augie borrowed an additional $300,000 from Union, secured by its inventory, equipment and accounts receivable. Union was unaware at the time that Augie had commenced negotiations with Restivo, and on November 27, 1984, entered into an agreement providing for Restivo's acquisition of all of Augie's stock in exchange for 50% of Restivo's stock. In the agreement Augie represented that it had receivables of over $630,000 and equipment and inventory valued at over $1.9 million. No provision for the legal transfer of Augie's real property or equipment to Restivo was made, and no such transfer was made.

After the exchange of stock on January 1, 1985, Restivo changed its name to Augie/Restivo Baking Company, Ltd., and moved its manufacturing operations and some of its equipment from Brooklyn to Augie's plant in Central Islip. Augie's affairs were wound up and Restivo became the sole operating

---

[36] *In re* Augie/Restivo Baking Co., Ltd. ("Augie/Restivo"), 860 F2d 515 (2d Cir. 1988).

company, keeping a single set of books and issuing financial statements under the name Augie/Restivo. Augie was not dissolved.

MHTC Leases to Augie/Restivo

From January through April 1985, MHTC extended further credit to Augie/Restivo of $750,000. MHTC also sought and received a guarantee of Augie/Restivo's obligations from Augie including a subordinated mortgage on Augie's property in Central Islip in the sum of $750,000. By March 1986, MHTC had advanced a total of $2.7 million to Augie/Restivo. During the period January 1985 through March 1986 various other firms extended trade credit to Augie/Restivo.

Separate Chapter 11 Cases

In April 1986, Augie/Restivo and Augie filed separate chapter 11 cases. Union was listed as a creditor only of Augie. Following a consolidation for procedural purposes, Augie/Restivo entered into a series of more than 25 cash collateral stipulations, in which it was agreed that Augie/Restivo's accounts receivable constituted cash collateral[37] which was placed in a special account at MHTC and from which MHTC agreed to make loans to Augie/Restivo in a sum equivalent to the cash collateral deposits. The loans were secured by the assets of Augie/Restivo as debtor in possession, and carried a superpriority administrative expense status. Over time, the cash collateral stipulations were renewed in greater and greater amounts until eventually the entire amount of MHTC's prepetition loans to Augie/Restivo of $2.7 million had been converted to postpetition superpriority administrative debt, secured by Augie/Restivo's accounts receivable and by the subordinated mortgage on Augie's real property.

---

[37] *Id.* at 517. *See supra* Chapter 12, this handbook, Use, Sale, and Lease of Property, subtitle "Cash Collateral (§363)."

Augie/Restivo Motion for Consolidation

A proposed sale for $7.7 million was in the offing at confirmation of Augie/Restivo but, evidently because Union might object to the sale and prevent confirmation of such plan with regard to Augie's creditors, Augie/Restivo moved for substantive consolidation of the two cases. Union opposed, but the bankruptcy judge granted the motion[38] finding that Augie and Restivo had merged and that the contemplated sale was in the interests of the creditors of both companies.

After the consolidation motion was granted, the sale fell through because of the difficulty in finding financing. Union appealed, and the district court affirmed. In discussing the problem, the court of appeals stated succinctly: "Substantive consolidation has no express statutory basis but is a product of judicial gloss."[39]

Dangers in Substantive Consolidation

The court of appeals held that the effect was to subordinate Union's unsecured claims against Augie to MHTC's superpriority administrative claims. The court stated that because of the dangers in forcing creditors of one Debtor (Augie/Restivo) to share on a parity with creditors of a less solvent Debtor (Augie), "we have stressed that substantive consolidation 'is no mere instrument of procedural convenience' . . . but, a measure vitally affecting substantive rights, . . ."[40] The sole purpose of substantive consolidation is to ensure the equitable treatment of all creditors. Numerous considerations have been mentioned as relevant to determining whether equitable treatment will result from substantive consolidation."

---

[38] *Id.* citing 84 BR 315.

[39] *Id.* at 518 (citing *In re* Commercial Envelope Mfg. Co., 3 B.C.D 647 (B. SDNY 1977). *See also, supra,* this chapter, notes 1 and 2.

[40] Citing Flora Mir Candy Corp. and Chemical Bank, *inter alia. See supra,* this chapter, subtitle "Chemical Bank and Flora Mir subtitle Refusal Consolidation—One of 12."

Factors Relevant to Substantive Consolidation

The court of appeals examined the three factors which were relevant. The first factor consists of creditors who make loans on the basis of the financial status of a separate entity and expect to look to a specific borrower for satisfaction of that loan. Such lenders structure their loans according to their expectations of that borrower and do not anticipate having the assets of a more sound Debtor compete for the borrower's assets.

The second factor, entanglement of the Debtor's affairs, involves cases in which there has been a commingling of two firm's assets and business functions. In such business functions the objection is that creditors will benefit because untangling is impossible or so costly as to consume the assets. "Commingling, therefore, can justify substantive consolidation only where 'the time and expense necessary even to attempt to unscramble them [is] so substantial as to threaten the realization of any net assets for all the creditors, . . .'"[41]

De Facto Merger

The court found that the third factor, a cornerstone of the bankruptcy court's decision with regard to the entanglement issue, was the bankruptcy court's finding that there had been a merger between Augie and Restivo. Such a finding was clearly erroneous, because "the two corporations were never legally merged: (i) they failed to comply with the laws of merger under New York law; (ii) neither corporation was ever dissolved; and (iii) Augies never formally transferred its assets and retained ownership of the Central Islip facility. Furthermore, the requirements for the finding of a *de facto* merger were not met.[42]

---

[41] *Id.* at 519 citing "Kheel [Chemical's Trustee], . . . and Commercial Envelope. . . ." *See also* this chapter, *supra,* subtitles "Chemical Bank and Commercial Envelope."

[42] *Id.* (citing "In . . . Ladjevardian v. Laidlaw-Coggeshall, Inc., 431 F. Supp. 834 (SDNY 1977), the prerequisites for a *de facto* merger were summarized. . . .") *See infra* Chapter 18, this handbook, Confirmation of Consensual Plan, subtitle "De Facto Confirmation."

The court of appeals also rejected MHTC's argument holding that the bank's reorganization plan and sale justified the consolidation because consolidation would benefit the creditors of both companies:

> Where, as in the instant case, creditors such as Union and MHTC knowingly made loans to separate entities and no irremediable commingling of assets has occurred, a creditor cannot be made to sacrifice the priority of its claims against its debtor by fiat based on the bankruptcy court's speculation that it knows the creditor's interests better than does the creditor itself. . . .[43]

"The plain fact is that Union's claim against Augie's assets is superior to that of MHTC, and, as a result, the undesirability of consolidation is as clear in the instant case as in our earlier decision in *Flora Mir*. . . ."[44] The court concluded its finding by holding Union was in the same position as were the debenture holders in *Flora Mir*. The result of substantive consolidation in the instant case would be to make Augie's assets available to pay the debts of Augie/Restivo, and to enrich MHTC (whose entire pre-petition loans to Augie/Restivo have been converted to fully-secured post-petition superpriority administrative debt pursuant to the cash collateral stipulations) at the expense of Union.

Observation

The cases show the need and benefit of substantive consolidation of a parent and subsidiaries with each other. A Debtor which maintains a number of subsidiaries may find it necessary to consider in its plan of reorganization a presentation of a consolidation of two or more groups of subsidiaries in order to provide for payment to the specific group which performed the services or became obligated to pay such specific creditor. This procedure avoids duplicate

---

[43] 860 F2d at 520.

[44] *Id.* at 520.

payments and eliminates guaranties by providing that the fundamental obligor pay the debt. Substantive consolidation aims at an equitable reassembling of each Debtor's balance sheet which becomes beneficial to the Debtor and its subsidiaries as well as creditors. In the *LTV* case, the grouping of a number of creditors in specific groups was designed to provide for equitable distribution or liability to each Debtor so that each group received equitable distribution.

Failure to observe the equitable doctrine among creditors, as the reader will recall, resulted in the denial of consolidation in the *Augie/Restivo* case. The effect of consolidation would have been to subordinate an unsecured claimant in the subsidiary, its only creditor, to the superpriority administrative claims of the parent thereby leaving no payment to the unsecured creditor.

Of course, a creditor may oppose substantive consolidation against Debtors in situations where the creditor claims, as in *Flora Mir,* that it dealt with one Debtor and had no relationship with the parent. The objective in excluding one or more with the group from consolidation is obviously sought for a greater return to the objector. In this day and age, such facts as lack of knowledge of the group appears to be difficult to prove considering the numerous credit agencies which have such expansive financial files of the standing of virtually every business seeking credit, as well as the banks requiring financial data for the issuance of credit cards.

Completing this chapter on Substantive Consolidation serves like a traveler's journey through many miles of road, and then stopping in an effort to arrive at Confirmation. Stopping at each inn, for inquiry and discussion, we have already acquired information along the way that aids us in arriving at Chapter 18, Confirmation of Consensual Plan.

Chapter 18
Confirmation of Consensual Plan

Requirements of §1129 for Confirmation

The reader will understand more fully the anxiety of Debtors and creditors to reach confirmation when the accomplishments of reorganization are defined in §1141[1] which discusses the effect of confirmation. However, before reaching §1141, necessity requires a discussion of the requirements that must be met for a plan of reorganization to be confirmed. Section 1129 deals with "Confirmation of Plan" and is composed of two subsections: subsection (a) contains paragraphs (1) to (13), and if a Debtor can comply with all the requirements of the paragraphs then the plan will be confirmed under §1129(a). We turn now to two subsections of §1129(a).

---

[1] *See infra* Chapter 20, this handbook, Post Confirmation Matters. *See also* Toibb v. Radloff, 111 S.Ct. 2197 (1991), holding that an individual, nonbusiness debtor can reorganize under chapter 11.

The court shall confirm a plan only if all of the following requirements are met:

. . .

(8) With respect to each class of claims or interests—

    (A) such class has accepted the plan; or

    (B) such class is not impaired under the plan.

. . .

(10) If a class of claims is impaired under the plan, at least one class of claims that is impaired under the plan has accepted the plan, determined without including any acceptance of the plan by any insider.

This problem involving the issue of impairment of the status of a secured creditor became the central issue in the confirmation of the plan in the *Madison Hotel* case[2] where Prudential[3] sought to enforce a foreclosure of MHA's property. Prudential was a secured creditor in a class by itself, but had not accepted the plan as required by §1129(a)(10), claiming it was an impaired creditor. However, MHA contested that position, claiming Prudential was not impaired and therefore, had been deemed to have accepted the plan.

Financing a Hotel

MHA was a limited partnership[4] organized under the laws of Wisconsin and consisting of two general partners, Darrell Wild and Wild, Inc., in addition to a number of limited partners. On December 11, 1972, MHA entered into a loan agreement with Citizens Mortgage Investment Trust ("CMIT") to finance the construction and operation of its Concourse Hotel. Pursuant to the terms of the agreement CMIT advanced funds to MHA for that purpose. In return, CMIT received a

---

[2] Madison Hotel Associates, d/b/a The Concourse Hotel ("MHA"), 749 F2d 410 (7th Cir. 1984).

[3] Prudential Insurance Co. of America ("Prudential").

[4] *See* 11 U.S.C. §101(13): "'Debtor' means person or municipality concerning which a case under this title has been commenced; . . ." and (41) "person includes individual, partnership, and corporation, . . ."

promissory note obligating MHA to repay the principal amount of the loan and the accrued interest. "CMIT secured its loan with a first mortgage and a first security interest in MHA's realty, and in the event of default an 'assignment of rentals' accruing from such property."[5]

Permanent Financing

"The parties agreed that CMIT would finance only the construction costs and upon completion of the hotel, the promissory note along with all of CMIT's security interests, would be assigned to Prudential who would, in turn, pay the outstanding balance of the CMIT loan and provide MHA with permanent financing for hotel operations."[6] Accordingly, on September 9, 1974, CMIT assigned to Prudential the promissory note in the sum of $7 million, the first mortgage and the first security interest in MHA's realty and the assignment of rentals. "Thereafter, under the terms of the Prudential financing agreement, MHA was obligated to pay Prudential monthly installments of principal and interest in the amount of $59,360."[7]

Foreclosure of Mortgage[8]

Shortly after opening in the summer of 1974, the Concourse Hotel began to experience operating problems and generated a negative cash flow resulting in MHA's defaulting in early 1976 on the payment of its monthly loan installments to Prudential. On October 16, 1978, notice of default and acceleration of the amount due was issued to MHA by Prudential. "Both the promissory note and the first mortgage provided that in the event of default, Prudential as mortgagee

---

[5] *Id.* at 413.

[6] *Id.*

[7] *Id.*

[8] *Id.* Although referred to in footnote 2 of the opinion by the court, it is of interest to consider a further transaction between MHA and CMIT. On September 13, 1974, MHA and CMIT entered into a sale-leaseback arrangement whereby CMIT purchased the parcel of land underlying the Concourse Hotel subject to Prudential's first mortgage.

could immediately accelerate the entire balance due and payable, including principal, interest and reasonable attorney's fees. . . . On February 1, 1979, Prudential commenced a foreclosure action in the United States District Court for the Western District of Wisconsin"[9] seeking foreclosure and collection under Wisconsin law, of the entire accelerated amount.

Loan not Usurious
Escrow Account Established

In the meantime, in May 1976, the general partners of MHA had filed a lawsuit in Wisconsin state court alleging that the interest rates charged by Prudential were usurious in violation of Wisconsin statute.[10] On July 20, 1978, the circuit court for Dane County, Wisconsin granted summary judgment for Prudential ruling that no issues of a material nature existed and the interest rates were not usurious. The Wisconsin Court of Appeals affirmed. The federal district court, however, reserved final disposition of the foreclosure action until the Wisconsin state court had resolved the issue. On February 11, 1980, before the Wisconsin Court of Appeals issued its decision, the parties agreed to establish an escrow account into which MHA paid the amount of principal and interest due Prudential under the promissory note and first mortgage.[11] As of August 1, 1983, MHA had made payments into the account which totalled $4,888,581.17.

Foreclosure Granted

Back again to the foreclosure case. On August 17, 1981, the judge of the Federal District Court considered the parties' legal and equitable arguments on the foreclosure issue, reviewed

---

[9] *Id.*

[10] *Id.* at 413. *See also* note 3 where the court stated that CMIT was also named as a defendant as the owner of certain parcels of MHA's realty as discussed in footnotes 2 and 10 of the opinion.

[11] *Id.* at 414. *See also* note 4 where the court stated that ". . . CMIT is also a party to the escrow account. . . ." *See* note 7.

the applicable Wisconsin state law of foreclosure,[12] and granted Prudential's motion for summary judgment to foreclose on the MHA mortgage. The court of appeals observed: "According to the [district] court, '[o]n the present record the equities are with [Prudential] who [has] been subjected to years of projected litigation pursued by [MHA] . . . in an obvious effort to extend [its] low cost use of the loan funds. . . .' The court ruled that 'because of the continuous and current default in the First Note, First Mortgage, and Security Agreement, [Prudential] may foreclose the First Mortgage by judicial proceeding under the terms of the mortgage and sell the collateral of the Security Agreement.'"[13] The district court granted Prudential time until August 24, 1981, to submit a form of judgment of foreclosure and sale of the realty described in the First Mortgage and the collateral described in the Security Agreement.

Chapter 11 Petition Filed

On August 24, 1981, before Prudential filed its judgment of foreclosure with the district court, MHA filed a chapter 11 petition in the United States Bankruptcy Court for the Western District of Wisconsin. This district court was the same district which had jurisdiction of the foreclosure proceeding. "The effect of MHA's Chapter 11 petition was to stay the foreclosure proceeding, . . .[14] transfer it to the bankruptcy court, . . .[15] and thereby preclude Prudential from obtaining a final judgment of foreclosure."[16]

---

[12] *Id. See* Wisc. Stat. 846.01 *et seq.* (1981–82).

[13] *Id.*

[14] *Id.* at 414 citing 11 U.S.C. §362(a) (1982). *See, supra,* Chapter 6, this handbook, Automatic Stay.

[15] *Id.* at 414 citing "28 U.S.C. §1478 (1982). (*See* West Publishing Co., *Federal Civil Judicial Procedure and Rules,* 28 U.S.C. §§1471 to 1482. Omitted). Transition to new court system. Pub. Law 95-598, Nov. 6, 1978, Bankruptcy Amendment Federal Jurisdiction Act 1984, . . ." *See* 28 USC §1334 (Bankruptcy cases and proceedings) and, *supra,* Chapter 7, this handbook, Jurisdiction of Court.

[16] *Id.* at 414.

Abstention or Dismissal

On December 22, 1981, MHA filed its proposed plan of reorganization with the bankruptcy court; and on the same day, the bankruptcy court conducted a hearing to address claims by CMIT and Prudential that the court should abstain[17] from considering MHA's Chapter 11 petition or, in the alternative, dismiss the entire case. Following the evidentiary hearing,[18] the court ruled that the case was not appropriate for abstention. "These are cases which exist which are not and nor can be better protected in another court. I'm satisfied with the Debtor as a person which may have relief under Chapter 11."[19]

Good Faith

Cause

Adverting to various subsections which provide for dismissal under §1112(b), the bankruptcy court stated that there had been no suggestions as to any specific subsection. Nonetheless, petitioners argued that there was available an additional category which would be found in "an absence of good faith." The bankruptcy court's response: "I'm satisfied that there has been sufficient efforts to reorganize undertaken by the Debtor to rebut any contention that there would be a lack of good faith in the initial filing of the Chapter 11."[20]

Throughout the pendency of the Chapter 11, the stay remained in effect on Prudential's foreclosure action in the United States District Court, although Prudential continued to seek relief from the stay. Finally, Prudential contended that it "would be delayed in the event the Chapter 11 case were dismissed if it were not permitted during the Chapter 11 proceeding to enter its foreclosure judgment"[21] and commence the period for equity of redemption allowed by Wisconsin law.

---

[17] *Id.* at 414 citing 11 USC §305(a)(1) (1982). *See supra* Chapter 5, this handbook, subtitle "Abstention of Chapter 11."

[18] *Id.* at 414–15 citing 11 USC §1112(b). Conversion or dismissal: "[T]he court may . . . dismiss a case . . . for cause; including— . . . (2) inability to effectuate a plan; . . ."

[19] *Id.* at 415.

[20] *Id.*

[21] *Id.* at 415.

"On March 5, 1982, the bankruptcy court ruled that Prudential lacked the 'cause' required under 11 U.S.C. §362(d)(1) to obtain relief from the stay. . . . [T]he occurrence of delay is speculative upon the failure of the Debtor's effort to reorganize under chapter 11. If those efforts are successful, Prudential will incur neither delay nor economic loss. Even if those efforts are unsuccessful, there is no contention that Prudential will incur unprotected or uncompensated economic injury."[22]

Constituents of Good Faith

The bankruptcy court conducted additional hearings on MHA's proposed plan of reorganization. At the July 9, 1982, hearing, Prudential presented an offer of proof that MHA had not acted in good faith when proposing the Plan of Reorganization. The bankruptcy court had noted that "Taking all of the offers of proof as proved, they must be applied against the legal standard for good faith in a Chapter 11. Also considered are matters which the Court has observed or has received evidence on either in this or in prior hearings which would be counter to the matters that are proved. . . ."[23]

The terms of the second amended plan also were considered by the bankruptcy court. These consisted of the history of the amendments to the plan and the conduct of the Debtor and Debtor's counsel throughout the bankruptcy proceedings. "[T]he fact that the plan calls for full payment to all creditors and specifically the treatment of MHA in the plan is considered. Also considered is the presence of an escrow fund that was created in prior proceedings."[24] In addition, the bankruptcy court held that essentially "a plan is proposed in good faith when there is a reasonable likelihood that the plan will achieve a result consistent with the objectives and purposes of the Bankruptcy Code.[25] Based upon these

---

[22] Id. at 415. See §362(d)(1) providing for the granting of relief from the stay for "cause, including the lack of adequate protection of an interest in property of such party in interest, . . ." See also supra Chapter 6, this handbook, Automatic Stay subtitles, "Foreclosure" and "Evidentiary Hearing."

[23] Id. at 415.

[24] Id. at 415.

[25] Id. at 415.

considerations, the [bankruptcy] court ruled that sufficient evidence existed to find that *MHA*'s plan of reorganization was proposed in good faith."[26]

Creditors Acceptance
Confirmation of Plan

The court of appeals remarked that the record revealed that all of MHA's creditors, except Prudential, affirmatively accepted the plan of reorganization. Following the July 12 hearing, the bankruptcy court ruled, from the bench, that MHA's plan satisfied the statutory requirements of 11 U.S.C. §1129(a)[27] and the court confirmed the plan. "Specifically, the bankruptcy court found that, in compliance with 11 U.S.C. §1129(a)(3), MHA proposed the plan in good faith."[28]

Alluding to §1129(a)(8), the bankruptcy court found that all classes of creditors accepted the plan or their claims were not impaired by the plan, as impaired is defined by §1124. The plan reinstated Prudential's position as it existed prior to the default; and did not otherwise alter legal, equitable, or contractual rights between MHA and Prudential. On July 14, 1982, the bankruptcy court entered a written order confirming MHA's plan of reorganization.[29]

Appeal To District Court
Reversing Bankruptcy Court

Prudential appealed to the district court and the case was assigned to the same judge who two years previously had granted Prudential's motion for summary judgment to foreclose on MHA's mortgage under Wisconsin state law. MHA

---

[26] *Id.* at 415–16.

[27] *Id.* at 416. The court of appeals cited the entire section listing the eleven subsections. "Title 11 U.S.C. §1129(a) provides that: (a) The court shall confirm a plan only if all of the following requirements are met: (1) The plan complies with the applicable provisions of this chapter. . . ."

[28] *Id.* at 416. *See* §1129(a)(3): "The plan has been proposed in good faith and not by any means prohibited by law."

[29] *Id.* at 417.

filed a motion "asking [the district judge] to disqualify herself[30] due to her apparent lack of impartiality on the issue of foreclosure and her statement that the case involved 'many years of delay and legal skirmishing' on the part of MHA. [The judge] denied the motion summarily . . . and overruled the bankruptcy court's holding that Prudential was not impaired under MHA's plan of reorganization. . . ."[31]

The district court held that: "'MHA's plan impairs Prudential's claim because it does not restore Prudential's judicially-recognized right to proceed with foreclosure of the real and personal property of the Concourse Hotel and because Prudential's right to foreclose does not arise merely from a contractual provision or applicable law, but is created by court order and is not simply a right to accelerated payments which can be cured, Prudential's claim does not fall within the exception created by §1124(2). Therefore, Prudential cannot be *deemed* to have accepted MHA's plan under §1126(f),[32] and this matter must be remanded to the bankruptcy court for a determination of the plan's validity under §1129(b)."[33]

In addition, the district court believed that there was sufficient indication of misuse to justify an evidentiary hearing to determine whether MHA's pre-filing conduct "'demonstrates by a preponderance of the credible evidence that its sole purpose in filing for Chapter 11 reorganization was to hinder or delay its secured creditors, Prudential and CMIT. The determination should not be limited to deciding only whether there is a reasonable likelihood that the plan will achieve a result consistent with the objectives and purposes of the Bankruptcy Code.'"[34]

---

[30] *Id.* at 417 citing 28 U.S.C. §455(a).

[31] *Id.* at 417.

[32] *Id.* at 417 §1126(f). Acceptance of plan: "[A] class that is not impaired under a plan and each holder of a claim or interest of such class are conclusively presumed to have accepted the plan and solicitation of acceptances . . . from the holders . . . of such class is not required.

[33] *Id.* (referring to §1129(b)). *See infra* Chapter 19, this handbook, Confirmation of Cram Down Plan.

[34] *Id.* at 417.

Nonimpaired Claimant Deemed to Accept Plan

On appeal to the court of appeals MHA claimed that (1) the district court erred in ruling that Prudential's claim was impaired for purposes of §1129(a)(8);[35] and (2) the district court improperly construed the good faith requirement of §1129(a)(3). The parties agreed, however, that Prudential, as holder of the first mortgage on MHA's realty, was the sole member of the class and that Prudential had not affirmed MHA's plan of reorganization. Therefore, the court held that "in order for MHA's Chapter 11 plan to satisfy the requirement of confirmation set forth in 1129(a)(8), Prudential's claim must be one that is 'not impaired' under the plan."[36] Presenting the entire section of 1124 in its opinion, the court of appeals opined: "Congress 'define[s] impairment in the broadest possible terms' and then carves out three narrow exceptions to that expansive definition[37].... These three exceptions, though narrow in scope, are of vital importance in Chapter 11 reorganization because, pursuant to 11 U.S.C. §1126(f), 'a class that is not impaired under a plan is *deemed* to have accepted the plan. . . .' (Emphasis added.)"[38]

Plan Causing Acceleration

The court of appeals reviewed the history of MHA's default on its loan payments which began in early 1976. Then Prudential accelerated the maturity of the loan in October 1978 and obtained a judicial order of foreclosure in August, 1981. Before Prudential reduced the order to a judgment of foreclosure, MHA filed a chapter 11. MHA's plan of reorganization sought to cure the default of Prudential's

---

[35] *Id.* at 417. *See* "§1129(a)(8): with respect to each claim or interest—(A) such class has accepted the plan; or (B) such class is not impaired under the plan."

[36] *Id.* at 418.

[37] *Id.* citing *In re* Taddeo, 685 F2d 24, 28 (2d Cir. 1982). *See also In re* Forest Hills Associates, 40 BR 410, 414 (B. SDNY 1984).

[38] *Id.* at 418.

accelerated loan and reinstate the maturity of that loan as it existed before the default.[39]

> Thus, the issue before this court is whether MHA's plan to cure the accelerated Prudential loan satisfies the four-prong test set forth in 11 U.S.C. §1124(2); if so, Prudential's claim is not impaired for purposes of 11 U.S.C. §1129(a)(8) and Prudential is deemed to have accepted the plan.[40]

According to the bankruptcy court, MHA's plan "did in fact satisfy the four-prong test of 11 U.S.C. §1124(2),[41] providing for full payment to Prudential of the claim it had filed based on default. . . ."[42] The court next found that even though the district court had entered an order of foreclosure, MHA's plan reinstates the maturity of Prudential's accelerated loan as such maturity existed before the default. . . ."[43] In addition, the bankruptcy court found that the plan properly provided for the payment of allowed costs and fees incurred by Prudential in enforcing the default.[44] Finally, the bankruptcy court found that none of Prudential's alleged alteration in rights were sufficient to demonstrate that Prudential would be impaired by confirmation of the plan.

The district court disagreed with the bankruptcy court's analysis of §1124(2). According to the district court:

---

[39] *Id.* at 419. *See also id.* at note 9. "It is well-recognized that a Chapter 11 Debtor's plan of reorganization may cure the default of an accelerated loan. Title 11 U.S.C. §1123(a)(5)(G)(1982) provides that: 'A plan shall—
    (5) provide adequate means for the plan's execution, such as—(G) Curing or waiving of any default.'"

[40] *Id.*

[41] *Id.* citing *In re Hewitt*, 16 BR 973 (B. D Alaska (1982)): "that a secured creditor is not 'harmed by the reversal of acceleration, . . . where . . . a court has simply applied the contractual provision or applicable law requiring acceleration and has embodied this application in a judgment of foreclosure.' 16 BR 977."

[42] *Id.* at 419.

[43] *Id.*

[44] *Id.* at 419. *See* §§1123, 327, and 328 (Employment of Professional Persons and Limitation on Compensation of Professional Persons).

Contrary to the language of *In re Hewitt*, . . . "[a] judicially-recognized right to foreclosure is something different from a right to accelerated payments that arises by operation of a contractual provision or of applicable law."[45]

Plan Considering Prudential Nonimpaired

The next question considered by the court of appeals was what effect the district court's order of foreclosure entered pursuant to Wisconsin state law would have upon MHA's attempt to cure the default of its accelerated loan and thereby render Prudential's claim "not impaired." The general rule is that a claim is impaired unless it falls within one of the three exceptions set forth in 11 U.S.C. §1124. "In the present case, the applicable exception is found in section 1124(2) which provides that "curing a default, even though it inevitably changes a contractual acceleration clause, does not thereby 'impair' a creditor's claim."[46]

Congressional Intent–Reorganization Superior to Liquidation

The court of appeals continued to support the Debtor's plan by citing from various Congressional discussions that "there was no doubt that §1124 embodied Congress' intent to allow the chapter 11 Debtor to cure the default of an accelerated loan and reinstate the original terms of the loan agreement, without impairing the creditor's claim. . . . The rationale underlying Congress' enactment of Chapter 11, including the 'impairment' exception of §1124(2), is the simple fact that reorganization is economically more efficient than liquidation."[47] As Congress expressed its thinking:

"Often, the return on assets that a business can produce is inadequate to compensate those who have invested in the business. Cash flow

[45] *Id.*

[46] *Id.* at 419. *See also In re* Taddeo, 685 F2d 24, 28–29 (2d Cir. 1982).

[47] *Id.* at 420.

problems may develop, and require creditors of the business, both trade creditors and long-term lenders, to wait for payment of their claims. If the business can extend or reduce its debts, it often can be returned to a viable state. It is more economically efficient to reorganize than to liquidate because it preserves jobs and assets.[48]

Effect of Obtaining Judgment of Foreclosure

After analyzing a number of cases, the court of appeals observed: "The point to be gleaned from the relevant case law is that a creditor, holding a final judgment of foreclosure, is not impaired under section 1124(2) if the Debtor's plan of reorganization cures the default of the accelerated loan before the foreclosure sale actually occurs or before the judgment merges into the mortgage under state law, thereby transferring title to the mortgagee."[49] The court went a step further: "We add that even if Prudential had obtained a judgment of foreclosure, that would not alter our analysis because '[u]nder Wisconsin law, a mortgagee has only a lien on the mortgaged property even *after a judgment of foreclosure is entered. Id.* at 871 (emphasis added).'"[50]

Good Faith–Dismissal or Confirmation Definition

The court of appeals referred to the district court's reasoning that §1129(a)(3) required the bankruptcy court to evaluate the Debtor's pre-filing conduct as well as the feasibility of the plan itself.[51] According to the district court, "'[i]n the assertions made by Prudential there are indications that MHA's filing for reorganization may have been motivated by the sole purpose of hindering and delaying its creditors.'"[52]

---

[48] *Id.* at 420 citing H.R. Rep. No. 595, 95th Cong., 1st Sess. 220, *reprinted in* 1978 U.S. CODE CONG. & AD. NEWS 5963, 6179.

[49] *Id.* at 422 citing *In re* Clark, 738 F2d 869 (7th Cir. 1984).

[50] *Id.* at 422 referring to *In re* Clark.

[51] *Id.* at 424.

[52] *Id.*

[T]he district court "concluded that [t]he indications of misuse of the bankruptcy court [were] sufficient to require an evidentiary hearing by the bankruptcy court to determine whether MHA's pre-filing conduct demonstrates by a preponderance of the credible evidence that its sole purpose in filing for Chapter 11 reorganization was to hinder or delay its secured creditors. . . ."[53]

The court of appeals indicated that an erroneous construction by the district court was its error in construing the good faith requirement of 11 USC §1129(a)(3) which is "generally interpreted to mean that there exists 'a reasonable likelihood that the plan will achieve a result consistent with the objectives and purposes of the Bankruptcy Code.'[54] . . . [T]he important point of inquiry is the plan itself and whether such plan will fairly achieve a result consistent with the objectives of the Bankruptcy Code. . . . The district court's decision failed to make this legal distinction between the good faith that is required *to confirm a plan* under section 1129(a)(3) and the good faith that has been established as a *prerequisite to filing* a Chapter 11 petition for reorganization [11 USC §1112]."[55]

The court of appeals held that the good faith requirement of §1129(a)(3) "looks to the Debtor's plan and determines, in light of the particular facts and circumstances, whether the plan will fairly achieve a result consistent with the Bankruptcy Code. The plan 'must be viewed in light of the totality of the circumstances surrounding confirmation' of the plan [and] . . . [t]he bankruptcy judge is in the best position to assess the good faith of the parties' proposals."[56] The bankruptcy judge had conducted three separate evidentiary hearings concerning the feasibility of the plan. The court considered the terms of the plan, the history of the amendments, and the conduct of the Debtor and its counsel, and concluded that there was sufficient evidence that the purposes of the Code were being met. At the July 12, 1982,

---

[53] *Id.*

[54] *Id.* citing *In re* Nite Lite Inns, 17 BR 367, 370 (B. SD Cal. 1982), *et al.*

[55] *Id.* at 424–25 citing E. DiDanato, *Good Faith Reorganization Petitions: The Back Door Lets the Stranger In,* 16 CONN. L. REV. 1, 3 (1983).

[56] *Id.* at 425 citing *In re* Jasik, 727 F2d 1379, 1383 (5th Cir. 1984).

hearing, when the plan was confirmed, the bankruptcy judge had stated that "*on the basis of the whole record in this case the good faith of the Debtor in proposing this plan to the standards required under [11 USC §1129(1)(3)] . . . was sufficiently evidenced. . . .*' (Emphasis added.)"[57]

The court of appeals then turned to the issue of whether the bankruptcy court needs to conduct an additional evidentiary hearing to determine if MHA originally filed its chapter 11 petition for reorganization in good faith. "It is generally recognized that 'good faith' is a threshold prerequisite to securing Chapter 11 relief. . . ."[58] The court of appeals alluded to the bankruptcy court's consideration on December 22, 1981, of Prudential's claim that the court should dismiss the case for MHA's lack of good faith under 11 USC §1112(b) in filing its petition and its finding that "'there had been sufficient efforts to reorganize undertaken by the Debtor to rebut any contention that there would be a lack of good faith in the initial filing of the Chapter 11.'"[59]

> MHA's actions are consistent with Congress' intent that a business organization experiencing cash flow problems be allowed to file a Chapter 11 petition for reorganization, extend the period of its debts, and return to the status of a viable entity while paying creditors in full. Based upon the evidence presented, we agree with the bankruptcy court that MHA's plan of reorganization was proposed in good faith. Accordingly, we hold that there is no reason to further burden the bankruptcy court with an evidentiary hearing concerning MHA's pre-filing conduct.[60]

---

[57] *Id.*

[58] *Id.* at 426, citing *In re* BBT, 11 BR 224, 235 (B. D Nev. 1981); *In re* Victory Constr. Co., 9 BR 549, 558 (B. CD Cal. 1981).

[59] *Id.*

[60] *Id.* at 426.

Court of Appeals' Decision

The court of appeals approved the bankruptcy court's findings that held that the plan satisfied all eleven requirements of §1129(a), and reversed the district court's ruling that Prudential was impaired under §1129(a)(8) and that there was not a proper determination of good faith under §1129(a)(3). The court of appeals held further that the district court was in error and rejected the district court's suggestion that MHA's plan "may also violate §1129(a)(7), . . . [and] even if Prudential is not impaired, it is entitled to reject any plan that provides it with less than it would receive upon liquidation."[61]

The court, however, held: "Prudential's claim is not impaired and thus, pursuant to the provisions of §1126(f) Prudential is deemed to have accepted the plan, *notwithstanding* any provision to the contrary. In light of this fact, Prudential cannot now reject the plan under 11 U.S.C. §1129(7). Accordingly, we agree with the bankruptcy court that MHA's plan of reorganization satisfies all eleven requirements of §1129(a) and we hold that MHA's plan of reorganization 'shall be confirmed.'"[62] The court of appeals thereupon reversed the district court with instructions to reinstate the order of the bankruptcy court dated July 14, 1982, confirming MHA's plan of reorganization.

Observation
Section 1129(b) as Alternative to §1229(a)

Section 1129(b) is correlated with §1129(a) as noted by the court of appeals in a footnote[63] in response to one of MHA's contentions that the district court improperly construed the

---

[61] *Id. See* 11 USC §502. Allowance of claims or interests. *See also* §1129(a)(7) for discussion of "effective date of plan" and other sections involving chapter 11. *See also* Weintraub & Crames, *Defining Consummation, Effective Date of Plan of Reorganization and Retention of Postconfirmation Jurisdiction: Suggested Amendments to Bankruptcy Code and Bankruptcy Rules*, 64 AM. BANKR. L.J. 245 (1990).

[62] 749 F2d at 426–27.

[63] *Id.* at 424 note 13.

"good faith" requirement of §1129(a)(2) which requires the court to confirm a plan "'only if *all* of the specific requirements are met including good faith and not by any means forbidden by law.' (Emphasis added.)" According to Prudential, "it cannot be *deemed* to have accepted MHA's plan under 11 USC §1126(f) because the section deals with acceptances of a plan and holds that a non-impaired creditor is conclusively deemed to have accepted the plan. Therefore, since it is impaired §1126(f) is not applicable and lacking the acceptance of all classes, the Debtor's petition must be considered under §1129(b). In light of this, Prudential argued that this matter must be remanded to the bankruptcy court for determination of the plan's *validity* under 11 USC §1129(b)."[64] We ask: What validity? Obviously, in anticipation of the dismissal of Debtor's petition based upon a finding that Prudential's claim was impaired.

The court of appeals response to §1129(b) appeared in footnote 13: "The district court's erroneous ruling that Prudential's claim was impaired for purposes of §1129(a)(8) did not end the analysis."[65] Section 1129(b) must also be considered. The court of appeals observed a correlation between the sections, by indicating that §1129(b) is predicated upon the requirement that all the sections of §1129(a) exclusive of §1129(a)(8) are required as a precondition for a Debtor's filing a §1129(b) plan. Under such circumstances, "then, the court shall confirm the plan, notwithstanding the requirements of such paragraph." The plan, however, must not discriminate unfairly and must be fair and equitable, to each class of claims or interests that are impaired under, and have not accepted the plan.

The footnote by the court of appeals served a double purpose. First, assume the court of appeals remanded the case finding Prudential's claim was impaired and a transfer to §1129(b) followed. The same findings would exist as in §1129(a), to wit, the Debtor's plan does not discriminate unfairly, and is fair and equitable to each class of claims or interests that is "impaired under, and has not accepted, the

---

[64] *Id.* at 424 (emphasis added).

[65] *Id. See* §1128(b) Confirmation Hearing: "(b) A party in interest may object to confirmation of a plan."

plan." Since the only complainant is Prudential, which is being returned to its original agreement without default, and since at least one impaired class has accepted the plan,[66] the plan will, nonetheless be confirmed under §1129(b).

Indeed, as we shall see under §1129(b), the objective is to give the Debtor a second opportunity to confirm a plan, but a price has to be paid. We repeat again, the cram down plan may not discriminate among classes and it must be fair and equitable to all classes. As we shall see in Chapter 19, some plans provide for an option: The creditors may accept a consensual plan or failing to accept the consensual plan, the cram down plan will be available for acceptance.

---

[66] *See* requirement of 11 U.S.C.(b)(I) ". . . [I]f all of the applicable requirements of subsection (a) of this section other than paragraph (8) are met with respect to a plan, the court, on request of the proponent of the plan, shall confirm the plan notwithstanding the requirements of such paragraph if the plan does not discriminate unfairly, and is fair and equitable, with respect to each class of claims or interests that is impaired under, and has not accepted, the plan."

Chapter 19
Confirmation of Cram Down Plan

Comparison:
Consensual and Cram Down Plans

The failure of a Debtor to present a consensual plan of reorganization does not mean that the Debtor's petition will be converted to a chapter 7 liquidation proceeding. Indeed, §1129(b) indicates Congress' intent to keep reorganization alive, by presenting the Debtor with another opportunity under chapter 11. The sharp distinction between the subsections is that in §1129(a) the Debtor presents a plan which the Debtor and its creditors deem to be acceptable after examination of the Debtor's financial status, hard negotiations, and "[c]onfirmation of the plan is not likely to be followed by the liquidation, or the need for further financial reorganization, . . . unless such liquidation is proposed in the plan."[1]

One more requirement is as to holders of impaired claims or interests who have not accepted the plan. As to these nonacceptors, they "will receive or retain under the plan on account of such claim or interest property of a value, as of the effective date of the plan, that is not less than the amount such holders would so receive or retain if the Debtor were liquidated under chapter 7 of this title on such date; . . ."[2] Thus, even though the Debtor is insolvent, the holders of claims or interests will receive property of a value at least as much as they would have received if the estate were liquidated. In such case, unsecured creditors would receive the full amount of their claims in the Debtor's property before the next class of subordinated creditors or shareholders would receive any distribution. This provision constitutes an inducement to interested parties and subordinated claimants to negotiate a consensual plan with senior claimants who in turn would be stimulated to accept a consensual plan to avoid the time and expense of a cram down plan.

The *Kham & Nate* case[3] defines the equitable requirements for cramming down a plan as follows: "There is one exception to the requirement of approval. 11 U.S.C. §1129(b)(1) provides that a fair and equitable plan may be crammed down the throats of objecting creditors."[4] First we cite the opening sentence of §1129(b)(1), which presents the requirements for compliance with cram down of a plan, a synonym that claims and interests will be adjusted to standards which do not discriminate unfairly and are fair and equitable.

Cram Down Defined

(b)(1) Notwithstanding section 510(a) of this title, if all of the applicable requirements of subsection (a) of this section other than

---

[1] *See* §1129(a)(11).

[2] *See* §1129(a)(7)(A)(i), (ii) and (B).

[3] Kham & Nate's Shoes No. 2 Inc. ("Kham & Nate" or "Debtor") v. First Bank of Whiting ("Bank"), 908 F2d 1351, 1359 (7th Cir. 1990).

[4] *See also infra,* this chapter, subtitle "Fair and Equitable—Absolute Priority Rule."

paragraph (8) are met with respect to a plan, the court, on request of the proponent of the plan, shall confirm the plan notwithstanding the requirements of such paragraph if the plan does not discriminate unfairly, and is fair and equitable, with respect to each class of claims or interests that is impaired under, and has not accepted, the plan.

Section 1129(b)—Kham & Nate's Case

We start then with *Kham & Nate,* a case in which three proposed plans under §1129(a) had failed to obtain acceptance under §1129(a)(8). The Debtor then turned to §1129(b). The court of appeals summarized the principal issues which hinged on whether a chapter 11 plan of reorganization, which could not be confirmed because of noncompliance with §1129(a)(8), could comply with the requirements of §1129(b). Kham & Nate operated four retail shoe stores in Chicago and had been in chapter 11 for 6 years operating as debtor in possession, and finally confirmed its plan under §1129(a).

First Bank of Whiting ("Bank"), one of Kham & Nate's creditors, appealed from the order confirming the fourth plan. The order of confirmation not only reduced the Bank's secured claim to unsecured status, but allowed Khamolaw Beard ("Beard") and Nathaniel Parker ("Parker"), the Debtor's principals, to retain their equity interests, notwithstanding the firm's inability to pay its creditors in full. The bankruptcy judge subordinated the Bank's claims after finding that the Bank behaved "inequitably." Moreover, he allowed Beard and Parker to retain their interests on the theory that their guarantees of new loans to be made as part of the reorganization were "new value."[5]

Bank's Financing to Debtor

The Bank started financing the Debtor in July 1981, extending credit of $50,000 which was rolled over with interest in 1983 to $42,000. Letters of credit were subsequently issued

---

[5] *Id.* at 1353. *See supra* Chapter 15, this handbook, Fraudulent Conveyances, subtitle "Bundles."

by the Bank in favor of the Debtor's creditors, which the Debtor supported with a note to the Bank. The Bank's security interest was limited to the goods the suppliers furnished. In late 1983, the Debtor experienced serious cash flow problems and asked the Bank for additional capital to which the Bank agreed if it could be made secure. This was difficult as the Debtor had been losing money in the previous 2 years and owed more than $400,000 for taxes. Any new loan would be subordinate to tax liabilities. The parties discussed two ways to make the Bank secure: by "a guarantee by the Small Business Administration ("SBA"), or by a bankruptcy petition followed by an order giving a postpetition loan superpriority to the Bank."[6]

Filing Chapter 11 Petition

While waiting for the SBA to act, the Debtor filed its petition under chapter 11 in January 1984. The bankruptcy court granted its application for an order under §364(c)(1),[7] giving a loan from the Bank priority even over the administrative expenses of the chapter 11. The Debtor and Bank then signed their loan agreement which opened a $300,000 line of credit. The contract provided for cancellation on 5 days' notice, and a clause which stated, "nothing provided herein shall constitute a waiver of any right of the Bank to terminate financing at any time."[8]

The parties signed the contract on January 23, 1984, and the Debtor took $75,000. Suppliers began to draw on the letters of credit. Quickly thereafter, on February 29, the Bank mailed the Debtor a letter stating that it would make no additional advances after March 7. After all was said and done, Debtor's ultimate indebtedness was $164,000: "$42,000 outstanding on the loan made in 1981, $47,000 on the letters of credit, and $75,000 on the line of credit."[9] The Debtor paid $10,000 against the line of credit in April 1985, but made no

---

[6] *Id.* at 1353.

[7] *See supra* Chapter 3, this handbook, subtitle "Creditor's Adequate Protection."

[8] 908 F2d at 1353. *See also supra* Chapter 3, this handbook, Use, Sale or Lease of Property.

[9] *Id.* at 1354.

further payments. "Debtor did not ask the court to order Bank to make further advances or to grant superpriority to another creditor to facilitate loans from another source."[10]

Subordination of Bank's Secured Debt
Evidentiary Hearing

No substantive change occurred until the spring of 1988, when the Debtor proposed its fourth plan of reorganization. Although the three previous plans provided for the Bank to be paid in full, the fourth plan proposed to treat the Bank's claims as general unsecured debts and also proposed to allow the shareholders to keep their stock in exchange for guaranteeing new loans to the Debtor.

Reasons for Subordination of Bank's Claim

In an evidentiary hearing the bankruptcy judge concluded that the Bank had behaved inequitably in terminating Debtor's line of credit and inducing Debtor's suppliers to draw on the letters of credit. These draws, the bankruptcy judge concluded, "converted Bank from an unsecured lender (the position it held before the bankruptcy) to a super-secured lender under [the] financing order."[11] After vacating the financing order, the judge, on the authority of §510(c), subordinated the Bank's debt because of its inequitable conduct.[12] Finally, the judge confirmed the plan, including the provision allowing the stockholders of Debtor to retain their interests, holding that their guarantees were "new value" equivalent to the worth of the interests they would retain, which the judge thought small. The district court affirmed.

The Bank's Appeal

In addition to the appeal from the order of confirmation, the Bank appealed the judge's order because the judge had not quantified Bank's entitlement since the Debtor had filed a counterclaim against the Bank contending that it was entitled

---

[10] *Id.*

[11] *Id.*

[12] *Id.*

to more than $300,000 in damages. As a result of the Bank's refusal to provide extra credit, the Debtor contended that it had to close several of its stores and suffered other damages. Essentially for these reasons, the judge subordinated the Bank's claims and issued an order requiring the parties "to brief anew the question whether the finding of liability—and implicitly the subordination of Bank's claims—was proper. Pending counterclaims usually prevent an order from being final. . . ."[13] This was the basis for the Bank's claim that the court of appeals lacked jurisdiction.

At this point the court of appeals "pretended puzzlement"[14] and asked: "Why does Bank not just withdraw its notice of appeal?"[15] The court of appeals held that because no one objected, Bank's claim had been quantified and the claim was allowed in full automatically.[16] "Nothing in the plan is contingent on the resolution of Debtor's counterclaim against Bank."[17] The court regarded Debtor's request for damages as a form of commercial litigation, demanding a remedy for breach of contract. Comparing such claim to the disposition of a controversy that would be a "standalone dispute out of bankruptcy," the court pointed out it would be appealable. "We need not decide whether a decision to subordinate a claim would be appealable in advance of quantification; here the subordination was accomplished as part of the plan, and the confirmation order is always appealable."[18]

Subordination of the Bank's claim required two steps: setting aside the financing order followed by the application of §510(c). Bank did not object to the setting aside of the financing order on the merits, but on a procedural issue which the court of appeals held was not substantiated. However, before the court would move on to the application of §510(c), the court observed an intermediate step namely, §364(e) which

---

[13] *Id.* citing *In re* Berke, 837 F2d 293 (7th Cir. 1988).

[14] *Id.* (author's analysis).

[15] 908 F2d 1354.

[16] *Id.* at 1355. *See* §502(a) Allowance of claims or interests: "A claim or interest, proof of which is filed under section 501 of this title, is allowed, unless a party in interest . . . objects."

[17] *Id.*

[18] *Id.* at 1355.

provides that reversal or modification of a financing order on appeal "does not affect the validity of any debt so incurred, or any priority or lien so granted, to an entity that extended such credit in good faith." As we indicated in our discussion in Chapter 3 of this handbook, the Seventh Circuit Court of Appeals stated:

> Section 364(e) "instantiates the principle that bankruptcy judges may make *binding* commitments to give priority to new credit. If creditors fear that the rug will be pulled out from under them, they will hesitate to lend. So §364(e) and companion provisions, *e.g.*, 11 U.S.C. §363(m)[19] . . . disable courts from backtracking on promises in the absence of bad faith, which is a very narrow exception.

Court of Appeals' Comment
The Power of §364(e)

The court of appeals observed that an order granting a priority was protected by §364(e) and could not be set aside on appeal without finding that the secured creditor acted in bad faith. The court of appeals found no such conduct on the Bank's part and was astonished that the Bank ignored the principle behind §364(e) and neglected to offer an objection to the bankruptcy judge to have its claim reclassified to its proper status. Failing, however, to take such action, the Bank had no such choice in the court of appeals. Such action would have disposed of the necessity of proceeding with the trial of the issues of confirmation.

Prepetition Draw on Letters of Credit

The bankruptcy court submitted two reasons for subordination of the Bank's claims: first, the Bank's awareness

---

[19] *See* §364(e): "The reversal or modification on appeal of an authorization under subsection (b) or (c) of this section of a sale or lease of property does not affect the validity of a sale or lease under such authorization to an entity that purchased or leased such property in good faith. . . ."

of Debtor's financial condition and Debtor's reliance upon the line of credit; and, second, the Bank obtained an unfair advantage by inducing suppliers to draw on the letters of credit after the financing order and thereby promoted its position on these advances from unsecured to supersecured. The Bank, however, disclaimed priority either for the $47,000 advanced to satisfy the letters of credit or the $42,000 outstanding on the loan made in 1981. "Sums paid out after bankruptcy on letters of credit issued before bankruptcy are prebankruptcy loans, to which §364 cannot apply. . . . So, although the financing order appears to give Bank priority on all of its loans, pre- and postfiling, Bank wisely concedes that the order could not have properly done so. . . ."[20]

Subordination, therefore, only concerned the $65,000 advanced under the line of credit granted by the financing order. Subordination agreements are enforceable in bankruptcy (§364(d)) as they are under applicable nonbankruptcy law, with certain exceptions. Specifically for this case, under principles of "equitable subordination, [the court may] subordinate for purposes of distribution all or part of an allowed claim to all or part of another allowed claim. . . ."[21]

Observing that §510(c) allows judges to subordinate claims but does not provide criteria for the exercise of the power, the court noted that the absence of such provisions "commits the subject to the courts to be worked out in the common law fashion. . . . Equitable subordination usually is a response to efforts by corporate insiders to convert their equity interests into secured debt in anticipation of bankruptcy. . . . Courts require the insider to return to their position at the end of the line. . . ."[22]

---

[20] *Id.* at 1356. However, the order granted Bank superpriority of administrative expenses under §364(d). But *see, supra,* Chapter 3, this handbook, Use, Sale, or Lease of Property, subtitle "Cross-Collateralization," indicating cases where cross-collateralization has been granted and rejected.

[21] *See* §510(c).

[22] 908 F2d at 1356.

Good Faith of Bank

The court continued: "'Inequitable conduct' in commercial life means breach *plus* some advantage taking. . . . Firms that have negotiated contracts are entitled to enforce them to the letter, even to the great discomfort of their trading partners, without being mulcted for lack of 'good faith.' Although courts often refer to the obligation of good faith that exists in every contractual relation[23] . . . 'good faith' is a compact reference to an implied undertaking not to take opportunistic advantage in a way that could not have been contemplated at the time of drafting, and which, therefore, was not resolved explicitly by the parties."[24]

The Bank's conduct under the financing agreement was reviewed by the court and all of the Bank's activities were found consistent with (except for a minor exception) the financing agreement. "Equitable subordination under [section] 510(c) is not a device to magnify the damages available for inconsequential breaches of contract."[25]

Fair and Equitable
Absolute Priority Rule

Having determined that there was not any inequitable conduct by the Bank, the court turned to a determination of the impairment of classes which would prevent confirmation. The reader will recall the same problem occurred in the *Madison Hotel* case which resulted in a finding that the Debtor's plan was properly in §1129(a) because there was no impairment of classes inasmuch as the plan had been accepted by all creditors, and the mortgagee, who claimed to be an impaired creditor, was not voting and, thereby, was considered consenting under §1124.

There is one exception to the requirement of approval. 11 U.S.C. §1129(b)(1) provides that a 'fair and equitable plan' may be crammed down

---

[23] *Id.*

[24] *Id.*

[25] *Id.* at 1359.

the throats of objecting creditors. The Code says that a plan treats unsecured creditors fairly and equitably if the 'holder of any claim or interest that is junior to the claims of such class will not receive or retain under the plan on account of such junior claim or interest any property.' 11 U.S.C. §1129(b)(2)(B)(ii). This is the 'absolute priority rule'. An objection to the plan may be overridden only if every class lower in priority is wiped out. Priority is 'absolute' in the sense that every cent of each class comes ahead of the first dollar of any junior class.[26]

The bankruptcy judge approved a cram down plan in the case. Here, unlike *Madison Hotel,* unsecured creditors would not be paid in full and cured of the mortgagee's payments to date. The judge overruled the Bank's objection after finding that the plan was fair and equitable. "Yet the court did not extinguish the interests of every class junior to the unsecured creditors. Instead it allowed the stockholders to retain their interests, reasoning that by guaranteeing a $435,000 loan to be made as part of the plan, Beard and Parker contributed 'new value' justifying the retention of their stock."[27]

New Value Defined

The reasoning in the judge's opinion that justified "new value" was that the size of the new debt made the risk of the guarantees "substantial." The risk also exceeded the value of the retained stock, because "'given the history of Debtor and the various risks associated with its business,' the stock would have only 'minimal' value. Beard and Parker thus would contribute more than they would receive, so the court allowed them to keep their stock."[28]

The shareholders reasoning as to value of their contribution seemed to be too clever by half. The court pretended to be meditating when it observed: "There is

---

[26] *Id.*

[27] *Id.*

[28] *Id.*

something unreal about this calculation. If the stock is worth less than the guarantees, why are Beard and Parker doing it? If the value of the stock is 'minimal,' why does Bank object to letting Beard and Parker keep it? Is *everyone* acting inconsistently with self-interest, as the court's findings imply? And why, if the business is likely to fail, making the value of the stock 'minimal,' could the court confirm the plan of reorganization?"[29]

Stock is Property

Seemingly the court of appeals had no difficulty in answering its philosophical meditation. "Confirmation depends on a conclusion that the reorganized firm is likely to succeed, and not relapse into 'liquidation, or the need for further financial reorganization. 11 U.S.C. §1129(a)(11).' If, as the bankruptcy court found, the plan complies with the requirement, then the equity interest in the firm *must* be worth something—as Beard, Parker, and the Bank all appear to believe."[30]

This led the court to observe: "Stock is 'property' for purposes of §1129(b)(2)(B)(ii) even if the firm has a negative net worth.[31] . . . An option to purchase stock also is 'property.' . . . [W]hether we characterize the stock or the option to buy it as the 'property,' the transaction seems to run afoul of §1129(b)(2)(B)(ii), for it means that although a class of unsecured creditors is not paid in full, a junior class (the shareholders) keeps some 'property'."[32]

Fair and Equitable
Insolvent Debtor's Status

Covering then the derivation of the meaning of "fair and equitable", the court of appeals turned to the Bankruptcy Act of 1898 which "required 'plans of reorganization' to be 'fair and equitable' but did not define the phrase. . . . The absolute

---

[29] *Id.*

[30] *Id.*

[31] *Id.* at 1360 citing Norwest Bank Worthington v. Ahlers, 108 S.Ct. 963, 969 (1988).

[32] *Id.*

priority rule came into being as a cross between the interpretation of 'fair and equitable' and a rule of contract law."[33]

In a cram down situation, how can shareholders retain any part of their stock, if the company is insolvent? The court opined that new capital contributed may allow the stockholders as investors to retain their interests which may be lower in value than a contribution. "Some firms depend for success on the entrepreneurial skills or special knowledge of managers who are also shareholders. If these persons' interests are wiped out, they may leave the firm and reduce its value. If they may contribute new value and retain an interest, this may tie them to the firm and so improve its prospects."[34]

The court of appeals next postulated that "the exchange of stock for new value may make sense. When it does, the creditors should be willing to go along. Creditors effectively own bankrupt firms. . . . If there are many creditors, one may hold out, seeking to engross a greater share of the gains. But the Code deals with holdups by allowing half of a class by number (two-thirds by value) to consent to a lower class's retention of an interest.[35] When there is value to be gained by allowing a lower class to kick in new value and keep its interest, the creditors should be willing to go along. . . ."[36] Supporting this position the court cited from the *Ahler*'s case: "A 'new value' exception means a power in the *judge* to 'sell' stock to the managers even when the creditors believe that the transaction will not augment the value of the firm. . . ."[37]

Fair and Equitable
Reorganization

Since contracts give creditors priority over shareholders, a plan of reorganization has to do the same. Also, under the 1898 Act bankruptcy was a branch of equity, "so it is not

---

[33] *Id.* citing Northern Pacific Ry. v. Boyd, 33 S.Ct. 554 (1913).

[34] *Id.*

[35] *Id.*

[36] *Id.*

[37] *Id.* Norwest Bank Worthington v. Ahlers ("Ahlers"), 108 S.Ct. 963, 968 (1991).

surprising that equitable modifications of the doctrine developed. One of these was the 'new value exception' to the absolute priority doctrine. So far as the Supreme Court is concerned, however, the development has been 100% dicta."[38]

The *Kansas City Terminal*[39] case was held by the court of appeals to be the genesis of the exception. "The [Supreme] Court conceived the absolute priority rule as barring any retention of interest by a shareholder if any layer of creditors is excluded. [The Supreme Court] used this rule to veto a decision by the secured creditor to allow the shareholder a stake when junior creditors were cut out and objected. Yet the senior creditor, which as a practical matter owned 100% of the firm, must have had a reason to suffer the continued existence of the shareholder. The plan in *Kansas City Ry.* was identical in principle to selling the firm to the secured creditor at auction, and the secured creditor giving some stock to the manager and former shareholder."[40] The court of appeals noted, however, that the Supreme Court stated in dicta that the "right to object did not give the junior creditor as potent a power as it might, because the judge could modify the strict priority equitably if the shareholder agreed to contribute new value."[41]

There was a time lapse until *Case v. Los Angles* was decided.[42] The Supreme Court reversed the holding in the bankruptcy court, which followed *Kansas City Ry.*, allowing shareholders to retain an interest in exchange for their promise to contribute value in the form of continuity of management, plus financial standing and influence in the community that would enable the Debtor to raise new money. The shareholders were allowed to retain their stockholdings even though the class of senior creditors objected—"a dramatic step from the suggestion in *Kansas City Ry.* that new value plus the *consent* of the creditor whose claim exceeded the value

---

[38] *Id.*

[39] *Id.* Kansas City Terminal Ry. v. Central Union Trust Co., 46 S.Ct. 549 (1926).

[40] *Id.* at 1360–61.

[41] *Id.* at 1361.

[42] *Id.* at 1361. Case v. Los Angeles Lumber Products Co., 60 S.Ct. 1 (1939).

of the firm would suffice. The Supreme Court reversed, holding that new value must mean 'money or money's worth.' . . ."[43]

"Cases in the lower courts proceeded to follow the dicta in *Case* and *Kansas City Ry.* without noticing the difference between consent and objection by creditors. . . . Perhaps this distinction was not an essential one in the administration of a common law doctrine, especially not when (a) the unanimity rule made the lack of consent the norm; and (b) bankruptcy was a branch of equity."[44] "Everything changed with the adoption of the Code in 1978. The definition of 'fair and equitable' is no longer a matter of common law; §1129(b)(2) defines it expressly. Holdouts that spoiled reorganizations and created much of the motive for having judges 'sell stock' to the manager shareholders no longer are of much concern, now that §1126(c) . . ."[45] requires numerical and value quantification for consent. "And bankruptcy judges no longer have equitable powers to modify contracts to achieve 'fair' distributions. Bankruptcy judges enforce entitlement created under state law. . . .[46] '[W]hatever equitable powers remain in the bankruptcy courts must and can only be exercised in the confines of the Bankruptcy Code.'"[47]

New Value's Existence

As to whether the "new value" exception to the absolute priority "survived the codification of that rule in 1978 is a question open in this circuit.[48] . . . The language of the Code strongly suggests that it did not and we are to take this language seriously even when it alters pre-Code practices."[49] The Bank had taken the position that the new value exception vanished in 1978.[50] "We stop short of the precipice, as the

---

[43] *Id.* citing 60 S.Ct. at 10–11.

[44] *Id. See supra* Chapter 16, this handbook, subtitle "Applicability of UFTA to Queen Elizabeth Statute."

[45] *Id.*

[46] *Id.* Butner v. United States, 99 S.Ct. 914, (1979); Levit v. Ingersoll Rand Financial Corp., 874 F2d 1186, 1197–98 (7th Cir.1988).

[47] *Id.* citing Ahlers, 108 S.Ct. at 968.

[48] *Id.*

[49] *Id.*

[50] *Id.* at 1362. *See supra* Chapter 7, this handbook, subtitle "BAFJA."

Supreme Court did in *Ahlers*,[51] . . . for two reasons: first, the consideration for the shares is insufficient even if the new value exception retains vitality; second, although Bank vigorously argues the merits of the new value exception in this court, it did not make this argument in the bankruptcy court. Despite Bank's failure to preserve its argument, the history and limits of the rule before 1978 are pertinent to our analysis because, as the Court held in *Ahlers*[52] . . . at a minimum the Code forbids any expansion beyond the limits recognized in *Case*."[53]

The court of appeals indicated that *Case* rejected the argument that continuity of management plus financial standing that would attract new investment constituted "new value," and instead held that only an infusion of "money or money's worth" would suffice. "*Ahlers* reinforce[d] the message, holding that a promise of future labor, coupled with the manager's experience and expertise, also is not new value. . . . The Court observed, . . . , again quoting from *Case*, that the promise was 'intangible, and in all likelihood, unenforceable. It has no place in the asset column of the balance sheet of the new [entity].'"[54]

Guarantees as New Value

The court used this analysis to review the guarantees of Parker and Beard. There was no indication of whether Parker and Beard had substantial assets at risk in the event of Debtors' default. "A guarantor who has *not* paid has no claim against the firm. . . . Debtor relies on *In re Potter*,[55] . . . but it does not support the bankruptcy judge's decision. The new

---

[51] *Id.*

[52] *Id.*

[53] *Id.* Case v. Los Angeles Lumber Products Co., 60 S.Ct. 1 (1939). *See also In re* Holiday Associates Limited Partnership, 39 BR 711, 716 (B. SD Iowa 1992) (Without deciding whether the new value exception survived the enactment of the Code, the court held that the Debtor's plan was unconfirmable since interest holders retained equity in the Debtor without contributing new value and there was not the appropriate consent of senior creditors.).

[54] *Id.*

[55] *Id. In re* Potter Material Service, Inc., 781 F2d 99 (7th Cir. 1986).

value in *Potter* was a combination of $34,800 cash plus a guarantee of a $600,000 loan. If Beard and Parker had contributed substantial cash, we would have a case like *Potter*. They didn't and we don't. To the extent that *Potter* implies that a guarantee alone is 'new value,' it did not survive *Ahlers*. *Potter* observed that the guarantor took an economic risk. . . . *Ahlers* holds that detriment to the shareholder does not amount to 'value' to the firm; there must be an infusion of new capital. . . . The plan of reorganization should not have been confirmed over Bank's objection."[56] The court of appeals vacated the order of confirmation and remanded it to the district court for transmission to the bankruptcy court.

Observation

Madison Hotel clearly indicates that any impaired class of creditors that does not accept a §1129(a) plan proffered by the Debtor, or any other proponent of a plan in the same position, may, nonetheless, have the plan considered under §1129(b). However, we again reiterate that the plan must not discriminate against any class and must be fair and equitable. Under §1129(b) if the creditors are not paid the full amount of their claims, the shareholders and/or the next higher class, preferred shareholders or junior claimants, must be eliminated from the plan, unless the impaired classes accept the same plan or another. A contribution that may induce creditors of each class to accept the plan may be money or money's worth added to the plan by the shareholders.

No free ride is allowed. Confirmation is a two way road, with both paths requiring the consent of creditors who control the road. If under §1129(a) the creditors of all classes waive the flag, the road is clear for the Debtor. *Madison Hotel* is a rarity in that creditors receive 100% payment. Other cases generally contain an inner feeling by creditors that the Debtor will succeed. Section 1129(b) indicates a demand to the Debtor to "show me how you're going to make it," without new value, money, or real guarantees which are necessary to sustain the business. No single group controls the case. The Debtor,

---

[56] *Id.* at 1362–63.

assisted by committees, runs the show monitored by the U.S. Trustee with Judge Fair and Equitable calling the shots.

Effective Date of Plan

Now let us consider the requirements of §1129, dealing with the effective date of a plan, which provides: "[w]ith respect to each impaired class of claims or interests . . . (A) each holder . . . (ii) will receive . . . property of a value as of the effective date of the plan. . . ." Effective date is repeated in several subsections of §1129.[57] Effective date is the date upon which a confirmed plan becomes operative and distribution of cash and property is commenced. In essence, it is the point in time "when the plan can and should be susceptible of implementation and commencement of the operation of its provisions."[58]

Section 1141—Effect of Confirmation

We turn our discussion to §1141, one of the postconfirmation sections of the Code, which is entitled: "Effect of confirmation of a plan." Section 1141(a), with certain exceptions, binds both the Debtor and participants in the plan who are not creditors, but are bound by the plan upon receiving property of the estate. All creditors or equity security holders, whether or not such creditors or equity security holders have accepted the plan, are similarly bound. In other words, the prepetition claims are discharged and secured and unsecured creditors and equity security holders receive the distributions set forth in the plan, unless the plan provides otherwise as to specific creditors. As for the Debtor, "[e]xcept as otherwise provided in the plan or the order confirming the plan, the confirmation of the plan vests all the property of the estate in the Debtor."[59]

---

[57] *See* §1129(a)(7)(B), *et al.*

[58] *See* B. Weintraub and M.J. Crames, *Defining Consummation, Effective Date of Plan of Reorganization and Retention of Post-Confirmation Jurisdiction, Suggested Amendment to Bankruptcy Code and Bankruptcy Rules,* 64 AM. BANKR. L.J. 245 (Summer 1990).

[59] *See infra* Chapter 20, this handbook, Postconfirmation Matters.

Plans also contain provisions which require an explanation. Consider §1101(2) "'substantial consummation', means—(A) transfer of all or substantially all of the property proposed by the plan to be transferred; . . ." Section 1127, "Modification of Plan," authorizes the proponent of a plan to modify the plan "at any time before confirmation, . . . [provided the plan meets] the requirements of sections 1122 and 1123 of this title. . . . After the proponent of a plan files a modification . . . the plan as modified becomes the plan."

Plans may be modified after confirmation but before substantial consummation, but the modified plan must meet "the requirements of sections 1122 and 1123. . . . Such plan as modified under this subsection becomes the plan only if circumstances warrant such modification and the court, after notice and a hearing, confirms such plan as modified under section 1129 of this title." Additionally, "[t]he proponent of a modification shall comply with §1125 of this title with respect to the plan as modified."[60] The modified plan is binding upon any holder of a claim or interest that has accepted or rejected the plan as before modification or change unless within a time fixed by the court such holder changes his previous acceptance or rejection."[61]

Confirmation:
Consensual and Cram Down Combined

The case of *In re Commodore*[62] sets forth a practical solution of the effective date in a modification of a plan which required a third party to make a contribution of funds to the Debtor upon the entry of a final order. The necessity for providing a definition of effective date in a plan is indicated by the following definition which was added to the plan in the *Commodore* case: "'Final Order' shall mean an Order entered and docketed by the Court on a certain date, from which certain date eleven business days have elapsed and on which Order (i) no stay, appeal or certiorari proceeding is in effect with respect to such Order and (ii) the Order has not been

---

[60] *See* §1127(c).

[61] *See* §1127(d).

[62] *In re* Commodore, 87 BR 62 (B. ND Ind. 1987).

vacated."[63] This provision gives the Debtor a short period of time, *e.g.*, 15 days leeway, or more if necessary, particularly if an appeal is pending, to prepare for its distribution procedure. The 6-month period in *Laventhal & Horwath*[64] was an unusually lengthy time, obviously due to the necessity of obtaining the many individual consents of nonparticipants to the plan. The reason is obvious as the factors in the *Commodore* case indicate: "appeal and stays hinder such distribution."[65]

Partnership Problems
Liability of Partners

Laventhal & Horwath was an accounting firm consisting of 629 partners. The partnership found it necessary to recover from its insolvent condition. Filing a petition under chapter 11 for the partnership seemed to be the answer,[66] but a hurdle had to be overcome: Would a discharge of the obligations of the partnership also protect the 629 partners from suits by all of the partnership's creditors? The Uniform Partnership Act ("UPA") presents answers: "(1) A partnership is an association of two or more persons to carry on as co-owners a business for profit."[67] The nature of the individual partner's liability for the partnership's debts is contained in §15 of the UPA: "[A]ll partners are liable (a) Jointly and severally, for everything chargeable to the partnership. . . ."[68]

---

[63] *Id.* at 63. *See also, infra,* this chapter, subtitle "Contents of Order of Confirmation."

[64] *See* Laventhal & Horwath ("Laventhal"), Case No. 90 B 13839 (CB) (B. SDNY 1992). *See also* Order Confirming Debtor's Amended Plan of Reorganization, August 24, 1992.

[65] 87 BR 63. *Cf. In re* Milleson, 83 BR 696, 699 (B. D Neb. 1988): "effective date held to be on or after the date on which the confirmation order is entered."

[66] *See* §§101(13): "'Debtor' means person . . . [and] (41) includes, individual, partnership. . . ."

[67] *See* WEST'S UNIFORM LAW'S ANNOTATED, Uniform Partnership Act §6: Partnership Defined.

[68] *See* UPA §15 (the liabilities referred to are under "sections 13 [Partnership Bound by Partner's Wrongful Act] and 14 [Partnership Bound by Partner's Breach of Trust]"). *See also In re* Pappas, 661 F2d 82 (7th Cir.

Filing of Chapter 11 by Partnership

Confronted with joint and several liability, the partners agreed to file a chapter 11 petition for the partnership in an effort to limit the liability of the partners by effectuating a consensual plan. Notwithstanding the number of partners, none filed an answer to the petition.[69] One can only be astonished and elated as to the distance travelled by §105(a) in its efforts not merely to resuscitate the partnership, but at the same time to protect the individual partners, all of whose personal assets could have been seized by recalcitrant creditors. The order of confirmation sets forth in detail how the power of the court solved the problem.[70] The scope of our handbook just permits some of the highlights.

Debtor's Plan—Order of Confirmation

The Debtor's plan provided for participation of all of the partners (Participants), and as to those of the 629 who did not accept the allocation formula (Nonparticipants), they would remain unprotected by the Permanent Injunction provided for in the plan. Creditors who accepted the plan did so with the understanding that each Participant would contribute a sum of money to the Debtor to substantiate a plan of reorganization under §1129.

The order of confirmation of the plan commenced with "Findings of Fact and Conclusions of Law" which summarized compliance with the various sections leading to the Disclosure Statement, the Order, and Acceptances of each class of the plan. "All of the conditions precedent to Confirmation . . . have been satisfied or are satisfied by virtue of this Order."[71] Left

---

1981).

[69] *See* §303(b)(3) Involuntary cases: "[a]n involuntary case against a person is commenced by the filing with the bankruptcy court of a petition under chapter 7 or 11 of this title—(3) if such person is a partnership—(A) by fewer than all of the general partners in such partnership; . . ." *See also* §303(d): "The Debtor, or a general partner in a partnership Debtor that did not join in the petition, may file an answer to a petition under this section."

[70] *See* Chapter 4, this handbook, Power of Court.

[71] Order at 3 ¶4.

open were a series of incomplete proceedings which the Debtor anticipated concluding before the "effective date of the plan."

Applicability of Cram Down

A novel provision in a §1129 plan where the creditors of each class had accepted the plan, was further fortified with a finding that "[e]ven though the Debtor has satisfied the requirements of Section 1129(a)(8) with respect to all Classes and therefore is not required to satisfy the 'cram down' standards set forth in Section 1129(b) of the Bankruptcy Code, . . . the Debtor has shown that it is able to satisfy such 'cram-down' standards with respect to (a) all classes of impaired unsecured claims . . . [t]he plan does not discriminate unfairly against, and is fair and equitable with respect to, each of [certain classes]. Accordingly, even if any or all of [these classes] were to have rejected the Plan, confirmation of the Plan would still be appropriate."[72]

The reference to the Debtor's compliance with the cram down provision of the Code was the equivalent of putting a double lock on the door, and at the same time served to fortify the necessity for contributions required from nonconsenting partners in order to satisfy the requirements for a consensual plan. Liquidation of the hard assets, accounts receivable, and completion of contracts required both support and contributions from the partners; thus, the creation of two groups, Participants and Nonparticipants. "The Debtor has sought substantial financial contributions from the Participants, which contributions are to be paid to the Debtor's estate for ultimate distribution to creditors under the Plan."[73]

"On January 8, 1991, as part of the Preliminary Injunction Order, the Court required the production of personal financial disclosure forms from the Participants (the 'Participant Disclosure Forms'). . . ."[74] These Participant Disclosure Forms are not to be passed over as simple verified statements of a partner's assets and liabilities. "The Debtor obtained financial statements from the vast majority of the Participants and

---

[72] *Id.* at 6 ¶6.

[73] *Id.* ¶8.

[74] *Id.* at 6–7 ¶9.

provided them to the Creditor's Committee and the Banks in redacted form. . . . In order to corroborate the financial information set forth in the Participant Disclosure Forms, . . . the Debtor obtained from the vast majority of the Participants (i) tax returns from the preceding two-year period and (ii) copies of the financial statements provided by the participants to other third parties. . . ."[75] The forms were examined by the Creditor's Committee and the Banks with the assistance of the committee's accountants who analyzed the Participants, Disclosure Statements.

Computation of Funds Necessary for Confirmation

The review of these documents having been completed, the Debtor, the Creditors' Committee, and the Banks "conducted arm's-length negotiations concerning the maximum amount which the Participants might be reasonably expected to voluntarily contribute to the estate, and ultimately agreed upon $47.3 million as the Aggregate Participant Settlement Amount."[76] As of the date of the Order, 507 of the 629 Participants, representing in excess of $40 million, had executed and delivered Participant Settlement Agreements to the Escrow Agent. Of the Non-Committed Participants approximately 20 were either (i) insolvent or administratively closed estates of deceased Participants or (ii) Debtors in personal bankruptcy. Lest there be any discrimination among partners, and anything but fair and equitable treatment, the Participant Settlement Amount from each Participant required an investigation and analysis of each partner's finances based on relevant factors extending from the partner's earnings during the period prior to chapter 11 and future earnings, as well as present net worth.

Nature of Causes of Action Settled

Not to be overlooked, as we discussed in previous chapters, the Debtors were compromising and settling causes of action that belonged to the Debtor's estate under §§541, 544, 547, and

---

[75] *Id.* at 7 ¶9.
[76] *Id.*

548 of the Bankruptcy Code and applicable state law.[77] All of the "level of payments to the Debtor's estate by the Participants are at least as much in the aggregate as the amounts which a chapter 7 trustee of the Debtor would be able to recover by exercising his or her rights under §723[78] of the Bankruptcy Code. Moreover, liquidation of all the Debtor's assets under chapter 7, including the amounts which could be recovered by a chapter 7 trustee from the individual Participants. . . ."[79]

Observation

The unusual and attractive feature of the *Laventhal* case is its ability to combine the subjects of consent and cram down into a single plan. The usual consensual confirmation plan generally creates value of assets by a combination of inventory, accounts receivable, real estate, and the continued profitable returns of future operations. *Laventhal* offers the same comparable value from its accounting firm—assets which have been earned by the parties in several past years (reflected in their savings) as well as part of those earnings estimated for several years in the future by each partner. The flexibility of the power of the court brings us back to §105(a) and a happy day: At this writing all partners have accepted the *Laventhal* plan[80] and the plan has been confirmed.

The Debtor is now on its way to benefit by a rehabilitation; business begins with the anticipation that reorganization has restored its financial condition in many of the aspects we have indicated for rehabilitation. The creditors also anticipate the sound status that they have helped to conceive, not only in the

---

[77] *Id.* at 9 ¶15. *See supra* Chapter 14, this handbook, Trustee's Strong-Arm Powers Marshaling of Assets; Chapter 15, this handbook, Preferences; and Chapter 16, this handbook, Fraudulent Transfers and Obligations.

[78] *See* §723, Rights of Partnership Trustee Against General Partners. *See also* §1129(a): "The court shall confirm a plan only if all of the following requirements are met: (7) with respect to each impaired class—(A) each holder of a claim or interest of such class—(ii) will receive . . . property of a value, . . . that is not less than the amount that such holder would so receive or retain if the Debtor were liquidated under chapter 7 of this title. . . ."

[79] *Id.* at 9 ¶16.

[80] *See supra* §105(a) discussed in Chapter 4, this handbook.

payment of the dividend, but in allowing these accountants to continue their lifelong professions.

Chapter 20
Postconfirmation Matters

Effect of Confirmation
The Bind on the Parties

As we completed the previous chapter we briefly commented concerning on the effect of confirmation. The legal significance of binding the parties and dealing with postconfirmation matters requires a clarification of the legal conclusions arising from the confirmation of a plan. Section 1141(a) provides for the entities who are bound by the confirmed plan: "[T]he provisions of a confirmed plan *bind* the debtor, any entity issuing securities under the plan, any entity acquiring property under the plan, and any creditor, equity security holder, or general partner in the debtor, whether or not [their claims or interests are impaired or they have accepted the plan. . . .]"[1] (emphasis added).

---

[1] *See* exception: "Except as provided in subsections (d)(2) and (d)(3) of this section. . . ." 11 USC §1141(c).

Failed Reorganization

The word "bind" is crucial to the meaning of the section. Simply defined, it means "constrained with legal authority."[2] *Paul v. Monts*[3] is a case which is a practical delineation of the entities that are bound by §1141(a). The case involved third parties who were not creditors nor had any interest in debtor's property, but were proponents of a plan. In a *per curiam* opinion, the Tenth Circuit, in its opening sentence, presented the problem:

> This case presents the issue of whether a failed Chapter 11 reorganization plan gives rise to a cause of action which the Chapter 7 trustee can enforce against proposed participants to the plan who were not themselves creditors and who did not acquire property under the plan.[4]

Proposed Plan of Reorganization

The material facts in the case were largely undisputed. International,[5] conducting a business of packaging fluorocarbon products, had obtained loans totalling $6 million from Southwest National Bank[6] secured by International's property. Ninety percent of this indebtedness was guaranteed by Farmers Home Administration.[7] All or substantially all of the loans had been purchased by Southern Investors.[8]

On March 18, 1980, International filed a chapter 11 petition. On July 21, 1980, Debtor filed its second amended plan of arrangement which provided that Titan,[9] a wholly owned subsidiary, was to be formed by Travenca[10] and would

---

[2] *See* WEBSTER'S NINTH COLLEGIATE DICTIONARY (1983).

[3] 906 F2d 1468 (10th Cir. 1990).

[4] *Id.* at 1469.

[5] *Id.* at 1470. International Plastico, Inc. ("International" or "Debtor").

[6] *Id.* Southwest National Bank ("Bank").

[7] *Id.* Farmers Home Administration ("FmHA").

[8] *Id.* Southern Investors Management Company, Inc. ("Southern Investors").

[9] *Id.* Titan Energy Co., Inc. ("Titan").

[10] *Id.* Travenca Development Corporation ("Travenca").

(1) assume Debtor's entire obligation to FmHA, (2) provide $2.5 million of new capital, and (3) obtain 51% of Debtor's common stock, 175,000 shares of preferred stock, and title to certain assets. The intention of the parties was that Debtor have $1.36 million as working capital for future operations of its packaging facility. The proposed plan further provided that when Titan assumed Debtor's $6 million indebtedness, the Bank would transfer its mortgage for these loans to assets to be thereafter acquired by Titan, which would free all of Debtor's assets under the proposed plan.

Hearing on Plan

On August 19, 1980, the day before the confirmation hearing, the FmHA set forth 13 conditions to be satisfied prior to the Bank's transferring its security in Debtor's property to assets subsequently to be acquired and developed by Titan. On the following day, at the hearing on confirmation of the second amended plan, in deposition testimony both Debtor's and the Bank's attorneys "indicated that before the hearing, Travenca's representatives knew of the new FmHA conditions and acquiesced to their inclusion in the overall plan."[11] During the hearing, T. Conrad Monts, of Travenca, stated that under any condition either Travenca or he personally would pay the $2.5 million to Debtor in exchange for stock. The FmHA requirements were neither introduced into evidence nor mentioned at the hearing.

Confirmation of Plan

On September 2, 1980, the bankruptcy court entered an order confirming the second amended plan.[12] On September 3, 1980, Southern Investors informed Mr. Monts of the 13

---

[11] *Id.* at 1470.

[12] *Id. See* note 1: "The copy of the plan included in the record on appeal provides only one signature line, that for debtor's attorney. The copy is unsigned. There is nothing in the Bankruptcy Rules or in the local rules for the Bankruptcy Court for the District of Kansas requiring the signature of a potential participant in the Plan and, indeed, no such copy of the Plan signed by Mr. Monts or by Travenca has been identified for us."

additional conditions it would require "before the loan agreement *envisioned* by the plan could be approved."[13]

Implementation of Plan

After the plan was confirmed the parties disagreed regarding the obligations under it and the responsibility for implementation. The parties made several proposals to modify the plan, but no confirmed plan was ever implemented and, accordingly, the Bank moved to implement the plan.[14] The Debtor opposed the motion, anticipating that a modified plan might be approved, but finally the Bank filed a motion to convert to chapter 7 which the Debtor did not oppose. The order, however, approving the motion found that the Debtor did not implement the plan due to the failure of Travenca and Monts to satisfy their obligations under the plan. A trustee was then appointed, and Debtor's assets were substantially liquidated without objection from the Debtor or the bankruptcy court.

Trustee's Declaratory Action

In December 1981, the chapter 7 trustee, as plaintiff, "filed a declaratory judgment action in the bankruptcy court to determine if any of the defendants had breached their respective obligations under the failed plan. The trustee's amended complaint also sought damages from the defendants."[15] Defendant Southern Investment had since filed its own petition and was no longer a party. The FmHA and the Bank were still parties but the trustee's arguments in the court of appeals were not directed to their actions. There remained three defendants—Travenca, Titan, and Monts (collectively, "Travenca").

---

[13] *Id.* (emphasis added).

[14] *Id. See* §1142(b).

[15] *Id.* at 1471.

Confirmed Plan: A Contract?

The court observed in a footnote[16] that the trustee in his brief "argues that a confirmed plan has the characteristics of both a contract and a judgment and that, therefore, his cause of action is tantamount to an action to enforce a judgment of the bankruptcy court. . . . [The court responded that] '[w]hile a confirmed plan functions as a judgment with regard to those bound by the plan, . . . we think the claim here is more analogous to a contract claim.[17] Although the bankruptcy court, does approve, reorganization plans, the essence of that action is to authorize the debtor to enter into the Plan and to approve the proposed financial structuring.[18]. . . A third party in the position of Travenca here has not submitted to the jurisdiction of the court[19] and is simply dealing with the matter on a contractual level.'"

Motion for Summary Judgment

The court then considered the trustee's motion for summary judgment stating that it would affirm the grant of a motion for summary judgment "if it is clear from the record that there are no genuine issues of material fact and the [moving party is] entitled to judgment as a matter of law."[20]

"We address first whether Travenca is bound by the terms of the confirmed reorganization plan. Section 1141(a) of the Bankruptcy Code details the effect of confirmation of a reorganization plan and 'provides in pertinent part . . . [that] [w]hile it is clear that the debtor and its creditors are bound by the plan, it is less certain that Travenca, as a third party investor in the potential reorganization, was bound by the

---

[16] *Id.* at note 3.

[17] *Id.* In fact, a confirmed plan may serve as *res judicata* to a party in interest who failed to object to the plan or confirmation until after confirmation. *See* United States Department of the Air Force v. Carolina Parachute Corp., 907 F2d 1469 (4th Cir. 1990).

[18] 906 F2d at 1471 citing *In re* Food City, Inc., 110 BR 808, 810 note 2 (B. WD Tex. 1990).

[19] *Id. See* Chapter 7, this handbook, Jurisdiction of Bankruptcy Court.

[20] *Id.* at 1471 citing Willner v. Budig, 848 F2d 1032, 1033–34 (10th Cir. 1988), *cert. denied,* 109 S.Ct. 840 (1989), *et al.*

plan.' The general rule is that a confirmed plan of reorganization is binding on the debtor and other proponents of the plan."[21]

Nonetheless, the court continued, "[w]hile section 1141 does not bind Travenca, this conclusion does not mean that, upon the proper evidentiary showing, Travenca could not be bound under general contract law."[22] The district court, however, found upon summary judgment, that the plan did not represent a contract between the parties. Its conclusion was based on evidence that "so many outstanding conditions existed to the transfer of Debtor's major loans and most of its assets to Titan, that no agreement on this key term of the transaction existed and that therefore no contract existed."[23]

The circuit court, however, found that there was evidence that Travenca may have agreed to be bound by the terms of the plan "despite the eleventh-hour conditions inserted by the FmHA and later by [Southern Investors]. . . . Monts testified at the confirmation hearing that he understood 'absolutely' that Travenca would be obliged, upon confirmation, to pay Debtor a total of $2.5 million . . ." for the stock.[24] "We hold that the evidence raises a genuine issue of material fact as to whether Travenca was only agreeing to negotiate toward a workable plan to rescue Debtor or whether it firmly intended to participate, notwithstanding the last minute conditions. Whether the conditions made a critical difference to Travenca's ability or willingness to participate in the reorganization is an issue of material fact which should not have been disposed of on a motion for summary judgment."[25]

Estoppel of Claim

"The district court found that, even if an enforceable contract did exist, the trustee's claim would be barred by estoppel. The trustee, as successor to the debtor in possession, is bound by his predecessor's authorized actions. . . . A litigant

---

[21] *Id. See* §1141(a) *See also* note 4: "There is no indication in the record that Mr. Monts or Travenca were creditors of IPI."

[22] *Id.* at 1472.

[23] *Id.* at 1473.

[24] *Id.*

[25] *Id.*

is required to be consistent in his conduct. He may not maintain a position regarding a transaction wholly inconsistent with his previous acts in connection with that same transaction."[26] In the course of the bankruptcy proceeding, the Debtor took several actions which the district identified as inconsistent with the position the trustee asserted: (1) Debtor never moved for implementation of the plan; (2) Debtor opposed Bank's motion for implementation in apparent hope that an alternate plan would gain approval; (3) Debtor did not oppose Bank's motion for conversion to chapter 7; and (4) Debtor did not contest the liquidation of its assets in direct contradiction to the plan.[27]

"In addition to inconsistent conduct, however, Travenca must also demonstrate a detrimental change in its position as a result of reasonable reliance on that conduct in order to maintain the defense of estoppel.[28] . . . It must also show it rightfully relied and acted upon such belief and would now be prejudiced if the other party were permitted to deny the existence of such facts. . . ."[29]

The court of appeals opined that neither the district court nor the other parties nor its review of the record "identified any detrimental change in Travenca's position in reasonable reliance upon Debtor's conduct. We find this lack of evidence of reliance fatal to Travenca's motion for summary judgment. 'Under Rule 56(c), summary judgment is proper' if the pleadings, depositions, answers, interrogatories, and admissions on file taken with the affidavits, if any, show that there is no genuine issue as to any material fact and that the moving party is entitled to a judgment as a matter of law."[30] The court concluded that since estoppel is an affirmative defense upon which Travenca, the moving party, had the burden of proof and since "Travenca's showing here is totally devoid of any evidence on an essential element of the proffered

---

[26] *Id.*

[27] *Id.* at 1473–74.

[28] *Id.* at 1474 citing McClintock v. McCall, 214 Kan. 764, 522 P.2d 343, 346 (1974).

[29] *Id.* citing United American State Bank & Trust Co. v. Wild West Chrysler Plymouth, Inc., 221 Kan. 523, 527, 561 P.2d 792, 795 (1977).

[30] *Id.* citing Celetex Corp. v. Catrett, 477 U.S. 317, 322 (1986).

affirmative defense of estoppel, it was error for the district court to hold that the trustee would be estopped as a matter of law."[31]

The court reversed and remanded the bankruptcy court's decision, "[b]ecause we hold: (1) that there is a genuine dispute over material facts concerning whether Travenca had entered into a binding contract with the debtor-in-possession; (2) that Travenca did not establish the absence of a genuine dispute of material facts concerning its estoppel defense; and (3) that the enforcement and modification provisions of the Bankruptcy Code pertaining to Chapter 11 plans of reorganization do not preempt a claim for breach of contract premised on the plan for reorganization. . . ."[32]

Observation

While the court of appeals in *Paul v. Monts* clearly explains facts which bind entities to a confirmed plan, it is difficult to understand how, at a hearing on disclosure of the plan, Travenca did not submit agreements that complied with §1125(a)(1).[33] As stated in the section "'adequate information' means information of a kind, and in sufficient detail, as far as is reasonably practicable. . . ."

Additionally, the order of confirmation was submitted with the record on appeal with an open space for the debtor's signature and remained unsigned. Section 1123(a)(5)(B) requires that a plan "provide adequate means for the plans implementation such as—(B) transfer of all or any part of the property of the estate to one or more entities, whether organized before or after the confirmation of such plan; . . ."

Consider also "§1129. Confirmation of plan.", which requires compliance with many subsections: "(a)(2) [t]he proponent of the plan complies with the applicable provisions of this title"; (a)(3) plan proposed in good faith; and (a)(11) confirmation "not likely to be followed by the liquidation, or

---

[31] *Id. See* note 7: "Because of our disposition of this case, we express no opinion as to whether the conduct identified by the district court is sufficient to estop the trustee."

[32] *Id.* at 1476.

[33] *See* §1125. Postpetition disclosure and solicitation.

the need for further financial reorganization, of the debtor. . . ."

The firm provisions of the Code make it difficult to understand how the case ever reached confirmation of the plan, let alone implementation. The absence of a creditor's committee, or its action if it existed, emphasizes its need.[34] Moreover, an additional duty has been added through Bankruptcy Rule 3017: "This rule is amended to enable the United States trustee to monitor and comment with regard to chapter 11 disclosure statements and plans."[35] The Amendment is a sound answer to the procedural problem for future cases but as to the proponents of the Debtor's plan, Travenca and Monts, it is difficult to hold that their actions did not bind them to liability by estoppel.

Applicability of Other Sections of 1141

Sections 1141(b) (Vesting of Property) and (c) (Property Free and Clear)

We turn now to the other subsections of §1141. Section 1141(b) provides: "Except as otherwise provided in the plan or in the order confirming the plan, the confirmation of a plan vests all of the property of the estate in the debtor." Section 1141(c) provides "Except as provided in subsections (d)(2) and (d)(3) of this section and except as otherwise provided in the plan or in the order confirming the plan, after confirmation of a plan, the property dealt with by the plan is free and clear of all claims and interests of creditors, equity security holders, and of general partners in the debtor."

---

[34] *See supra* Chapter 10, this handbook, Committees of Creditors and Equity Security Holders.

[35] *See* Advisory Committee Note–1991 Amendment, citing: 28 USC §586(a)(3)(B) ("Each United States Trustee, . . . , shall— . . . supervise the administration of cases and trustees in cases . . . by . . . monitoring plans and disclosure statements. . . .").

Section 1141(d)
Discharge of Debtor

Section 1141(d)(1) provides that "[e]xcept as otherwise provided in this subsection, in the plan, or in the order confirming the plan, the confirmation of a plan—(A) discharges the debtor from any debt that arose before the date of such confirmation, and any debt of a kind specified in section 502(g), 502(h), or 502(i) of this title,[36] whether or not—(i) a proof of the claim based on such debt is filed or deemed filed under §501 of this title;[37] (ii) such claim is allowed under §502 of this title; or (iii) the holder of such claim has accepted the plan; and (B) terminates all rights and interests of equity security holders and general partners provided for by the plan."

Discharge of All Claims and Exceptions

Section 1141(d)(2) provides: "[t]he confirmation of a plan does not discharge an individual debtor from any debt excepted from discharge under Section 523. . . ."[38] As for all debtors subsection (d)(3) provides: "[t]he confirmation of a plan does not discharge a debtor if—(A) the plan provides for the liquidation of all or substantially all of the property of the estate;[39] (B) the debtor does not engage in business after

---

[36] *See* §502(g), (h), and (i) holding status of certain claims arising in chapter 11 to be considered as claims that had arisen prior to the filing of the petition: (g) claim resulting from rejection of executory contract under §365; (h) recovery of property under §522 (Exemptions); §550 (Liability of transferee of avoided transfer), or §553 (Setoff); (i) claim arising after commencement of case for a tax entitled to priority under §507(a)(7) (allowed claims of governmental units).

[37] *See* §501 (Filing of proofs of claim or interests); §502 (Allowance of claims or interests); and §503 (Allowance of administrative expenses).

[38] *See* §523. "Exceptions to discharge. (a) A discharge under sections 727, 1141 . . . does not discharge an individual debtor from any debt—(1) for a tax or a customs duty— . . . (2) for money, property, services (among others) . . . to the extent obtained by—(A) false pretenses . . . or actual fraud. . . ."

[39] *See* "§1101. Definitions for this chapter." *See* §1101(2): "[S]ubstantial consummation means—transfer of all or substantially all of the property proposed by the plan to be transferred; (B) assumption by the debtor or by the successor . . . of the business or of the management of all or substantially

consummation of the plan; and (C) the debtor would be denied a discharge under Section 727(a) of this title[40] if the case were a case under chapter 7 of this title." Subsection (d)(4) authorizes the court to approve a written waiver of discharge executed by the debtor after the order for relief under this chapter.

Section 1141 Clarifies Priority Sections

Section 1141 clarifies prior sections of the Code, namely, two other priority sections which are helpful for confirmation of the plan. First, we consider the priorities of claims set forth in §507 in a sequential order. The first priorities are expenses of administration set forth in §503—Allowance of administrative expenses. Such expenses are included under §503(b) with the exception of §502(f):[41]

> After notice and a hearing, there shall be allowed administrative expenses . . . including—(A) The actual, necessary costs and expenses of preserving the estate,[42] including wages, salaries, or commissions for services rendered after the commencement of the case; (B) Any tax—(i) incurred by the estate, except. . . ; or (ii) attributable to an excessive allowance of a tentative carryback adjustment

---

all of the property dealt with by the plan; and (c) commencement of distribution under the plan."

[40] *See* §727(a). "The court shall grant the debtor a discharge unless—(1) the debtor is not an individual."

[41] *See* §502(f). Claims incurred in the ordinary course of business after the chapter 11 petition is filed but before a trustee (or debtor becomes debtor in possession) is appointed ("gap claims") have a priority over general claims.

[42] *See* §327. Employment of professional persons; §328, Limitation on compensation of professional persons; §329, Debtor's transactions with attorneys; §330, Compensation of officers; and §331, Interim compensation. *See also* §507(a) Priorities: "The following expenses and claims have priority in the following order: (1) First, administrative expenses allowed under section 503(b) . . . (2) Second, unsecured claims allowed under section 502(f) of this title. . . ." *See also In re* The George Worthington Co., 921 F2d 626 (6th Cir. 1990), allowing the administrative expenses of a Chapter 11 Committee.

that the estate received. . . ; and (C) any fine, penalty or reduction in credit relating to a tax in subparagraph (B) of this paragraph.

Taxes

The scope of this handbook is far too limited to discuss the subject of taxes in depth. We do, however, consider several statutory sections benefiting the debtor through extending the time for payment of taxes upon confirmation. Upon completing this observation, we will continue with the *Wilson* case[43] dealing with competitive jurisdiction with the Tax Court. The Seventh priority, deals with allowed unsecured "claims of governmental units, only to the extent that such claims are for—(A) a tax on or measured by income or gross receipts—for a taxable year ending on or before the date of the filing of the petition. . . ; (B) a property tax assessed before the commencement of the case. . . ; (C) a tax required to be collected or withheld. . . ; (D) an employment tax on a wage, salary or commission. . . ; (E) an excise tax on—. . . ; [and] (F) a customs duty arising out of the importation of merchandise—. . . ."[44]

Deferment of Payment of Tax Claim—6 Years

For the debtor, this brief statement of tax claims is of importance because the Code provides for a deferment which would ordinarily be paid in cash upon confirmation. Subsection 1129(a)(9)(A) provides not only for an extension of time for payment of taxes, but also for other claims "[e]xcept to the extent that the holder of a particular claim has agreed to a different treatment of such claim, the plan provides [for a specified extended payment]: (A) with respect to a claim of a kind specified in section 507(a)(1) [administrative expenses] or §507(a)(2) ["Gap" claims] of this title, on the effective date of

---

[43] U.S. Internal Revenue Service v. Wilson and Guinee Jr., 974 F2d 514. (4th Cir. 1992), *cert. denied* 113 S.Ct. 1352 (1993). *See, infra,* this chapter, subtitled "Jurisdiction—Wilson Case Tax Court Versus Bankruptcy." *See also supra* Chapter 7, this handbook, Jurisdiction of Bankruptcy Court.

[44] 11 USC §507(a)(7)—Priorities.

the plan,[45] the holder of such claim will receive on account of such claim cash equal to the allowed amount of such claim; . . ."

Subsection 1129(a)(9)(C) provides that with respect to a claim specified in §507(a)(7)[46], "the holder of such claim will receive on account of such claim deferred cash payments, over a period not exceeding six years after the date of assessment of such claim, of a value, as of the effective date of the plan, equal to the allowed amount of such claim."[47] Since §507(a)(7) refers to governmental claims, the usual procedure between the debtor and the government is an extension of the payment of the claim in serial payments with accrued interest from the date of confirmation.

Implementation of Plan

With the plan of reorganization in place, it is now necessary to put the plan into action.[48] For this we look to §1142(a) which provides that "the debtor and any entity organized . . . for the purpose of carrying out the plan shall carry out the plan and shall comply with any orders of the Court." The section further provides in subsection (b) that "[t]he court may direct the debtor and any other necessary party to execute or deliver . . . any instrument required to effect a transfer of property dealt with by a confirmed plan, and to perform any other act, including the satisfaction of any lien, that is necessary for the consummation of the plan." With such authority in hand the debtor may begin the process of implementing the plan of reorganization.

---

[45] *See* discussion in Chapter 19, this handbook, Confirmation of Cram Down.

[46] *See* §507(a)(7) "Seventh, allowed unsecured claims of governmental units, only to the extent that such claims are for—(A) a tax on or measured by income or gross receipts. . . ."

[47] *See In re* Energy Resources, 871 F2d 223 (1st Cir. 1989), *aff'd,* 110 S.Ct. 2139 (1990), application to manager's personal liability in first priority.

[48] *See supra,* this chapter, Paul v. Monts under subtitle "Implementation of Plan."

Additional Postconfirmation Sections

Section 1143, Distribution, contains a provision concerning a plan's requirement of presentment or surrender of a security or the performance of any other act as a condition to participation in distribution under the plan, and sets a 5 year limitation on such performance, or any other action. Otherwise, the owner of such security "may not participate in distribution under the plan."[49] Section 1146 provides: "Special Tax Provisions" which apply in a case under chapter 11.

Jurisdiction—Wilson Case
Tax Court Versus Bankruptcy

Before we arrive at the "Final Decree" which terminates the chapter 11 proceeding, it is important to consider the *Wilson* case,[50] which is fundamental not only in considering the bankruptcy court's jurisdiction to administer tax claims, but also its concurrent jurisdiction with the tax court. The Fourth Circuit opens the issue: "We are presented with the question of whether a bankruptcy court has jurisdiction to resolve the tax liability of a debtor in bankruptcy, when the same issue is pending before the United States Tax Court and the automatic stay against the tax court's proceeding has been lifted."[51]

Filing of Chapter 11

"On April 15, 1983, the Internal Revenue Service issued two notices of deficiency against Edwin P. Wilson ("Wilson") in which it determined that Wilson was liable for federal income taxes, interest, and penalties totalling almost $30 million for the taxable years 1977 through 1981. Contesting the amount claimed by the IRS, Wilson filed a petition in the United States Tax Court to redetermine the tax deficiency."[52]

---

[49] *See* "§102. Rules of Construction, section (4): 'may not' is prohibitive, and not permissive; . . ."

[50] U.S. Internal Revenue Service v. Wilson and Guinee Jr., 974 F2d 514 (4th Cir. 1992), *cert. denied*, 113 S.Ct. 1352 (1993).

[51] *Id.* at 515.

[52] *Id.*

While the tax court proceeding was pending, Wilson filed a chapter 11 case and shortly thereafter John W. Guinee, Jr. was appointed trustee. "The IRS filed a proof of claim in the bankruptcy court to recover the taxes assessed, which after amendment reflected a tax liability in excess of $28 million. Pursuant to 11 U.S.C. §362(a)(8), the tax court proceeding was automatically stayed."[53]

Lifting the Automatic Stay

Since the tax liability would consume virtually the entire bankruptcy estate, a determination of the liability became essential to the administration of the estate. The parties, therefore, submitted an order to be signed by the bankruptcy court lifting the automatic stay. The next step was an attempt to place the tax liability issues upon the tax court's 1986 docket. The trustee agreed to intervene in the tax court proceeding to protect the estate's interest because (1) "a determination of the validity and amount of the IRS tax claims against the debtor is essential to the administration of the estate," and (2) if invalid, "or valid only in part, there may be sufficient funds to pay all other claims against the estate in full."[54] The bankruptcy court lifted the stay on March 11, 1986.

Settlement of Case

"After more than three years of pretrial proceedings in the tax court without a trial date being scheduled, the trustee and the IRS began negotiating a settlement of the tax claim, and on December 12, 1989, they arrived at a settlement which they believed was in the best interest of the estate. The settlement limited the amount that the IRS could collect; provided for full payment of secured and administrative claims and payment to the general and unsecured creditors of 85% of their claims; and

---

[53] *Id. See* §362(a)(8): "[A] petition filed under §301 [voluntary cases]; 302 [Joint cases]; or 303 [Involuntary cases] of this title . . . operates as a stay, applicable to all entities, of (8) the commencement or continuation of a proceeding before the United States Tax Court concerning the debtor." *See also supra* Chapter 10, this handbook, Committees of Creditors and Equity Security Holders.

[54] *Id.*

discharged Wilson from the post-bankruptcy liability to which he otherwise would have been subjected if the IRS had prevailed on its tax claim."

"The IRS then moved the bankruptcy court to reinstate the automatic stay of the tax court proceeding, pursuant to the court's equitable powers under 11 USC §105,[55] and, in order to obtain court approval for the settlement, filed a complaint seeking a determination of Wilson's tax liability for the years 1977 through 1981 under 11 USC §505 and of the dischargeability of that liability under 11 USC §523. In lieu of an answer, the trustee filed a stipulation setting forth the terms of the settlement agreement."[56]

No creditors objected to the settlement, but Wilson did object. "Opposing the government's motion to reinstate the automatic stay and moving to dismiss the complaint, Wilson contended that the bankruptcy court lacked subject matter jurisdiction[57] over the complaint and personal jurisdiction over him, that the settlement violated due process, and that the government was collaterally estopped by the bankruptcy court's earlier decision in an action by the trustee to 'pierce the corporate veil in reverse' so that the estate could collect from creditors of Wilson's alleged alter ego corporation. . . ."[58]

Jurisdiction in Both Courts

Wilson's first contention was lack of jurisdiction in the bankruptcy court of the tax claim because the tax claim in the tax court proceeding was pending prior to the filing of the chapter 11 petition. The court disagreed with such exclusivity stating that there is no such statutory language or principles. "In the absence of language conferring jurisdiction on a mutually exclusive basis, we conclude that the jurisdiction of each court is determined by the plain meaning of the applicable jurisdiction-conferring statute, and in any given

---

[55] *Id.* at 515–16. *See supra* Chapter 4, this handbook, Power of Court.

[56] *Id.* at 516.

[57] *Id. See supra* Chapter 7, this handbook, Jurisdiction of Bankruptcy Court.

[58] *Id. See supra* Chapter 14, this handbook, Trustee's Strong-Arm Powers Marshaling of Assets.

circumstance more than one court may and does have jurisdiction over a claim."[59]

The court of appeals then cited the basis of original jurisdiction in §1334[60] for the district courts and its reference to the bankruptcy judges in the appropriate district.[61] "Bankruptcy judges can hear and determine all cases and core proceedings arising under the Bankruptcy Code, subject to review by the district courts. . . . Core proceedings include, but are not limited to, the 'allowance or disallowance of claims against the estate,'[62] . . . and 'the dischargeability of particular debts.' . . ."[63]

The court emphasized that §505[64] of the Bankruptcy Code specifically addressed the bankruptcy court's jurisdiction to determine the amount or legality of any tax. Section 505(a)(2)(B) limits the bankruptcy court's jurisdiction in cases where the claim was adjudicated before the commencement of the case. Applying the facts to the law, the court concluded that (1) Wilson's claim in the tax court had not been adjudicated before the commencement of the chapter 11; (2) the IRS's proof of claim and complaint with the bankruptcy court to recover the amounts assessed properly invoked the jurisdiction of the bankruptcy court to resolve Wilson's tax liabilities; and (3) the claim instituted a core proceeding within the bankruptcy court's jurisdiction.[65]

The court also disposed of Wilson's argument that the tax court had jurisdiction since the automatic stay[66] had been lifted, by observing that the effect was only that the jurisdiction of both courts was concurrent. "The legislative material cited by Wilson only demonstrates that the general

---

[59] *Id.*

[60] *Id. See supra* Chapter 7, this handbook, Jurisdiction of Bankruptcy Court.

[61] *Id.* citing 28 USC §157(a).

[62] *Id.* citing 28 USC §157(b)(2)(B).

[63] *Id.* citing 28 USC §157(b)(2)(I).

[64] *Id.* §505 Determination of tax liability.

[65] *Id.* at 517 citing American Principals Leasing Corp. v. United States, 904 F2d 477, 481 (9th Cir. 1990) (Section 505 does not authorize the bankruptcy court to determine tax liabilities of nondebtors).

[66] *Id.* at 518. *See supra* Chapter 4, this handbook, Power of Court.

purpose of lifting the automatic stay is to allow a matter to be decided by a tribunal with special expertise. . . . Nevertheless, it will often be more appropriate to permit proceedings to continue in their place of origin, when no great prejudice to the bankruptcy estate would result. . . . In this case, however, where the administration of the estate depended on resolution of the tax liability issue and the issue had been pending in the tax court for over three years, the bankruptcy court properly exercised its power to adjudicate the tax liability of the debtor. . . ."[67]

Lifting of Stay for Debtor's Additional Points

The lifting of the stay did not "deprive the bankruptcy court of jurisdiction to resolve Wilson's unadjudicated tax claim when the chapter 11 petition was filed and the IRS filed a proof of claim and a complaint to determine that liability."[68] We have not concluded with all of Wilson's arguments raised on appeal, especially when he received a discharge of all his obligations, including the tax claims. A sketch of these additional arguments includes other sections of the Code.

Lack of Jurisdiction

Wilson challenged the bankruptcy court's approval of the settlement claiming the bankruptcy court lacked personal jurisdiction to determine his tax liability and the dischargeability of the liability. Response: Under §541(a) a debtor's estate is comprised of "all legal or equitable interests of the debtor in property as of the commencement of the case."[69] The agreement limited IRS to recovery from assets of the estate and Wilson was not subject to any further liability.

---

[67] *Id.* at 518.

[68] *Id.* at 517. *See supra* Chapter 11, this handbook, Trustees, Examiners, and Officers of the Court, subtitle "Effect of Filing Proof of Claim."

[69] *Id.* at 519.

Due Process

Wilson claimed a lack of due process when the IRS effectuated a taking of his property by approving the settlement without his "participation and consent." Response: "Procedural due process generally requires adequate notice and a hearing before there is a taking of property.[70] . . . Here, Wilson was afforded all the process that was due. He was served with each pleading, filed two motions, and was represented by counsel at all hearings. Although Wilson opposed the settlement agreement, his consent was not necessary to the approval of the agreement by the bankruptcy judge. . . . Objection by the debtor is not fatal to [the] settlement if 'it is found to be in the best interests of the estate as a whole.'"[71]

Collateral Estoppel

Finally, Wilson argued the IRS was "estopped from asserting any tax claims against him because the issue of corporate control, allegedly relied upon by the IRS as the exclusive basis for Wilson's tax liability, had already been decided by the bankruptcy court."[72] This issue involved (1) the piercing of the corporate veil by the trustee; (2) a finding that a corporation was the alter ego of Wilson; and (3) a finding that the estate was entitled to funds due on contracts entered into by the corporation. The case was dismissed by the bankruptcy court "for failure to state a cause of action reasoning that there was no right of action allowing a party to 'pierce the corporate veil in reverse'. . . . The court did not decide whether Services Commerciaux [a corporation] was in fact the alter ego of Wilson. Because the issue was not actually decided and, moreover, the IRS was not shown to have been in privity with the trustee in that action, collateral estoppel

---

[70] *Id.* citing Mullane v. Central Hanover Bank and Trust Co., 339 U.S. 306, 313 (1950).

[71] *Id.* citing St. Paul Fire & Marine Ins. Co. v. Vaughn, 779 F2d 1003, 1010 (4th Cir. 1985), *et al.*

[72] *Id.* See *supra* this chapter, Paul v. Monts under subtitle "Estoppel."

cannot be applied now to bind the IRS."[73] "In conclusion, finding no merit to any of Wilson's claims, we affirm the judgment of the district court."[74]

Final Decree

Several additional postconfirmation sections are still to be considered. A final decree terminates a chapter 11 proceeding which has already been confirmed. In the *Jordan* case,[75] a proceeding was brought by the debtors in various chapter 11 actions for the entry of a final order closing the chapter 11 cases pursuant to §350 of the Code and Bankruptcy Rule 3022. Several creditors objected. In one case, the debtor was in default in payment of the monies due pursuant to the plan, but in another a balance was still due although there was no default. In the latter instance, creditors objected to the closing of the case on the following grounds: "(1) Under Section 350 of the Bankruptcy Code and prior[76] Bankruptcy Rule 3022, a final decree was not entered until 'after an estate is fully administered' and to be in compliance with prior Bankruptcy Rule 3022 the debtor submitted to the court a confirmation order which retained jurisdiction in the court 'until all claims have been paid in full' and 'after the debtors successfully completed the plan.'"[77]

Case not Fully Administered

The court cited the statutory provisions of §350(a): "After an estate is fully administered and the court has discharged the trustee, the court shall close the case." Its complementary Rule 3022 contains similar language: "After an estate is fully administered, including distribution of any deposit required by the plan, the court shall enter a final decree (1) discharging

---

[73] *Id.* citing Virginia Hosp. Assoc. v. Baliles, 830 F2d 1308, 1311–12 (4th Cir. 1987), *aff'd* in part Wilder v. Virginia Hosp. Assoc., 110 S.Ct. 2510 (1990).

[74] *Id.*

[75] *In re* Jordan Mfg. Co. Inc., 138 BR 30 (B. CD Ill. 1992).

[76] *Id.* at 32. The court observed that no change existed between the prior §350 and the present version.

[77] *Id.*

any trustee; . . . (2) making provision by way of injunction or otherwise as may be equitable;[78] and (3) closing the case."[79]

Amendments to Bankruptcy Rule 3022

In 1991, Bankruptcy Rule 3022 had been amended to read: "After an estate is fully administered in a Chapter 11 reorganization case, the court, on its own motion or on motion of a party in interest, shall enter a final decree closing the case." The first objection considered by the court: "Should current Bankruptcy Rule 3022 be applied retroactively to these confirmed Chapter 11 proceedings?"[80]

Application of Retroactive Amendment

"As a general rule, an amendment will be applied retroactively, absent express statutory language to the contrary, where the amendment relates only to remedies or procedures and where retroactive application would not destroy a substantive right. . . . This general rule is embodied in the directive of the Supreme Court, concerning the application of the 1991 amendments to the Rules of Bankruptcy Procedure: . . . Thus, the current rule will apply to these cases if its application is 'just and practicable.'"[81]

Amendment—A Procedural Remedy

The bankruptcy judge then considered the holding in the *Stroop* case,[82] in which the court considered whether the application of an amendment to the Code to a pending case would result in manifest injustice. The *Stroop* Court identified three factors to be considered: "1. The nature and identity of the parties; 2. the nature of the rights affected; and 3. the impact of the change in law on preexisting rights."[83]

---

[78] *Id.* at 32–33. *See supra* Chapter 4, this handbook, Power of Court.

[79] *Id.* at 33.

[80] *Id.*

[81] *Id.* citing Ambrosino v. Rodman & Renshaw, Inc., 635 F. Supp. 968 (ND Ill. 1986), *et al.*

[82] *In re* Stroop, 47 BR 986 (DC Colo. 1985).

[83] *In re* Jordan Mfg. Co., Inc., 138 BR at 33.

Closing the Case: Procedural Levels

Turning to each factor, the court opined that the status of the parties had no impact where the dispute is a routine one between private parties, as in this case. As to the second factor, whether the rights involved have matured or become unconditional, the court noted that the right at issue in the *Stroop* case was more a procedural remedy than a substantive right and therefore, "absent manifest injustice, no one has a vested right in a given mode of procedure. In the cases before this Court, the entry of a final decree under Bankruptcy Rule 3022 is procedural in nature as it involves the 'ministerial act' of closing a case after it is fully administered. B. Weintraub and M.J. Crames, *Defining Consummation, Effective Date of Plan of Reorganization and Retention of Post Confirmation Jurisdiction, Suggested Amendments to Bankruptcy Code and Bankruptcy Rules,* 64 Am. Bankr. L.J. 245 (Summer, 1990)."[84]

As to "[t]he third aspect[, it] focuses upon any injury to pre-existing rights caused by the change in the law. As in *Stroop,* the amendment to Rule 3022 will have no impact on any preexisting rights of the creditors in these cases. Therefore, because the application of the current Rule 3022 is 'just and practicable' it should be applied in these cases."[85] Other issues were discussed by the court. Consider, for example, some of the final decrees which creditors contend should not be entered because the debtors have defaulted under their plans. "Apparently the creditors want to be able to resort to this Court to remedy the defaults. . . . The answer is that a creditor may resort to Section 1112(b) of the Bankruptcy Code, . . . which permits conversion to Chapter 7 or dismissal or may resort to state court, but may not resort to the bankruptcy court to collect an individual obligation arising out of a reorganization."[86]

---

[84] *Id.*

[85] *Id.*

[86] *Id.* at 36. *See* §1112(b) Conversion or dismissal. "[O]n request of a party in interest or the United States Trustee, and after notice and a hearing, the court may convert a case under this chapter to a case under chapter 7 of this title or may dismiss a case under this chapter whichever is in the best interests of creditors and the estate, for cause, including—" subsections (2), (4), (7) and (8) "material default by the debtor with respect to a confirmed plan." *See also Id.* at note 3: "This court merely selected

"A bankruptcy court has a third option under Section 1112(b). That section is not mandatory in requiring conversion or dismissal. It provides the court 'may' do either. So a bankruptcy court could elect to do neither, and leave the creditor with its state court remedies."[87]

In conclusion the court stated that "[t]his Opinion is to serve as Findings of Fact and Conclusions of Law pursuant to Rule 7052 of the Rules of Bankruptcy Procedure."[88]

Revocation of an Order of Confirmation

What if the order of confirmation is entered and a party in interest believes it was fraudulently obtained? Under such circumstances, the party in interest would look to §1144. Under this section, a party in interest may request the court to revoke such order "at any time before 180 days after the date of the entry of the order of confirmation." After notice and a hearing, "the court may revoke such order if and only if such order was procured by fraud." However, the revocation order doesn't completely abandon all parties previously protected by the plan. Under subsections (1) and (2) the order shall "contain such provisions as are necessary to protect any entity acquiring rights in good faith reliance on the order of confirmation and revoke the discharge of the debtor."

We arrive now at Chapter 21, Before and After Chapter 11. First, we will discuss the problems involved in the days before the existence of chapter 11 and then the problems overcome by its provisions. From there we go further to consider some of the comments, both "pro and con," for its continuance.

---

certain subsections of Section 1112(b) to make its point that Section 1112(b) encompasses both pre and post confirmation situations."

[87] *Id.*

[88] *Id.* at 40.

Chapter 21
Before and After Chapter 11

Much has been written about the origin and necessity of the continuance of chapter 11 for the business world. It is important to review some of chapter 11's origin because, as we shall shortly indicate, the thought does exist that its elimination or modification is a creature not only of modern day discussion, but interest. To understand the need for chapter 11, we shall consider its predecessors, bankruptcy without chapter 11 and the commercial laws of the states.

Early Stages

State Law

"In the United States, prior to the recent[1] amendments in 1934 of §77B of the Bankruptcy Act, an arrangement for

---

[1] *See* Levy & Moore, *Bankruptcy and Reorganization: A Survey of Changes II (1938) United States prior to the Depression,* 5 CHI. L. REV. 219 (1938) (reference to "recent" refers to Bankruptcy Act of 1934). *See also* 6 COLLIER ON BANKRUPTCY 5, note 1 (14th ed. 1978).

settlement of debt between a Debtor and creditor could be consummated through one of three methods: (1) a voluntary adjustment, (2) bankruptcy, or (3) an equity receivership. . . ." Each state had a version of the law for settlements of debt among creditors, *i.e.*, the common law consensual arrangements which toiled with the serious problem of the nonaccepting creditor who waited to levy upon the Debtor's property after agreement had been reached with accepting creditors.

Additionally, statutory bulk transfers were occasionally employed by Debtors to transfer their property to a controlled entity to avoid nonconsenting creditors levying upon the Debtor's property.[2] Add to these nonstatutory arrangements, state court statutes for the liquidation of assignments for the benefit of creditors.[3] These were liquidating statutes and left no opportunity for Debtors to rehabilitate their businesses for more advantageous returns for the Debtors as well as their creditors. Moreover, assignments for the benefit of creditors were acts of bankruptcy which were subject to bankruptcy liquidation.[4]

Bankruptcy Act Method

The Bankruptcy Act provided the second method for consummating an arrangement to settle debt between a Debtor and its creditors, either through a voluntary petition seeking liquidation, or an involuntary petition for creditors. There was included "a section 12 of the Act, the composition section. . . . The chief defect of the bankruptcy forum for reorganization, however, was that bankruptcy as it had developed, was a mechanism for liquidation. . . ."[5]

---

[2] *See* Weintraub and Levin, *Bulk Sales Law and Adequate Protection of Creditors,* 65 HARV. L. REV. 418 (1952).

[3] *See* Weintraub, Levin & Sosnoff, *Assignments for the Benefit of Creditors and Competitive Methods for Liquidation of Insolvent Estates,* 39 CORNELL L.Q. 3 (1953).

[4] *See supra* Levy & Moore at 224.

[5] *Id.*

Equity Receivership

"The third method of reorganization existing in this country prior to the depression was the equity receivership.[6] Upon application of a creditor's bill to the United States District Court a receiver of the Debtor's property was appointed. The Debtor was protected from the attacks of separate creditors by the equity receivership. The Debtor's business was continued under the supervision of the receiver. The assets were sold at auction and the income delivered to the receiver. After paying the expenses of administration and of the business operations, the proceeds went toward the claims of the creditor or of the creditors for whom the bill was filed."[7]

The equity receivership terminated "in a judicial sale whereby part or all of the old security holders became (oftentimes in conjunction with others) the purchasers under a new arrangement or plan evolved for that purpose and contemplating the continuance of the business in the form of a new company."[8] Creditors' committees were not forgotten in the equity receivership. "While the business was being conducted by the receiver and expenditures were being made for its rehabilitation, the reorganizers had formed a committee for each class of security and stock and were soliciting the deposit of these securities and shares."[9]

Section 77B

Of the three methods, the equity receivership, administered in the federal courts was the more feasible and most frequently employed. "But the blight of the depression and the consequent multitude of business failures, together with the abuses prevalent in many receivership cases compelled a search 'for a practice more open, more responsible,

---

[6] *Id.* at 225.

[7] *Id.* at 227.

[8] *Id.*

[9] *Id.*

more efficiently and closely regulated, and with all more surely valid, under the supervision of a court of bankruptcy.'"[10]

Bankruptcy Act

With this blight of the economy and the inadequacy of the bankruptcy law to provide for a sound reorganization, §77 (railroad reorganization) and §77B (general corporate reorganization) were enacted by the Act of June 7, 1934, under the title of "Emergency Legislation."[11] In 1938, replacing §77 and §77B were Chapters X and XI ("Chandler Act") which, in turn, in 1978, were replaced by Chapter 11 of the Bankruptcy Code, the present reorganization law. What we have presented in this book projects the necessity of rehabilitation and reorganization by the Bankruptcy Code of the United States encompassing states' commercial businesses.

Pro- and Anti-Chapter 11

However, several newspaper reports and law review articles have suggested Chapter 11's fall from grace. Such thinking on Chapter 11's survival bears discussion. We now proceed to consider first a presentation for extinction and then two for survival, each bearing meaningful headnotes.

B&R Article—Anti
Losers

In an article in the NEW YORK TIMES, *Time to Scuttle Chapter 11*,[12] Professor Bradley and Counsellor Rosenzweig endeavor to promote the title of their column by pouncing on

---

[10] *See* 6 COLLIER ON BANKRUPTCY 7 (14th ed. 1978).

[11] *See supra* Levy & Moore note 1 at 229.

[12] *See* NEW YORK TIMES FORUM, March 8, 1992, at 13, by Michael Bradley, Professor of Business, Finance, and Law at the University of Michigan, and Attorney Michael Rosenzweig. "This is adapted from an article to be published this month in the Yale Law Journal." The article was published as *The Untenable Case for Chapter 11*, 101 YALE L.J. 1043. *See also* "Developments" section, 78 ABAJ 32 (July 1992).

the *Eastern Airlines* case[13] for having lost huge sums in operations which led to liquidation of the company. "In the two years of operations in Chapter 11 the bankruptcy court released more than $4 billion in cash over the objections of creditors to finance Eastern's failing operations and pay the fees of lawyers and financial advisers. If the company had been forced to liquidate in 1989 [date of filing the petition], this cash would have gone to investors. Instead the court postponed liquidation until there was no money left."[14]

Winners

From this observation, Bradley and Rosenzweig contend that creditors' weakening influence in bankruptcy is due essentially to the fact that managers and professionals control the operations. "One set of winners consists of the lawyers, accountants, and financial advisors who earn big fees from bankruptcy reorganizations. But we believe that the principal beneficiaries are corporate managers. During reorganization managers can operate without the restraints ordinarily imposed by creditors. Chapter 11, far from preserving valuable assets, in fact serves mainly to protect managers' jobs."[15]

Changing Laws—Bradley and Rosenzweig's Proposal

The authors proceed with a question and answer: "How should the law of corporate bankruptcy be changed to address these problems? In our view, Congress should repeal Chapter 11 and bar corporations from obtaining protection from creditors. Put simply, corporations should be forced to pay their bills as they become due. Under such a regime, [with chapter 11 repealed], creditors would demand debt covenants restraining managers from running the company into the ground. If these debt covenants precluded asset sales and the

---

[13] Eastern Airlines, Inc. (*In re* Ionosphere Clubs, Inc.), 134 BR 515 (B. SDNY 1991). *See supra* Chapter 11, this handbook, subtitle "Ionosphere Clubs—Refusal to Appoint Trustee."

[14] NEW YORK TIMES FORUM, March 8, 1992, at 13. *See supra* Chapter 1, this handbook, Prepackaged Chapter 11, and Chapter 2, this handbook, Lender's Participation, discussing the *Southland* case involving "the necessity of new capital which required a change of control of the company."

[15] *Id.*

company lacked cash to pay its creditors and could not generate more by attracting new equity investors, then common stockholders would be forced to give up all claims to the assets."

Then up the ladder: "[O]wnership of the corporation would pass to the next higher priority security class (usually preferred stockholders), who would then face the same choice: pay the current debt obligation or pass control to claimholders ranking next highest in priority." Control would continue to pass to a class "able to sell new equity and pay the current debt; failing that, control would then pass to the most senior creditors, for whose exclusive benefit the company would then be liquidated."

"The most important feature of our [Bradley and Rosenzweig's] proposal is that the market, not bankruptcy judges, would determine the net equity position of a financially troubled company. In addition, passing corporate control up the priority ladder of the company, capital structure would provide those in control at any point with appropriate incentives to allocate the company's resources optimally." The final word: "This would prevent debacles like the Eastern Airlines reorganization and significantly reduce society's bill in cases of financial distress."

Westbrook Article—Pro
Think Again Before Scuttling

Professor Westbrook, answered Professor Bradley and Mr. Rosenzweig by a letter to the NEW YORK TIMES which the editor identified with the above subtitle. Prof. Westbrook replied that the "reorganization proposed by [Bradley and Rosenzweig] is unfair and unworkable. The authors ignore the exquisitely difficult problem of organizing a salvage under intense pressure. . . . Eastern Airlines is a dramatic, but poor, example. Most of the operational decisions in that case were approved by the creditors. The case is a salutary reminder that not all companies can be saved. The fact that many patients die on the operating table does not persuade us to close the hospitals, and I am confident that we will not scuttle Chapter

11, no matter how many theorists fantasize simple solutions to complex problems."[16]

Warren Article—Pro
Bankruptcy is a Better Alternative

In a column in THE NATIONAL LAW JOURNAL bearing the above subtitle, Professor Warren[17] presents the problem criticizing Bradley and Rosenzweig: "Everyone wants payment on time and in full for every obligation owed to them. And if they don't get it they are understandably angry. The bankruptcy courts are full of late payers and nonpayers with businesses filing for Chapter 11 to try to restructure some debts and discharge others. . . . The businesses that wind up in Chapter 11 often deserve harsh criticism for the mismanagement or lack of foresight that led them to the brink of collapse. But in the era of blame-the-system, a new complaint is afoot. Chapter 11 is at fault when creditors suffer losses because their Debtors fail."

Bankruptcy does not Cause Failure

"Bankruptcy does not cause failure; failure causes the losses creditors and others complain about. . . . There is much wailing about the fact that Debtors have gone to Chapter 11 with their underfunded pension plans, environmental disasters, massive torts, and huge liabilities under the labor contracts. But the blame is misplaced—these businesses have the same problem with or without Chapter 11."

---

[16] *Id. See supra* Chapter 14, this handbook, Trustee's Strong-Arm Powers Marshaling of Assets, subtitle "Foreclosure of Mortgage."

[17] Elizabeth Warren, William A. Schnader Professor of Commercial Law at the University of Pennsylvania, *Bankruptcy Is a Better Alternative,* NATIONAL L.J. at 15, April 20, 1992. *See also* her article in Yale Law Journal, published in December 1992, *The Untenable Case for Repeal of Chapter 11,* 102 YALE L.J. 437 (1992). *See* note 12, *supra,* B&R's article in the Yale Law Journal which is the subject of Prof. Warren's article rejecting the principles set forth in the B&R article.

State Law no Bed of Roses

"Creditors complaining about Chapter 11 would be well to remember that state law is no bed of roses. With a Debtor in full control of its business, operating without restrictions as it moves property, shuffles assets, encumbers property, buys and sells, and buys again, it can be almost impossible for some creditors to collect. State law process can be lengthy and arcane. Corporate shells and subsidiaries give a determined Debtor the opportunity to evade payments for years."

"A business that wants to resist paying its obligations can consume enormous resources by moving, hiding and litigating. When people speak of the nightmares of the *Johns Manville Trust*[18] or the *Eastern Airlines* debacle, it is well to think of the debacle outside of bankruptcy. No doubt some asbestoses claimants would have collected big judgments in full, but at some point—at the 100th, or 1,000th or 100,000th—*Manville* would have been out of money and the later victims would have received nothing. The attorney fees to resolve all those claims against Manville—one lawsuit at a time, a team for Manville and a team for the victims—would long ago have surpassed what has been spent in bankruptcy."

No Deadbeat Debtors

Prof. Warren continued observing: "Some creditors complain bitterly about the bankruptcy process, noting . . . the benefits deadbeat Debtors enjoy: . . . hold[ing] off foreclosures, resist[ing] debt collection, continu[ing] to operate, borrow[ing] more money, and—most galling—pay[ing] staggering attorney fees . . . [are] a one way street, full of benefits for the Debtor."

"What does business give up in return—a good deal. A Chapter 11 Debtor has an obligation to make full and continuing disclosures about its operations that it would otherwise never have to make. . . . The business becomes property of the estate, and management control . . . is restricted. A number of business activities can be undertaken only with court—and creditor—approval."

---

[18] *See, e.g.*, Johns-Manville, 26 BR 420 (B. SDNY 1983), *aff'd* 40 BR 219 (SDNY 1984), and *aff'd* 843 F2d 636 (2d Cir. 1988).

Moreover, "[a] Chapter 11 process may oust management from control and may wipe out equity interests.[19] It is a big gamble for a failing business—a time bomb in the center of a business, which will go off unless management can negotiate a successful reorganization plan."

Prof. Warren continued: "[F]or most companies Chapter 11 is the beginning of the end. . . . They liquidate[20] despite the breathing space and a high proportion of plan confirmations involve downsizing or selling the business. More critical for managers are recent studies showing that more than two-thirds of all managers are publicly replaced within two years of the bankruptcy filing."

"Chapter 11 is not perfect. . . . It is appropriate to study the system, to criticize it and to make it better.[21] But it is wise to remember that ultimately we are talking about failing businesses and a business failed imposes losses on those to whom it owed obligations—regardless of whether the business files for Chapter 11." Professor Warren concluded: "Without Chapter 11 businesses would still fail. But without Chapter 11, few Debtors or creditors would be better off."

Need for Automatic Stay and Other Provisions of the Code

Let us conclude with the article by Attorney Leonard Rosen:[22] "One recent proposal goes beyond reform. Michael Bradley and Michael Rosenzweig . . . call for repealing chapter 11. . . . [They] say we would be better off avoiding chapter 11 or any other judicial intervention in the restructuring of a company. . . . Unfortunately, it is far too simplistic to think

---

[19] *See* §1129(b).

[20] *See supra* Chapter 18, this handbook, Confirmation of Consensual Plan subtitle "Congressional—Intent Reorganization Superior to Liquidation."

[21] *See supra* Chapter 13, this handbook, Assumption or Rejection of Executory Contracts and Unexpired Leases of Real Property, subtitle "Observation."

[22] Leonard Rosen is a practicing attorney and adjunct professor of bankruptcy law at New York University Law School, and a former chairman of the National Bankruptcy Conference. *See* Rosen, *Book, Chapter and Worse,* BUSINESS LAW TODAY, Vol. 1, 203, p. 47, July/August 1992.

that such a process could work. Is there to be no stay[23] of actions by secured or unsecured creditors during the process of eliminating junior interests?[24] . . . Is there to be any ability to reject onerous contracts and leases (such as is provided for in Section 365 of the Bankruptcy Code)?[25] How will disputes about priority, liens, and equitable subordination be resolved?[26] What Bradley and Rosenzweig suggest is just not workable."[27]

With the overall experience of an expert in the insolvencies of commercial enterprises, Mr. Rosen's article encompasses important problems in the Bankruptcy Code considering the preservation of the sections of the Code needed to rehabilitate an insolvent Debtor. "One recent proposal goes beyond reform, [Bradley and Rosenzweig's] writing in the March 1992 issue of the Yale Law Journal calling for repealing chapter 11. . . ."[28] Piercing the article, Attorney Rosen replies to other matters of importance that were raised by Bradley and Rosenzweig.

Attorney Rosen also commented: "One wide-ranging set of proposals to reform chapter 11 is working its way through Congress. It is Senate Bill 1985. . . . The bill . . . began as a legislative initiative to establish a commission to review and propose changes in the Bankruptcy Code. . . . By the time the Senate passed it on June 17, 1992, Senate Bill 1985 contained five titles, with many sections. The bill would significantly change almost every chapter of the Bankruptcy Code and would add a completely new pilot chapter 10 for small businesses." Mr. Rosen continued:

> Senate Bill 1985 presumes the need for a new Bankruptcy Commission, although no one has clearly demonstrated such a need. What needs

---

[23] *See supra* Chapter 6, this handbook, Automatic Stay.

[24] *See supra* Chapter 15, this handbook, Preferences.

[25] *See supra* Chapter 13, this handbook, Assumption or Rejection of Executory Contracts and Unexpired Leases.

[26] *See supra* Chapter 14, this handbook, Trustee's Strong-Arm Powers Marshaling of Assets.

[27] *See* Rosen, *Book, Chapter and Worse*, BUSINESS LAW TODAY, Vol. 1, 203, p. 47, July/August 1992.

[28] 5 YALE L.J. at 1043.

to be done to the Bankruptcy Code does not require a commission. The Code has only been in operation for about 12 years. Its basic structure does not appear to be in question. It was the product of years of work, many days of hearings, and many pages of testimony and written submissions. It is too soon to go through that process again.[29]

Observation

Prof. Warren's law review article concludes with an emphasis on the mathematical data supplied by Bradley and Rosenzweig to sustain their position. The use of "credible empirical data, more than anything else scholars bring to the table, can drastically change the terms of a debate. . . . The data produced by Bradley and Rosenzweig are unsound, too unsound to earn a place in the Chapter 11 debate."[30]

Let us not forget that history has depicted the sorrowful trend of commercial law in the early years of our country. Chapter 11 stands for growth, an advancement in reorganization, the need for aiding an insolvent Debtor in this quest for rehabilitation and avoiding liquidation where reorganization is in sight. Our chapters are designed to show what rehabilitation means to Debtors, creditors, employees, tort victims, taxing authorities, and a host of other entities.

Chapter 11 has reframed bankruptcy's stature: a second opportunity to restore to life a business which needed financial support which was unavailable except through the medium of chapter 11. Without the aid of the federal court, it is impossible to imagine a cure. One need only remember that state law does not approach the boundaries of bankruptcy powers.

---

[29] *Book, Chapter and Worse* at 49. *See also* 1993 Report of Committee on Legislation of "The National Bankruptcy Conference," analyzing S.540, the "Bankruptcy Amendments Act of 1933," introduced by Chairman Heflin. On September 15, 1993, the Senate Judiciary Committee voted to pass the bill to the Senate floor.

[30] Bradley and Rosenzweig article at 479.

Index

(References are to page numbers)

Confirmation of Cram Down Plan

Consolidation